CONTENTS

A DISCLAIMER

Readers are advised that prices and conditions change over the course
of time. The restaurants, hotels, shops and other establishments reviewed in this book have been reviewed over a period of time, and the
reviews reflect the personal experiences of the reviewers. The reviewers
and publishers cannot be held responsible for the experiences of the
reader related to the establishments reviewed. Readers are invited to
write the publisher with ideas, comments and suggestions for future
editions.

INTRODUCTION

AN EXPERIMENT IN LIVING

When you scan the skyline of giant office buildings and gawky hotels, San Francisco seems to share the blockbuster blight of every major metropolis. Skyscraping slabs of glass and concrete compete for airspace with awkward postmodern monstrosities. The graceful slopes of the city's hills are hidden by the ungainly architectural marks that marks 30 years of unchecked development. But as soon as your eye drifts beyond the "Manhattanized" downtown and catches sight of the Bay Bridge, curving silently over the glistening waters between Yerba Buena Island and the waterfront, the bright-orange span of the Golden Gate Bridge arching majestically from Fort Point to the Marin headlands, or the wisps of fog hugging Twin Peaks and sneaking into town under a clear blue sky, you begin to sense the magic that makes San Francisco "everybody's favorite city."

Even among the towering "triumphs" of contemporary urban design, you glimpse the wonders that make San Francisco unique. The Ferry Building, a modestly elegant clock tower on the Embarcadero, no longer welcomes transbay commuters by the thousands, but it stands as a beacon of history against the encroaching high-rise businesses and condominiums. Coit Tower, a finely proportioned memorial column, beautifully illuminated at night, still owns the peak of Telegraph Hill. Even the alabaster TransAmerica "Pyramid," once the bane of heritage-minded San Franciscans, has been accepted as one of the more attractive modern additions to the city's contour. Away from downtown, you can still discern the shape of the rest of San Francisco's 43 hills as they roll westward to the Pacific Ocean. Bound by the sea and San Francisco Bay, the city is situated on a hospitable (if quake-prone) peninsula, blessed with built-in limitations on growth and breathtaking vistas that no visitor ever forgets.

Charlie Chaplin, recording his impression of his first visit to San Francisco in 1910, described its charm at the expense of the too-often-maligned city to the south. "San Francisco, the gateway to the Orient, was a city of good food and cheap prices; first to introduce me to frogs' legs à la provençale, strawberry shortcake and avocado pears. Everything was new and bright, including my small hotel. Los Angeles, on the other hand, was an ugly city, hot and oppressive, and the people looked sallow and anemic. Nature has endowed North of California with resources that will endure and flourish when Hollywood has disappeared into the prehistoric tar pits of Wilshire Boulevard." What nature endowed upon San Francisco has been brought to life by people who share Chaplin's affection. On 29,000 acres of prime real estate, originally populated by Costanoans and settled by Spanish expeditionaries during the year of the American Revolution, some 700,000 people go about their daily lives while commuters, tourists and dream-chasers accelerate the bustling pace. Somewhere between the anonymous details of statistics and the grand scope of the skyline, you find the pulse of what has long been known as "The City." It's down on the streets in the artificial canyons of the

Financial District, where bicycle messengers zoom around corners at breakneck speed while a conga player bangs out rhythms to the beat of footsteps on the sidewalk; over in the bookstores and espresso cafés of North Beach, where writers linger over cappuccinos and unfinished verse; at night out at a punky dance club in burgeoning SOMA (South of Market); among the chockablock Chinatown restaurants and markets, where ducks and dried fish hang in the windows; in a walk down the Filbert Steps on Telegraph Hill and a trip back in time along sheltered Napier Lane; in the posh shops around Union Square; in the smell of steaming clams and Dungeness crab at Fisherman's Wharf; in the brightly painted facades of remodeled Victorian row houses; or out in the Castro District, where gay pride animates one of the city's many vibrant neighborhoods.

Writer William Saroyan called San Francisco "a city that invites the heart to come to life . . . an experiment in living." And ever since the first civilian settlers built their homes on Yerba Buena cove in the 1830s, each generation has conducted its own remarkable experiment, flavoring the city's cosmopolitan character with new hopes and visions, until, it seems, every strain of political thought, every crackpot idea and every international culture has been represented at one time or another in the city that columnist Herb Caen calls "Baghdad-by-the-Bay."

San Francisco's history is speckled with colorful figures, emblematic of the city's welcoming embrace and expansive tolerance. Through the ambitious Mormon colonist Samuel Brannan, who arrived just in time for the great Gold Rush of 1849, and such entrepreneurs-turned-millionaires as Charles Crocker and James Flood, as well as such lovable charlatans as Emperor Joshua Abraham Norton, San Francisco embodied, in exaggerated form, the boom-town and gilded-age mentalities of the 1800s. The Barbary Coast was notorious for its rough-and-tumble bars and gambling dens. North Beach grew into an enclave for Italian immigrants. Chinatown emerged as its own city–within–The City.

The parade of characters and waves of immigration didn't let up at all after the turn of the century, even after the devastating earthquake and fire of 1906. Whether real, like Mayor James "Sunny Jim" Rolph, or fictional, like Dashiell Hammett's hardboiled sleuth Sam Spade, San Francisco's celebrities were the stuff of legend. Harry Bridges organized the waterfront and made the city a solid union town. Sally Rand, with her infamous fan dance, and Sally Stanford, with her high-profile brothel, continued the tradition of notorious nightlife. Jake Erlich and Melvin Belli gained more publicity as attorneys than anyone since Clarence Darrow or Perry Mason. Businessmen, such as Louie Lurie and Cyril Magnin, proved that millionaires could still be civic icons.

In the '50s, Jack Kerouac, Allen Ginsberg, Lawrence Ferlinghetti and other Beats (immortalized as "beatniks") challenged the establishment culture's gray-flannel suits, fur coats and martinis with cool poetry at the Caffè Trieste and City Lights Bookstore and hot jazz at the Blackhawk and Jazz Workshop. In the '60s, while Don Sherwood bedazzled and befuddled a generation on mainstream pop radio, Tom Donahue expressed the free-form culture of another by pioneering underground rock radio, while the Jefferson Airplane, Grateful Dead, Moby Grape, Big Brother and the Holding Company, Mother Earth and Quicksilver Messenger Service took their music to LSD-tripping, tie-dye-clad fans in Golden Gate Park. Meanwhile, the Willies—Mays and McCovey—kept hitting the baseball out of Candlestick Park, maintaining the city's legacy of sports heroes, which reaches back to Joe DiMaggio and Lefty O'Doul and extends forward to Joe Montana, Kevin Mitchell and Will Clark.

The '70s came to an early and brutal ending in late 1978, when Dan White, a disgruntled and disturbed city supervisor, shot and killed Mayor George Moscone and supervisor Harvey Milk, San Francisco's pioneering gay politician. Another tragedy occurred that year when People's Temple preacher Jim Jones led his flock from The City to the jungles of Guyana, where 900 drank poisoned fruit punch in a mass suicide.

Every decade, indeed every year, seems to bring another enormous issue or new set of values to the fore in San Francisco, from the Beats, through the free-speech, flower-power and antiwar movements, to gay pride, the specter of AIDS, the plight of the homeless and, most recently, earthquake preparedness. But it is also "the city that knows how"—how to host elegant bashes for the opening of the boating season on the Bay and the opera season at the Civic Center; how to turn the hills into the challenging Bay-to-Breakers foot race, in which hundreds of thousands run seriously or simply dress in outlandish costumes; how to celebrate Carnaval and Chinese New Year with music and parades in the Mission District and Chinatown; how to dine graciously on every type of cuisine imaginable; even how to make light of the impossible task of finding a parking place by turning it into a contest. And all the while, San Francisco never forgets how to be what California poet George Sterling called "The Cool, Gray City of Love."

In one of his many sentimental odes to San Francisco, Herb "Don't Call It Frisco" Caen wrote, "The Saroyan–Sam Spade city—perhaps that was the last of it, as far as storybooks are concerned, but there is no way to give up on San Francisco, once you have fallen under its spell." And that is why residents, tourists and travelers will find a city that is immeasurably full yet so strikingly unfinished, preserving elements of its past while straining toward the future, a city that even native San Franciscans regard as their favorite destination.

RESTAURANTS

INTRODUCTION

SAN FRANCISCO: A QUEST FOR QUALITY

That San Francisco is a restaurant town, nobody can deny. At least, not statistically. At last official count, there were 4,200 restaurants in the city, or about one for every 98 persons. Lined up kitchen-to-kitchen, these restaurants would form a chain stretching roughly from Anchorage to Zanzibar. But is this impressive ratio enough to light up the San Francisco restaurant scene in the '90s? The almost ideal environment created by a near-blessed climate, the fertility of the gardens and of the orchards, the lightness of the air, the purity of the springs, fuels here a permanent quest for quality. The wines from nearby counties have developed a gentle culture of their own, with followers eager to supplement the bounties of the table by a dedicated pursuit of viniculture. With so many resources and so much energy devoted to a search for the best in food and wine, it would be inconceivable not to find here the will, the talents and the tastes to fulfill the secret dream—dominance over the ovens of the rest of America. This is why San Francisco has been, and is, an extraordinary playground, a school, even a university, for all sorts of chefs.

In recent years, it has been said frequently that San Francisco's chefs are seated atop the Mount Olympus of American cuisine. But new talents in other cities are now emerging—and seriously challenging the city's lofty position. Today, rare ingredients are flown in at jet speed in a perfect state of freshness from everywhere to nowhere, making it possible to throw a gala event in, say, the middle of Death Valley. And two decades ago, a chef from Los Angeles who dared to cross the Golden Gate with his pots and pans would have received only snickers from the local press and the populace. But today, Los Angeles's kitchen wunderkind, Wolfgang Puck, can break new ground here to the sound of raucous applause.

San Francisco has the means to remain on the cutting edge of culinary innovation—in fact, today it's being forced to do so. Business headquarters are disappearing from the city—often moving to Los Angeles—and with the businesses go the hefty corporate expense accounts. But as corporate dining tapers off, tourism is on the up—and it's our guess that as a result, San Francisco's chefs will devote more attention to food. Though tourists may spend less than businesspeople do, they are looking for the best cuisine, and they have the time to savor it.

In the past two decades, thanks in good part to Gault Millau, restaurants and restaurateurs have been accepted as necessary components in any definition of true civilization. San Francisco has contributed to this elevated status of food-givers with its Jeremiah Towers and Alice Waterses (not to mention the late Masa)—chefs whose faces are as familiar on magazine covers as those of rock stars.

What has made America great is obvious in San Francisco, even on the restaurant scene. The constant stream, mostly from the East, of influences, ideas and cultures, with their implications for cuisine, is transformed here into something special—something essentially new—with the unmistakable stamp of the city upon it. The '90s will provide San Francisco with an extraordinary opportunity to take American cuisine one step farther along the path of progress.

As our editors put it, "The city's first restaurant was probably a room off the saloon in the long-gone Bella Union Hotel at Portsmouth Square, which was succeeded shortly thereafter by the original Poodle Dog, Maison Dorée and the fabulous Palace Hotel, where the legendary Lucien Heyraudt created a grand cuisine that routinely impressed visiting European royalty.

"Today, stalwart survivors of that tradition are scattered about town. Such places are often fondly described as 'truly San Franciscan,' that is, possessing a reassuring aura generated by dark polished wood, plenty of brass, frosted glass and mirrors, light fixtures made from old gas jets, waiters in starched jackets, espresso machines huffing like brass locomotives and well-heeled crowds clamoring for tables. Few, if any, of these places serve truly distinguished food, though it's hard to go wrong with fresh Dungeness crab or that nearly eclipsed delicacy, Rex sole." The editors go on to give you this precious tip: "one frequents such establishments not to worship the food, but to cut the fog with whiskey and catch the spirit of the old days, good and otherwise, in the 'City That Knows How.' "

As in show business, new faces come and go. Sometimes, they come and stay. Is San Francisco's restaurant scene changing? In a city that has never been discouraged, let us assume it's for the best.

André Gayot
Gault Millau, Inc.
5900 Wilshire Blvd.,
29th Floor
Los Angeles, CA 90036

ABOUT THE REVIEWS

Restaurants are ranked in the same manner that French students are graded, on a scale of one to twenty. The rankings reflect *only* the quality of the food; decor, service, wine lists and atmosphere are explicitly commented on within each review. Restaurants that are ranked thirteen and above are distinguished with toques (chef's hats), according to the table below:

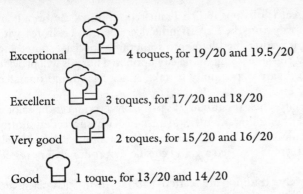

Exceptional 4 toques, for 19/20 and 19.5/20

Excellent 3 toques, for 17/20 and 18/20

Very good 2 toques, for 15/20 and 16/20

Good 1 toque, for 13/20 and 14/20

Keep in mind that we are comparing San Francisco's restaurants to the best in the world, and that these ranks are *relative*. One toque for 13/20 is not a very good ranking for a highly reputed (and very expensive) restaurant, but it is quite complimentary for a small place without much culinary pretension.

Unless otherwise noted, the prices given are for a complete dinner for two, including an appetizer and a main course and dessert per person, along with tax, tip and a bottle of wine. It is, naturally, hard to estimate the cost of wine; for our purposes we assume a modest bottle at a modest restaurant and a good California wine (usually $20 to $30 a bottle) at a more serious place. Lovers of the great Burgundies, Bordeaux or Champagnes will find their tabs higher than our estimates; conversely, those who like to eat lightly, sharing appetizers and desserts, will spend less. However, prices continue to creep up, so forgive us if a restaurant has raised its prices by the time you visit it.

TOQUE TALLY

18/20

Masa's

17/20

Acquerello
Amelio's
Chez Panisse

Fleur de Lys
Zola's

16/20

Ernie's
La Folie
Fresh Cream
Lalime's
Lark Creek Inn
Stars

15/20

John Ash & Co.
Cafe at Chez Panisse
Cafe Beaujolais
Campton Place
Château Souverain
Donatello
Fourth Street Grill
French Room
The Grille
↗Hayes Street Grill
Miramonte Hotel
Pierre
PosTrio
690
Square One
Le St. Tropez
Tra Vigne
Trilogy
Le Trou
Truffles
Victor's
Zuni Cafe

14/20

Act IV
Angkor Palace
L'Avenue
Bay Wolf Café
Bistro Rôti
Blue Fox
La Boucane
Caffe Sport
Le Castel
The Covey
Domaine Chandon
Fog City Diner
Fuku-Sushi
Golden Turtle

Gulf Coast Restaurant & Oyster Bar
Harry's Bar & American Grill
Lisa Hemenway's
Khan Toke Thai House
Modesto Lanzone
Matisse
Mustards
Narai
Phnom Penh
Royal Thai
Santa Fe Bar & Grill
Sedona Grill & Bar
Silks
Starmont
Stars Cafe
Yaya Cuisine

13/20

Alioto's Restaurant
Auberge du Soleil
Bayon
The Big Four
Butler's
Cactus Cafe
Café Majestic
California Culinary Academy
Carrara's Café
Celadon
Chef Paul
China Moon Café
Christopher's Café
Ciao
Circolo Restaurant & Champagneria
City Block
La Crème de la Crème
Eddie Jacks
Elite Café
L'Etoile
Il Fornaio
French Laundry
Garden House
Greens

Harbor Village Restaurant
Ironwood Café
Jimmy's American Place
Julie's Supper Club
Kabuto Sushi
Kenwood
Kim's
Kuleto's
La Lanterna
Madrona Manor
Mai's
Monsoon
Nob Hill
North China
North India
Ocean Restaurant
Oliveto
Pacific Cafe
Pacific Heights Bar & Grill

Peacock
Piatti Ristorante
Plaza Grill
Prego
Regina's
La Roca
Scott's Seafood Grill & Bar
Sun Dial Grill
Tadich Grill
Thep Phanom
Tre Scalini
Union Hotel
Vanessi's
Wu Kong
Yujean's Modern Cuisine of China

NO RANKING

Embarko

THE WORLD'S CUISINES

ALSATIAN

Le Castel

AMERICAN

Augusta's
Avenue Grill
Bistro Rôti
Bix
Blue Light Café
Butler's
Cafe Beaujolais
Campton Place
Embarko
Faz
Fog City Diner
Gertie's Chesapeake Bay Café
Harris'
Harry's on Fillmore

Hog's Breath Inn
Ironwood Café
Jack's
Julie's Supper Club
Lark Creek Inn
MacArthur Park
Marin Joe's
Mission Ranch
Pat O'Shea's Mad Hatter
Perry's
Plaza Grill
Savannah Grill
Stars
Stars Cafe
Vanessi's

ASIAN

Monsoon
Trader Vic's

BRAZILIAN
De Paula's

BURMESE
Mandalay

CAJUN
Elite Café
Gulf Coast Restaurant & Oyster Bar

CALIFORNIAN
Ace Cafe
Act IV
John Ash & Co.
L'Avenue
Bay Wolf Café
The Big Four
Bistro Rôti
Café at Chez Panisse
Café Majestic
California Culinary Academy
Carrara's Café
Casa Madrona
Château Souverain
Chez Panisse
China Moon Café
Christopher's Café
City Block
Corona Bar & Grill
La Crème de la Crème
Domaine Chandon
Eddie Jacks
565 Clay
Fourth Street Grill
French Laundry
French Room
The Grille
Hayes Street Grill
Lisa Hemenway's
Janot's
Jimmy's American Place
Kenwood

Madrona Manor
Masa's
Matisse
Monsoon
Mustards
Nob Hill
Pat O'Shea's Mad Hatter
Pacific Heights Bar & Grill
The Portman Grill
PosTrio
Eddie Rickenbacker's
Santa Fe Bar & Grill
Silks
690
Starmont
Sun Dial Grill
Truffles
Union Hotel
Victor's
Yaya Cuisine
Zuni Cafe

CAMBODIAN
Angkor Palace
Angor Wat
Bayon
Cambodia House
Cambodiana
Phnom Penh

CARIBBEAN
Miss Pearl's Jam House

CHINESE
Celadon
China Moon Café
Harbor Village Restaurant
Hong Kong Flower Lounge
Hunan
The Mandarin
North China
North Sea Harbor Village
Ocean Restaurant
Ton Kiang

11

Tommy Toy's Chinoise
Vegi Food
Wu Kong
Yuet Lee
Yujean's Modern Cuisine of China

CONTINENTAL
The Covey
Nob Hill

CREOLE
Elite Café
Gulf Coast Restaurant & Oyster Bar
Regina's

CUBAN
Cuba

FRENCH
Act IV
Amelio's
John Ash & Co.
Auberge du Soleil
Bayon
The Big Four
La Boucane
Brasserie Tomo
California Culinary Academy
Caprice
Carnelian Room
Le Castel
Cendrillon
Le Central
Chef Paul
The Covey
La Crème de la Crème
Le Cyrano
Domaine Chandon
L'Entrecôte de Paris
Ernie's

L'Etoile
Fleur de Lys
La Folie
Fournou's Ovens
French Room
Fresh Cream
Janot's
Kenwood
Lascaux
Masa's
Matisse
Oliveto
Pierre
The Portman Grill
Rodin
Silks
South Park Café
Starmont
Le St. Tropez
Trilogy
Le Trou
Victor's
Zola's

GERMAN
Swiss Alps

HAKKA
Ton Kiang

INDIAN
Bombay Palace
Gaylord's
North India
Peacock

INTERNATIONAL
Avenue Grill
Butler's
Embarko

PosTrio
690
Square One
Stars
Stars Cafe
Terra
Truffles
Zuni Cafe

ITALIAN

Acquerello
Alioto's Restaurant
Blue Fox
Buca Giovanni
Bucci's
Caffe Sport
Carrara's Café
Ciao
Circolo Restaurant & Champagneria
La Crème de la Crème
Donatello
Il Fornaio
Giuliano's
Harry's Bar & American Grill
Jackson Fillmore Trattoria
Kuleto's
La Lanterna
Modesto Lanzone
Lascaux
Little City Antipasti Bar
Little Italy
Little Joe's
Marin Joe's
Oliveto
Original Joe's
La Pergola Ristorante
Piatti Ristorante
Prego
Ristorante Giramonte
Terra
Tra Vigne
Tre Scalini
Tutto Bene

Vanessi's

JAPANESE

Fuku-Sushi
Kabuto Sushi
Mitoya
Osome
Sanppo
Yamato
Yoshi's Restaurant & Nightspot

KOREAN

Korea House
Seoul Garden

MEDITERRANEAN

Atrium
L'Avenue
Faz
Lalime's
Maltese Grill

MEXICAN

Alejandro's Sociedad Gastronomica
Cactus Cafe
Chevys
Corona Bar & Grill
Guaymas
La Rondalla

MIDDLE EASTERN

Yaya Cuisine

NICARAGUAN

Nicaragua

OYSTER BAR

Elite Café
Gulf Coast Restaurant & Oyster Bar
La Rocca's Oyster Bar

PERUVIAN
Alejandro's Sociedad Gastronomica

POLYNESIAN
Trader Vic's

SALVADORAN
La Roca
El Tazumal

SEAFOOD
Alioto's Restaurant
Cliff House
Gertie's Chesapeake Bay Café
Gulf Coast Restaurant & Oyster Bar
Hayes Street Grill
Ocean Restaurant
Pacific Cafe
Pacific Heights Bar & Grill
La Roca
Sam's Grill
Scott's Seafood Grill & Bar
Tadich Grill

SHANGHAI
Wu Kong

SOUTHWESTERN
Santa Fe Bar & Grill
Sedona Grill & Bar

SPA
The Grille

SPANISH
Alejandro's Sociedad Gastronomica

STEAKHOUSE
L'Entrecôte de Paris
Harris'
Original Joe's

SUSHI
Fuku-Sushi
Kabuto Sushi
Mitoya
Osome
Sanppo

THAI
Khan Toke Thai House
Manora's Thai Restaurant
Nakapan
Narai
Neecha
Royal Thai
Siam Cuisine
Thep Phanom

VEGETARIAN
Greens
Vegi Food

VIETNAMESE
Aux Delices Vietnam
Cordon Bleu Vietnamese
Garden House
Golden Turtle
Kim's
Mai's

RESTAURANTS

Ace Cafe
1539 Folsom St.,
South of Market
• 621-4752
CALIFORNIAN

11/20

What would it be like if the Jetsons (of TV-cartoon fame) opened a hof brau, then became enamored of Mexican and Carribean cuisine? The result would be something like the Ace. The espresso-joint ambience (showing through from a former incarnation) and funky furniture are down-to-earth without seeming completely real. It's lots of fun, though. The crowd ranges from laid-back hip to corporate, the food is tasty, and the service is sharp and friendly. Spicy Cajun shrimp and marinated flank steak with salsa go well with the draft beers—Cooper's Nut Brown Ale and Späten. The focaccia pizza topped with black beans, cilantro pesto and tomato con queso goes well with an Oregon Pinot Noir; we've also enjoyed capellini with creamy red-pepper sauce along with a buttery Chardonnay. An appetizer specialty is toast—with garlic, tapenade, or tomatoes and mozzarella. The sound system favors jazz, but don't be surprised if a bunch of people with vintage accordions burst in to play a rousing "Beer Barrel Polka"—it happens all the time in this neighborhood. Dinner for two, with beers, can be gotten for about $25.
Open Mon.-Thurs. 11:30 a.m.-12:30 a.m., Fri. 11:30 a.m.-2 a.m., Sat. 6 p.m.-2 a.m., Sun. 6 p.m.-10 p.m. All major cards.

Acquerello
1722 Sacramento St.
• 567-5432
ITALIAN

When Zola's vacated its longtime Sacramento Street premises last year, this distinguished Italian restaurant moved right in. The two partners, Giancarlo Paterlini, former general manager of The Donatello hotel and its lauded Ristorante, and Suzette Gresham, former executive chef at Ristorante Donatello, are a perfect pair: Paterlini has always been the consummate host, a Bolognese who knows Italian food and insists on a European standard of excellent service. Gresham, though not Italian, has an instinctive understanding of Italian cooking—in fact, to us, her dishes say "Mama mia." When you walk into this tiny, intimate restaurant—which takes its name from the *acquerellos*, or watercolors, hung on the whitewashed walls—you can almost feel how happy these two are to be working in their own restaurant. The greeting—and the service—is very personal: rather than rattle off a list of specialties, Paterlini will have you tell him what you'd like to eat, and he'll recommend dishes along those lines. Every night the menu features a half dozen appealing antipasti: spinach salad with pears and

Parmesan, a masterful sea bass carpaccio drizzled with extra-virgin olive oil, fresh goat's milk mozzarella with tomatoes. Pastas include an elegant salmon-and-scallop ravioli in a sauce of vermouth and dill, and heavenly little pillows of spinach gnocchi in a sweet Gorgonzola sauce. On a recent visit, a stunning pasta special—handmade ravioli filled with chopped shiitake and ricotta and served in a deeply flavored spinach-and-herb sauce—just barely won out over the more rustic, but absolutely delicious, penne in a rabbit-rosemary sauce. Some Italian menus lose interest after the pasta course; this one, happily, does not. Here, the choices are mostly excellently prepared classics. Who wouldn't enjoy the thick, tender lamb chops seared with olive oil, herbs and juniper berries, or the simple filet of beef flavored with shallots and a drop of aceto balsamico? The menu is so well orchestrated that the desserts fit in seamlessly. Caramelized rice pudding, studded with raisins and cooked properly al dente, is served in a mound with poached peaches on the side. Chocolate truffle cake here is the best we can remember—a densely textured bottom layer topped with a very dark silken chocolate mousse. Bravo! The wine list, while not overwhelming, has an extremely good selection of Italian wines, though it's difficult to find something really interesting under $20. Good choices here include Barbera d'Alba from Elio Altare, Dolceti d'Alba from Pasquera and any wine from Mastroberardino. Dinner for two, with wine, will run between $85 and $110.
Open Tues.-Sat. 6 p.m.-10:30 p.m., special Sun. regional dinners on occasion. Cards: MC, V.

Act IV
333 Fulton St.,
Civic Center (in the
Inn at the Opera)
• 863-8400
FRENCH/CALIFORNIAN

Act IV is aptly named as the after-performance spot par excellence in the Civic Center's cultural nexus. Snugly ensconced in the cozy, antique-studded Inn at the Opera, one of the city's most charming small hotels, Act IV offers full à la carte dinners and special three-course beat-the-curtain quickies, as well as substantial late-night snacks. Recently overhauled under the direction of Robert Lyon, who took over as chef in July 1989, its menu is moving from old-fashioned French toward something more fresh and modern. Traditional local fare is updated with a lighter hand and a grand cornucopia of ultra-fresh produce, meats, poultry and fish from Northern California growers and purveyors. During the opera season, Chef Lyon whets the appetite with special "theme" dinners keyed to the performances. The "Falstaff" menu, for instance, opens with a sturdy savory pie of rabbit "Henry IV" with ginger mus-

tard; a G-clef crowns the "Merry Wives of Windsor" bavarois of chocolate and vanilla mousses that close its curtain. These theme dinners are priced at $26 and $29; unlimited wine costs an additional $9. A la carte items, especially "late-night specials," are moderately priced.
Open daily 6:30 p.m.-midnight (late-night menu served after 10:30 p.m.). Cards: AE, MC, V.

Alejandro's Sociedad Gastronomica
1840 Clement St.,
Richmond District
• 668-1184
SPANISH/MEXICAN/
PERUVIAN

12/20

We aren't exactly sure what the "Sociedad Gastronomica" is or whether, in fact, it really exists. But we're told it is an association of Latin American gourmets and that Alejandro Espinosa, a Peruvian of Spanish descent, is a member of it. Society or not, some superb high-Spanish dishes are served here, as well as some competent Mexican "common" fare to satisfy those whose taste for Hispanic food only goes as far as enchiladas and tacos. Among 40 different *tapas* available, the alejandrinos, little fried pastries filled with cheese, egg or peppers, make an excellent starter. The entrées—barring the competent but unexciting Mexican dishes—can be astonishingly good, such as the best paella Valenciana in San Francisco: fresh fish and shellfish, good chorizo, fresh vegetables, chicken, and rice golden with saffron. A house favorite is the amusingly named "pescada a la macho," a hot, spicy (and *muy macho*) fisherman's stew of red snapper and tomatoes in a wine-herb sauce. The wine list includes picks from California, Spain and Chile, and the bar knows how to whip up an excellent pitcher of sangria. Desserts are typically Spanish; flan is the specialty. The slightly kitsch decor (cheap ironwork and tile, heavy wood, heavy chandeliers) and the sometimes-indifferent service detract from the experience, but we still think the paella is marvelous. About $50 for two, with wine.
Open Mon.-Thurs. 5 p.m.-11 p.m., Fri.-Sat. 5 p.m.-midnight, Sun. 4 p.m.-11 p.m. All major cards.

Alioto's Restaurant
2936 Hyde St.,
Fisherman's Wharf
• 673-0183
ITALIAN/SEAFOOD

Ask about Italian restaurants on Fisherman's Wharf and any native San Franciscan worth his saltimbocca will probably cringe with contempt. The overwhelming majority of so-called restaurants in this sorry tourist trap operate under the unspoken guideline that out-of-towners will eat anything. Alioto's, family owned since 1928, is a rare exception. Not only does it treat visitors with great respect, educating them in what seafood, Italian style, should be, but it attracts a loyal following of locals who return again and again for the fresh-only ("fresh-frozen" is an oxymoronic no-no) fish and shellfish. The varied menu doesn't stop at the shoreline, however: pasta, chicken and humanely raised veal round out the standard Italian fare. What most distinguishes Alioto's from its run-of-the mill neighbors, beyond its high standards and attention to ingredients, is its nostalgic submenu of Sicilian favorites that hark back to Rose Alioto, the restaurant's founder. Not surprisingly, many new dishes star the saltwater fish that grace both Sicily and California: notably carpaccio di pesce spada, thinly sliced raw swordfish marinated in lemon and oil; gramigna Charleston, elbow pasta sauced with swordfish, eggplant, mint and garlic; and mollusco Mediterraneo, marinated shellfish and Mediterranean vegetables that are skewered and grilled. Credit the manager, Nunzio Alioto, for the first-rate wine list (he's one of only eleven Master Sommeliers in the United States). And the view on the water's edge can't be beat. A dinner for two will easily be $75.

Open Mon.-Fri. 11 a.m.-11 p.m., Sat.-Sun. 11 a.m.-midnight. All major cards.

Amelio's
1630 Powell St.,
North Beach
• 397-4339
FRENCH

A week after the earthquake—that's last year's, not the one at the turn of the century—Amelio's lost a $5,000 bottle of wine. It simply fell from its perch to the floor. Aftershocks can be expensive. But that's about all that has changed for the negative since our last visit. In fact, we find improvements worthy of another point. We're still not quite sure whether chef Jacky Robert is a cuisinier or a magician. This gentleman has an uncanny knack for bringing lifeless dowager restaurants back into the full bloom of youth. Some eight years ago, his rather nouvelle ideas put Ernie's, then in a sad state of culinary dilapidation, at the top of the city's restaurant ladder. Hungry for a restaurant of his own, Robert left Ernie's a few years ago to resurrect Amelio's, an Italian-Continental remnant of many decades past. With charming co-owner Chris Shearman, Robert has done the near-impossible: only a few months after he donned his toque, the raves came in and this tiny, elegant dining room (magnificent old woods, floral fabrics and dramatic flower arrangements, all skillfully and softly lit) was full once again. The food is still an interesting blend of nouvelle cuisine and classic French, with a few Asian touches—Robert's lovely wife, Chong, is Korean, and he attributes much of his style to what he has learned from her. The best way to sample this eclectic cuisine is to order the often-changing dégustation menu. It may start with Robert's signature woven bicolor pasta with huge, barely cooked Hawaiian prawns and sea scallops in a light cream sauce with caviar. Then it may progress to crisp little deep-fried quail in a ginger-soy-molasses marinade served atop snow peas, followed by an intermezzo of a grape and Champagne sorbet. You then have a choice of entrées; the sautéed deer loin comes in a juniper berry sauce, the pheasant is cooked with truffles in a sealed casserole, and the lobster is served with a natural butter sauce. Then the kitchen sends out a lovely little salad—one night it included three delightful imported cheeses, another night an astounding Brie "pancake." Finally, you will be served dessert, perhaps an avocado mousse in a pool of Champange or a Grand Marnier soufflé in an orange shell. Ordering à la carte, one gets half the number of dishes for the same price (or more)—and it seems like most of Jacky Robert's attention is devoted to creating a fabulous dégustation menu. Still, we had a roasted rabbit loin with sesame sauce that was excellent, followed by one of the chef's fabled chocolate mousses. The wine list includes every treasure imaginable. The service is young, a tad pretentious and not always knowledgeable about the menu, but they're trying harder all the time. The tab will be about $130 for an à la carte dinner for two, with wine; menus are $36 and $57 per person, without wine or tip. *Open nightly 6 p.m.-10:30 p.m. All major cards.*

Angkor Palace
1769 Lombard St.,
Marina District
• 931-2830
CAMBODIAN

14

In an intimate dining room upstairs from street level, guests sit at low tables with foot wells to be served by the owner-chef's family. The decor is palatial, fitting the name and the food. This is stylized Cambodian palace cuisine, with its lasting French colonial influence, which transports the concept of *la cuisine* to a place where the richest cream comes from coconuts. In the hushed atmosphere, one hears quiet exclamations of delight as the dishes are served. We've enjoyed marinated pork chops on a bed of shredded cabbage, brilliant green papaya salad, a pot of fish mousse surrounded by cleverly cut vegetables for dipping. In our repeated visits the food has been as good as it looks. The short but deft wine list includes an amusing mousseux from Bordeaux that can be drunk throughout dinner—it matches the whole range of flavors. With Bordeaux, dinner will be about $40 for two.
Open daily 5 p.m.-10:30 p.m. All major cards.

Angor Wat
4217 Geary Blvd.,
Richmond District
• 221-7887
CAMBODIAN

12/20

This restaurant has inspired some local restaurant critics to proclaim Cambodian cuisine the most exciting new cooking to hit these shores. But authenticity isn't one of Angor Wat's strong suits; to the best of our knowledge, poached salmon, Cornish game hen and vegetables sautéed in olive oil (all found on the menu here) have never been Cambodian staples. Nonetheless, the food here is expertly prepared and seasoned with such Southeast Asian basics as tamarind, ginger, lemon grass, coconut milk and chili peppers. It's all tailored to the American palate—meats and poultry are boned, fish are fileted and no innards are offered—but it's all delicious: stir-fried pork and prawns with winter-melon sauce, five-spice broiled chicken, salmon with lemon-grass sauce and much more. Chef-owner Keav Ty has combined the cuisine of his heritage with his training as a French chef, and the result is largely successful. The setting is pleasant, with pictures of Angor Wat (the temple) on all the walls, and the price is quite fair: $40 for dinner for two, with wine. *Open Tues.-Sat. 5 p.m.-10:30 p.m., Sun. 5 p.m.-10 p.m. All major cards.*

Atrium
101 California St.,
Financial District
• 788-4101
MEDITERRANEAN

12/20

Northern California boasts a balmy Mediterranean climate, with the same produce, the same wealth of seafood, even the same love of the local wine. What, then, could be more natural than for San Francisco to embrace the rich and varied cuisines of the Mediterranean coast? At Atrium, the aromas of garlic, roasting lamb and grilling fish set the tone the moment you step inside. The open, airy feel, accented by lush greenery and full-length windows, enhances the effect. You could be in Portofino. Chef Sheila Marques, a Jeremiah Tower protégée, serves a mostly Italian menu with Californian touches. In such novel combinations as asparagus-mint soup with lemon cream, grilled duck-breast salad with oranges and olives in citrus vinaigrette, and marinated free-range chicken and spring vegetables baked in parchment with feta cheese, she emphasizes fresh, mostly organic, produce along with seafood, poultry and lamb. Have the zuccotto, a chocolate cream-filled sponge cake soaked in Grand Marnier. For $80, two will eat and drink heartily. *Open Mon.-Fri. 11:30 a.m.-2:30 p.m. & 5:30 p.m.-9 p.m., Sat. 5:30 p.m.-9 p.m. Cards: AE, MC, V.*

L'Avenue
3855 3rd Ave.,
Richmond District
• 386-1555
CALIFORNIAN/
MEDITERRANEAN

We've all been waiting for a restaurant like this, a little romantic place on a quiet street, with moody lighting, a lot of soft wood and brass, cloth-covered tables, candlelight—and great food. It's a dream. Chef Nancy Oakes knows just what lovers (and others) want to dine on: Californian cuisine, or, let's say, regional American cuisine—but always with a French touch. Our favorite appetizer is the Maryland crabcakes with red-onion-and-black-pepper dressing and roasted pepper aïoli. Balance that with a salad of vine-ripened tomatoes and goat-cheese mozzarella. Maybe share a fig-and-prosciutto salad with ginger crème fraîche, greens

and roasted walnuts. Then move on to pan-roasted squab stuffed with apple-and-onion confit, on a bed of roasted potatoes, artichoke hearts and peppers with Burgundy sauce. Linger over dessert, then stroll out into the Paris—make that San Francisco—night. Dinner for two, with wine, will be about $80.
Open Mon.-Sat. 6 p.m.-10 p.m., Sun. 5:30 p.m.-9:30 p.m. All major cards.

Bayon
2018 Lombard St.,
Cow Hollow
• 922-1400
CAMBODIAN/FRENCH

This charming neo-Cambodian place was a well-kept secret until an indiscreet restaurant critic blew the cover. Now Bayon is charming and packed. Incredibly, the effect of popularity on the quality of Bayon cuisine has been, if anything, positive. Ingredients are as fresh as can be, and the preparations are as dazzling and tasty as ever; more important, the kitchen has become ever more deft and confident. Aside from the excellent food, one of the main reasons we like Bayon is the decor. Pastel walls and beams lit by mixed blue and pink track lights, Bhuddist artifacts and ethereal music create a rarified feeling, like an art gallery inside a temple. Chef Dean Leng uses fresh ingredients and favors organic produce. One side of the dual-culture menu is Cambodian palace cuisine, the other side unadulterated (well, only a little) French. On the Asian end, we love the lawt, crispy little blossom rolls with fragrant stuffing. Sach cheam aing is a flavorful grilled lamb chop marinated in herbs and spices, and trobs mean samras is baked eggplant with minced pork and diced prawns. On the French end, the catfish filet meunière and rack of lamb are straightforward and tasty. Dinner for two, with wine, is $40.
Open Tues.-Sun. 5 p.m.-10:30 p.m. All major cards.

The Big Four
1075 California St.,
Nob Hill
• 771-1140
CALIFORNIAN/FRENCH

You've got to love the theme here. But what Big Four are we talking about? The four basic food groups? A new basketball conference? Absolutely not, for this is San Francisco, and the four in question were powerful men, nay robber barons, who poured millions into building it. Indeed, the cornerstones for the place are Mark Hopkins (as in the hotel), Charles Crocker (as in the bank), Leland Stanford (as in the university) and C.P. Huntington (as in the library in Pasadena—he had a particularly long reach). Inside, everything's all dark and moody à la the Edwardian era. Think of it as robber-baron club chic. There are pompously comfortable green leather chairs and banquettes. Plenty of dark wood sets off scads of beveled-glass mirrors. The Big Four were meat-and-potatoes kinds of guys, and for a long while the menu reflected their tastes.

But no more. Someone has let a woman into the club and made her chef at that. We were delighted to find that Diane Ciccaroni now showcases seasonal cuisine that changes four times a year. She also conjures daily specials that are lighter than anything else offered here in recent memory. For example, avocado, pink grapefruit and endive salad with lime-poppyseed dressing was a refreshing mix of soft and crunch, though a bit unnerving at that price; chilled drunken oysters with minted cucumber-tequila salsa were fresh and zippy. Main courses are better than they were. We particularly enjoyed the game—Muscovy duck breast with citrus-honey glaze, steamed greens and herbed polenta was wholly satisfying. Expertly grilled venison with wild-rice pecan pancakes was matched with dried sour cherries on a raft of raddichio. One problem: you still need a robber baron's cash flow to afford the wine list. The food cries out for red, and it's difficult to find an appealing bottle for under $45. Desserts are a mixed bag. Yes, some of the pastry-tray offerings are from the bake shop, La Nouvelle Pâtisserie, but at triple the retail price. Others are made in-house. We loved the mousse with dar, hazelnut and white chocolate served in a luscious chocolate tulip cup. Service throughout the meal was excellent. For dinner expect to pay a baronial $130 for two, including wine.

Open Mon.-Fri. 7 a.m.-10:30 a.m., 11:30 a.m.-3 p.m. & 5:30 p.m.- 10:30 p.m., Sat.-Sun. 11:30 a.m.-3.p.m. & 5:30 p.m.-10:30 p.m. All major cards.

Bistro Rôti

155 Steuart St.,
• 495-6500
AMERICAN/CALIFORNIAN

Opened in the spring of 1989, this bistro is the latest production from the enormously successful team of Cindi Pawlcyn and company (founders of Fog City Diner and Bix in the city, Mustard's and Tra Vigne in Napa Valley, and so on). Rôti—short for "Rôtisserie"—is located in the lobby of the new Hotel Griffon, on the site of one of the first sailors' boarding houses built after the Great Earthquake and Fire in 1906. The decor is men's-club classic with brass overhead racks for your briefcase, wood bistro chairs and imitation-leather banquettes and booths.

The centerpiece here is an open fireplace where spits laden with chickens, ducks and Rock Cornish game hens turn in front of a hardwood fire. This display smells wonderful and appears incredibly inviting—the only problem is that it's difficult to actually snare an order of those tasty-looking birds. The fireplace simply isn't big enough to handle the demand. It's much easier to savor the grilled veal chop (marinated in black peppercorns and served with a braised-artichoke-and-pearl-onion stew) than the orange-and lemon-scented duck or the chicken infused with mint and garlic. Pawlcyn always includes enough daily specials to keep it interesting, and among the best choices here are plump, tender mussels in a saffron broth; house-cured salmon with herb-infused Mascarpone; and Santa Barbara escargots with walnuts and whole roasted garlic cloves. Seafood is almost always a good bet at Rôti, whether it's crimson tiger prawns, swordfish with smoked onion and esacarole, or fresh sweet scallops seared on the griddle and served in a delicate beurre blanc with a pile of eggplant and red-pepper strips. Straightforward desserts include straw-berry-rhubarb tart, coffee pot-de-crème, and an eggy lemon soufflé with raspberry sauce. The well-edited wine list includes several gems like the Cru du Coudelet, a Côtes-du-Rhône from Beaucastel, one of Châteauneuf-du-Pape's best properties.

Rôti has had to work out a few kinks in its first months. There were problems mastering the difficult art of roasting over a wood fire (some of the birds came out with blackened skins), and we experienced a few problems with the service and with inconsistent quality. Still, with a half chicken priced at $9.50, Rôti is one of the few bistros in the city with real bistro prices—and it's open all day long. Dinner for two, with wine, will cost between $60 and $75.
Open Sun.-Thurs. 11:30 a.m.-11 p.m., Fri.-Sat. 11:30 a.m.-midnight. All major cards.

Bix
56 Gold St.,
North Beach
• 433-6300
AMERICAN

12/20

Squint a little bit, order another martini and you'll swear a Raymond Chandler novel has come to life around you. Dark burnished wood, brass and frosted glass, a white-jacketed wait staff, torch singer Mary Stallings (formerly of the Count Basie band, among others) crooning by the piano—it's all there. The food in this classic speakeasy isn't inspired, but it is tasty. It might be described as imaginative home-style cooking, similar to the fare at the backing partnership's other properties: Fog City Diner, Rio Grill, Mustards, and so on. Proprietor Doug Biederbeck knows spirits the way a sommelier knows wines, and the gleaming back bar is a potable wonderland. Biederbeck is also known to appear tableside with his trademark silver tray to mix his famous dry martinis on the spot. Dinner runs about $60 to $70 for two, with martinis.
Open Mon.-Fri. 11 a.m.-11 p.m., Sat. 11 a.m.-midnight, Sun. 11 a.m.-10 p.m. All major cards.

Blue Fox
659 Merchant St.,
Financial District
• 981-1177
ITALIAN

The name is venerable, but the restaurant inside is new. None of the many previous Blue Foxes were in the same class as Gianni Fassio's stylized temple of *cucina nobile Italiana*. While being seated in one of two palatial, softly lit dining rooms, we always have an exciting sense of being at center stage amid amplified elegance. The supporting cast offers enthusiastic, impeccable service. And the food is edible art—make that edible, delicious art. One hates to sink a fork into a radiant creation such as the terrine of white and green asparagus with red potatoes, but it has to be done—and the result is heavenly. On a recent visit, our risotto with Stracchino cheese was rich and plentiful enough to be a meal in itself, although it was nicely balanced by a simple and flavorful red mullet with bitter greens. The selection of Italian wines is among the best in this Italian-oriented city. The little bar, with its white piano and pale neoclassical motif, is considered a most elegant spot for after-work martinis. Dinner for two, with a couple of martinis, is about $130.
Open Mon.-Sat. 6 p.m.-10:15 p.m. Major cards.

Blue Light Café
1979 Union St.,
Marina District
• 922-5510
AMERICAN

11/20

We've heard more than one story of people arriving at the Blue Light with dinner reservations, only to give away their table because they were having so much fun in the bar. But that's not the best way to do it; the best way is to make a reservation and show up early for a little prepandial tequila, raucous talk and rock and roll. As is appropriate in a place owned by Boz Scaggs, there's a steady backbeat pulsing through the multilevel, industrial-tech restaurant. Galvanized aluminum, high ceilings and low light (abetted by skylights before dark) give the Blue Light a lazy Southern feel, as if it occupied an old warehouse on the bayou end of the Mississippi. On the other hand, it fits the upscale Union Street milieu as well—quite a trick. Steaks, chicken, spicy sausage and fresh fish are grilled over mesquite. There's basic, hearty fare like pork ribs with homemade barbecue sauce, and there are dishes with flair: grilled pork chops stuffed with dried apricots and Sonoma dry jack and brushed with a glaze of apple cider and bourbon. We love the slightly sweet cornbread and the tangy, creamy coleslaw that comes with most entrées. Mesquite-grilled steaks are the most consistently good dishes, especially in the form of fajitas. Service is generally efficient, but on a busy evening it's wise to order some of Boz's patented buttermilk onion rings to keep hunger at bay while perusing the menu.

Dinner for two, with beer, will run about $50.
*Open Sun.-Wed. 6 p.m.-10 p.m., Thurs.-Sat. 6 p.m.-11 p.m.
Cards: MC, V.*

Bombay Palace
600 Beach St.,
Fisherman's Wharf
• 776-3666
INDIAN

11/20

Ah, the enveloping aroma when we enter the Bombay Palace, as if the very air were an hors d'oeuvre preparing us for the meal to come! The marble-dense, maroon-and-gray dining room may be somewhat chilly and austere, though elegant, and the efficient service may be always a bit on the unctuous side; but the savory Indian food is among the most reasonably priced in the Bay Area. We like the flavor of the appetizer samosas, deep-fried pastry triangles stuffed with potatoes, peas, cloves and spices. From the tandoor oven, the meats and poultry are excellent, especially the robustly flavored chicken tikka and the succulent thighs of chicken tandoori with lots of good grilled sweet onions. Two vegetable dishes shine—the eggplant, sophisticated and spicy, which makes an excellent accompaniment to the grilled meats; and the mixed vegetables, a blend of cauliflower, potatoes, carrots, onions and green beans, seasoned with just enough golden curry to be interesting without obscuring the delicate flavors. Lentil dhals can be weak and watery. A recent order of vegetarian thali was not as interesting as some we've had, and the breads, particularly the onion kulcha, though tasty, don't hold their texture well. Indian desserts are not a strong point here, although there is a lovely creamy cardamom-scented rice pudding with moist raisins and almonds. Dinner for two, with beer or wine, $50.
Open Mon.-Sun. 11 a.m.-2:30 p.m. & 5 p.m.-10 p.m. Cards: AE, MC, V.

Brasserie Tomo
745 Columbus Ave.,
North Beach
• 296-7668
FRENCH

12/20

This relative newcomer to San Francisco's haute cuisine scene is certainly haute-minimalist chic in its angular, assymmetrical use of space. It's one of the weirdest, most chilling restaurants around, like a cross between a hospital and a Japanese art statement. The only pleasure is the high-tech gray leather chairs, which are a lot more comfortable than they look. Hopefully, all the good stuff will be on the plate; and, occasionally, it is. But Brasserie Tomo, the creation of Japanese-born Tomo Okuda, who studied cooking in France, is also a study in inconsistency. When Okuda is good, he's superb, undeniably a terrific chef. But when his dishes don't work, which is frequently, it's embarrassing. Despite its thick covers, the wine list is minimalist as well, with mostly serviceable—and a few excellent—vintages from France and California. The service is incredibly efficient, undercut with a bit of anxiety. Brasserie Tomo's specialty is a choice of three eight-course prix-fixe dinners, for $40, $55 or $70. There is also a small but interesting range of à la carte dishes. The entire menu changes completely every two weeks. It's much more fun to sample Okuda's concepts through the set dinners, but alas, the only one that really delivers his genius is the $70, which makes for a pricey meal.

A recent splurge starred a seafood terrine of halibut with a tiny man sculpted from radish walking an oyster-mushroom path under a broccoli tree, warmed by a carrot sun. Visually it was precious enough to make our teeth hurt. Flavor-wise it was bland and overcooked enough to border on the rubbery, served in a tomato-herb sauce that was way too watery. A grilled foie gras on daikon in its own natural juice and perfumed with shallots was marvelous. Sweetbreads served in a fragrant sauce with small bâtons of carrots and green beans were full of flavor and joy. Delicately sliced shrimp, scallops, mixed Oriental mushrooms, diced carrots and tomatoes in a delicate vinaigrette, served amusingly in martini glasses, were beautifully balanced in texture and flavor. Sadly, a vichyssoise was dreadful, flabby and bland, and sweet enough to be like a serving of melted potato ice cream. Granita of grapefruit was meant to be refreshing but it suffered from a freezer-burn aftertaste. So it went up and down until the final whopping bill. We hope that Okuda warms up his place and cleans up his act, because Brasserie Tomo could be one of the more remarkable restaurants in Northern California. But he's got a long way to go. Dinner for two, with wine, runs from $150 to $180.

Open Mon.-Sat. 5:30 p.m.-10:30 p.m. Cards: AE, MC, V.

Buca Giovanni

800 Greenwich St.,
North Beach
• 776-7766
ITALIAN

12/20

Once a fixture at Vanessi's (a popular North Beach eatery), Giovanni Leoni disappeared from the culinary scene for a few years and then resurfaced as owner of this most enjoyable restaurant, Buca Giovanni. As the name suggests, the dining room is below street level and was designed to resemble a Toscana dungeon, with scoured brick substructures decorated with memorabilia and scenes from Lucca. The menu features many items from Tuscany rarely seen on San Francisco menus. An antipasto misto has a generous amount of aromatic bresaola and wonderfully sweet dried tomatoes with olive oil. The pastas are all a delight; we especially like the panzerotti salsa di noci, perfectly al dente ravioli pockets filled with seasoned veal and graced with a delicious, nutty sauce. Entrées range from rabbit porcini, which is sautéed with porcini mushrooms in a white-wine

sauce, to roast lamb stuffed with porcini, herbs and morta-della and wrapped in grape leaves. To finish, try the ball of good chocolate gelato rolled in semi-sweet shavings. Buca Giovanni is also notable for its low-fat and low-salt daily specials. A moderately priced wine list with good California selections makes for a pleasurable and affordable evening. About $80 for dinner for two, with wine.
Open Mon.-Thurs. 5:30 p.m.-10:30 p.m., Fri.-Sat. 5:30 p.m.-11:30 p.m. Cards: AE, MC, V.

Café Majestic
Hotel Majestic,
1500 Sutter St.,
Civic Center
• 776-6400
CALIFORNIAN

It didn't take long for former theater critic Stanley Eichelbaum to change careers and fix his indelible stamp on the San Francisco food scene. After making a name for himself at the tiny take-out café Eichelbaum & Co., he seemingly breezed into the Café Majestic in the turn-of-the-century Hotel Majestic. There's nothing old-fashioned about Eichelbaum's menu, though—even the old San Francisco favorites are reworked with a contemporary flair. The grilled chicken Nellie Melba, for example, substitutes lychee fruit for the usual grapes, and the "toasted angels" wraps sautéed oysters in prosciutto instead of yesteryear's anonymous cured meat. These succulent little morsels are finished with a zesty slathering of lime-cilantro butter and shredded chili. Wow! The remainder of the menu is pure Californian, with the requisite nods to Asia and the Mediterranean. Lamb-lovers will dote on the grilled chops à la Reine, served with a tangy fig-blueberry chutney. Even dieters eat well, with several starred dishes (the grilled chicken Maria Callas with roasted garlic, apple and papaya salsa is a standout) weighing in at under 300 calories. Desserts are worth a splurge, especially if the Linzertorte's among them. The wine list stars some lesser-known, reasonably priced California gems. About $80 for dinner for two, including wine.
Open Mon. 6 p.m.-midnight, Tues.-Sat. 7 a.m.-10:30 a.m., 11:30 a.m.-2:30 p.m. & 6 p.m.-midnight, Sun. 6 p.m.-midnight. Cards: AE, MC, V.

Caffe Sport
574 Green St.,
North Beach
• 981-1251
ITALIAN

This is a place of near-legendary status, often spoken of in hushed tones. When revered New York restaurant critic Mimi Sheraton was in town for a brief guest stint at the San Francisco *Examiner*, these were her words on Caffe Sport: "I wanted to try it, but I couldn't get in." That may be hard to believe, but anyone who's withstood the Caffe Sport ordeal knows two things: getting in can be a battle, and the management could care less about restaurant critics. Even if you're wise to the reservation system (begin calling at noon Tuesday for a spot that week; reservations are not

accepted for parties of less than four), you'll have to wait outside for a half an hour or so. Once in, you may be crammed into a table designed to accommodate half your party, and you may turn gray before a hand-scrawled menu is made available. Pass the time by admiring the chaos of toys, knickknacks and Italian artifacts plastered to the walls and ceiling. The fun really begins when the waiter comes for your order. Let's say four of you have chosen four dishes. The waiter will tell you that you must order two single-size dishes and one double. If you have trouble deciding which item to order double size, he'll decide for you and will try to bully you into agreeing. But take as much time as you need, even if your waiter gets in a snit. There are no appetizers here, not even salads, and bread will arrive at your table with no butter. But as soon as the large, colorful platters of food are brought out, all angst and confusion are washed away in a sea of garlic. You may be put off by the quantities of garlic at first bite, but it soon becomes clear that chef Antonio La Tona is working on a rarefied plane where high-impact flavors blend explosively. The pasta con pesto—a staple here—is laden with the traditional riches of olive oil, Parmesan and, of course, garlic, but it attains an ethereality that we can only attribute to the addition of stock. Caffe Sport's finest triumph, also stunningly rich, is the scampi—gigantic, tender prawns served in a creamless white sauce that defies explanation. The calamari all'Antonio comes with the same sauce, and we've seen people swoon over it. We've swooned ourselves over the and the coziche, mussels bathed in a simple sauce of lemon, wine, garlic and olive oil. As we've felt in the past, desserts are uninteresting; instead, end with an espresso. Dinner for two, with wine, will run about $60.
Open Tues.-Sat. noon-2 p.m. & 6:30 p.m.-10:30 p.m. No cards.

California Culinary Academy
625 Polk St.,
Civic Center
• 771-3500
FRENCH/CALIFORNIAN

On a recent visit to this unusual place, we were delighted to find it vastly improved over the California Culinary Academy of old: a few years back, dining at the CCA called for a colossal appetite for heavy, tedious, overcomplicated French cooking and a sense of humor generous enough to forgive the student chefs their culinary sins. Of course, if you demand perfection and uniformity of a kitchen, your needs are probably better met by one of the city's "name" French restaurants. But if you have an open mind and a sense of adventure, you'll spend far less while getting a feel for the behind-the-scenes aspects of restaurant dining—and you'll enjoy cooking that is lighter and more innovative than it was in the past. The CCA is one of America's top training grounds for professional chefs, and all the meals served in its three restaurants (plus the goodies in its café-deli) are prepared by students in its sixteen-month program. Under rigorous supervision, these chefs-in-training apply their newly learned skills to the three very different menus. In the Academy Grill, freshmen practice on simple salads, soups and grilled dishes such as lamb brochette with mint hollandaise and ahi tuna with fresh salsa. Cyril's, named for the late San Francisco bon vivant Cyril Magnin, brings a "gourmet light" menu that manages to substitute flavor for calories in its satisfying fare. Cumin and garlic enliven the smoked eggplant timbale with yogurt, and a fresh relish of minced apple, red onion and corn adds both crunch and a nice balance of sweetness and zest to a grilled chicken breast. A compelling dessert teams a cinnamon-topped poached pear with a crisp multilayered wafer of phyllo brushed with walnut oil and sprinkled with pistachios before baking, then presents them in a pool of apricot purée squiggled with raspberry highlights. In the main restaurant, now called the Careme Room after the legendary chef, juniors and seniors produce an ambitious, ever-changing menu that recently has included roast monkfish with caviar in puff pastry; sautéed quail with mushrooms, ginger and apples; and venison in strudel dough with mushrooms.

On Thursday and Friday evenings, Careme offers one of San Francisco's greatest unsung bargains in its $25.95 buffet. This is a chance for the garde-manger (cold appetizer) and pastry classes to strut their stuff via twin groaning boards of delicacy upon delicacy that begin and end the meal. Your servers are also students, who must learn all aspects of restaurant operation to earn their degree. They're generally helpful and earnest, if not yet totally polished. If you time your visit right, you might be able to peer into one of the demonstration classrooms that overlook the grand, high-ceilinged dining room. Expect to pay, for two, $80 for dinner in the Careme Room, $40 for lunch at Cyril's and $60 for dinner at the Academy Grill (all prices include wine).

Careme Room: open Mon.-Fri. with seatings at noon, 12:30 p.m., 6 p.m., 6:45 p.m., 7:30 p.m. (& an additional seating on Fridays at 8:15 p.m.). Cyril's: open Mon.-Fri. 11:30 a.m.-1:30 p.m. Academy Grill: open Mon.-Fri. 11:30 a.m.-1:45 p.m., 6 p.m.-8 p.m. Cards: AE, MC, V.

Cambodia House
5625 Geary Blvd.,
Richmond District
• 668-5888
CAMBODIAN

11/20

The food is appealing in this family-run Cambodian restaurant in the outer Richmond district, and the dining room has a pleasant feel. An emphasis on fresh ingredients and light, delicate preparations is the Cambodian touch here. Otherwise, the menu has a broader Southeast Asian character. The curries and sweet-tangy dipping sauces are particularly fine, and for that reason they are perhaps better complemented by a light, fruity white wine than by beer. This isn't within walking distance of anything notable but, like the nearby Khan Toke Thai House, is worth the drive. Dinner runs about $35 for two, with wine.
Open Sun-Thurs. 11 a.m.-3 p.m. & 5 p.m.-10 p.m., Fri.-Sat. 11 a.m.-3 p.m. & 5 p.m.-10:30 p.m. All major cards.

Campton Place
Campton Place Hotel,
340 Stockton St.,
Union Square
• 781-5155
AMERICAN

Fans of the exquisite Campton Place were crushed when executive chef Bradley Ogden left to open his own restaurant, Lark Creek Inn. Everyone wondered what the fate of this little jewel would be. Well, acolytes need not worry: Campton's new chef, Jan Birnbaum, who served as sous-chef to Ogden for a year and developed a very similar style, is filling his predecessor's toque nicely—the menu hasn't changed all that much, but he is adding some personal touches. Prior to coming to Campton, Birnbaum, a native of Baton Rouge, plied his trade at New Orleans' infamous K-Paul's, then at New York's Quilted Giraffe and Denver's Rattlesnake Club. The emphasis is still on what's freshest and finest at the market, and on dishes that sound simple, such as grilled quail or fish, but are served with marvelously inventive accompaniments, light sauces and witchy reductions. We love coming here for lunch to sample Birnbaum's fabulous salads—one of which, consisting of tender quail with crisp skin the color of mahogany, candied yams, fresh figs and mixed greens in a huckleberry vinaigrette, was an incredibly sensuous dish. Another nice pick contains turkey and Maytag blue cheese with fat chunks of smoky-sweet bacon and tiny yellow tomatoes—who ever said that turkey was bland? As always, the pastries and breads are very good at Campton—that basket of luscious poppyseed bread, teeny garlic biscuits and earthy corn sticks is addictive. We especially appreciate the homemade ice creams and flaky tarts. Dinner for two, with wine, will run about $150.
Open Mon.- Fri. 11:30 a.m.-2:30 p.m. & 5:30 p.m.-10 p.m., Sat.-Sun. 5:30 p.m.-10:30 p.m. All major cards.

Carnelian Room
355 California St.,
Financial District
• 433-7505, ext. 211
FRENCH

9/20

To dine on the 52nd floor of the Bank of America World Headquarters building in downtown San Francisco is to have one of the great urban views on Earth—like dining in the first class section of a good airliner. Unfortunately, at a recent dinner in the Carnelian Room, we felt as if we might as well have been on an airliner, because the food was just about at that level. Or let us put it this way: if dinner were a car, it would be a 1969 Lincoln Continental—big, serviceable, nothing to be excited about and certainly not the most appealing option out there. In all fairness, the Carnelian Room's menu reads better than it used to; many of the dishes, like poached tiger prawns with lobster mousse and roast squab with endive-and-red-onion confit, sound like an appealing amalgam of French and Californian cuisines. We do like the Carnelian Room's sunset dinner special because we've found it's the only way to dine adequately without being horrified by the price-quality ratio. For $28 each we ate a three-course dinner and watched the waning sun turn Berkeley the color of passion-fruit mousse.

A small cup of crab-and-seafood chowder was loaded with chunky goodies but the broth tasted like an experiment in the executive dining room of the Campbell Soup Company. Terrine of salmon and watercress was a satisfying slab nicely surrounded by spiky field greens, but the overchilled temperature and monochromatic flavor made it dull. When it came to main courses, a fine New York steak with béarnaise sauce was expertly medium-rare but was lukewarm, and we could hardly get the waiter's attention to send it back. We had a choice of three desserts. Strawberries Carnelian turned out to be plain vanilla ice cream topped with a few slightly sour fresh strawberries in a port-wine sauce. A smooth-textured cheesecake on an overly gluey and sweet raspberry sauce wasn't worth finishing.

One thing that redeems the Carnelian Room is a superb wine list, rich with Californian and French selections—some rare and exquisite vintages going back to the turn of the century and, like a Château Lafitte Rothschild 1945, selling for hundreds of dollars. The wine bottles are on display in a glass-fronted "cellar in the sky" that is fascinating to peruse. We had a rich, buttery Château Montelena 1986 Chardonnay for a pricey $38, which, to tell the truth, tasted better than anything on our plates. Sunset dinner for two, with wine, costs $90. Regular dinner for two, with wine costs about $140.

Open Mon.-Sat. 6 p.m.-10:30 p.m., Sun. 10 a.m.-3 p.m. & 6 p.m.-10:30 p.m. All major cards.

Le Castel

3235 Sacramento St.,
Presidio Heights
• 921-7115
FRENCH/ALSATIAN

The postcard-perfect upper Sacramento neighborhood boasts some of San Francisco's most impressive Victorian houses. One of them is Le Castel. Just being in one of the three parlor-like dining rooms is so delicious that owner Fritz Frankel could probably serve trail mix and still have to turn away business. But the food's merit has increased so substantially since our last visit that Frankel could probably serve it in a garage and still be booked every night. Truly, this is the best of both worlds. The classical French and Alsatian menu offers the kind of sumptuous, unabashedly real dishes that most people still associate with the cuisine after countless new waves of "art" cooking. We adore the bone marrow on toast and the incredible potato pancakes. The specialty here is game: roast mallard duck with red cabbage, tender milk-soaked venison with pears poached in Riesling, roast pheasant with a dark, piquant sauce. Le Castel provides such a lovely French holiday of an evening that we have to recommend it as of one San Francisco's most enjoyable restaurants. Dinner for two, with wine, is a worthwhile $125.

Open Tues.-Thurs. 6 p.m.-9:30 p.m., Fri.-Sat. 6 p.m.-10 p.m. All major cards.

Celadon

881 Clay St.,
Chinatown
• 982-1168
CHINESE

The name refers to an elegant gray-green porcelain glaze that somehow captures the ambience in this courtly Chinese restaurant. Behind the dramatic bronze doors are cool, intimate and handsomely detailed dining rooms, candlelit and gleaming with fine linen, silver and lacquered woods. The food has provincial roots but the style and standards come from Hong Kong. Dishes are presented and served with ceremony. Peking duck, for example, is carved in the traditional manner "at tableside" and deftly packed into rice pancakes and steamed buns with black-bean sauce. The delicious squab shatin is an unadorned, strongly flavored bird that is deep-fried and served plain with little bowls of salt and white pepper. The house specialty is fresh lobster steamed with garlic. As is the norm in good Chinese restaurants, expect those little hot towels that follow finger foods. This is not a place to go for a fast meal; it's ideal for an absorbing evening if you have the time (and appropriately absorbing company). It's less expensive than it seems—about $45 for two, with wine.

Open daily 8 a.m.-3 p.m. & 5 p.m.-11 p.m. All major cards.

Cendrillon

1130 Valencia St.,
Mission District
• 826-7997
FRENCH

9/20

Once upon a time there was a restaurant called Cendrillon—Cinderella, as you'd read it in English. And once upon a time the restaurant was a real Cinderella story—a small unpretentious find in the Mission district where you could get an excellent and creative French three-course dinner for under $20 per person. It was popular, and it was praised. But these days Cendrillon needs a fairy godmother to transform it back to the high-quality, charming little restaurant it once was. The restaurant was taken over recently by Thai management, and they mean well. They really do. We can see this in the menu, which tries to offer some interesting options. It is built around five appetizers and eight entrées plus daily specials. Appetizers are uneven. For example, we enjoyed a light puff pastry stuffed with a garlic mayonnaise and a whole hard-boiled quail egg; however, the accompanying quail leg stuffed with lobster mousse was overcooked and rubbery. Dragon escargots were deep-fried snails studded with rice noodles. A garlicky mayonnaise worked well but the snails were gritty. Who's doing the washing back there, anyway? Rack of lamb was served rare as ordered, beautifully cooked though not all that tender; the accompanying fettuccine, unfortunately, was oversalted. Desserts were another disappointment—a dark-chocolate charlotte, which used to be marvelous, rich and black as a dark night in a wealthy city, had become pale as milky coffee and far too sweet. Dinner for two, with wine, comes to $75.
Open Mon.-Sat. 5:30 p.m.-10:30 p.m. Cards: AE, MC, V.

Le Central

453 Bush St.,
Union Square
• 391-2233
FRENCH

12/20

More than most of San Francisco's "great" French restaurants, this simple bistro with its menu scrawled on blackboards and on mirrors reminds us of dining in France. Situated downtown, Le Central overflows at lunchtime, largely with business and political figures. Although they come here to do some political moving and shaking, they also come to nourish their bodies and souls with delicious and honest French country cooking. Starters include crabcakes in a beurre blanc; strips of Norwegian smoked salmon; a salad of grilled eggplant, tomatoes and fresh herbs; and, maybe best of all, a rich, spicy saucisson chaud in an abundant cream sauce. The simpler entrées are a glorious herbed roast chicken, cold salmon with sauce verte, rack of lamb. There is boudin noir aux pommes, and specialties like grilled coho salmon with beurre rouge, and tortellini with prosciutto and chanterelle mushrooms. Desserts, if chosen carefully, are terrific, especially the tarte tatin

with crème fraîche. With this food we would like some wonderful fruity Alsatian wines, but the wine list leans heavily toward Californian selections, and not the best ones. However, if you ask, there is an unlisted stock of mostly French wines—including a bottle or two from Alsace—that can be had. The service, though frenzied at lunch, is friendly and efficient to newcomers as well as to the famous clientele. About $70 for dinner for two, with wine.
Open Mon.-Sat. 11:30 a.m.-10:30 p.m. Cards: AE, MC, V.

Chevys

150 4th St.,
South of Market
• 543-8060
MEXICAN

11/20

The noise level around 5 in the evening is exceeded only by the noise level around 8 p.m. Still, it's not as noisy as the Cadillac Bar & Grill, which Chevys is trying, with some success, to replace as the yuppie cantina of choice in the downtown area. The formula for this one of three restaurants in the chain was concocted by Pier 39 entrepreneur Warren Simmons. The gist is something like Hard Rock Café goes south of the border. The neon desertscape over the bar is funky and interesting, but the overwhelming presence of the Corona beer logo is depressing. The food is better than it needs to be—in fact, it's acceptable. Fresh tortillas and tortilla chips, spicy nachos, mesquite-grilled fajitas (excellent marinated flank steak and chicken) and good enchiladas are the main fair. Seasonal fresh fish such as swordfish and salmon are grilled and served with fresh, spicy salsas. The no-reservations policy makes for a high profit margin on tequila and beer—there's always a long wait for a table, and most of the crowd passes the time at the bar. Two will spend about $40 for dinner and beers.
Open Mon.-Thurs. 11 a.m.-10 p.m., Fri.-Sat. 11 a.m.-11 p.m. Cards: MC, V.

China Moon Café

639 Post St.,
Union Square
• 775-4789
CHINESE/CALIFORNIAN

We were hoping that Barbara Tropp would perfect her intriguing cuisine and she has. Behind the neon moon on Sutter Street is a convivial restaurant for people who prefer flavors and textures to bulk. Tropp's spacy interpretation of Chinese cuisine has its own sensibility—she knows how to tease the taste buds and tickle the palate by combining distinctively flavored ingredients to create unexpected and delightful harmonies. For example, the divine duck soup is based on roast garlic broth with shreds of roasted duck, fried ginger, fresh water chestnuts, carrots and celery. Dishes are often whimsically or poetically named. From the day the place opened we were fans of chaos soup (which has now disappeared). We also are intrigued by the "strange flavor sauce," a concoction of garlic, soy sauce, vinegar and sugar that is not nearly as strange as it is tasty, especially in the "strange flavor eggplant" appetizer. The dim sum items at lunch are exquisite, particularly the jewel-like spring rolls with interesting fillings and chili-ginger sauce. When it's in season, don't miss the steamed salmon with fresh coriander pesto, served with sautéed blue-lake beans and pearl onions. The storefront space can only be called happy: the servers moving among the crowded tables are happy; the cooks in their exotically equipped open kitchen are happy; and the eaters are very happy indeed. That pleases us, because we consider China Moon to be one of the city's little treasures. Dinner with wine costs about $50 for two.

Open Mon.-Sat. 11:30 a.m.-2 p.m. & 5:30 p.m.-10 p.m., Sun. 11 a.m.-2 p.m. & 5:30 p.m.-10 p.m. Cards: MC, V.

Ciao
230 Jackson St.,
Financial District
• 982-9500
ITALIAN

An Italian visitor recently remarked, "Italian restaurants in the Bay Area have such strange names in translation— 'Please,' 'Plates,' 'Skewers,' 'Coffee with Milk.' " Well, this one means both "hi" and "good-bye," and it has the breezy, high-tech look you might expect from such insouciance. The approach in the kitchen, however, is anything but casual, and the problems we encountered in the past have smoothed considerably. Ciao routinely garners "best pasta in the city" honors, and such well-executed dishes as tortelli ai carciofi (pasta filled with artichokes, Parmesan and cream, topped with browned butter and sage), pappardelle con gamberetti (fresh herb pasta with fresh rock shrimp and tomatoes) and an old standby, linguine alle vongole (with clams, herbs and olive oil) show why. Grilled specialties, especially the huge veal chops, fork-tender lamb chops with thyme and honey, and fresh local salmon steaks, are cooked carefully (even extra-rare upon request). The saltimbocca Ciao, tender veal rolled around sage, prosciutto and Fontina, does just about leap into your mouth. Risotto tends to vary in texture from one visit to the next, but this is a dish that's hard to get perfect every time. Portions are more than ample, but be sure to save a little nook for some sacripantina (yellow cake with marsala, rum and whipped cream), tiramisu (ladyfingers with Mascarpone, espresso, rum and cocoa) or the highly unusual torta mezzaluna di mele (apple-and-pine-nut tart with vanilla gelato). The California-Italian wine list has some real finds; with a modest bottle, the tab for two runs about $80.

Open Mon.-Sat. 11 a.m.-midnight, Sun. 4 p.m.-10:30 p.m. Cards: AE, MC, V.

Circolo Restaurant & Champagneria

161 Sutter St.,
Financial District
• 362-0404
ITALIAN

Who would have believed that an Iranian-born restaurateur with a penchant for *la cucina Italiana* could have changed the culinary face of the staid old Financial District? That's exactly what Fazol (Faz) Poursohi has done with Faz, Caffe Latte and, most recently, Circolo in the Crocker Galleria. With its stylish peach hues, art deco accents, custom-built wood-burning oven and skeins of freshly cut multicolored pasta draped on drying racks, Circolo has helped breathe new life into this fossilized cranny of the city. Its menu centers around pizza, pasta (try the linguine with sea scallops and sun-dried tomatoes) and alla griglia (grilled) specialties ranging from fat jumbo prawns with basil-butter sauce to duck legs with rosemary, apple and pomegranate. Watching the pizza chefs is a treat, and tasting their perfectly crisp-edged, chewy creations is a pizzaholic's nirvana; the melanzana pizza, with grilled eggplant, garlic, tomato, basil and mozzarella, says it all. Plan to spend about $50 to $60 for two, with gelati and a wicked tiramisu as a sweet finale. *Open Mon.-Fri. 11:30 a.m.-11 p.m., Sat. 5 p.m.-11 p.m. All major cards.*

City Block

101B S. Park,
South of Market
• (415) 543-3663
CALIFORNIAN

Walk into City Block and the place feels like a hybrid created from a railroad station and a modern art gallery. "Ah," you think, "trendy." Yes, City Block is trendy. And City Block serves exceptional food, most of the time. And City Block is very, very noisy. At peak capacity, you need to block your ears. Forget talking business or philosophy or having an emotional breakdown—at a recent dinner we had a 60-watt conversation. But we sure do like the food, with enough creativity in the dishes both at lunch and dinner to balance the excesses or the combinations that get overly inventive. Nearly half the menu changes daily and the steady dishes, like poussin, lamb, fish pasta and risotto, are prepared somewhat differently every day. The goat-cheese wonton appetizer is piquant and lively, strewn with pine nuts, sautéed spinach and red peppers.Main dishes vary. We particularly like what's done with poussin. A recent version was roasted, with corn fritters and a tangle of City Block's own coleslaw. A seafood stew of custardy oysters, scallops, mussels and andouille sausage in a savory chili- and cilantro-scented tomato stock was a masterful marriage of ingredients. Lamb chops with apricots, coconut, almonds and couscous were expertly cooked, but the portion was insultingly small. (Lunch is a much better buy than dinner; just about the same food is served in slightly smaller portions, and priced between $2 and $7 lower per item.) Then there is the dessert. City Block does lovely things to fresh fruit.

Gingerbread with poached nectarines and Chantilly cream was dense, fragrant, spicy and delicious. A seasonal pie of blueberries, blackberries and apples with homemade vanilla-bean ice cream suffered from a slightly stodgy crust but the fruit was incredibly fresh and still chewy enough to be interesting. A small but select wine list, with a mix of French, Italian and California wines, offers a better choice of whites than reds. There's an extremely reasonable corkage fee of $5—they're very open to people bringing in their own wines. Once they make the noise level manageable, this will be a truly special, innovative little restaurant. Dinner for two is $110. Lunch runs about $75.

Open Mon.-Thurs. 11:30 a.m.-2:30 p.m. & 5:30 p.m.-9:30 p.m., Fri. 11:30 a.m.-2:30 p.m & 5:30-10:30 p.m., Sat. 5:30 p.m.-10:30 p.m. Cards: DC, MC, V.

Cliff House
1090 Point Lobos Ave.,
Ocean Beach
• 386-3330
SEAFOOD

8/20

There is a long history of catastrophies here: Once a ship full of dynamite ran aground and wrecked the place. Another time it burned on Christmas. The next disaster in the saga of this oft-rebuilt Victorian masterpiece was the progressive floundering of its restaurants (the Seafood & Beverage Company and Upstairs at the Cliff House) from mediocre levels to scary abysses. We hate to say it, but they're charging for the view while only going through the motions of running restaurants. There are two ways to proceed here. The obvious course is to fight the hordes of tourists for a table at sunset and enjoy a gorgeous view with Seal Rock in the foreground—if you get lucky, it will be most pleasant. But believe us, the seals out there eat better than the customers in the dining room upstairs—at least, they never have to pay a hefty tab. The other best bet is to show up midmorning for breakfast in the downstairs dining room. If you arrive between tour buses, it's a nice way to start the day. Breakfast for two runs $20; dinner for two, with wine, is about $50.

Seafood & Beverage Company: open daily 9 a.m.-10:30 p.m.; Upstairs at the Cliff House: open daily 11 a.m.-10:30 p.m. All major cards.

Cordon Bleu Vietnamese
1574 California St.,
Polk Gulch
• 673-5637
VIETNAMESE

11/20

Cordon Bleu Vietnamese is not about great food, and it's definitely not about terrific ambience. We'll describe it in two sweet words: good and cheap. This cramped but cozy cookhouse, with two tables and a wooden counter, is right next to the hip Lumière movie-theater complex. That makes it a perfect stop for tasty five-spice roast chicken. Even better, the food can be ordered to go, on the way to the beach or a picnic. To eat in, one orders from a list of combination plates that include such morsels as country chicken salad, spicy imperial roll, and beef marinated in lemon grass. Keep in mind that they don't serve alcohol here, and only cash is accepted. About $10 for two.

Open Tues.-Thurs. 11:30 a.m.-2:30 p.m. & 5 p.m.-10 p.m., Fri.-Sat. 5 p.m.-11 p.m. No cards.

Corona Bar & Grill
88 Cyril Magnin Pl.,
Union Square
• 392-5500
MEXICAN/CALIFORNIAN

10/20

We used to love the Corona when it opened a couple of years ago as one of restaurant designer Pat Kuleto's megasuccesses. We still love the Southwestern decor, with masks, beautiful lighting and comfortable booths. And a few dishes still stand out, like the fat shrimp, crab and corn burrito that's served at lunchtime, and a cajeta flan with chocolate, almonds and fresh whipped cream. A new chef, Reed Hearon, has taken over in the kitchen, and though he turns out the most elaborate Mexican menu in the Bay Area, the dishes often fall short of their toothsome descriptions. Quesadillas, though filled with exotica like chanterelles, Fontina cheese, chorizo and corn, we have found to be tough and a bit soggy. The black-bean pancake appetizer, one of our former favorites, is now served with seared, peppered ahi tuna and pineapple-tomatillo salsa, and has been mushy the last few times we've ordered it. Main dishes can be okay but they can also be a hit-or-miss experience, especially as the menu changes so often that a favorite, enjoyed one night, might never show up again; this might include dishes like grilled breast of duck with cured duck leg and peppered Pacific salmon grilled with mole verde. But do order dessert here. There are such novelties as chocolate–ice-cream taco with fresh berries. Dinner for two, with wine, will cost about $90.

Open Mon.-Sat. 11:30 a.m.-5 p.m. & 5:30 p.m.-10:30 p.m., Sunday 5:30 p.m.-10:30 p.m. Cards: AE, MC, V.

Cuba
2886 16th St.,
Mission District
• 864-9871
CUBAN

11/20

Though Cuban cuisine is very popular on the East Coast, it is rarely seen in San Francisco—which is reason enough to visit this simple little Formica-and-linoleum eatery in the Latino Mission District. The most unusual and often quite good dishes—prepared by the same chef for the past eighteen years—are another reason. There are copious Cuban seafood soups, tasty meat dishes (Cuban roast pork and beef served with superb black beans), paella Valenciana, paella marinada. The service is—we'll be kind—relaxed; there are some good beers and only a few wines. Dinner with beer will cost two people $25.

Open Mon.-Thurs. 11 a.m.-10 p.m., Fri.-Sat. 12 p.m.-10 p.m. Cards: AE, MC, V.

Le Cyrano
4134 Geary Blvd.,
Richmond District
• 387-1090
FRENCH

12/20

Little neighborhood restaurants come and go, but Le Cyrano has been around for decades. The food is French ancien, the clientele merely ancient and the room a bit gloomy despite good lighting. Dinner is prix fixe only, starting with soup—cream of leek or onion—and continuing with a simple butter-lettuce vinaigrette. Main courses are the best part of the meal: a long-simmered stew of beef or veal, nice sautéed frogs' legs or a small individual rack of lamb. Desserts are basic (crème caramel, sherbets, raspberry or chocolate sundaes), but the short wine list is reasonably priced—and the prix-fixe meals are downright cheap at $9 to $17.50 a person, without wine.
Open Tues.-Sat. 5 p.m.-10:30 p.m., Sun. 4:30 p.m.-9:30 p.m. Cards: MC, V.

Aux Delices Vietnam
2327 Polk St.,
Polk Gulch
• 928-4977
1002 Portrero St.,
Portrero Hill
• 285-3196
VIETNAMESE

12/20

The primary location on Polk Street is a snappy neighborhood Vietnamese place—stylish and friendly, with yummy food. Located in a storefront, Aux Delices is a small restaurant with a row of partitioned booths down one side. Fashion prints enliven the walls, and elegant foliage blends with the plain wood to create a cool tropical feeling. The best bet on the menu is the fresh seafood—for instance, a whole crab sautéed in its shell with a nicely balanced salt-and-pepper sauce. Crab also figures in a number of tasty soups, such as fresh asparagus and crab in a dark, rich broth. Service is quick and friendly, and the beer is always cold. You'll spend about $25 for two, with beer.
Polk St. branch: open Mon. 5 p.m.-10 p.m., Tues.-Sun. 11:30 a.m.-2:30 p.m. & 5 p.m.-10 p.m. Portrero St. branch: open Mon. 5 p.m.-10 p.m., Tues.-Sat. 11:30 a.m.-2:30 p.m. & 5 p.m.-10 p.m.

De Paula's
2114 Fillmore St.,
Upper Fillmore
• 346-9888
BRAZILIAN

12/20

Tucked away in the trendy upper Fillmore area, this little place serves food that tops most of what we sampled last time we visited Brazil. Chef Franco Rodriguez, who joined the restaurant in January 1988, hasn't tampered much with the menu yet, but he plans to introduce rotisserie meats and daily fresh-fish specials in the summer of 1990. (Also, look for a name change around the same time—most likely to Restaurante Brasil.) The entrées can be exciting: camarãos a bahiana (prawns sautéed in a sauce of tomatoes, coconut milk and red palm oil), wonderful marinated pork, chicken marinated in dark beer and sautéed with peppers, onions and cream, and a fine feijoada, the black-bean and pork stew that is Brazil's national dish. Entrées have some unusual accompaniments, such as refried beans with yucca flour; the flour is fried with bacon, olives and spices. There are some

good beers, a few wines and delicious Brazilian soft drinks. The desserts are too sweet by American standards, but the splendid chocolate from Cocolat ends the meal on a high note. About $40 for dinner for two, with beer.
Open Mon.-Thurs. 11:30 a.m.-2:30 p.m. & 5 p.m.-11 p.m., Fri. 11:30 a.m.-2:30 p.m. & 5 p.m.-midnight, Sat. 5 p.m.-midnight, Sun. 5 p.m.-11 p.m. All major cards.

Donatello
501 Post St.,
Union Square
• 441-7100
ITALIAN

We know that Donatello has developed a reputation as one of the pre-eminent Italian restaurants in Northern California. We know that Donatello, as a hotel dining room, is one of the most stuffily beautiful, with its eighteenth-century walls and rich touches of gilt. However, we feel rich touches of guilt in evaluating the menu. Yes, the food is generally exquisite and unusual. But in simple terms of value for cuisine, Donatello is way out of line. Maybe Ron Miller, a native San Franciscan who has been named the new executive chef of Donatello, will do something about improving the minuscule portions that annoyed us so on a recent visit. The sautéed fresh shiitake mushrooms with garlic, spinach and pancetta were beautifully tender and flavorful, as was the fresh eggplant and zucchini with tomato sauce, Fontina cheese and oregano. However, we also would have enjoyed a side order of a couple of magnifying glasses. When it comes to main courses, we've experienced a similar parsimony: boneless quail stuffed with quail-and-chicken farce, scented with fresh thyme and served with polenta was delicious, but it was barely enough to satisfy the appetite. Roast rack of lamb with rosemary, pancetta and garlic was buttery-tender and fragrant, but there wasn't much going on with the accompanying side dishes.

In all fairness, the level of cooking is remarkable. Each dish finds the right balance between the main flavor motifs and their enhancements. And one cannot doubt Miller's consciousness of—and interpretation of—Italian cuisine; every time we've dined at Donatello we've cleaned our plates. But that's part of the problem: every time we've dined at Donatello we've wanted to go out and fill up on a hamburger afterward. And it seems that in a restaurant where a prix-fixe dinner for one is $65 and the average dinner for two (with wines from the extraordinarily detailed and exciting list) comes to about $200, our stomachs should be as full as our pockets are empty.
Open daily noon-2 p.m. & 6 p.m.-11 p.m. All major cards.

Eddie Jacks
1151 Folsom St.,
South of Market
• 626-2388
CALIFORNIAN

This fun and very stylish SOMA restaurant is an offshoot of the renowned Wolfdale's in Lake Tahoe. Proprietors Deborah Dale and Jerry Wolf named it after their respective fathers, Eddie and Jack. Wolf and Tim Dale, Deborah's brother, gutted the existing site and built the definitive glass-and-marble art gallery–cum–restaurant. We like the food, too. Chef Tom Fox, a longtime family associate, is a culinary intellectual with a flair for flavor. He smoke-cures meats and makes pastas, often topping them in an Asian manner, such as with smoked duck with stir-fried vegetables and hoisin sauce. The best-selling lunch item is an open-face lamb sandwich with goat cheese and red onions. Some people go just to sit at the bar and satisfy their addiction to the sweet potato chips, or eat fried polenta sticks with Gorgonzola sauce. The wine list is one of the sharpest in town, and the bartenders pour rare and fabulous wines by the glass as well as make spectacular martinis. When Eddie Jacks is packed, which it usually is, the atmosphere is upbeat, sexy and comfortable. Dinner for two can cost anywhere from $40 to $70, with wine.
Open Mon.-Thurs. 11:30 a.m.-2:30 p.m. & 6 p.m.-10 p.m., Fri. 11:30 a.m.-2:30 p.m. & 6 p.m.-11 p.m., Sat. 6 p.m.-11 p.m. All major cards.

Elite Café
2049 Fillmore St.,
Upper Fillmore
• 346-8668
CAJUN/CREOLE

This is one of those rare places where you don't mind waiting—where, in fact, the wait often turns out to be one of the high points of the evening. Since reservations aren't taken, the Elite Café is constantly jammed, and there are abundant fresh oysters, shrimp and crawfish, an excellent bar and bartenders that talk good baseball to help pass the time. The Elite is an integral part of the lively yuppie scene along Fillmore; Harry's Saloon, a preppy hangout, is just across the street, and the Pacific Heights Bar & Grill ("Pacbag" for short) is just beyond Rory's, one of the city's best ice cream parlors.

Starting with the obvious in Cajun cuisine, there are a few redfish dishes on the menu—foremost among them, redfish Caroline, a filet fried in a mélange of spices and covered with a creamy, piquant fresh crab sauce. But this Cajun/Creole menu makes good use of many other entrée ingredients. For instance, filet mignon and fresh salmon are also blackened, and the thick, spicy gumbo alone is worth a visit. Other tempting main dishes include grilled T-bone lamb chops with rosemary butter, and crabcakes topped with a caper sauce tartare. Once the site of the Asia Café, a 1920s hot spot, the Elite has preserved much of the handsome dark-wood paneling, deep booths, mirrors and fixtures from that era. Service is unfailingly efficient; the white-jacketed waiters are young and sharp. Having gone on about all that, we must now admit that we go to the Elite more for the Cajun martinis (made with pepper vodka) and the house-made desserts—bread pudding with bourbon sauce and Creole cream-cheese pecan pie—than for anything else. Dinner for two, with wine, will run $65. *Open Mon.-Sat. 5 p.m.-11 p.m., Sun. 10 a.m.-3 p.m. & 5 p.m.-10 p.m. All major cards.*

Embarko
100 Brannan St.,
South of Market
• 495-2120
AMERICAN/
INTERNATIONAL

Proprietor Joe Leis sees the anything-goes concept behind Embarko as "chopsticks and a fork marching hand in hand over the Golden Gate Bridge." In a new, yupscale corner of the city, right smack against the Bay, he and his partners aim to blast the Bay Area's jaded palates with "everything from rodeo to Tokyo," in an offbeat, fast-paced setting. Embarko follows closely on the heels of its Mill Valley predecessor, The Avenue Grill, where Leis and his entourage parlayed a similar formula into one of Marin County's hottest eateries. At both places, the food pulls no culinary punches, as shown by such bold Embarko signature dishes as beer-batter coconut prawns with mango-mustard mayonnaise; spicy all-American meatloaf with garlic mashed potatoes and gravy; and sautéed peppery prawns, "spiced with no apologies." Whether or not the formula works is yet to be seen, so we're withholding our rating—after all, something this wild and crazy needs a bit of time to settle in. Plan to spend $90 for dinner for two, including wine. *Open Mon.-Fri. & Sun. 11:30 a.m.-3:30 p.m. & 5:30 p.m.-11 p.m., Sat. 5:30 p.m.-11 p.m. Cards: AE, MC, V.*

L'Entrecôte de Paris
2032 Union St.,
Cow Hollow
• 931-5006
FRENCH/STEAKHOUSE

11/20

Americans have been eating less beef in recent years, and aside from much-touted health reasons, we suspect this is partly due to the increasing unavailability of good beef. We have never thought of San Francisco as a great beef eater's town and were curious to see whether a French-style steakhouse could prosper here. After more than six years, L'Entrecôte is still alive and cooking, and has expanded to serve dishes like sautéed salmon in a tangerine sauce with almond wild rice, and roasted rack of lamb au jus. The real reason to come here, however—and the sole attraction for about 80 percent of L'Entrecôte's customers—is still for the French steak dinner. It starts with a nice little butter-lettuce salad with chopped walnuts and a tangy vinaigrette; then comes the steak itself, which is tasty though not outstanding, and french fries, which, in the true French style, are greaseless and delicious. Homemade desserts are

beautiful to look at (profiteroles, tarte tatin) but unexceptional. The wine list, while not long, is well priced, with several premium wines available by the glass. The serving staff is competent. About $85 for two, with wine.
Open Mon.-Sat. 11:30 a.m.-midnight, Sun. 11:30 a.m.-10 p.m. All major cards.

Ernie's
847 Montgomery St.,
Financial District
• 397-5969
FRENCH

Remember that scene in *Vertigo* where Kim Novak walks into the classic San Francisco restaurant and Jimmy Stewart falls for her like a ton of bricks? It was shot upstairs at Ernie's 30 years ago, in the sumptuous Ambrosia Room. That private dining room's Victorian splendor has remained intact since then, but the rest of the house, and the cuisine, have evolved with the times. The modern Ernie's is still the classic San Francisco restaurant, primarily because owners Victor and Roland Gotti haven't missed a beat in over a half century of ownership. One enters into a pale marble foyer shining with tall mirrors. Down a short staircase, the dining room is all peach and sea green, with champagne-hued silk walls and high-backed chairs upholstered in silk brocade. The service is swift, sure, warm and—best of all—practically invisible. Dishes come and go, silverware is replaced, wine is poured, and it's all just part of the comfortable hum of a well-oiled mechanism. Chef Marcel Cathala's menu is more adventurous than those of his predecessors. He works closely with sommelier Steve Taylor to make the most of the magnificent wine cellar the Gotti brothers have built. Among appetizers, we've liked the pheasant pâté en croûte with seasonal mushrooms, and ravioli stuffed with Petaluma snails. Grilled tuna with a tropical fruit coulis was outstanding one night, although we had a hard time not ordering our favorite rack of lamb in puff pastry, with veal mousse and garlic sauce. Desserts are terrific, and there's a fine selection of Cognacs and other spirits. Dinner for two, with wine, will set you back $140, but it's worth it.
Open daily 5:30 p.m.-11 p.m. All major cards.

L'Etoile
1075 California St.,
Nob Hill
• 771-1529
FRENCH

A San Francisco classic, not only because of the food, but because the room is a kind of time warp opening into the late 1950s. Yes, the wild and innocent city that Herb Caen fondly depicts in his Sunday columns in the *San Francisco Chronicle* is still alive and well on Nob Hill, down a flight of red-carpeted stairs from California Street. The room is dressed in slightly unreal vivid colors, anchored by a central island of vast brass-riveted red-leather banquettes, with little tasseled lampshades on the candles at each table. The unwordly yellowish lighting and hushed air (even the clink

of silverware is muted) add to an atmosphere of subdued elegance. On the other hand, a lot of people think the place is stuffy, and we admit that the service, at least, can seem so. But that's just the style. As for the food, chef Claude Bougard presents a classically based French menu. You might start with an appetizer of fresh scallops on a bed of linguine, in a Champagne-herb sauce. Among the main courses, we've especially enjoyed the quail pâté "Luculus," the quenelles of fish, truffles and lobster sauce, and filet mignon flamed in Armagnac with pepper sauce. Bougard also offers a filet of lamb in a spicy red-wine sauce with a purée of chestnuts and berries, and braised lobster, served out of shell on a bed of pasta, with a tarragon-and-white-wine sauce. The wine cellar is a vault full of treasures—and the bottles priced accordingly. If you can stand another ounce of richness, among the desserts are hot soufflés flavored with various liqueurs. For a truly splendid evening, dine late on steak tartare, then go upstairs to the colonial French/African lounge and listen to maestro Peter Mintun tickle the ivories for the classiest crowd in town. With vodkas, dinner for two is about $120.
Open daily 5:30 p.m.-11 p.m. All major cards.

Faz
132 Bush St.,
Financial District
• 362-4484
AMERICAN/
MEDITERRANEAN

12/20

This is a popular spot in the Financial District, despite being noisy and crowded. Or maybe because of that. At any rate the food is good, especially the grilled shrimp, a house specialty. Fish and meats smoked on the premises are another strong suit. The decor falls between high-tech café and diner, which fits the creative, upscale American cuisine with a slight Middle Eastern influence. The upbeat ambience reflects the ebullient personality of Iranian chef-owner Faz Pourshoi. A big crowd shows up after work for happy hour with free appetizers and the bar specialty, yummy fresh-fruit margaritas. Apple Brown Betty is one of the popular desserts. Dinner and margaritas for two comes in at $40.
Open Mon.-Fri. 11:30 a.m.-3 p.m. & 5 p.m.-10 p.m.. All major cards.

565 Clay
565 Clay St.,
Financial District
• 434-2345
CALIFORNIAN

9/20

They do try hard. We like the decor enormously, particularly at night when the knife-edged voices of people doing business over lunch give way to the softer tones of simply eating dinner. The umber ceiling, russet-wood pillars and open racks of glassware make for exciting, warming visuals, while the modern abstract art on the walls is colorful yet nondescript enough not to interfere with the feeling of relaxation. It's just too darn bad the food isn't tastier. The menu, which changes both at lunch and at dinner, displays trendy foodie hallmarks like complete pedigrees for the beef and salad greens, and detailed descriptions of what's in each dish that stop just short of mentioning salt and pepper. On several visits, our dishes didn't taste nearly as scrumptious as their descriptions. The Caesar salad was a huge pile of impeccably fresh romaine with a just-mixed dressing and curly shreds of Parmesan, but the taste was one-dimensional. An order of grilled swordfish with a pepper butter was moist and appealing, though the accompanying steamed vegetables weren't as tasty as they looked. Like the rest of the menu, the desserts are valiant efforts, but they don't quite come off. Fresh raspberries in Frangelico cream proved to be uninspired. The only sin about a double-chocolate sin cake was that it tasted oily. Clay's wine list offers more than a dozen fine, reasonably priced California vintages by the glass, and a wide range of California reds and whites by the bottle. Dinner for two, with wine, costs $90. *Open Mon.-Fri. 11:30 a.m.-2:30 p.m. & 5:30 p.m.-9:30 p.m., Sat. for private parties only. Cards: AE, MC, V.*

Fleur de Lys

777 Sutter St.,
Union Square
• 673-7779
FRENCH

Chef-partner Hubert Keller will never leave his patrons indifferent. Keller, in addition to working under Roger Vergé at the Moulin de Mougins, opened two restaurants himself, in São Paulo, Brazil, and in San Francisco (the financially troubled Sutter 500). He was much influenced by Vergé's cuisine, as well as by his training, at a tender age, at some of the other best houses in France, including Haeberlin and Bocuse. You can taste the results. Consider his signature lamb chops. Arriving inside fragrant clouds of herbed mousseline, the roast chops are butter-tender and scrumptious with a simple but absolutely ethereal wine sauce. Every dish is a treat for the eye as well as the palate. One night an appetizer plate included a little fish sculpted from horseradish purée, with a caviar eye and tomato fins. It served as the focus, both visually and on the palate, for thin slices of cured salmon which melted in the mouth with an impression that was more fragrance than flavor. The purée was equally delicate, with just the slightest punctuation of horseradish, and those two simple currents developed into a sea of sensation. That sensual synergy is the most amazing thing about Keller's wizardry: with deft combinations of aroma, flavor, texture and color—sometimes complemetary, sometimes in contrast—he summons dazzling special effect from a few well-chosen elements. A baked potato standing on end had a cap like a magic mushroom, and its hollow interior contained an herbed breast of squab. There was a world of delight in those few quick bites. Foie gras sautéed in butter and salt was displayed on broad lettuce leaves with sliced duck breast. We would have been happy with the foie gras alone, as rich as it was, although the texture of the duck breast helped define the richness and amplified its dimensions. For dessert there was a chocolate mousse and a meringue swan gliding on a raspberry lake. You get the picture. Needless to say, the wine list is a wonderland in its own right. The 10,000 bottles are evenly divided between France and California, and the list features around 40 California Chardonnays. The Michael Taylor–designed interior is a large flowery tent of silk-screened fabric, draped to create a main dining room and several discreet alcoves. Just the sort of pavilion in which a French knight might throw a feast before riding out to quest for the Grail. Dinner for two, with wine, costs $150. *Open Mon.-Sat. 6 p.m.-10 p.m. All major cards.*

Fog City Diner
1300 Battery St.,
North Beach
• 982-2000
AMERICAN

Part Empire Diner, part Dashiell Hammett and part yuppie grazeteria, the Fog City Diner gets our vote for the most fun restaurant in town. For one thing, it's great-looking—a gleaming, low-slung, romantic cross between a '30s roadside diner and a '40s big-city bar and grill. For another, the dressed-up clientele is as handsome and lively as the restaurant. Add to this a well-staffed and well-stocked bar, a counter from which you can watch the intricate but frenzied ballet in the kitchen, and an irresistible, reasonably priced menu of contemporary American food, and you'll understand why you need dinner reservations days (even weeks) in advance. Seemingly all of San Francisco is willing to put up with long waits, a cool welcome and sometimes perfunctory service to hang out in one of the classic wooden booths and sample from the menu of "small" and "large" plates. (Everything, even the herb-scented bread, is à la carte, so before long you'll have a table full of little plates.) Co-owner and chef Cindy Pawlcyn, also the owner of the wine country's Mustards, has created a menu with something for everyone, from the trendy to the traditional: crisp Caesar salad with homemade croutons, fried mozzarella with a vibrant tomato sauce, a grilled pasilla pepper stuffed with jack cheese, a strange but tasty garlic custard with shiitake mushrooms and walnuts. Specialties include some of the best crabcakes anywhere; a dish of grilled pork chops in a soy-ginger marinade, served with applesauce and mashed-potato pancakes. Our favorite dessert is the smooth-as-silk crème brûlée. The size of your tab depends on your appe-

tite: two can have a snack and a glass of wine each for $20 or a feast with a bottle of wine for $60 or so.
Open Sun.-Thurs. 11:30 a.m.-11 p.m., Fri.-Sat. 11:30 a.m.-midnight. Cards: MC, V.

La Folie
2316 Polk St.,
Russian Hill
• 776-5577
FRENCH

Chef Roland Passot, his wife Jamie (the host) and his brother-in-law Georges (the sommelier) have created a two-year-old gem of a restaurant on the site of Camargue, which in its day was one of the more enjoyable bistros in San Francisco. La Folie, its successor, is even better. The Passots have created an environment that is a sort of casual dining playpen for rich people. The one open room is gloriously lit so that a peachy-gold glow suffuses everything and everybody. Customers dress in everything from business suits to open-necked shirts and slacks. The fanciest thing in the restaurant, in fact, is the way Passot puts his plates together. There's a keen mind at work here, with a sense of humor. He surprises with herringbone patterns, swirls of vegetables, architecturally arranged appetizers, plates designed like collages . . . so inventive is the presentation that even when a dish doesn't quite come together, the visual and aromatic appeal is most inviting. The smallish menu changes regularly, and tends to focus on seasonal ingredients. The best deal is the five-course prix-fixe for $45. For a recent dinner, this included an exquisite fall salad with roast rabbit loin and chanterelles in a hazelnut vinaigrette, and a less successful salad of salmon, avocado and lobster with an obscurely flavored nage of caviar. Parsley-and-garlic soup with ragoût of snails and shiitake mushrooms and a corn-and-Belgian-endive soup with oyster flan were two of the most unusual and complex soups we've ever eaten, incredibly provocative in textures and contrasts. A vanilla-bean-dotted Champagne sorbet was the perfect palate cleanser—light and fragrant, cooling and not too sweet. La Folie's desserts are as appealing as its main courses; meal-size plates arrive covered with color, shape and texture. Individual tarte tatin on a fragile puff pastry came with cinnamon ice cream, caramel sauce, almond tuile and strawberries. If there's a fault to La Folie, it's the folly of Passot's humor and playfulness. Sometimes the dishes are just *too* gorgeous, just *too* complex and even *too* filling. But oh, what delicious fun. Dinner for two, with wine, $165.
Open Mon.-Sat. 6 p.m.-10:30 p.m. Cards: AE, MC, V.

Il Fornaio
1265 Battery St.,
Levi's Plaza
• 986-0100
ITALIAN

San Francisco went gaga over this place when it opened. It's definitely a crowd-pleaser, going as far as any establishment in town toward being all things to all meals, Italian style. Breakfast, lunch and dinner are each totally different experiences, thanks to lots of big windows, dramatic lighting and vast stretches of pale, softly polished marble. There's food everywhere—ingredients like pasta, garlic, cured meats and herbs hang in a working display, their pungent aromas pervading the restaurant. Breads and pastries baked daily draw a big breakfast crowd. The long marble bar is a favorite place for cocktails and wine beginning in midafternoon. Tables on the sunny, sheltered patio are objects of fierce competition at lunch, but it's a languid hangout after the young execs scurry back to their lairs. Owner-chef Larry Mindel is a self-styled culinary Renaissance man who gets involved in every phase of the operation, to the point of growing some of his own herbs and vegetables himself. Dinner doesn't approach the fabulous *cucina nobile* of the Blue Fox or Donatello, but it's hearty, varied and delicious. We've been impressed by a thick soup of vine-ripened tomatoes and fresh bread, with herbs and olive oil, and a whole salmon roasted in a clay pot with herbs and olive oil. Pasta has been inconsistent in texture but mostly firm, and the sauces are exquisite. Agnolotti (pasta pouches filled with lamb) has a knockout fennel cream sauce. Tagliolini di pane is an interesting bread-crumb pasta that we had with a tangy sausage-and-wine sauce. Pizzas can be inspired or merely delicious, depending on . . . Mindel's mood? The wait staff is knowledgeable about matching foods with the excellent Italian wine selection. Dinner is $65 to $80 for two, with wine.
Open Mon.-Thurs. 7 a.m.-10 a.m. & 11:30 a.m.-11 p.m., Fri. 7 a.m.-midnight, Sat. 8 a.m.-10:30 a.m. & 11:30 a.m.-midnight, Sun. 3:30 p.m.-11 p.m. All major cards.

Fournou's Ovens
Stanford Court Hotel,
905 California St.,
Nob Hill
• 989-1910
FRENCH

10/20

What has happened to Fournou's Ovens? Once the toast of the town, the restaurant now has lost its luster. Still, it is better than when we were last here. The service is professional as ever—one is made to feel quite comfortable, almost like an honored guest. Yet there is something claustrophobic about all this etched glass, copper and tile that we just can't put our finger on. The breads, especially the sourdough, are tasty, and our appetizer of smoked salmon and sour cream on warm potato pancakes with Manchurian osetra caviar was good. The grilled shiitake mushrooms washed in olive oil and balsamic vinegar were flavorful, and the lobster salad with mussels served with peppered brioche points was fine. The main courses followed suit, providing good food without much excitement. The free-range chicken, served on two heart-shaped leek-garlic waffles with ham maple sauce, was interesting, and our venison with parsnip purée, sausages and potato pancakes was a good mix of flavors; there was absolutely no gaminess to the venison.

Desserts are still a strong suit here: we enjoyed the lemon angel food cake with fresh strawberry purée and the intense, tequila sunrise–colored blood orange sorbet. The wine list is strong, with a good selection of half bottles. Dinner for two, with wine, will run approximately $130.

Open daily 5:30 p.m.-11 p.m. All major cards.

French Room

Four Seasons Clift Hotel,
495 Geary St.,
Union Square
• 775-4700
FRENCH/CALIFORNIAN

Hotel restaurants have been making a comeback in San Francisco, and the Clift Hotel's French Room is foremost among them. The glorious room, newly minted in the image of a gracious bygone era, serves one of the city's freshest and most creative menus. Chef Kelly Mills satisfies the old-money set with deft executions of standbys like Caesar salad (served with fresh Dungeness crab in season), garlic-crusted rack of lamb and prime rib with English popovers. On the other hand, his interest in Asian cuisines gives rise to such delights as an appetizer of crabcakes with papaya and fresh coriander relish or a special of fresh scallops and Chinese broccoli in black-bean-and-ginger sauce with rice noodles. Seafood is abundant on the menu: Pacific oysters are sautéed in a cornmeal batter with a goat cheese dressing; fish such as Chilean sea bass or fresh salmon are served with a variety of sauces; and every Friday Miller offers a special of fresh abalone sautéed in a citrus butter. The stunning silver dessert cart is not for the faint of heart, although there are usually gleaming bowls full of plump, seasonal berries hidden among the really dangerous stuff. Service is perfectly unobtrusive, and each formally dressed table is like a little private dining room. Spend some time perusing the exceptional California wine list. Dinner runs about $140 for two, with wine.

Open daily 6:30 a.m.-2:30 p.m. & 6 p.m.-10:30 p.m. All major cards.

Fuku-Sushi

Japan Center West,
1581 Webster St.,
Japantown
• 346-3030
JAPANESE/SUSHI

The sushi here is perhaps the best in town, but what doubly attracts us is the place's gestalt. From the moment you step into the dimmed, romantic interior you are treated like an emperor (or an emperor's mistress), with full attention lavished on you by the waitress and the sushi chef. The latter is a true master, gracefully assembling his creations out of the freshest of ingredients. After you start feeling your sake and get bolder in your ordering, the chef may offer you his finest creation: a piece of uni (sea urchin) topped with a raw quail egg. The merry atmosphere and great food are conducive to prodigious ordering, so the bill can add up fast. Expect to pay from $45 to $70 for two, with sake.
Open Wed.-Mon. 5:30 p.m.-10:45 p.m. Cards: AE, MC, V.

Garden House

133 Clement St.,
Richmond District
• 221-3655
VIETNAMESE

Precious few good things have resulted from the troubles in Southeast Asia, but this gem of a regional restaurant in the inner Clement Street shopping district is one of them. Owner Nguyen Ngoc Ut fled Vietnam with his family during the war, bringing with him a marriage of cuisines that goes back to the time when Vietnam was part of French Indochina. The Vietnamese sensibility is seen in the emphasis on the freshest seafood and vegetables—including, naturally, hot chili peppers—while the French influence shows in what might be termed the conceptual sophistication: clever, often amazing flavor combinations and gorgeous presentations. The dining room leans toward a European aesthetic with wood-paneled walls and pristine linen tablecloths. One major quibble is the music: insidious, nonstop, contemporary Vietnamese pop music. Shut out the sound, however, and focus on the goi cuon appetizer, shrimp and pork rolls wrapped in paper-thin rice skins and served with a savory-sweet dipping sauce. Cilantro is the key flavor in this and many other dishes. The flavors of the lemon beef salad (a "salad" of sliced beef in a lemon-mint dressing) telescope outward in a hot pepper glow. Entrées—like cha ca (broiled fish with dill-and-rice pancakes), lua hong (flaming prawns and beef) and ca xao lan (sautéed monkfish in a coconut-curry sauce)—tend not to be as enthralling, but the curries are very good. It's also worth noting that Garden House does a great job of packing food to go, making it one of our favorite stops on the way out to Golden Gate Park. About $30 for two, with drinks.
Open Mon.-Thurs. 5 p.m.-10 p.m., Fri.-Sat. 10:30 a.m.-10 p.m. Cards: AE, MC, V.

Gaylord's

**900 North Point St.,
Ghirardelli Square,
Fisherman's Wharf
• 771-8822**
INDIAN

12/20

Originally started in New Delhi, this worldwide chain now has representatives in Bombay, London, New York and Los Angeles, as well as several Bay Area locations. Though the individual restaurants are privately owned, the chefs are trained in India, and each has a specialty. This Gaylord's boasts three chefs, one who specializes in tandoori, one in curries, one in desserts. The place is elegantly and comfortably appointed, with bay windows overlooking the harbor. The food is as reliable and respectable as Gaylord's reputation, though none of it will dazzle you. Starters include vegetable samosas (deep-fried pastry pockets stuffed with curried tomatoes, potatoes and peas) and assorted tandoori (bite-size pieces of chicken and lamb marinated overnight in yogurt and spices, then barbecued). The best entrée is the chicken tandoori, which is cooked in the tandoor oven after marinating for hours in a curry sauce. Indian desserts can be over-rich; try the delicious farmer's cheese instead. About $50 for two, with beer.
Open Mon.-Sat. 11:45 p.m.-1:45 p.m. & 5 p.m.-10:45 p.m., Sun. noon-3 p.m. & 5 p.m.-10:45 p.m. All major cards.

Golden Turtle

**308 5th Ave.,
Richmond District
• 221-5285
2211 Van Ness Ave.,
Van Ness
• 441-4419**
VIETNAMESE

The classical image of an ibis depicted on a screen in the entrance to the original Golden Turtle says something about the cuisine at both locations. The menu designed by chef-owner Kimquy Tran and her family is an array of variations on the classsical Vietnamese theme of balanced opposites. Simple, fresh flavors are ingeniously combined to play both with and against one another, developing a marvelous complexity that is further enhanced by sweet and savory sauces. The grill is an important part, as are mysterious concoctions in which the meats are marinated before going over the coals. The grilled shrimp appetizer, served with tiny rice pancakes, vegetables and plum sauce, is flavorful. Don't miss house specialties such as five-spice chicken and Saigon pork chops, or the shrimp-and-pork salad roll with its pronounced cilantro tang. Another winner is sunshine chicken: marinated thighs baked with garlic. The original location just off Clement Street is small and intimate, while the newer and more spacious Golden Turtle, in a large house on Van Ness Avenue, is a showier fantasy in carved wood. Two can dine for $35 (including wine).
5th Ave. branch: open Tues.-Sun. 5 p.m.-10:30 p.m. Van Ness branch: open Tues.-Sun. 11:30 a.m.-3 p.m. & 5 p.m.-10:30 p.m. All major cards.

51

Greens

Building A,
Fort Mason
• 771-6222
VEGETARIAN

This is probably the most talked-about upscale vegetarian restaurant in the nation. The menu changes weekly at this attractive, view-struck converted warehouse, reflecting the season and the availability of fresh local foods. Our favorite time to visit Greens is in the fall, when the kitchen does marvelous things with mushrooms. Pizza is offered perennially and is always exceptional, as are (appropriately enough) the salads; we recall a particularly delightful salad of lettuces, mango and pecans in a balsamic-shallot vinaigrette. Homemade desserts (apricot and cherry cobbler, sorbets, chocolate hazelnut cake) will quickly rid you of any virtuous feeling you may have after a meatless Greens meal. You'll feel even less virtuous if you succumb to the temptations of the wine list, one of the best in town. On à la carte weeknights, expect to spend $50 for two, with wine; the weekend prix fixe is $25 a person, without wine.
Open Tues.-Sat. 11:30 a.m.-2:30 p.m. & 6 p.m.-9 p.m., Sun. 10 a.m.-2 p.m. Cards: MC, V.

Harbor Village Restaurant

4 Embarcadero Center,
Financial District
• 781-8833
CHINESE

Harbor Village is the first American outpost of the Harbor View Group, which owns hotels and restaurants in Hong Kong. Its interior—teak, rosewood, crystal, carpeting, bar, piano and perhaps even the hostesses in slinky gowns—was shipped across the Pacific in three huge cargo containers and plopped down in the middle of the Financial District. The result is a sort of Chinese nouveau opulence that only borders on the tasteful. Harbor Village was carefully thought out and is skillfully run—service is quietly attentive, the kitchen is efficient and the food is consistently very good. Everything we've tried has been tasty and fresh, but we can especially recommend anything with bones or shells: squab, duck, whole catfish, rock cod and crab netted from an immaculately maintained aquarium. A special of live prawns can be had either sashimi style, steamed with minced garlic, or poached. Soups are exceptional, especially the shark's fin and the conpoy, which contains pricey dried scallop shreds. And for those who opt for the wilder side of Chinese cuisine, snake soup is offered during the winter months; it employs either Texas rattlesnake or imported Chinese snake meat. A regal Chinese dinner for two, with wine, will cost about $70.
Open Mon.-Fri. 11 a.m.-2:30 p.m. & 5:30 p.m.-9:30 p.m., Sat.-Sun. 10:30 a.m.-2:30 p.m. & 5:30 p.m.-9:30 p.m. All major cards.

Harris'
2100 Van Ness Ave.,
Van Ness
• 673-1888
AMERICAN/STEAKHOUSE

10/20

We know beef isn't socially correct these days, but a lot of people still like it. Its fans are middle-aged people, mostly, and yet the number of hip-looking young people settling into the banquettes here is surprising for an old-fashioned steakhouse that looks as if it had come through the Twilight Zone from the '50s. The uniformed waiters would be at home in an old Santa Fe Railroad dining car. All the high-quality beef is raised by Harris Ranch in central California and aged in Harris's temperature-controlled cases, some with display windows. Stick to the steaks and chops, or if you don't have an appetite for red meat, treat yourself to the daily fresh catch of Maine lobster. By all means have a cocktail in the bar (that reminds us of a perfect movie set) and exploit the excellent offering of red wines. Oh—gentlemen, please wear jackets. You'll spend $75 to $80 for two, with wine.
Open daily 5 p.m.-10 p.m. All major cards.

Harry's Bar & American Grill
500 Van Ness Ave.,
Civic Center
• 864-2779
ITALIAN

Ernest Hemingway wouldn't have liked this Harry's very much. He would say that both the clientele and the food were putting on airs, and we agree, which is why we've lowered our ranking. But a lot of corporate and professional San Franciscans and well-heeled out-of-towners seem to like this Spectrum Foods–owned version of Harry's as well as the classic Venetian original. It has a watering-hole feel about it, a little bit of singles action and a swirl of performing-arts cachet when the nearby symphony and opera are in session. The rooms, with peachy walls and shell sconces, brass touches and wide windows on Van Ness Avenue (a canal, of sorts, for rubber-tired gondolas), are appealing when they're full of people. The interesting northern Italian menu was designed by chef Patrizio Sacchetto before he was lured away to the new Blue Fox. Appetizers include oysters with basil butter, grilled radicchio, and salmon cured in grappa and served with a mustard-dill sauce. Tender loin of venison in a rich Barolo wine sauce is delicious, as is black-and-white pasta with fresh scallops. Special risottos can be excellent but also can be on the gloppy side. Dinner comes in at about $70 for two, including wine.
Open Mon. 11:30 a.m.-10 p.m., Tues.-Thurs. 11:30 a.m.-11 p.m., Fri.-Sat. 11:30 a.m.-midnight, Sun. 11:30 a.m.-10 p.m. All major cards.

Harry's on Fillmore
2020 Fillmore St.,
Upper Fillmore
• 921-1000
AMERICAN

12/20

Several nights a week the line of preppies and yuppies goes halfway up Fillmore Street outside Harry's. They're waiting to get into one of the town's true hot spots in order to party with like-minded and like-funded souls, to the wistful strains of "Louie Louie." Harry's isn't big—two limousines disgorging at once can just about pack the place—but that's part of its charm. Another part of its charm is the excellent, if limited, menu served during all but the peak hours. Harry's cheeseburger is more than respectable; the fries are magnificent. A juicy little pepper steak is aged beef with a liberal coating of fresh-cracked pepper. Fine wines are available by the glass. The dining area is a raised section, enclosed by railings, like a room within a room. A light meal, with wine, runs about $25 for two.
Open Mon.-Sat. 5 p.m.-11 p.m., Sun. 5 p.m.-10 p.m. All major cards.

Hayes Street Grill
320 Hayes St.,
San Francisco
• 863-5545
CALIFORNIAN/SEAFOOD

It's hard to believe that this thriving bistro—owned in part by Patti Unterman, the *San Francisco Chronicle*'s popular restaurant critic—is just ten years old. The black-and-white photos of San Francisco celebrities, the comfortable setting and the easy pace of the place evoke the feeling of a decades-old haunt. People come back to the Hayes Street Grill time and time again for food that's straightforward and always on the mark. For starters, there are those impeccably fresh oysters, plus an array of appealing first courses: grilled scallops and an avocado salad with a tomatillo-papaya salsa; Dungeness crab–and-artichoke salad. Reasons in themselves to visit the Hayes Street Grill are the classic burger, the sharply seasoned Caesar salad and, above all, the mesquite-grilled fish. Up to a dozen fish are chalked on the board each day, and can be ordered with one of a half dozen sauces—everything from a béarnaise or a hand-made tartare sauce to an herb-shallot butter. All fish plates come with excellent frites, and are priced in the $11 to $18 range. For those craving anything *but* seafood, the menu offers handsome dry-aged New York steak; grilled whole chicken breast; lamb chops with arugula and roasted potatoes; and either whisky-and-fennel sausages or tender boudin blanc. As for the dessert menu, the heavenly crème brulée is, hands-down, the best in the city. And something as simple as the raspberry tart, made with truly flavorful raspberries, can be revelatory. There are always a half dozen attractive wines available by the glass. Dinner for two, with wine, runs about $75.
Open Mon.-Fri. 11:30 a.m.-3 p.m. & 5 p.m.-10 p.m., Sat. 6 p.m.-11 p.m. Cards: MC, V.

Hong Kong Flower Lounge

51 Millbrae Ave.,
Millbrae
• 692-6666
CHINESE

11/20

Hong Kong Flower Lounge is one of those special finds—a suburban restaurant with genuine style, charm and better-than-average food. An always-crowded dining room with a mixture of well-dressed Asian and Caucasian clientele is one tip-off. Another is the fanciful, brightly lit dining room with glossy green-tiled roofs, pale wooden pillars and dull salmon-colored walls hung with the odd Chinese painting or two; it's all a bit wacky, extremely comfortable, and it works. Further, unlike most Bay Area Chinese restaurants with enormous menus that are impossible to work through, Hong Kong Flower Lounge offers a comparatively small range of dishes, but everything reads well and the lovely multipaged presentation in both Chinese and English is reassuring. Everything is attractively presented, competently seasoned and appealing in texture. There are no extraordinary dishes, no gastronomic epiphanies, yet it doesn't matter. It's just so pleasant to be here that the dinner is satisfying even with glitches. Egg rolls, though slightly greasy, are crunchy appetizers. Spareribs look good: glossy, juicy and mahogany-colored, though at a recent dinner they were too salty and were served cold. "I can put them in the microwave," suggested our excellent waiter. It helped. Minced squab in iceberg lettuce leaves was edible but murky in flavor; the overall impact was that of warm, brown indistinction. The crystal shrimps dish was a large serving of plump, perfectly fresh prawns, so delicately cooked in a light cornstarch-based coating that, except for the odd pungent wand of green onion or aromatic jolt of fresh ginger, the dish tasted of nothing but warm, slippery shrimp. Portions of everything, from appetizers to main dishes, are exceedingly generous. And the waiters are courteous and prompt. With beer, dinner for two is around $40. *Open Mon.-Fri. 11 a.m.-2:30 p.m. & 5 p.m.-9:30 p.m., Sat.-Sun. 10:30 a.m.-2:30 p.m. & 5 p.m.-9:30 p.m. Cards: AE, MC, V.*

Hunan

924 Sansome St.,
North Beach
• 956-7727
853 Kearny St.,
Chinatown
• 788-2234
5723 Geary Blvd.,
Richmond District
• 221-3388
CHINESE

9/20

The Chinatown branch of Hunan is the place where many of us on the West Coast first tasted the pleasures of hot, humid Hunanese cuisine, and this small chain still remains one of the best practitioners of that particular culinary style. Our favorite branch remains the one on Kearny Street—not because the food is any better than at the other two, but because it's got the most authentically funky atmosphere, and it is in the heart of Chinatown. If you love super-heated food, this is the place for you; plan on drinking lots of Tsing Tao beer to quench the fire of the artfully used peppers here. The dumplings are fabulous, the kung pao chicken dissolves

the top layer of your tongue and the shrimp in the various fiery stir-fries are fresh and fat. Since the prevailing flavor here is hot, what you order is practically moot. Food comes out at a breakneck pace, making it a good bet for premovie dining. Dinner for two, with beer, will cost about $30.
Sansome St. branch: open Mon.-Sat. 11:30 a.m.-9:30 p.m.; cards: AE, MC, V. Kearny St. branch: open Mon.-Sat. 11:30 a.m.- 9:30 p.m.; no cards. Geary St. branch: open daily 11:30 a.m.-9:30 p.m.; cards: AE, MC, V.

Ironwood Café
901 Cole St.,
Haight-Ashbury
• 664-0224
AMERICAN

Named after a town on Michigan's northern peninsula, the Ironwood Café was designed to look like a north-woods lumber-town café. The high-ceilinged, two-level dining room is filled with oldtime touches—antique oil lamps, a wooden mannequin, knotty pine booths—that give it a warm, cozy feel. Much attention is given to the food, as evidenced in all the details: spiced breads are baked here daily; ice creams are homemade; even the pickles are pickled here on the premises. The kitchen has a deft hand with seafood; the daily changing menu offers such dishes as mahi-mahi, charbroiled and served in a scallion vinaigrette, and swordfish with a green-peppercorn mayonnaise. Also, try one of the creative vegetarian dishes here: a wild-mushroom stew combines chanterelles, white mushrooms, carmelized onions, crème fraîche and herb dumplings, and homemade ravioli is stuffed with pumpkin and Parmesan cheese. The dessert selection changes frequently and is always worth sampling, and the wine list is well chosen. About $65 for a tasty dinner for two, with wine.
Open Mon.-Thurs. 5:30 p.m.-10 p.m., Fri.-Sat. 5:30 p.m.-10:30 p.m. All major cards.

Jack's
615 Sacramento St.,
Financial District
• 986-9854
AMERICAN

10/20

In business at one location or another since 1864, Jack's is an old–San Francisco darling of the Montgomery Street financial community. The room is austere, with linoleum floors and bright lights. We've known the waiters to be rude, on occasion, to unknowns; and the food ranges from the sublime to the merely acceptable. Best bets are the incredible fresh cracked crab with scrumptious homemade mayonnaise, the fried eggplant and superb au gratin potatoes. Main dishes consist of simple, solid fare: broiled English mutton chops, sautéed crab legs with béarnaise, poached salmon in hollandaise. Don't let the cheesy decor fool you into a casual approach—men without ties won't be seated (though Jack will discreetly loan you one, if

needed). Dinner for two, with wine, is $80.
Open Mon.-Fri. 11:30 a.m.-9:30 p.m., Sat.-Sun. 5 p.m.-9:30 p.m. Cards: AE.

Jackson Fillmore Trattoria
2506 Fillmore St.,
Upper Fillmore
• 346-5288
ITALIAN

11/20

Owner Jack Kreitzman covers most of the bases in this rollicking trattoria. We've never had a bad time here, though we've had trouble getting in and have never found the food inspired, just good. Anchoring the northern boundary of the Upper Fillmore neighborhood, within walking distance of such popular watering holes as Harry's Saloon and Alta Plaza, Jackson Fillmore has been packed from the minute it opened. The cuisine is southern Italian—not always the best, given that region's overdependence on olive oil. It's authenticity is evidenced by the many times we've overheard parties reminiscing about Roman holidays past. Especially good are the antipasti, which can be a nice light meal: try the eggplant saltimbocca and the insalata di pomodori, a salad of tomatoes, tiny zucchini, red onion and garlic marinated in olive oil and vinegar—the essence of late summer, even if it is foggy outside. In the past, we have experienced curt service, but that, too, is authentically Roman. The large portions, reasonable prices and festive atmosphere keep them coming. Two can eat well for $30, with a glass of wine each.
Open Tues.-Thurs. 5:30 p.m.-10:30 p.m., Fri.-Sat. 5:30 p.m.-11 p.m., Sun. 5 p.m.-10 p.m. Cards: MC, V.

Janot's
44 Campton Pl.,
Union Square
• 392-5373
FRENCH/CALIFORNIAN

12/20

Imagine you've just spent hours trudging around the Paris shops, and you drop into a little bistro for some sustenance. Look again—this is San Francisco, but the feel of Janot's is pure France. It's casual, it's noisy, it's fun—and the food is creative and good. We're happy to report that the place has lightened its cuisine and cleaned up its Gallic-superiority act since our last edition. The Californian touch is evident in fresh ingredients like naturally raised beef, an unsullied taste treat. Service is now refreshingly courteous, although the harried wait staff doesn't always take time to explain unfamiliar dishes. The appetizer of roulade de saumon is light and flavorful, the salmon juicy and flaky; the rich calf's liver and calf's brains are delectable dishes, if a bit heavy on the butter. Do try the venison and duck when they're offered as specials. Drink a good Beaujolais and you'll forget you've just braved I. Magnin and Neiman-Marcus and will probably wander off in search of the Métro. Expect to pay $80 for dinner à deux (wine included).
Open Mon.-Sat. 11:30 a.m.-2:30 p.m. & 6 p.m.-10 p.m. Cards: AE, MC, V.

Julie's Supper Club

1123 Folsom St.,
South of Market
• 861-0707
AMERICAN

Julie's sends up the '50s, embraces the '60s, ignores the '70s—and isn't that what the '80s were all about? This restaurant for the '90s has been called a terrific dive, and that about sums it up. The bar is a fine place to sip a martini or three and thrill to the sounds of lounge acts like the Dinos, who lend a perfectly sleazy, bowling-alley ambience to the front of the house. There are two dining rooms, usually packed with an extremely diverse if all-white clientele. Call the decor camp, demented, cheap—it's just a lot of fun. Owner Julie Ring's solid American food is consistently tasty. The meatloaf is how Mom used to make it, but the best thing on the menu may well be the San Francisco-style burger (served on a sourdough baguette), which is perfect with a glass of Zinfandel from the short but excellent wine list. A dinner for two, with wine, comes in at $45.
Open Mon.-Thurs. 5:30 p.m.-10:30 p.m., Fri.-Sat. 5:30 p.m.-11:30 p.m. All major cards.

Kabuto Sushi

5116 Geary Blvd.,
Richmond District
• 752-5652
JAPANESE/SUSHI

Although the star chef at this small, fashionable sushi joint was long a prime attraction at Kinokawa, Kabuto still has its little problems. One great ringmaster does not a circus make, or something like that. The inestimable Sachio Kojima, from Hokkaido, is a true sushi samurai, and a consummate showman to boot. Knives seem to sprout from his hands as he slices, shapes, wraps and presents pelagic morsels. His ceremonial cries are from the heart, as are occasional outbursts of applause from awestruck patrons. Although he makes no personal claims, Sachio is credited by his fans with having invented the California maki—maguro, crab and avocado surrounded by rice and wrapped in seaweed. His tiger eye, a psychedelic treasure of smoked salmon and poached squid, is hypnotic. A dinner menu is also offered, but sushi is the best bet here. About $50 for two, with sake.
Open Tues.-Sat. 5 p.m.-3 a.m. Cards: AE, MC, V.

Khan Toke Thai House

5937 Geary Blvd.,
Richmond District
• 668-6654
THAI

Wear slip-on shoes and clean socks to Khan Toke, because the first thing you'll do is hand your footwear over to be checked until after dinner. The age-old custom has been upheld in this Thai enclave since its opening in 1974. Though it disconcerts some people, we always look forward to padding into the lushly carpeted, candlelit labyrinth of dining rooms in our stocking feet to begin what has never failed to be a resplendent feast. Diners are seated on floor cushions at low tables (some have wells for feet) with padded back supports. Appetizers are generally the best part of an outstanding menu; one could make a memorable meal

with a few openers (Thai crab with a cucumber salad, or a spicy squid salad shot with mint) and an order of the exquisite pad Thai noodles. One must is the green papaya salad, a piquant dish laced with fresh chilis, and a specialty is pong pang, a seafood concoction indundated with "secret" spices. The artfully layered flavors that give each dish a special character induce us to drink wine here rather than beer, as with most Thai food. And the wine list is up to it: delicate Sauvignon Blancs and perfumed Gewürztraminers are just right to boost the dynamics, point up the subtleties and, not least, extinguish the flames just short of causing serious mental damage. A special treat on Sunday evenings is provided by temple dancers, who perform sinuously against the backdrop of intricate hardwood wall carvings and windows overlooking as tropical a garden as one will find in San Francisco. Romance addicts: this place is for you. About $40 for two, with a modest wine.
Open nightly 5 p.m.-11 p.m. All major cards.

Kim's
508 Presidio Ave.,
Presidio Heights
• 923-1500
VIETNAMESE

This utterly charming little Vietnamese restaurant suffers from its difficult location. We think it's a terrific neighborhood place; it's just that the neighborhood (très chic upper Sacramento Street) is about a block away on the other side of the busy California-Presidio intersection. Don't let that keep you away. Kim's predecessor in the venue was Bodega, a seafood restaurant that has since moved to roomier quarters, but that left behind its decor of exposed wood. It gives the dining areas a seaport feel, which is accented around sunset by the building's western exposure. Kim is vivacious and her family is wonderful. The food has been consistently fine—delicate, fresh, satisfying Vietnamese-French cuisine. The sophisticated French influence even shows up in such simple items as the tender spring rolls. Our hands-down favorite dish is the succulent catfish baked with vegetables and a fragrant sauce in a clay pot. A reasonable $35 for two, with wine.
Open Mon.-Sat. 11 a.m.-2:30 p.m. & 5 p.m.-10 p.m. All major cards.

Korea House
1640 Post St.,
Japantown
• 563-1388
KOREAN

12/20

This is Asian soul food, with enough heat to blow both Thailand and Hunan Province right off the map, and some delicacy of flavor to boot. The pale-wood decor of the large upstairs room (a nightclub is downstairs) is beautiful in a stark, mountainish way, though there's little to stare at but other patrons, a reassuring number of whom look Korean. Each of the many tables has its own gas barbecue for personal immolation of various marinated meats and fish.

Squid, in a sweet-hot marinade, is particularly satisfying to grill. It puffs up and turns purple, echoing the reaction of some Westerners to the fierce spiciness of most of these dishes. Aside from the barbecue selections (all served with pickled vegetables and a peppery broth), there are such magnificent traditional dishes as sang sum chi gaw, a stew of fish, greens, mushrooms, noodles and tofu that is guaranteed to clear blocked sinuses. And don't neglect mun aw hwe, defined on the menu as "steamed ugliest fresh octopus with hot sauce." Gnarly, perhaps, but ugly? No way—it tastes too good. Service is lickety-split. Best of all, Korea House is open until 3 a.m. Two can have dinner and plenty of cold Korean beer and still get out for $35.
Open daily 11 a.m.-3 a.m. Cards: MC, V.

Kuleto's
221 Powell St.,
Union Square
• 397-7720
ITALIAN

Pat Kuleto is the designer behind such popular haunts as Lascaux and PosTrio, among others. Kuleto has such a knack for setting a mood that Bill Kimpton, the owner of this good northern Italian restaurant, gave it the designer's name. This may not be the most dramatic of Kuleto's venues, but it's quintessentially his in its use of marble and wood, subtle color schemes and such clever spatial arrangements as the raised section at the rear of the long room. The focal points are a high Florentine ceiling and a magnificent wooden bar from San Francisco's great nineteenth-century Palace Hotel. The bar is a great place to hang out, drink wine and nibble antipasti beneath a hanging forest of salamis, pastas, herbs and garlic. But, most important, the menu: if sautéed radicchio is offered, embrace it—there's none better this side of Tra Vigne. Another great thing about Kuleto's is the light but delicious California extra-virgin olive oil produced by Pat Kuleto especially for the restaurant; it's served for bread-dipping in lieu of butter. Our favorite Kuleto meal consists of nothing more than the house-made focaccia, a head of roasted garlic and an order of fried calamari, which is served with creamy, tangy aïoli. We also love the torta rustica, a thick-crust pizza with cheese, pancetta and pine nuts. The wine list is mostly Italian and California, and modestly priced. Dinner is about $40 for two, with wine by the glass.
Open Mon.-Fri. 7 a.m.-10:30 a.m. & 11:30 a.m.-11 p.m., Sat. 11:30 a.m.-11 p.m., 8 a.m.-11 p.m. All major cards.

REFLECTIONS OF GRANDEUR.

CHAMPAGNE

Veuve Clicquot Ponsardin

MAISON FONDÉE EN 1772

REIMS
FRANCE

"Une seule qualité:
la toute première"

"One quality...
the very finest"

Madame Veuve Clicquot Ponsardin

Lascaux
248 Sutter St.,
Downtown
• 391-1555
FRENCH/ITALIAN

12/20

If there had been a restaurant scene in the movie *Quest for Fire*, it would have been filmed here. Lascaux is yet another triumph for restaurant designer Pat Kuleto. Faced with a low-ceilinged subterranean space downstairs from Sutter Street, he came up with a neo-neolithic motif that really does evoke the famous painted cave of France. Rock-textured walls and columns with glowing red sconces flicker with firelight from open hearths. The noise level is deafening when the house is more than half full, which makes it hard to hear the live jazz from the bar—much less the person across the table. But it's fun. The country European menu is simple and well executed. Spit-roasted meats such as chicken, rabbit and venison are consistently juicy and tender. Salmon, mahi mahi and other fresh fish are grilled and served with rice and vegetables. Side dishes like vegetable purées and roasted garlic are tasty if uninspired, and there are different soups and pastas every night. The fairly priced wine list excels in reds, especially some undervalued Bordeaux. Dinner for two, with wine, will run about $70. *Open Mon.-Fri. 11:30 a.m.-3 p.m. & 5:30 p.m.-11 p.m., Sat. 5:30 p.m.-11 p.m. All major cards.*

Modesto Lanzone
601 Van Ness Ave.,
Civic Center
• 928-0400
ITALIAN

From the moment you step into Modesto Lanzone's namesake restaurant in Opera Plaza, expect a singular dining experience. A whimsical Robert Arneson bust of Lanzone, spattered with "tomato sauce" paint and dripping with strands of sculpted "pasta," sets the mood right in the entryway. In the dining room, additional artwork from Lanzone's vast collection greets you from every possible angle. Far from being overwhelming, however, the effect is thoroughly delightful, enriching even further the artistry on which the kitchen justly prides itself. Classic northern Italian dishes, such as herb-scented roast rabbit and juicy roast chicken with artichokes, join a long and practically alphabetical list of pastas made fresh daily by Modesto's two aunts. The delicate cannelloni alla Rossini, stuffed with minced veal, vegetables and cheeses, is outstanding. Order anything made with porcini mushrooms, those woodsy, densely flavored delights, when they're available. As for wine, why not keep it in the *paese* and try a fine Italian bottle—a Barbaresco, perhaps—to add the finishing touch. About $100 will buy a sumptuous, varied dinner for two, including wine.
Open Tues.-Sat. 3 p.m.-10:30 p.m. All major cards.

Little City Antipasti Bar

673 Union St.,
North Beach
• 434-2900
ITALIAN

12/20

This unambitious watering hole and meeting place with, well, fairly nourishing Italian food is a real North Beach gem. A lot of places have opened and closed around this Washington Square location without developing the kind of scene that Little City enjoys, with loyal regulars and the reputation of a satisfactory rendezvous. The narrow stand-up bar area and a number of tables devoted to the libations trade are always crowded at lunch and at cocktail hour with stylish San Franciscans. What's the draw? Simply that old-time formula of good food, moderate prices and snappy service. Antipasto is the big deal, obviously, and it's well done. There are also pastas with sauces ranging from savory clams and garlic to tangy bolognese. And you'll find good wines by the glass. Dinner runs about $40 for two, with wine.
Open Mon.-Thurs. 11:30 a.m.-2:30 p.m. & 6 p.m.-11 p.m., Fri.-Sat. 11:30 a.m.-2:30 p.m. & 6 p.m.-midnight. All major cards.

Little Italy

4109 24th St.,
Noe Valley
• 821-1515
ITALIAN

11/20

Nestled in one of the city's yuppie enclaves, Little Italy is immensely popular with both neighborhood residents and outsiders. They love the generous portions, affordable prices, homey atmosphere and country-style ("contadina") cooking. So do we; the food is simple, and always infused with generous amounts of garlic. (Little Italy uses up more than 200 pounds of the precious stuff *weekly*.) One sure winner is the prosciutto and cheese–stuffed artichoke. The signature dish here is spaghetti and prawns g.o.a., which is prawns sautéed in olive oil with crisped slivers of garlic and anchovies (thus, the initials) and served on a bed of spaghetti. Dessert is, predictably, limited to zabaglione—with good fresh fruit. About $60 for dinner for two, with wine.
Open Mon. 6 p.m.-10 p.m., Tues.-Thurs. 6 p.m.-10:30 p.m., Fri. 6 p.m.-11 p.m., Sat. 5:30 p.m.-11 p.m., Sun. 5 p.m.-10 p.m. Cards: MC, V.

Little Joe's

523 Broadway,
North Beach
• 433-4343
ITALIAN

11/20

Just as there are cult films, so there are cult restaurants. Little Joe's many followers swear this is the best restaurant in San Francisco, nay, the best in the country. But though one can have a very nice meal here, it just isn't worth the potential two-hour wait for a table. The restaurant's motto, "Rain or Shine, There's Always a Line," is unfortunately all too true. The no-reservations policy and the refusal to provide any kind of waiting area (instead, customers form a long, snaky line around the bar, getting entirely sloshed before finally being seated) considerably mar our enjoyment of a meal here, though we suspect that the loyalists consider the wait half the fun. Pastas are always correctly al dente, and any of the pastas with mussels or clams are memorable. The veal dishes, the best of which are the saltimbocca and a big, saucy parmigiana, are all admirable. Surprisingly, the Italian fish stews are made to order. Vegetables are always well prepared and abundant. In fact, all the portions are abundant, making dessert unnecessary—a blessing, since they are mundane. The waitresses are friendly but dreadfully hurried; the whole mood of Little Joe's is too frantic for those who enjoy relaxed meals. Still, no matter what we say, there will still always be an interminable line here. About $30 per person for dinner with wine. *Open Mon.-Thurs. 11 a.m.-10:30 p.m., Fri.-Sat. 11 a.m.-11 p.m., Sun. noon-10 p.m. No cards.*

MacArthur Park
607 Front St.,
North Beach
• 398-5700
AMERICAN

11/20

There is no park in San Francisco named MacArthur, but there is a large converted warehouse named MacArthur Park in North Beach that serves fashionable American cuisine. Although the small front dining room faces a lovely wooded square, the three back dining areas are more elegant. First-rate ingredients are clearly used here. The best entrées are from the oakwood smoker—a superb chicken in a barbecue sauce, a delicious spicy sausage. From the mesquite grill emanates a parade of honest steaks, chops and fresh fish. Whatever you order, make sure to accompany it with the best dish in the house, the side of crisply fried Bermuda onion "strings." Desserts are homemade and satisfying (apple pie, shortcake), and the service is amicable, if rushed. Dinner for two, with wine, will be about $60. *Open Mon.-Thurs. 7 a.m.-10 a.m., 11:30 a.m.-2:30 p.m. & 5:30 p.m.-10:30 p.m., Fri. 7 a.m.-10 a.m., 11:30 a.m.-2:30 p.m. & 5:30 p.m.-11 p.m., Sat. 4:30 p.m.-11 p.m., Sun. 10 a.m.-2:30 p.m. & 4:30 p.m.-10 p.m. All major cards.*

Mai's
1838 Union St.,
Cow Hollow
• 921-2861
316 Clement St.,
Richmond District
• 221-3046
VIETNAMESE

When you've had enough of the trendy shops along Union Street, seek respite in this charming little hideout. The sign might not attract you, but the handsome bistro setting (burnished wood, copper fixtures, a few outdoor tables) will. This decor might lead you to expect provincial French fare, but the kitchen produces a remarkably skilled Vietnamese cuisine. Everything here is wonderful: crisp rolls stuffed with shrimp, pork, noodles and bean sprouts; spicy prawns sautéed in a garlic-wine sauce; fresh salads dressed with Vietnamese fish sauce and rice-wine vinegar; aromatic soups poured over rice noodles; and la lot beef, a marvelous blend of ground beef and spices wrapped in la lot leaves and charbroiled. If you're in the do-it-yourself

mood, try the Vietnamese-style shabu, a bubbling chicken broth in which you cook morsels of meat, fish, tofu and vegetables, then dip them in soy sauce. The waiters may not speak fluent English, but they are full of smiles and are most attentive. Unusual for a Vietnamese eatery, this Mai's boasts a full bar. Dinner for two, with beer, is about $30.
Open daily 10 a.m.-10 p.m. All major cards.

Maltese Grill
20 Annie St.,
Financial District
• 777-1955
MEDITERRANEAN

12/20

This downstairs place in an alley off Market Street blows both hot and cold. When the house is full and the kitchen is on, it can offer a rollicking and lip-smacking good time. When the large, low-ceilinged dining rooms are less than three quarters full, it somehow seems dismal, despite the heartwarming Mediterranean (primarily Provençal) thrust of the kitchen. Because of the location, it's more of a happening place on weeknights, when the stand-up Pasatiempo Bar is lively and the cooking staff can be seen performing its frantic ballet in the open-view kitchen. Ratatouille and a pungent tapenade are good appetizers. A very garlicky roast chicken is great with a lean California Sauvignon Blanc, and the roast lamb can be truly succulent. You'll spend about $45 for a dinner for two, with wine.
Open Mon.-Thurs. 11:30 a.m.-3 p.m. & 5:30 p.m.-10 p.m., Fri.-Sat. 11:30 a.m.-2:30 p.m. & 5:30 p.m.-10:30 p.m. All major cards.

Mandalay
4348 California St.,
Richmond District
• 386-3895
BURMESE

12/20

Behind the colorful exterior is an equally colorful interior, with cheery paper lanterns setting off blond wood. Mandalay has a carefree feel about it that comes partly from the whimsical decor and partly from an unusually eclectic menu. We've loved the salads every time. They're colorful, too, and toothsome once one gets used to the prevalent influence of Nga-Pi, a fermented shrimp paste that's liberally applied and haunts most Burmese dishes with its indescribable flavor. Try Lap Path Thok (Burmese tea-leaf salad), which is artfully arranged little mounds of peanuts, split beans, garlic, fried coconut, roasted sesame seeds, the ubiquitous dried shrimp and special tea leaves that have been soaked in Burmese water. Dinner for two comes in at $20 for two, with a couple of Chinese beers.
Open Tues.-Sun. 11:30 a.m.-3 p.m. & 5 p.m.-10 p.m. Cards: MC, V.

The Mandarin
Ghirardelli Square,
900 North Point St.,
Fisherman's Wharf
• 474-5438
CHINESE

8/20

The Mandarin has two things going for it. One is the decor—it just might be one of the most beautiful Chinese restaurants in America, with exquisite details in antique pottery, wooden beams, deep-rose walls, carvings, lacy bamboo and leather chairs. It's worth a trip just to see the room and its sweeping view of San Francisco Bay during the day. The other thing going for The Mandarin is the fact that it's located in Ghirardelli Square, so you can go out and buy yourself a consoling trinket in one of the dozens of surrounding shops if you get as dreadful a meal as we did on a recent noontime visit. A chicken egg-drop soup was as appealing as dishwater full of shredded tissue. Assorted appetizers consisted of indifferently seasoned fried shrimp balls, greasy egg rolls without distinctive flavor and spare-ribs as brown and dry in appearance as if they'd been excavated from a Ming tomb. They tasted fine, but so what? An order of Mongolian lamb was visually unappealing and stringy with a slightly burnt taste, and came with lardy uncrisp pastry buns. Diced chicken with almonds was a mixture of diced vegetables and meat with soggy nuts, all so uninspired in seasoning that the flavor was simply brown and there wasn't even enough texture to make up for it. If Gertrude Stein had eaten this meal, she would have said, "There is no there there." But the prices sure are there. This depressing lunch for two, with beer, was $40. Double that price for dinner and take a chance, if you dare. Cecilia Chiang, The Mandarin's owner, was once known for her exquisite Cantonese and Mandarin specialties. What happened?
Open daily noon-11 p.m. All major cards.

Manora's Thai Restaurant
3226 Mission St.,
Mission District
• 550-0856
THAI

9/20

Manora's Thai has been a Mission District favorite for years, and has become so successful that they've opened a couple of other branches. But this is still the parent eatery, and it still does offer some interesting, though occasionally inconsistent, Thai cooking. If we have one criticism of Manora's to make, it's that we find so many of the dishes just a bit too sweet. Thai cuisine does involve a fair amount of sugar, but at Manora's we sometimes find ourselves too aware of it. Presentations here are lovely: the vibrant reds, greens, golds and browns of Thai cuisine stand up magnificently against china patterned with cobalt-blue flowers. Chicken saté on a recent visit was overgrilled and the peanut sauce with it was unattractively gluey. On the other hand, a bowl of lemon-chicken soup with coconut was liquid perfection, full of hefty chunks of dark-meat chicken in an aromatic

broth that was silky and satisfying. Pad Thai, chewy opaque noodles in a tomatoey sauce with thin strips of fried omelet, red and green peppers and shrimp, is a well-cooked version of this Thai standard, though, as usual, slightly too sweet for our taste. We particularly like the mild chicken curry with coconut milk, cucumber and potato, as well as the roast-duck curry with coconut, pineapple and red chili sauce. Desserts are generally weird and forgettable—like the Siam gems (red tapioca beads with water chestnuts, coconut meat, jackfruit and toddy palm seed in sweet iced coconut milk). For a Thai restaurant, there's a decent selection of wine, more than a dozen moderately priced California varietals available by the bottle or by the glass. Dinner for two, with beer, will run about $40.
Open Mon.-Fri. 11:30 a.m.-2 p.m. & 5 p.m.-10 p.m., Sat.-Sun. 5 p.m.-10 p.m. Cards: M, V.

Masa's
Hotel Vintage Court,
648 Bush St.,
Union Square
• 989-7154
CALIFORNIAN/FRENCH

Masa's opened to great acclaim in 1983 with founding chef Masa Kobayashi, who had previously been at Auberge du Soleil in Napa, performing amazing feats of alchemy in the kitchen. However, his tragic—and still-mysterious—death in 1984 led foodies to cast doubtful speculation on the culinary future of the restaurant. But, in the tradition of the world's great chefs, Kobayashi had carefully and painstakingly trained his brigade, especially Julian Serrano, who was Kobayashi's protégé, currently the restaurant's executive chef. This small (65 seats) restaurant really is no beauty, but neither is it offensive-looking. The table silver is Christofle; the china is Hutschenreuther. We felt rich just sitting here—even richer once we'd tasted the food. First came an *amuse-gueule* (literally, a "taste-tickler") of a croûte topped with a slice of lovely coral salmon, a dab of caviar, a button of dressing and a sprig of dill—a perfect lagniappe. The bread was yeasty and soft inside, with a crisply browned crust. Care was taken even with the butter—gorgeous, sweet and fresh, formed in a rooster-shaped mold. Salads here are raised to chef's d'oeuvre. The lobster salad was constructed of perfectly cooked lobster meat, pale, ivory-like leaves of endive and subtly zesty pink peppercorns. Another salad was a sensual affair—a soft bed of mixed greens topped with rich foie gras.

We're often afraid—and not without good cause—that after we've been so aroused by the opening courses, we're doomed to be disappointed by entrées. Not here. A miasma of fragrant mushrooms surrounded the côte de veau; the veal was whimsically laid out in the shape of a crab, nestled next to an inky, earthy morel mushroom filled with a musky sauce that emerged like a hidden prize upon the first bite. The veal was showered with slivers of fresh black truffles that made us recall why this tricky, elusive fungus is so highly prized—its deliciousness is like nothing else in the world. Tender oyster mushrooms, tiny bundles of slender French green beans, a creamy carrot purée and a mash of beets also graced the plate. The duck breast was beautifully pink and succulent, lacking any overt gaminess. It was thinly sliced and fanned out on the plate, sharing space with a mellow, poached winter pear.

Masa's is one of the few restaurants in this country that breeches the cheese course—rather, that serves a cheese course at all. The plateau du fromage features an herbed, creamy chèvre, a deeply veined, voluptuous Roquefort and a luxurious, satiny triple crème, as well as a perfect bunch of tiny grapes and thin, crisp slices of apple. Desserts don't go bump in the night, either. The crème brûlée is silky, flecked with vanilla beans, and fired under the salamander, rendering its sugary topping a crackling, caramelized glaze. A quartet of sorbets refreshed our overstimulated palates— gem-colored, egg-shaped scoops of strawberry, cranberry, peach and green apple. A delicate, almond-flavored tuile cookie filled with a tart, clear-tasting apple sorbet, surrounded by sautéed apples, fresh figs and sugared pecans, was one of those dishes we never want to finish eating: layer upon layer of tastes and textures—a truly stunning dish. There are also eight dessert wines that can be ordered by the glass, including various vintages of Château d'Yquem. While the Masa's experience does not come cheap (the prix-fixe menu is $65 per person; ordering à la carte can rack the tariff up considerably higher, to about $250 for two, with wine), the evening is more than worth its price. *Open Tues.-Sun. 6 p.m.-9 p.m. All major cards.*

Miss Pearl's Jam House
601 Eddy St.,
Civic Center
• 775-5267
CARIBBEAN

11/20

This happening new place is either a fantasy or a nightmare, depending upon your viewpoint. Some people are unnerved to find themselves swimming in a wall-to-wall, homogenous crowd of beautiful and affluent young white people. Others feel right at home, and that's the key to enjoying the Jam House. Owner Julie Ring (see Julie's Supper Club) took over a defunct sleazy motel and went tropical in a trashy, fun way with two bars and an inside-outside restaurant. The all-appetizer menu is full of tasty surprises like deep-fried catfish fingers with cilantro-and-roast-pepper purée, and tangy fritters of black-eyed peas. More substantial dishes include duck with sweet-potato

fries and tamarind-cherry sauce. The coconut-onion dressing on the hearts of palm is wild stuff. The preppy waiters take their sweet time getting around; the wine list is fine, but it's a beer-oriented place. You'll spend about $40 for two, with beer.
Open Mon.-Sat. 8 a.m.-10:30 a.m., 11:30 a.m.-2:30 p.m. & 6 p.m.-11 p.m., Sun. 10:30 a.m.-3 p.m. All major cards.

Mitoya
1855 Post St.,
Japan Center,
Japantown
• 563-2156
JAPANESE/SUSHI

12/20

This is a slice from Tokyo's fast lane, the Ginza, where eating as entertainment is taken seriously. Mitoya occupies two rooms on the second level of Japan Center; the larger room is a coffeehouse by day and a sing-along karaoke bar and disco by night. The smaller, more attractive room is a robata-yaki bar, similar to a sushi bar but offering, in addition to sushi and sashimi, a range of meats, vegetables and what have you that are grilled to order over open flames and served in bite-size portions. Even a bite at a time, the most eclectic eaters are sated long before running out of dishes to try. One delicious tidbit is a thin slice of lean beef wrapped around a young asparagus spear and briefly fired. Slices of sweet yam, cooked quickly and served with butter melting over them, are divine. The robata-yaki master can recommend the evening's most propitious choices, which are also posted on a board overhead. But a warning: Sophisticated as you may be, East is East and West is West. Avoid fermented bean curd unless you've had it before and you like it. Shoes are removed before entering, and guests sit before the bar with feet dangling in a well. The decor resembles a set from a Kurosawa epic about the Shogunate. Feel free to point and gesture—the universal language where food is concerned. About $35 for two, with beer.
Open Sun.-Thurs. 6 p.m.-2 a.m., Fri.-Sat. 6 p.m.-2:30 a.m. All major cards.

Monsoon
601 Van Ness Ave.,
Opera Plaza,
Civic Center
• 441-3232
ASIAN/CALIFORNIAN

A comprehensive tea list is one of the touches that distinguishes this place from ordinary East-West restaurants. Another is a respect for the classical forms of several Asian cuisines, which are enhanced rather than corrupted by the creativity of proprietor Bruce Cost (an Asian food scholar) and chef Tony Gulisano (formerly of Il Fornaio). The decor is a not-unpleasant cultural chaos featuring marble floors, lacquered pillars, a glassed-in kitchen and a Chinese dragon painted on the ceiling over the raised dining room (there are also little booths). Unfortunately, large windows offer nothing but a view of Opera Plaza's inner courtyard, and it's not a pretty sight. We visited just after Monsoon opened, and the service was still on the rough side—a rather uncoordinated staff struggled to keep things together. But we liked the food with its fresh Californian ingredients and distinctive Asian flavors. Outstanding were cold noodles with a Thai pesto of peanuts, ginger, mint, coriander, basil and garlic, and a tasty venison saté with peanut-coriander sauce for dipping. There are also some interesting little Chinese hamburgers, flecked with ginger and served with a hot mustard dipping sauce. Our favorite main dish was grilled lemon duck, a crispy bird with fresh, zesty lemon sauce. Desserts include a scrumptious Asian tiramisu made with coconut custard, rum, and tropical fruits. Once the service smooths out a bit, this will be a fine place to dine. Dinner is $85 for two, with wine.

Open Mon.-Thurs. 11:30 a.m.-11 p.m., Fri. 11:30 a.m.-midnight, Sat. 5:30 p.m.-midnight, Sun. 5:30 p.m.-11 p.m. Cards: MC, V.

Narai

2229 Clement St., Richmond District
• 751-6363
THAI

Run by a family of Chiu Chow Chinese, Narai is one of the very best Thai restaurants in San Francisco, and one of the few patronized by Asians. It is also the only Bay Area restaurant that dares serve the notorious durian fruit. Banned from public transportation and hotels in Thailand because of its awful odor, durian nonetheless has many addicts; eating it is said to be like eating custard in a sewer. Narai's menu offers both Thai and Chinese dishes; we prefer the Thai, though everything here is fresh-tasting and well prepared. It's hard to find better squid: still translucent, yet tender and warm, it is poached for a matter of seconds before being tossed in a piquant salad or into the magnificent hot-and-sour seafood soup. The soup is loaded with clams, shrimp, shark's fin and scallops and is rich with the fragrance of kaffir lime, lemon grass and coriander. (If only the kitchen would omit the mock crab!) Start your meal with the New Zealand mussels, which are steamed in a clay pot and served with a chili paste. Try one of the good curries, made with pastes of fresh seasonings instead of Indian-style spices. If you want to sample one of the Chinese offerings, there are deep-fried whole pompano in a sweet-hot sauce and steamed whole crab with minced pork, on a bed of silver noodles. Besides the exotic durian, which is served with glutinous rice flavored with sweetened coconut milk, Narai's warm taro, gingko nut and red-date pudding is one of the city's most unusual desserts. Since there are only twelve tables, you may have to wait. About $40 for dinner for two, with Thai beer.

Open Tues.-Sat. 11 a.m.-10 p.m., Sun. 11 a.m.-9:30 p.m. Cards: AE, MC, V.

Neecha

2100 Sutter St.,
Western Addition
• 922-9419
THAI

10/20

This homey little storefront Thai place scores well on several counts. The dining room is dim and cozy; one can be anonymous, two can be intimate. It has true neighborhood personality (Western Addition with Pacific Heights overtones). And the food is good and inexpensive. So although Neecha doesn't ring the exalted bells of gastronomy, it offers a genuine and satisfying Thai meal and is, for instance, excellent for a lunch stop during a shopping spree on nearby trendy upper Fillmore Street. The appetizers and salads in particular are excellent, especially yam pla mak (spicy squid salad) and yam neur (a salad of marinated grilled sirloin). Dinner for two, with a couple of beers, costs about $22. *Open Mon.-Fri. 11 a.m.-3 p.m. & 5 p.m.-10 p.m., Sat.-Sun. 5 p.m.-10 p.m. All major cards.*

Nicaragua

3015 Mission St.,
Mission District
• 826-3672
NICARAGUAN

10/20

A steady fixture in one of the outer Mission District's banana belts, Nicaragua has that no-frills cantina feel of a regional family restaurant—that is to say, greasy but friendly, even if you don't speak Spanish. We stop in frequently for an afternoon beer with ceviche, a tasty mixture of marinated rockfish and salsa, with plenty of cilantro and, on the side, freshly made corn chips. Tamales are tops, in two varieties: nacatamal (beef) and yoltamal, the purist's tamale (all cornmeal). We've also enjoyed vigoron, a combination of tender steamed yucca and crispy fried pork. The fried bananas served with most dishes are terrific when eaten with a side order of sour cream. If there's any fresh, whole-fried snapper offered, accept; likewise the staple, indio viejo con arroz y maduro (spiced beef with rice and fried bananas), which is hearty and cheap. Two can eat and drink quite well for $20. *Open Mon.-Thurs. 11 a.m.-9:45 p.m., Fri.-Sun. 11 a.m.-10:45 p.m. No cards.*

Nob Hill

Mark Hopkins
Inter-Continental Hotel,
999 California St.,
Nob Hill
• 392-3434
CONTINENTAL/
CALIFORNIAN

This elegant house restaurant of the Mark Hopkins Inter-Continental Hotel has had trouble establishing and maintaining an identity. Talented young chefs seem to consider it a way station before they move on to greater glory. When this review was written an English chef, Ward Little, was doing wonderful things with fresh local ingredients, what we'd call continental cuisine with a strong Californian regional character. Among appetizers, we loved salmon cured in ginger and lemon juice, and sautéed duck foie gras that melted like butter in our mouths. A creamy banana-squash soup was also very good. Sea scallops and lobster with green lentils and a light herbed cream was a nice marriage of flavors and textures, while roast rabbit with

rosemary and little artichokes was on the dry side. Late one evening during crab season, a Dungeness crab mousseline with delicately perfumed vermouth sauce was outstanding. The room itself is handsome and sensitively lit, with dark-wood panels dividing luxuriantly upholstered booths. The service is hotel-professional: it's good but not overly warm. Dinner is about $125 for two, with wine.
Open daily 6:30 a.m.-10:30 a.m., 11 a.m.-2 p.m. & 4:30 p.m.-10 p.m.

North China
2315 Van Ness Ave.,
Van Ness
• 673-8201
CHINESE

North China's location on north Van Ness Avenue, which doubles as Highway 101 along that stretch, is the worst thing about it. We love the place, but, frankly, that busy drag is a drag. There's nowhere to stroll after dinner, even though the neighborhood is relatively safe at any hour. Even the restaurant's tasteful, soothing interior provides only a temporary respite from the lurching traffic outside. But we keep returning because the food is so wonderful. The mandarin crêpes are the best we've encountered. They're offered with an unprecedented range of fillings—served warm with hoisin sauce and a choice of chicken, shrimp, mushrooms or mu shu pork, or stir-fried with egg and bean curd. Like the crêpes, steamed buns are made on the premises daily and are served with such entrées as smoked tea duck, which is perfectly crisp on the outside and tenderly moist inside. A cold plate, North China's equivalent of antipasto, offers delectable glazed short ribs, spiced beef, smoked fish and sesame chicken salad. All in all, the meticulous use of fresh and first-quality ingredients makes the food consistently pleasing. Service is extremely efficient, and the price is right at about $35 for dinner for two, with a moderate bottle from the superb wine list.
Open Mon.-Sat. 11:30 a.m.-2 p.m. & 4 p.m.-10 p.m. Cards: AE, MC, V.

North India
3131 Webster St.,
Cow Hollow
• 931-1556
INDIAN

If you stay away from Indian restaurants because you have an aversion to the *faux* Raj scenario (and the outrageous prices that usually go with it), you'll love this warm, lively, handsome family-run storefront in a quiet block of Webster Street. Call it a northern Indian bistro. But it's not just ambience that keeps the white-clothed tables in two dining rooms full most nights: the cheerful glassed-in kitchen and its tandoor oven turn out delicious food. The curries have a delicate, complex spiciness that develops in the mouth. There is also surprising subtlety in the Boti kebab, skewered spice-marinated lamb from the tandoor oven. Classic accompaniments include matar paneer—cheese and peas in a mild sauce—and the breads are exceptional, especially the warm, puffy pooris. Dinner will be about $35 for two, with wine.

Open Mon.-Fri. 11:30 a.m.-2:30 p.m. & 5 p.m.-11 p.m., Sat. 5 p.m.-11 p.m., Sun. 5 p.m.-10 p.m. All major cards.

Ocean Restaurant
726 Clement St.,
Clement District
• 221-3351
CHINESE/SEAFOOD

Have you ever noticed how a lot of plush, fancy restaurants will be empty while some plain little hole-in-the-wall has a line out the door? You can't eat decor, and the Cantonese-style fish emporium called Ocean proves the point. This place features bamboo and linoleum, poor lighting, and a lot of noise. But you'll find absolutely fresh fish and seafood that is expertly prepared—grilled, steamed and pan-fried—with divine results. (The same concept as Pacific Café, which also has a line out the door at all hours—funny coincidence.) Large saltwater tanks hold live fish such as sea bass and catfish until each is called upon to meet its noble fate. Look for steelhead salmon, and order it steamed with no accompaniment but a touch of soy sauce. Crustacean frenzy invades here during crab season. The delectable Dungeness are served a number of ways, including chopped and braised with garlic, ginger and onion, or steamed and served whole with black-bean sauce. Dinner costs about $35 for two, with wine.

Open daily 11:30 a.m.-3 p.m. & 4:30 p.m.-9:30 p.m. All major cards.

Original Joe's
144 Taylor St.,
Union Square
• 775-4877
ITALIAN/STEAKHOUSE

10/20

Located on one of the sleaziest blocks in San Francisco, just steps away from several of the city's busiest porno theaters, this landmark has been serving generally fine grills and generally questionable Italian food for more than half a century. The steaks here are still huge and very reasonably priced, and the chicken sauté sec and veal cacciatore are both eminently respectable dishes. But, as always, think twice before ordering seafood here, except for the greaseless and quite lovely deep-fried calamari. Entrées are served with your choice of four accompaniments; skip the greasy fried potatoes, mushy vegetables and ravioli filled with something unidentifiable, and have the spaghetti instead—the meat sauce is delicious. The waiters, many of whom have been here for eons, range from friendly to amusingly gruff. The room itself is rather grim, with lots of red vinyl and a '50s cocktail-lounge look. There is no wine list to speak of, but the drinks are strong and cheap. This place is not bad at all if you order properly, and the price is certainly right:

your bill will be about $35 to $40 for dinner for two, with drinks.
Open daily 10:30 a.m.-1 a.m. Cards: MC, V.

Pat O'Shea's Mad Hatter
3848 Geary Blvd.,
Richmond District
• 752-3148
AMERICAN/CALIFORNIAN

12/20

WE CHEAT TOURISTS AND DRUNKS, says the sign over the door, but don't believe it. They do not discriminate at the Mad Hatter. What they do, more than anything, is deliver fair value in food and libations, not to mention nonstop sports on several prominent high-resolution TV monitors fed by satellite. If the Giants or the 49ers are in the playoffs, this is the next best place after Candlestick to watch them. Come to think of it, the Mad Hatter may be better than the stadium, because the food is good. Daily specials, like the daily sports roster, are listed on a blackboard. Offerings typically include fresh, honestly prepared fish, meat and pasta creations, along with good salads. This is a hungry person's pub in the true Irish tradition, offering just about everything you'd expect to find in a yupped-up bar and grill except attitude and high prices. We've had superb rack of lamb, excellent anglerfish and salmon, and a good salad of tender greens with sun-dried tomatoes, sweet red onions and peppery nasturtiums (edible flowers being a delightful incongruity here). Roasting potatoes is a high art, particularly when the tasty tubers are set off by succulent slices of roast beef. The waitresses are formidable in their green Mad Hatter T-shirts, but if you don't give them any trouble, they won't have to slap you around much. Good California wines are available, as well as such fresh, creamy draft beers as Guinness, Bass and San Francisco's own Anchor Steam. After dark the tables are folded away, a cover charge is instituted, and, presumably, the posted motto goes into effect for the evening. About $25 for two, with a beer.
Open daily 11:30 a.m.-3 p.m. & 4 p.m.-9 p.m. Cards (lunch only): MC, V.

Osome
1923 Fillmore St.,
Upper Fillmore
• 346-2311
JAPANESE/SUSHI

12/20

The austere surroundings may be uninviting and the service may be indifferent, but this is some very fine sushi. Order an assorted sushi or sashimi dinner and you'll get a sampling of the extremely fresh tuna, octopus, salmon, shrimp and mackerel accompanied by pungent sliced ginger and fiery wasabe. Sushi-lovers should stay at the bar, the better to appreciate chef Toshi's considerable talents; others should take one of the tables and try the traditional eight-course kaiseki meal. About $45 for a sushi-and-sake dinner for two.
Open daily 5:30 p.m.-11 p.m. All major cards.

Pacific Café
7000 Geary Blvd.,
Richmond District
• 387-7091
SEAFOOD

There are two locations, but the original one out near the beach is the best. That's why there's always (read always) a line out the door. We're not talking about a sophisticated cuisine but one that is extremely attractive because of the absolute and divine freshness of the fish and other seafood offered. Much of the catch comes from the restaurant's own boat. Although seafood is currently flown in fresh from all over the world, the Pacific Café concentrates on denizens of, where else, the Pacific Ocean. The beach-house decor is simple, all wood, with each table in its own little booth. Fresh bread and butter is served right away. Green salads can be had with that delightful anachronism, Thousand Island dressing (it's creamy and oh-so-delicious). Look at the blackboard immediately for the day's catch. If sand dabs are listed, order them—they're increasingly rare little morsels with delicate, snowy flesh, perfect with a dry Sauvignon Blanc from the excellent list of California white wines. Broiled swordfish and salmon are sure bets, too. Fish is served with french fries, the classic seafood accompaniment. And do have cheesecake for dessert. The only problem is parking, but then a good brisk walk in the Pacific breeze is the perfect setup for this kind of meal. About $40 for two, with wine.
Open daily 5 p.m.-10 p.m. Cards: MC, V.

Pacific Heights Bar & Grill
2001 Fillmore St.,
Upper Fillmore
• 567-3337
SEAFOOD/CALIFORNIAN

Oysters are the name of the game here, or at least one of the games. The other one has more to do with birds and bees than bivalves, for upper Fillmore can be a very amorous street indeed, and the PacBag (as it's known around town) is one of its primary venues. (Perhaps the oysters have something to do with that.) In any case, the curved small bar in the front window of this charming neo-Victorian building is a restaurant within the restaurant, offering a comprehensive selection of West Coast oysters on any given day, in addition to mollusks from the East Coast and the Gulf of Mexico. Tempting are the Hog Island Sweetwaters from Tomales Bay, Kumamotos, Willapa Bays, Westcot Bays, Golden Mantles, Blue Points, and more—opened on the spot, mixed and matched as desired, served with a variety of mignon nettes and salsas. There are two dining rooms: a narrow Victorian-style parlor that is sunny at lunch and romantic at dinner, and a smaller, more modern room upstairs at the back, which has less natural light but more dramatic track lighting. The regular menu concentrates on seafood. There are usually several fish available for grilling over mesquite, with a choice of toppings such as coriander-ginger butter, shallot sauce, tangy salsa, or sauce verde.

Fresh prawns are prepared in a number of ways—for example, braised in Anchor Steam beer—usually with garlic figuring in somehow. Crabcakes are excellent, too. Owners Craig and Suzie Bashel take an active interest in wine, and feature a rotating selection of good wines by the glass—which, if drunk with dinner, bring the tab to about $50 for two.

Open Mon.-Thurs. 11 a.m.-3 p.m. & 5 p.m.-10 p.m., Fri.-Sat. 11 a.m.-3 p.m. & 5 p.m.-11 p.m., Sun. 10:30 a.m.-2:30 p.m. All major cards.

Peacock
2800 Van Ness Ave.,
Van Ness
• 928-7001
INDIAN

Located in a restored Victorian mansion, the Peacock's lovely setting exudes a continental formality not often found in ethnic (even Indian) restaurants. The second-floor dining room is quite posh, with floor-length drapes, thick carpets, commodious chairs and fresh flowers, all in shades of peach and pink. Expect to be kept waiting for at least a short while in the first-floor anteroom; this wait will give you time to peruse the voluminous wine list. Once you're seated, let the waiter know how sturdy your palate is, since the kitchen is very good about keeping hotness to a minimum upon request. Interestingly, the tandoori chef here has permanently added a layer of mesquite to his oven, imbuing the tandoori meats and breads with a smoky aroma and taste. Nearly everything is good: masala kulcha, the tandoor-baked bread stuffed with herbs and onion; juicy, tandoori chicken that has been marinated for hours in yogurt and spices; barra kebab, tandoor-baked lamb chops marinated in a mildly spiced cream sauce; and murgh sagwala, a wondrous combination of chicken and spinach. A favorite side dish here is a lesser-known regional Indian treat: spicy, tandoor-smoked chicken wings that have been marinated with nutmeg and green chilies. The Indian desserts are typically very sweet. About $60 for a delicious dinner for two, with wine, in a lovely setting.

Open Sun.-Fri. 11:30 a.m.-2:30 p.m. & 5:30 p.m.-10:30 p.m., Sat. 5:30 p.m.-10:30 p.m. All major cards.

La Pergola Ristorante
2060 Chestnut St.,
Marina District
• (415) 563-4500
ITALIAN

12/20

As neighborhood restaurants go, La Pergola is one of the most delightful finds in San Francisco. It has its inconsistencies and there is a tendency in the kitchen to get slap-happy with the extra-virgin olive oil, but the room is elegantly casual, light and appealing to the eye, the waiters are charming and obliging, and there are some unusual dishes that you won't often find in a small bistro-style, moderately priced café like this. The entire restaurant is kept as a nonsmoking environment, which we very much appreciated, as the tables are close together.

We liked the shiitake mushrooms, eggplant, and small whole onions that were combined with another appetizer, bresaola con fagioli, which is air-cured beef with dried beans. The two were served together on a large metal platter and had the visual and gustatory appeal of a summer picnic served on a dining room table. La Pergola's pastas can be either sublime or overreaching. Duck pasta is made up of big, magnificent pillows stuffed with loosely ground and well-seasoned duck in a vibrant but not remotely overpowering tomato sauce. The richness and meatiness of the filling is wholly satisfying. Seafood ravioli isn't as successful—so densely stuffed that the shellfish flavors are indistinguishable, and dressed in a lush saffron cream sauce that can be a tad cloying. Of the regular main dishes, we were particularly impressed with braised rabbit with polenta, black olives and vegetables, reminiscent of the best of the Tuscan countryside. This is filling food. However, two of the desserts are worth a little excess—a house-made tiramisu, fluffy, flavorful and rich without heaviness, and La Pergola's own crème caramel, smooth but not remotely rubbery and sprinkled with slivered almonds. A small but excellent wine list balances California and Italian vintages. The bigger Italian reds can get pricey, but you can get a lovely bottle of white wine for under $25. Dinner for two, with wine, is a well-spent $82.
Open Mon.-Thurs. & Sun. 5:30 p.m.-10:30 p.m. & Fri.-Sat. 5:30 p.m.-11 p.m. Cards: AE, MC, V.

Perry's
1944 Union St.,
Cow Hollow
• 922-9022
AMERICAN

10/20

During the wild and crazy '70s, Perry's was known for having the most salacious cruising scene on Union Street (quite an achievement). That is to say, few patrons admitted to going there just for the victuals. Now that things have cooled down in the bar, one hears more raves about the food. Admittedly, Perry's hamburger is one of the best bar burgers in town, a generous one-third pound of prime beef on a poppyseed egg roll, appropriately messy with the traditional burger trimmings and cheese on request. The cottage fries are great, too. We've enjoyed the robust, scintillating Chinese chicken salad, garlicky fettuccine with white clam sauce, good, crisp salads and well-aged steaks, which are usually cooked more or less to order. Sample from the good California wine list, but skip the pasty desserts and head out onto Union Street to satiate your sweet tooth elsewhere. Anywhere from $30 to $50 for two, with wine. *Open daily 9 a.m.-midnight. Cards: AE, MC, V.*

Phnom Penh

631 Larkin St.,
Polk Gulch
• 775-5979
CAMBODIAN

Widely credited as being the city's first Cambodian restaurant, Phnom Penh is still among the best. The little corner storefront, with its blue-and-white curtains and tablecloths, square windows and rustic wood decor, has a friendly feel about it (although the neighborhood—borderline Tenderloin—does not feel friendly). Chef Bony Tsang knows how to create subtly spiced, satisfying dishes, all the flavors purely Southeast Asian. We love baked eggplant simmered in lemon sauce; chopped pork and shrimp with garlic sauce, which makes the difference between fragrance and flavor academic; and pan-fried whole fish with a spicy, piquant sauce. Charbroiled marinated lamb and grilled salmon with coconut-tamarind sauce, Phnom Penh style, are two house specials, and dishes we return for again and again. Everything reflects the freshness of the foods and herbs, and a deft touch with spices. And don't miss water-chestnut pudding for dessert (there's nothing crunchy about it, believe us). The wine list here is French and California, and it suits the food well. The tab comes to about $30 for two. *Open Mon.-Thurs. 11 a.m.-3 p.m. & 5 p.m.-9:30 p.m., Fri.-Sat. 11 a.m.-3 p.m. & 5 p.m.-10 p.m. All major cards.*

Pierre

Meridien Hotel,
50 3rd St.,
South of Market
• 974-6400
FRENCH

So, you didn't win the lottery this year? You didn't luck out in the drawing for a week in Paris, complete with all the three-toque meals you could digest? No problem! If you time it right, some of the top chefs of France can come to you via the Meridien's Celebrated Women Chefs of France program. As part of this, every two months a top *cuisinier* will fly in and take over Pierre's kitchen to create her own prix-fixe menu, offered for one week. The most recent series has included notables such as Adrienne Biasin of Chez La Vielle in Paris. Michel Richard of Citrus in Los Angeles also made a guest appearance (as part of the former Master Chefs program) with a lavish menu highlighted by Maine lobster en croûte and sautéed duck breast with duck cannelloni in Pinot Noir sauce. But don't worry if you miss these visits. Pierre's chef, Sebastien Urbain, not only duplicates their menus faithfully, he has crafted a fine menu of his own that interprets classic French favorites with skill, imagination and a light touch. His duck foie gras, which is sautéed and topped with a not-too-sweet port-wine sauce, is ambrosial. He also has a special way with game birds—roast breast and leg of pheasant with orange-green peppercorn sauce are both tender, delicate and juicy, and roast squab always comes out rare and densely meaty without being tough. Service is impeccably formal and the dining room is a study in quiet, understated elegance. With dinner for two, with wine, running about $120, Pierre ranks as an occasion place, although you'll dine every bit as well here as at most of the pricier spots around town.

Open Tues.-Sun. 6 p.m. to 11:00 p.m. All major cards.

The Portman Grill
The Portman Hotel,
500 Post St.,
Union Square
• 929-2887
CALIFORNIAN/FRENCH

12/20

As most things do, hotel dining has come full circle. Hoteliers have realized that a good deal of their bread and butter (literally) was slipping away from them; many of them now want their restaurants to have credibility and cachet as well as the rubber-chicken banquet business. The Portman Grill is a very bright light in the hotel dining renaissance. Rather than being an ultra-fancy, brocade-and-draperies type of environment, the Grill opts for a sophisticated yet informal look, taking full advantage of its atrium location with lots of greenery and ficus trees, and dressed in gleaming travertine. But the environment isn't the only element that's modern and young; chef Fred Halpert, 35, orchestrates the kitchen here with a sure yet innovative hand. After studying extensively in France (with master chef Roger Verge, among others), Halpert did a couple of stints in Los Angeles; he then moved to San Francisco in 1984 and opened the much-lauded Restaurant 101 with his friend and colleague Gerard Michler. In 1987, when the Portman asked him to open the Grill and become the hotel's executive chef, Halpert couldn't refuse the challenge.

For a first course, we devoured the risotto with smoked chicken and buffalo mozzarella, the risotto creamy and perfectly cooked, the chicken and melting cheese wonderfully blended additions. The Provençal salad of warm goat cheese with mixed field greens was a simple, lightly dressed delight—the tangy chèvre offsetting the peppery snap of the greens. We couldn't resist the grilled filet of beef served with a ragoût of wild mushrooms and lentils du Puy. The filet was buttery and rich, and the mixture of earthy mushrooms and mellow lentils an inspired touch—we mopped up every last drop of sauce. The roasted Muscovy duck breast served with a confit of onions was delicious—nongamy, and enhanced by the almost-sweet onions. The desserts may be the only weak link here. Our pear tarte with a raspberry coulis, for example, was beautifully presented with the pear fanned out over the pastry, but with a grainy texture. The ice creams, however, are wonderful, as we sampled in the sautéed apples with vanilla ice cream. A prix-fixe dinner for two costs $120, with wine.

Open daily 11:30 a.m.-10 p.m. All major cards.

PosTrio

**The Prescott Hotel,
545 Post St.,
Union Square
• 776-7825**
CALIFORNIAN/
INTERNATIONAL

Life is filled with little ironies, isn't it? Who would think that San Francisco, which has held the culinary whip over Los Angeles for decades, could be brought to its foodie knees by L.A.'s hottest, trendiest (and many would argue best) chef? Up until now, the smart money would snort and guffaw in derision at such a blasphemous thought—but the unheard of has happened: Wolfgang Puck, chef to the stars, took San Francisco by storm in 1989 with his first Bay Area restaurant, PosTrio. Located in the recently refurbished, cozy Prescott Hotel (yet another of Bill Kimpton's small hotel renovations paired with an excellent restaurant), a stone's throw from Union Square, PosTrio's kitchen is helmed by the husband-and-wife team of Anne and David Gingrass, both Spago alumni, under Puck's aegis. The restaurant's whimsically offbeat yet sophisticated decor is another feather in Pat Kuleto's already well-feathered hat—there are three dining levels that encompass a beautiful copper-and-hardwood bar that is currently the hottest, most happening boîte in town.

The menu is just as diverse and fresh as the decor. While there are some references to Puck's L.A. eateries, Spago and Chinois on Main, vis-à-vis the smoked-salmon-and-cream-cheese pizza served in the bar, and the barbecued Chinese sausage with sweet-and-sour cabbage offered as an appetizer, Puck and the Gingrasses have given PosTrio its own identity with its own dishes. To begin with, there's the thick, wheaty grain bread studded with bits of olive and wheat kernels that is so fragrantly delicious, one could almost be happy dining on bread alone. The giant blini with smoked salmon, sour cream, a generous dollop of salmon caviar and a sprinkling of radish sprouts is truly a dish for the gods. The crabcakes with arugula leaves and a smoky, sexy red-pepper sauce are perfectly crispy outside, the chunky crab on the inside moist and well spiced. And the aforementioned Chinese sausage, which is served sliced and beautifully arranged on barely warm, limp cabbage, is sweet, hot and peppery-spicy, in the best Chinese fashion, and its tiny accompanying salad is goosed with cilantro—a truly wonderful dish.

The main courses fulfill the promise of the appetizers. The Dungeness crab curry risotto with dry-fried spinach is marvelous, musky with just enough heat, and with the Chinese-style, cellophane-like spinach that Madame Cecilia Chiang perfected long ago in both her San Francisco and L.A. branches of The Mandarin. The lamb, with which Puck has proven to be a wonder at his other restaurants, is typically exquisite—tender, pink and juicy—served with creamy, garlicky mashed potatoes and a tangle of slivers of crackling fried parsnips.

The desserts prepared by pastry chef Barbara Ury are a sugar-plum vision come true: warm berry summer pie with homemade ice cream, poppyseed shortcake with strawberry-swirl ice cream and a strawberry compote, an ice cream sundae with bananas, brownies, whipped cream and hot fudge. Of course, there are more sophisticated desserts, such as orange-chocolate Cognac mousse with candied orange sauce, and crème brûlée, but who could resist those simple American pleasures? As would be expected, the wine list here is quite extensive and well chosen (heavy on the Californias), with quite a selection of reasonably priced bottles. Breakfast here is also wonderful, though it lacks the bustle and sparkle of the chic evening crowd. For $100 for two, including wine, you'll eat a memorable dinner.
Open daily 7 a.m.-midnight. All major cards.

Prego
2000 Union St.,
Cow Hollow
• 563-3305
ITALIAN

Part of a consortium that runs several San Francisco and Los Angeles establishments (Ciao, MacArthur Park, Harry's Bar), Prego is known as a singles' bar and a place to have good open-fired pizza or calzone. But it should be known for its fine meals served in several bright, smartly styled dining rooms. Chef Bobby Estenzo, who has been running the show in Prego's kitchen for more than six years, undoubtedly puts together some of the best pasta creations to be found in San Francisco. Estenzo came from Oakland's Bay Wolf Café via a six-month stint in Italy, where he studied with the esteemed chef Giuliano Bugialli. Among Estenzo's most exquisite dishes is the agnolotti d'aragosta, half-moon pockets filled with lobster and prosciutto in a light, lemony cream sauce. Spinach raviolis are stuffed with lamb, veal and goat cheese, and topped with a porcini mushroom sauce. Less exciting than the pastas, though still very good, are the entrées; from classic osso buco served with soft polenta to a dish of free-range chicken roasted in a white-wine mustard. Among the antipasti treasures are chilled prawns in a lime-mint marinade with feta cheese, and bocconcini in camicia (a hunk of mozzarella, wrapped in radicchio and stuffed with sun-dried tomatoes and capers, then grilled with polenta.) The best of the desserts is the tiramisu, the Italian classic that combines ladyfingers, espresso, chocolate and Mascarpone cheese. An inexpensive wine list has a good selection from both Italy and California. A reasonable $70 for dinner for two, with wine.
Open daily 11:30 a.m.-midnight. All major cards.

Regina's
490 Geary St.,
Union Square
• 885-1661
CREOLE

Take a French Creole gal from Natchez, train her in Paris, send her on a side trip to Anchorage and then plunk her down on San Francisco's Theater Row and what do you have? An instant success! With visions of creating the San Francisco equivalent of Sardi's, Regina Charboneau opened her namesake restaurant in 1987. Like Sardi's, it's a great hangout for theatergoers and performers alike, with its collection of masks and theater memorabilia. The food, however, is something else entirely: a potpourri of classic Creole favorites with more than a nod toward California freshness. Eggplant Lafayette combines thinly sliced fried eggplant with shrimp and crab in both a light cream sauce and a spiced tomato coulis. Grilled lamb chops come with a lively tomato-mint marmalade. The biscuits and corn muffins are dynamite but don't fill up, because you can't say no to the rum-flamed bananas Foster or the mile-high pie, a delight filled with chocolate and mint ice creams and drizzled with hot fudge sauce. Who needs Sardi's? Come for a platter of oysters before the show ("Oysters 2, 2 & 2" brings two each of Bienville oysters with artichoke hearts, Cheddar and cream sauce; Rockefeller oysters with spinach and Romano; and Ohan oysters with eggplant, bacon and Provolone). Regina's also offers lighter postperformance snacks and a jazz brunch on weekends. Plan to spend about $100 on a full dinner for two; jazz brunch entrées run $9 to $16.
Open Tues.-Fri. 6 p.m.-midnight, Sat.-Sun. 10 a.m.-2 p.m. & 6 p.m.-midnight. Cards: AE, MC, V.

Eddie Rickenbacker's
133 2nd St.,
South of Market
• 543-3498
CALIFORNIAN

12/20

If the Banana Republic people opened a restaurant, it would look something like this. A real biplane suspended over the bar elevates that part of the premises from a mere fern bar to a truly theatrical fern bar, which at times holds the potential for truly theatrical rowdiness. The separate dining room extends a wartime hero theme that really is evocative, if not nostalgic. Owner Norman Hobday (whose Henry Africa's was the granddaddy of fern bars) is banking, quite astutely, on the gentrification of a currently nondescript neighborhood that will eventually welcome the new San Francisco Museum of Modern Art. The food is straightforward, revolving around grilled meats and fish on one hand, and creative salads on the other. The Caesar salad is a palate-pleaser; ditto the cheeseburger; encore the peach cobbler.
Open Mon.-Fri. 11 a.m.-3 p.m. & 5 p.m.-8 p.m., Sat. 11 a.m.-3 p.m. All major cards.

La Roca
4288 24th St.,
Noe Valley
• 282-7780
SALVADORAN/SEAFOOD

This simple little seafood restaurant is the only good thing known to have come from the troubles in El Salvador, which sent the delightful owner and her family north to us. The name refers to a large rock that sits in the window and may or may not have some significance, depending on which family member one talks to. What is significant is the awesome amount of garlic in La Roca's ubiquitous sauce, a green concoction of chiles and various herbs and spices that accompanies everything. One orders from a selection of seafood, especially fresh calamari and prawns, and specifies one of several sauces all based on more or less the same ingredients (the red one is tomato-based). Take our advice, don't let anyone talk you out of La Roca sauce. Be sure to say you want it very spicy. Then order a Sauvignon Blanc or Chardonnay from the excellent wine list, or a couple of cold beers, and try to make a little conversation above the roar. The place does get crowded, and it does not take reservations. Never mind—tables in the two dining rooms occupying the bottom floor of a Victorian building are set so closely together that turnover is fast, and it's definitely worth a short wait. If the line is out the door, put your name on the list and go down the street for a quick drink. The tab for dinner will be about $35 for two, with wine.
Open Tues.-Sat. 5:30 p.m.-11 p.m., Sun. 5:30 p.m.-10 p.m. All major cards.

La Rocca's Oyster Bar
3519 California St.,
Laurel Village
• 387-4100
OYSTER BAR

12/20

La Rocca's is located as close to the upper Sacramento neighborhood as it could be without being part of it. Actually, it's on the flip side, in tiny Laurel Village shopping center on California Street, which is probably why it doesn't have the higher profile it deserves. Location aside, we think La Rocca's is as good as Swan Oyster Depot, which it is accused of imitating. (The truth is that both are representatives of the traditional Northeast-style oyster bar.) The comfortable, harboresque ambience could use a large window overlooking a working marina, but otherwise it's a great place to sit and banter with the personable shuckers while you feast. Like Swan, La Rocca's serves only Blue Point oysters from the East Coast, and while we feel there are also good oysters grown on the West Coast, these have been consistently fresh and saltwater-tangy. The cocktail sauce served with oysters, shrimp and clams has a nice zip to it. La Rocca's real glory, however, is a creamy, buttery, fragrant oyster stew. Price is about $22 to $40 for two, with wine.
Open daily 11 a.m.-8:30 p.m. All major cards.

Rodin
1779 Lombard St.,
Marina District
• 563-8566
FRENCH

11/20

Perhaps the fact that the restaurant is named after one of the most powerful, visually provocative sculptors of the last hundred years is meant to make you feel that the food will be as shapely and potent as, say, *The Thinker*. Well, it certainly made us think—predominantly about why restaurants that set themselves up as museums of haute cuisine think they can get away with skimping on the food because they've got a concept.

The menu is small but reads enticingly. You can order à la carte or from the four-course prix-fixe menu ($39 without wine), which allows you to choose from a variety of dishes. When we last dined here, oysters Rockefeller en croûte with golden caviar was a satisfying and substantial appetizer: barely poached oysters with spinach and a touch of hollandaise sauce, wrapped in unexciting short-crust pastry with the salty zip of yellow roe. An uninspired but adequate wine list wasn't as tempting as the possibility of ordering by the glass, so we had Michel Tribault sparkling wine, 1985, with our appetizers. It had all the depth and finish of ginger ale. Main courses were by far the best part of the meal. Boneless quail stuffed with shiitake mushrooms and wild rice with a green-and-red-grape sauce was nicely cooked, tender, full of autumnal intrigue on a wine-dark, slightly sweet sauce that hinted of black currants. Spring rack of lamb marinated and served medium rare in a red-wine herb sauce was tender and rosy, accompanied by a sad lineup of baby poached vegetables that looked as if they were about to face a firing squad. Dinner for two, with wine, comes to $80 or so.
Open Mon.-Sat. 5:30 p.m.-10:30 p.m. All major cards.

La Rondalla
901 Valencia St.,
Mission District
• 647-7474
MEXICAN

12/20

This mad crazy-quilt of a restaurant, open into the early morning, serves some of the best Mexican food in town. The atmosphere is zany: there's a long counter in the front room facing the open kitchen and three back rooms decorated with Christmas-tree lights, balloons, stuffed birds, cheap fake Tiffany lamps and other assorted junk. La Rondalla consistently puts out fine dishes: one of the best guacamoles north of the border, glorious asado (thin rare grilled steak smothered with fresh onions, potatoes and tomatoes) and equally good adobada, marinated pork filets topped with the same combination. The strolling and not-too-competent mariachi band and the confused waitresses attired in red blouses and black skirts add to the fun. The Mexican beers are fine and cheap and the noise level only mildly excruciating. A wonderful place for a

late-night meal, especially when you receive the check: a mere $25 for dinner for two, with beer.
Open Tues.-Sun. noon-3:30 a.m. No cards.

Royal Thai
951 Clement St.,
Richmond District
• 386-1795
THAI

There used to be only one San Francisco restaurant—Khan Toke—that dished out both marvelous Thai food and great ambience. Now Royal Thai rivals Khan Toke on both counts. Pat and Jamie Disyamonthon (both alumni of Khan Toke Thai House) opened this chic place in early 1988 after several successful years with their first Royal Thai in San Rafael. The food here is just as good, and the ambience is much better. Like sex appeal, terrific restaurant ambience is hard to define, but this place definitely has it. The same air of excitement that animates the room when it's packed (that is, most of the time) is still there later on, when only one couple is left in one of the elevated niches feeding slivers of hot pepper to each other by candlelight. On one side is a narrow but comfortable bar-waiting area. The main dining room's split-level configuration cleverly gives most tables a feeling of intimacy. Soft illumination from a variety of sources, including candles, glass lamps and neon, is quietly dramatic and flattering, too. One wall is mirrored, and a stained-glass lobster presides over all. The food looks and tastes good, from the initial basket of crispy krupuk with savory tamarind dipping sauce, all the way through the final touch of coconut ice cream. A trademark appetizer is marinated squid, barbecued on skewers and served with a tangy-sweet green sauce. The papaya salad is colorful, crunchy and hot. Special dishes can excel—fresh salmon in a sauce of coconut and red curry, for one, or deep-fried soft-shell crab with deep-fried sweet potato. About $45 for dinner for two, with wine.
Open Mon.-Fri. 11 a.m.-3 p.m. & 5 p.m.-10:30 p.m., Sat.-Sun. 5 p.m.-10:30 p.m. All major cards.

Sam's Grill
374 Bush St.,
Financial District
• 421-0594
SEAFOOD

11/20

In business at various locations since 1867, Sam's Grill has established itself as one of the revered old–San Francisco seafood restaurants. With reasonable prices, unpretentious and efficient service and a commitment to using quality fresh fish, Sam's has a regular following among the denizens of the Financial District. These business-wise regulars know the secret to enjoying Sam's: always ask what is fresh, ask for it rare and, above all, avoid all sauces. Generous portions of sautéed rex sole, sand dabs or broiled swordfish will delight. Start with East Coast oysters or the fresh asparagus in a mustard sauce, order your fish carefully and finish with

the exceptionally good cheesecake, and you will leave Sam's very contented. For two, it's $50, with wine.
Open Mon.-Fri. 11 a.m.-8:30 p.m. Cards: DC, MC, V.

Sanppo
1702 Post St.,
Japantown
• 346-3486
JAPANESE/SUSHI

12/20

Who says fine Japanese food has to cost a fortune? Lately it seems that modestly indulging oneself at a San Francisco sushi bar will bring a check that may cause heart failure. Not so at Sanppo. Although the decor is modified Formica and the presentation is not as elaborate as at more elegant Japanese restaurants, there is artistry in the kitchen combined with very low prices. Sushi and sashimi are perfectly fresh and quite fine, but Sanppo's real forte is tempura. It makes some of the best in town: lobster tempura is a fabulous indulgence, and the more standard prawn and vegetable tempuras are a delight. Also showcasing the kitchen's exceptional talent for frying are the amazing fried oysters, which have not a trace of grease. Recommended too are the traditional long-simmered noodle dishes. Expect friendly if somewhat rushed service, a wait at peak times and a low tab: $30 for two, with sake or beer.
Open Tues.-Sat. 11:45 a.m.-9:55 p.m., Sun. 3 p.m.-9:55 p.m. No cards.

Scott's Seafood Grill & Bar
2400 Lombard St.,
Marina District
• 563-8988
SEAFOOD

Incredible as it may seem, there aren't many good seafood places in the City by the Bay. In fact, the rule of thumb is that the farther a seafood restaurant is from Fisherman's Wharf, the better it will be—and Scott's is a good distance from the wharf. This Cape Cod house is somewhere between kitschy and comfortable, the service is friendly but rushed, and the wait at peak hours (no dinner reservations are taken) can be very, very long. The food, however, justifies the wait. To start, have the fine varietal oysters on ice, the wonderful clam chowder, or broiled prawns in a Cajun rémoulade. The fried seafood dishes (oysters, calamari), a disaster at most places, are greaseless and wonderful; live Maine lobsters are available daily; and a fresh-fish menu changes twice a day, with specials such as poached salmon in herb beurre blanc or various preparations of halibut, tuna or mahi mahi. But the stars of this show are the seafood sautés: the sauté of scallops and prawns with marvelous saffroned rice is sheer perfection. There are some nice but overpriced California wines and a few uninteresting desserts. About $60 for dinner for two, with wine.
Open Sun.-Thurs. 11:30 a.m.-10:30 p.m., Fri.-Sat. 11 a.m.-11 p.m. All major cards.

Seoul Garden
22 Peace Plaza,
Japantown
• 563-7664
KOREAN

12/20

The best Korean restaurants always somehow suggest that country's harsh highland landscapes with spare designs incorporating pale wood, rock, and iron. Seoul Garden does that, but it also evokes a sumptuous palace set in that landscape. It is large and noisy, with many roomy tables filled with people enthusiastically grilling squid, beef, chicken and vegetables on gas barbecues set into the table-tops. The food is cut into strips and brought to table in bowls by authentically garbed servers. In addition to the grilling material, there are kitchen-prepared specialties: miso-based soups and delicate seaweed soup, hot kim chee (pickled vegetables), spicy braised ribs and steamed whole fish, to name a few. About $40 for two, with a glass of wine. *Open daily 11 a.m.-midnight. All major cards.*

Silks
Mandarin Oriental Hotel,
222 Sansome St.,
Financial District
• 885-0999
CALIFORNIAN/FRENCH

The chef who first gave the Silks menu its eclectic spin has gone on to other venues, but the kitchen has maintained reasonable consistency pending the impact of a new executive sensibility. It's still one of the best hotel restaurants in San Francisco. Silks offers what every such establishment should offer: rarified ambience. It's a beautiful room with a spacious feeling, though it's not actually very large. The sense of openness comes from cleverly planned decor: harmonious colors and plush upholstery and carpeting. The visual centerpiece is a striking display of flowers and desserts. Service is professional—unobtrusive and sharp. Some winners on the menu include a grilled vegetable terrine with chèvre, grilled chicken wings in red sesame mole, and roast squab with chèvre beneath the skin. Desserts, such as the chocolate decadence cake with fresh seasonal berries, are to die for.
Open Mon.-Fri. 7 a.m.-10:30 a.m., 11:30 a.m.-2 p.m. & 6 p.m.-10 p.m., Sat. 6 p.m.-10 p.m., Sun. 8 a.m.-2 p.m. & 6 p.m.-10 p.m.

690
690 Van Ness Ave.,
Van Ness
• 255-6900
CALIFORNIAN/
INTERNATIONAL

First off, let's begin with the name "690." Originally, culinary empire-builder and chef extraordinaire Jeremiah Tower named his newest restaurant "Speedo 690," as the building it's housed in is a former carburetor-repair shop that was named Speedo. Well, the folks at the Speedo swimwear company took umbrage, and threatened all sorts of unpleasant nonsense against Tower if he didn't change the name. So now the restaurant's official name is simply 690 and with this eatery, the formidable Tower can add another notch to his belt of successes. From the Santa Fe Bar & Grill through Stars (and its progeny, Stars Cafe and the recently closed Starfish), Tower has made a point of not repeating himself, and that credo holds true at 690. The influences here are Southeast Asian, Middle Eastern, Caribbean and Indian, with touches of Morocco thrown in for good measure.

Tower hasn't let his Dewar's Scotch–ad fame go completely to his head; on our visit to 690, he was greeting and seating patrons—a very nice, personal touch. The staff is friendly, and the menu is one of those from which it's nearly impossible to make a choice, since everything sounds so good (and the menu changes regularly, just to complicate matters of decision). The lentil cake appetizer is not to be missed—the cake itself is spicy and piquant, and the fresh salsa of red and yellow tomatoes and the smoky sour cream served with it take this dish way over the top in the pantheon of earthly delights. The smoked, curried chicken wings, served with a chrome-yellow mayonnaise also infused with curry, are sticky, addictive wonders, and the smoked-chicken salad with a black-bean purée, saffron and a mildly nutty toasted cashew cream really blew us away—even though the portion was big enough for three people, we felt compelled to finish it. Main courses do not disappoint, as they do all too often these days. For instance, the grilled pork chop with buttered corn, mushrooms and a finger-lickin'-good tropical barbecue sauce tastes mighty good. Tower has always done a particularly good job with gilled and finned creatures, and at 690 there's a school of delicious fish dishes. The grilled Pacific snapper with coconut rice, ancho chile sauce and papaya salsa has so much going on at once—the cool of the coconut against the heat of the chile; the subdued snapper against the sweet bite of the salsa—that it's a truly thrilling dish, and the sautéed Szechuan salmon with crisp, stir-fried vegetables, a hint of soy sauce and ginger butter is light, fresh and terribly good. The yummy desserts here include a fluffy tropical trifle with a puckery mango purée, a whimsical frozen ice-cream sandwich with shaved chocolate, and a Jamaican chocolate rum cake, but we'll put our money on the homemade ice creams here—they're served with a variety of fresh-fruit sauces and soft, molasses-sweetened ginger cookies. The wine list here is small but well chosen, and prices are quite reasonable for a restaurant of this caliber, and one that serves food this spectacular: dinner comes to about $100 for two, with wine.

Open daily 11:30 a.m.-midnight. All major cards.

South Park Café
108 S. Park,
South of Market
• 495-7275
FRENCH

10/20

Bistros have a charm all their own. From the type of clientele they attract to the type of straightforward, full-bodied food they serve, they fill a necessary niche in an urban setting. South Park Café is one of San Francisco's best, bringing a little bit of Paris to this serenely unexpected park in the industrial heart of the area south of Market Street. There are even Parisian and San Franciscan newspapers hanging on a magazine rack by the front door. Lunches are great if you get there early enough; otherwise, the noise level is a problem. Dinners are much more relaxing. One added plus to South Park is its cocktail-hour menu of well-prepared inexpensive tapas, such as steamed mussels with garlic and steamed potatoes with garlicky aïoli. You'll also find the cheapest blini with caviar and smoked salmon in town. The baguettes are pure Paris—airy, crusty, simple in flavor. Servers mean well but can be forgetful or clumsy—at a recent lunch, a busboy dropped a buttered knife on some-one, mumbled a hasty apology and rushed away. Many of the dishes have a rough country appeal that we particularly like, though the kitchen has a tendency to get carried away with flavors. At lunch, a lamb sandwich with caramelized onions and red peppers was powerfully appealing, but the bread was much too soggy and the accompanying fresh baby greens were drowning in vinaigrette dressing. Boudin noir with cooked apples and potatoes is one of the finer examples of a blood sausage in town, and an excellent choice at dinner. We like the desserts as well. Marquise au chocolat is a South Park signature—a dense, flourless but not sludgy slab of chocolate cake floating on a soothing lake of pistachio-studded crème anglaise. Lunch for two will be about $35. Dinner for two, with wine, $62.
Open Mon.-Fri. 8 a.m.-10 p.m. & Sat. 6 p.m.-10 p.m. Cards: AE, MC, V.

Square One
190 Pacific Ave.,
Financial District
• 788-1110
INTERNATIONAL

From the day it opened in 1984, Square One has been one of San Francisco's most successful restaurants. Owner-chef Joyce Goldstein had a big following when she managed the Chez Panisse café for several years, before she branched out on her own. Her idea was to expand from the staid French and Italian repertoire and really present home cooking from the Mediterranean—the kind of cooking Goldstein had been doing at home for years before she ever ventured behind a restaurant stove. There's always something fasci-nating: a Sephardic dish from Spain, a Brazilian feijoada of black beans slow-cooked with dried meats and sausages presented with all the fixings. She composes her plates with a painter's eye for color, shape and texture, in startling juxtapositions, but she never short-circuits the flavors.

Goldstein is compulsive and a perfectionist. When she decided to put burgers on the menu, she ended up making her own ketchup. But her flavor treasure house is not always translated by the staff. This is a big restaurant, turning out several hundred meals a day. And the menu is not only large in scope; at least half of the dishes change each and every day. Sometimes her young cooks are just not up to it.

Desserts, however, never disappoint, whether you order a housemade sorbetto or gelato served with tender home-made cookies, a slab of scrumptious berry pie or the heavenly nut torte. Still, it's amazing to see two people managing to work their way through the dessert sampler plate. This could be a meal on its own.

Joyce's son Evan was the youngest ever to pass the prestigious Master Sommelier exam in London; now he teaches courses for other aspiring sommeliers. And his wine list, which he is continually refining and redefining, is a dream for wine-lovers—it's priced fairly, and because the food is so eclectic, he manages to include lovely obscure little wines from southern Italy and Portugal. Dinner for two, with wine, will cost $75 to $90.

Open Mon.-Thurs. 11:30 a.m.-3 p.m. & 5:30 p.m.-10 p.m., Fri. 11:30 a.m.-3 p.m. & 5:30 p.m.-10:30 p.m., Sat. 5:30 p.m.-10:30 p.m., Sun. 5:30 p.m.-9:30 p.m. All major cards.

Stars
150 Redwood Alley,
Civic Center
• 861-7827
AMERICAN/
INTERNATIONAL

If Ayn Rand were still alive today and writing contemporary novels, surely one of her characters would be a Jeremiah Tower–like mogul—even his name is in Rand's style. King of all he surveys, at least in the Bay Area restaurant scene, Tower has been systematically expanding his empire to include, aside from Stars, the late Starfish (closed in January 1990), Stars Café and his new baby, 690. And he has crossed the Pacific into Hong Kong, where he is opening The Peak Cafe. Stars itself was a hit from the moment it opened a few years back, the power restaurant to which the heavy hitters of San Francisco society and industry come to be seen. There's a palpable buzz about this casually elegant, com-fortable room that emanates from both the diners and the kitchen. The food here never fails to astound (the menu changes daily), whether it's a perfectly cooked hot dog or the roast veal rack with wild rice, potato au gratin, Swiss chard and black-truffle aïoli—everything is as it should be, Zen dining at its best. Dishes like the Hawaiian tuna tartare with cilantro-chili vinaigrette, sesame cucumbers and gin-ger cream, and the dill gnocchi with smoked sturgeon, gravlax, mushrooms and chili cream must have other top chefs wondering in frustration why they didn't come up with them. Salads are marvelous at Stars: pear and radicchio salad with toasted pine nuts, bacon, garlic toast and blue-cheese vinaigrette. The black-bean soup with sour cream and tomato salsa is inky and muskily captivating, and if there's a risotto available, don't miss it. Desserts are terrific, especially the fresh berry pies. Tower takes great pride in his wine list (heading the daily menu are his suggested wine selections for that particular *carte*). Stars is a must for anyone who claims to be a gastronome, and while the experience doesn't come cheap, it's certainly worth the tariff. Dinner for two, with wine, will run about $120. *Open Mon.-Fri. 11:30 a.m.-2:30 p.m. & 5:30 p.m.-11 p.m., Sat.-Sun. 5:30 p.m.-11 p.m. All major cards.*

Stars Cafe
555 Golden Gate,
Civic Center
• 861-8521
AMERICAN/
INTERNATIONAL

Stars's bon vivant chef-owner, Jeremiah Tower, first branched out with a modest fish-and-chips take-out dubbed Starfish (which closed in early 1990). Next, he opened Stars Cafe. An architect by training, Tower has had a lot of fun with the café's decor, putting in a corrugated tin roof and splashing the pale, plastered walls inside with giant vintage French posters and whimsical high-tech lights. The best spots to eat are at the bar or on one of a row of galvanized-metal-topped tables lining one side of the storefront.

Wage mules can be found here in the morning, filling up on house-made muffins, crumbly oatmeal scones loaded with currants, and perfect scrambled eggs; unfortunately, the caffè and espresso drinks fall way short of the mark. For lunch, Tower always offers a soup: baked pumpkin with sage cream is good, but his minestrone—a few paltry vegetables afloat in a thin broth—can't help but disappoint. The best bet is the ancho-chile-and-chicken sandwich, or any of the fish, chicken or beef paillards in interesting sauces (teamed with a slab of bread, the paillard also makes a great sandwich). Tower also makes a "mixed light fry," which substitutes a light dusting of corn flour for the traditional fish-and-chips beer batter. One day it might include oysters, calamari, bass and salmon, the next day an entirely different mix, but it's always served with a lovely handmade tartare sauce and a mountain of thick-cut fries. From 5 p.m. on, Tower offers a daily changing menu of tapas and "small dishes": grilled bread rubbed with tomato and drizzled with olive oil, shrimp sautéed in olive oil with hot pepper and garlic, spinach sautéed with pine nuts, raisins and apricots.

The house wine list is short and succinct, but you may

also request anything on Stars's extensive wine list. Desserts are consistently good: warm plum napoleon with orange sabayon cream, raspberry Linzertorte with crème Chantilly, a superlative tiramisu or a plate of delicious little cookies. Everything at Stars Cafe comes in under $10, but sometimes it's not such a bargain—when a minute portion of pasta arrives, or when your braised meat with polenta is mostly polenta with a few dabs of meat. But despite its inconsistencies, this young offshoot of the lauded Stars's restaurant is a good bet for a quick, less expensive meal put together with panache. Dinner for two, with wine, is $45. *Open Mon.-Fri. 7:30 a.m.-10 p.m., Sat.-Sun. 10 a.m.-10 p.m. Cards: MC, V.*

Le St. Tropez
126 Clement St.,
Richmond District
• 387-0408
FRENCH

In all honesty, we love this place. It's like one of those little neighborhood places in the Marais or St.-Germain-des-Prés. Not the gastronomic theater of Fleur de Lys or Amelio's, perhaps, but grand in its own way and so utterly, so warmly romantic with candlelight shining on copper and dark stone. But keep it a secret, please. The food is some of the most deft and harmonious French fare to be had in this or any other city. We love the lobster and vegetable soup, sprinkled with truffles and fresh foie gras. A warm salad of duck giblet confit is perfumed with ginger and thyme. There are poached quail eggs with cucumber and tomato coulis, wrapped in a jambon of smoked duck and smoked salmon. The rack of Sonoma lamb, in its own juices with a confiture of fresh vegetables, is always exquisite; likewise smoked duck with fresh mango, pepper, honey and saffron sauce. For dessert, don't pass up the coconut-and-mango charlotte with a pineapple coulis. Dinner for two, with wine, will be $70 to $80.
Open Mon.-Sat. 5:30 p.m.-10 p.m. All major cards.

Swiss Alps
605 Post St.,
Union Square
• 885-0947
GERMAN

12/20

Lucerne native Heinz Oetiker's cozy little restaurant in the theater district is as stable as the Matterhorn itself. The service is very friendly (they clearly anticipate and expect a tourist trade and will probably ask you where you're from), and the ambience is decidedly alpine: inside, the walls of the tiny dining room are decorated with murals proclaiming folksy Swiss maxims, and outside, the marquee boasts of the "Fondue Specialties," which are not bad at all. However, as often happens in the nearby theaters, the real stars don't get top billing—the veal, not the fondue, is the reason to visit Swiss Alps. Oetiker is clearly comfortable with both the French and Germanic aspects of Swiss cuisine, as evidenced by two fine veal dishes: on the French side, a superb veal

Cordon Bleu (stuffed with the thinnest, most delightful ham and a nice Gruyère), and on the German side, the delicious Geschnetzeltes Kalbfleisch (veal in a rich cream sauce). Oetiker also prepares admirable sweetbreads (which can be so often ruined by a heavy hand) and fine lightened versions of such old German warhorses as Sauerbraten. Starters are less interesting—simple salads and adequate homemade soups—and the desserts (crème caramel, poire belle Hélène) will never set the world on fire. On the other hand, neither will the check: dinner for two, with beer or wine, will run about $45.
Open Tues.-Sat. 5 p.m.-10 p.m. Cards: AE, MC, V.

Tadich Grill
240 California St.,
Financial District
• 391-2373
SEAFOOD

Tadich Grill has been around in one incarnation or another since the Gold Rush of 1849, and it is much revered by its legion of fans, both locals and regular visitors to the city, for whom Tadich epitomizes San Francisco. Count us among those fans. Although there are some lapses, most meals we've had here have been terrific. And we will always love the charming, old–San Francisco ambience: the private wooden booths, the chummy counters, the financial district lunchtime chaos and the very professional waiters. Fond gustatory memories from this menu of honestly prepared, high-quality seafood include robust, incredibly delicious cioppino, flavorful calamari steak and juicy grilled swordfish. Specials on a particular day might include charbroiled offerings of ahi tuna, Cajun catfish or orange roughy, prawns sautéed in Chardonnay and fresh salmon in a lobster sauce. Great French bread is served in abundance, and wine is poured Italian style in small tumblers. Our bad meal may have boded ominously of inconsistency, but we can assure you that it won't drive us away. Desserts are as solidly simple as the rest of the menu: Roman Beauty apples baked and served in their own juice, with a sprinkling of sugar, as well as rice-custard pudding, cheesecakes, sundaes, sherbets. Expect to spend about $50 for dinner for two, with a modest wine, and about $30 for lunch, with a glass of wine.
Open Mon.-Fri. 11 a.m.-9 p.m. No cards.

El Tazumal
3522 20th St.,
Mission District
• 550-0935
SALVADORAN

12/20

This little neighborhood restaurant in the Mission District serves the cuisine of El Salvador, which is not too common in San Francisco. The dining room is homey and nicely decorated, a nice change from the omnipresent Formica and linoleum. For those not accustomed to (or curious about) Salvadoran cooking, El Tazumal also serves some very good Mexican food (for example, superb enchiladas). But it would be foolish to pass over such Salvadoran specialties as beef tongue in a garlicky red tomato sauce. Also offered is a Nicaraguan-style churrasco, a charbroiled steak accompanied by black beans, rice, and green fried plantains (a more savory relative of the banana). Ice-cold beer is the best accompaniment to this cuisine; try one of the Mexican brands. About $30 for dinner for two, with beer; you can sample some of these dishes for less at the neighboring taquería.

Open daily 10 a.m.-10:45 p.m. All major cards.

Thep Phanom
400 Waller St.,
Lower Fillmore
• 431-2526
THAI

The big drawback to Thep Phanom is its location in a low-down corner of the city. Otherwise, this Thai restaurant is tops. The dining room is dramatically lit and lively. There are plenty of carved wood accents, and fresh flowers on the glass- and cloth-covered tables. Chef-owner Pathama Parikanont has a wily way with spices and chilies, setting up a complex and subtly mounting fire on the palate; ingredients are invariably fresh and of highest quality. We liked her tom kha gai, chicken stewed in coconut milk with galanga root, citrus and peppers. Larb ped is a gently fiery salad of ground duck tempered by cool mint leaves. The beer is always cold, and some thought obviously went into selecting a few good wines to match the range of food. You'll spend about $35 for two, including beer or wine.

Open daily 5:30 p.m.-10:30 p.m. All major cards.

Tommy Toy's Chinoise
655 Montgomery St.,
Financial District
• 397-4888
CHINESE

12/20

Imagine dining in Gump's, among the Asian exotica. One is almost surprised at the lack of price tags on the many objets d'art displayed in this glittering, windowless Chinese fantasy of a dining room. Tommy Toy is first and foremost a showman, and that's what makes eating here almost worth the breathtaking prices and often-surly treatment from the waiters. Among the showier dishes is a whole coconut with a cap of pie crust. Break the crust to reveal the hollow full of steamy, fragrant chicken stewing in coconut milk. Toy's signature tenderloin of veal sautéed with tree ears, black fungi, tiny carrots and the inspirational ingredient, pecans, is delicious. The menu often reads better than it tastes, however, and many dishes are overwhelmingly sweet. It's cheaper, and as much fun, to watch the elegant circus from a seat at the fabulous bar. If you dine, the tab will be about $120 for two, with drinks.

Open Mon.-Fri. 11:30 a.m.-3 p.m. & 6 p.m.-10 p.m., Sat. 6 p.m.-10 p.m. All major cards.

Ton Kiang

3148 Geary Blvd.,
Richmond District
• 752-4440
CHINESE/HAKKA

10/20

Ignore the harried waiters and the decor (there really isn't any unless you count the tanks of live catfish and crabs balefully awaiting their culinary fate), and go to Ton Kiang for the flavorful, sometimes irresistible Chinese food. The long and detailed menu of regular dishes is enhanced by specials like minced squab in lettuce leaf served with plum sauce, one of the best versions of this dish in San Francisco. Steamed oysters with black-bean sauce serves up six of the biggest oysters we've ever seen. They are pungent, custardy, oily and sensational over simple steamed rice. We've returned to Ton Kiang again and again for our favorites: salt-baked chicken, the steamed Dungeness crab with fresh ginger and scallions, spicy braised eggplant and earthy country-style Hakka dishes that include fat Chinese bacon with red cabbage and a range of clay-pot mixed-meat casseroles. The down side is that sometimes the food falls flat. Some dishes can be way too oily, and with such a wide range of menu selections to choose from, unless you are a regular and simply work your way through by trial and error to determine your favorites, dinner can be a gastronomic roulette, equally weighted with wins and losses. Most appetizers we have found to be undistinguished, like the potstickers or the greasy, uninspired spring rolls. Stick to the main dishes, and if you're allergic to MSG, make sure to specify that you don't want it—they'll oblige. Dinner for two, with beer, will be $35.
Open daily 11 a.m.-10 p.m. Cards: MC, V.

Trader Vic's

20 Cosmo Pl.,
Nob Hill
• 776-2232
POLYNESIAN/ASIAN

10/20

May Trader Vic's eternally endure the vicissitudes of changing tastes, soaring rents and earthquakes; forget the food and the coma-inducing cocktails—this place is a piece of living history and should be revered and fêted. Although certain concessions to modern tastes have been made here (more selections of grilled and poached seafood, for instance), the pseudo-Polynesian food for which you have come since time immemorial is still here. Yes, the pupu tray is perhaps a little more onomatopoeic than one would wish (although the spareribs are still terrific, and the crab puffs shall always remain one of our favorite guilty pleasures). Some of the more ambitious Chinese and Asian dishes are just so-so. Stick to the roast Indonesian lamb (minus the peanut sauce), the poached salmon and the steamed Chinese fish of the day, and you'll dine very nicely.

As ever, the heart of Trader Vic's remains the Boathouse Bar. We love walking into it—sneaking through the mysterious, fog-shrouded alleyway entrance, turning a blind eye to the souvenir-packed cases near the door and snuggling into a cozy banquette. And even if you don't drink liquor, the bartender will happily, if rather suspiciously, mix up virgin versions of the drinks that made the late Vic Bergeron famous, things with names like the Suffering Bastard, and all manner of concoctions served in coconut shells or hollowed-out pineapples or glasses the size of birdbaths. It's fun to dine in the bar as well (it has a separate menu)— the fresh oysters on the half shell, the smoked salmon and the bedspring potatoes and onion rings make for very yummy snacks. Dinner for two, with drinks, will run $100. *Open Mon.-Fri. 11:30 a.m.-2:30 p.m. & 5 p.m.-midnight, Sat.-Sun. 5 p.m.-midnight. All major cards.*

Le Trou
1007 Guerrero St.,
Mission District
• 550-8169
FRENCH

Le Trou may be one of the most unique restaurants in all of San Francisco. The spirit behind Le Trou is Robert Reynolds, who was a longtime apprentice to San Francisco's beloved and legendary French chef and teacher, Josephine Araldo. Reynolds first opened the restaurant as a training ground for his own students, and for years it remained more of a cooking-school–cum–restaurant than a full-fledged restaurant. Now Le Trou has grown up, and the menu— one that will bring joy to any true lover of regional French food—has developed along with the restaurant. Tuesday through Friday, in the restaurant's latest configuration, Reynolds offers either a three-course, one-wine menu for $25, or a four-course, two-wine menu for $35. Saturday is the blowout night here, with five courses, two wines, and both an apéritif and a dessert wine included in the $45 prix-fixe. The menu now includes three or four choices each for the first and main courses (before, there was simply one set menu). While service can be slow, and the very occasional dish not up to par, it is such a pleasure to sit down to the kind of meal a French grandmother would prepare that these minor flaws can be overlooked. While so many restaurants today maintain crowd and noise levels that prohibit real conversation, it's also a delight to find a place like Le Trou where you can count on a relaxed, intimate evening.

The meal might begin with melon drenched in pineau des Charentes, or a wisp of Roquefort tart, followed by braised duck legs with beans simmered in a tomato-lamb sauce; rabbit in pipérade with thyme-scented potatoes; or, perhaps, roast leg of lamb with garlic-rosemary sauce served with chard and sautéed apples. Reynolds always has a homemade bread; often he'll plait two different doughs together for a lovely effect. And his desserts are homey and comforting: a true gâteau basque with a custardy center, pear tart with Madeira cream, or strawberries and citrus-spiked red wine served with spongecake and orange cream. Like a shrewd French housewife, Reynolds has been running his restaurant on a shoestring for years. He does all his shopping in the city on his motorcycle, and his encyclopedic knowledge of "petits vins" results in some of the most interesting food-and-wine matches to be found in the city. A cozy dinner for two, with wine, will be $50, $70, or $90. *Open Tues.-Sat. 6:30 p.m.-10 p.m. No cards.*

Tutto Bene
2080 Van Ness Ave.,
Van Ness
• 673-3500
ITALIAN

12/20

Yes, this is another gem in the Spectrum restaurant chain's crown, and yes, it really is tutto bene. This very handsome room looks authentically Italian—albeit Italy via hip San Francisco—warm with lots of wood and marble, and a wonderful mural depicting culinary bounty. The menu is great for grazing and sharing dishes. One of our favorite appetizers is the gioielli del vagabondo—little purses fashioned out of carpaccio and stuffed with celery, grana cheese and capers. Another is the melazana Marco Polo, a mix of marinated eggplant, rosemary, mint, garlic, sesame oil, soy sauce, hot peppers and oranges, which is truly delicious. Your best bet might be to order the piatto del vicino, which is a sampler of the vagabond purses, bruschetta with fresh mozzarella, the melazana Marco Polo and the rotolino ai quattro formaggi. And as a second course, don't miss the polenta alla montanara, a terrific dish of soft polenta, Stracchino cheese, sautéed mushrooms and a head of buttery roasted garlic. Pastas here are quite good, especially the tagliarini neri Tutto Bene, a toss of black pasta, calamari, tomatoes, hot peppers, olive oil, garlic and basil; and the gnocchi stuffed with potato and rabbit. Main courses range from a simply grilled chicken breast dressed with sun-dried tomatoes, garlic, olives and grilled zucchini to wonderful grilled sweet-hot Sicilian sausages served with braised red cabbage; while the entrées are first-rate, we have more fun ordering appetizers and pastas. Desserts are dazzling—try the frozen hazelnut cream with honey zabaglione and chocolate sauce, and the alla luna, Tutto Bene's version of tiramisu. But the best dessert is the bill—dinner for two, with wine, will run to about $50.
Open Mon.-Thurs. 11:30 a.m.-11 p.m., Fri. 11:30 a.m.-midnight, Sat. 5 p.m.-midnight, Sun. 5 p.m.-11 p.m. All major cards.

Vanessi's
1177 California St.,
Nob Hill
• 771-2422
ITALIAN/AMERICAN

You won't receive a warm, robust welcome from Mama herself here—the restaurant is run by a father-daughter team—but this isn't a cozy home-style place. Regardless of ambience, Vanessi's is one place where the food is so good it doesn't matter. The mixed antipasto—Italian meats, cheeses, cold prawns, scallions, olives—is a little mundane, and the pastas, a tortellini Alfredo for example, are competent but not creative (though the carbonara is one of the best we've had). But the main courses are quite remarkable. Fish and shellfish are handled beautifully. A sauté of scallops *agrodolce* in garlic butter is perfectly prepared and of the very highest quality. The meats—prime steaks and sweet young lamb chops—are expertly grilled and are among the best in the city. And those little new potatoes fried with onion, garlic, peppers and parsley—we dream of them! Most desserts, though not made in-house, are delicious, especially the chocolate cake from the nearby Victoria Bakery. Don't miss the warm zabaglione, the best in the city, which is for once not over-liquored. The Italian offerings on the wine list are only moderately overpriced; the California wines, more so. Dinner for two, with a simple wine, will run about $70.
Open Mon.-Thurs. 11:30 a.m.-10 p.m., Fri. 11:30 a.m.-11 p.m., Sat. 4:30 p.m.-11 p.m., Sun. 4:30 p.m.-10 p.m. All major cards.

Vegi Food
1820 Clement St.,
Richmond District
VEGETARIAN/CHINESE

12/20

A perennial favorite with hippies, Zen Buddhists and vegetarians, this good little spot on busy Clement Street is becoming more and more popular with foodies, too. The appeal is not decor (it's obvious that this was once a pizza parlor), but inventive Chinese vegetarian food. The deep-fried walnuts, found on so many trendy menus these days, originated here. So did the concept that gorgeously fresh broccoli, cauliflower and snow peas can be quickly wokked and served al dente as a perfectly respectable main course. Not to mention the tofu, which was adding flavor and substance to dishes here long before it became a chic item on other restaurants' menus. The food is modest yet comforting; the tab is comforting in its modesty—about $16 for two, with wine.
Open Tues.-Fri. 11:30 a.m.-3 p.m. & 5 p.m.-9 p.m., Sat.-Sun. 11:30 a.m.-9 p.m.

Victor's

**Westin St. Francis,
335 Powell St.,
Union Square**
• 956-7777
CALIFORNIAN/FRENCH

Victor's is named for the original chef of the fledgling St. Francis Hotel when it opened in 1904. Known as a culinary innovator, Victor Hirtzler set the tone for fine dining in San Francisco during his twenty-year reign at the St. Francis stove. His namesake restaurant now crowns the hotel's 32-story tower, and the view alone is worth the trip up the outside elevator. The food is too good to take second billing, though, thanks to chef Joel Rambaud's overlay of traditional French technique on prime California ingredients. His modernized coulibiac, for instance, wraps fresh Pacific salmon in phyllo dough, with a sauce of California caviar. He hot-smokes his rack of lamb over mesquite and serves it, rare and juicy, over a four-bean ragoût with sweet garlic sauce. In addition to his comprehensive à la carte menu, Rambaud also offers a seasonal five-course (plus sorbet) Californian dinner selection that includes such luxuries as foie gras, lobster bisque and veal medallions with morels in brandy sauce. If you can manage dessert, be sure to order a hot soufflé (30 minutes' preparation required) as you start your entrée. The top-notch wine list at Victor's is presided over by Master Sommelier David O'Connor. The setting is opulent and the service formal without being pompous. Count on spending $150 for a complete à la carte dinner for two, with wine; the prix-fixe meal costs $47 (without wine). A Sunday brunch buffet, with champagne, is priced at $25 per person.
Open Mon.-Sat. 6 p.m.-11 p.m., Sun. 10 a.m.-2 p.m. & 6 p.m.-11 p.m. All major cards.

Wu Kong

**1 Rincon Center,
101 Spear St.,
Financial District**
• 957-9300
CHINESE/SHANGHAI

Now that Wu Kong has opened in the posh Rincon Center, San Francisco has its first restaurant serving Shanghai cuisine—the lush, elegant cooking of what was once Asia's most sophisticated city. From the noisy, informal tables in the enclosed atrium to the solemnly elegant indoor dining room, we've consistently found good service and food at Wu Kong. We like the fact that, far more than most Chinese restaurants, Wu Kong serves with style. All the plates have artful blue lotus blossoms twining around the rim. The jasmine tea is delicately fragrant, clearly of a fine grade of tea leaf. You won't find spring rolls or potstickers here, or any of the appetizers normally associated with San Francisco Chinese restaurants. Instead, there are appetizers like vegetable goose, wrapped in a deep-fried sheet of bean curd and stuffed with chopped shiitake mushrooms. Chicken with wine sauce is subtly flavored and becomes increasingly exciting as the flavors of rice wine, peanut oil, sesame oil and rice vinegar complement the juicy meat. Main dishes,

when they work, are equally mouthwatering. The vegetable rice here is light and wonderful, steamed and mixed with Chinese cabbage leaves and chunks of smoky ham. "Eight precious hot sauce" is a mélange of chicken, pork and shrimp—only mildly spicy, and full of flavor and chewy textures. We didn't care at all for half a sweet-and-sour fish with pine nuts. The sauce was incredibly sugary and gluey, and the fish was so thickly fried that it tasted like junk food. Pine nuts and peas were a nice touch. The wine list at Wu Kong is excellent, with a particularly diverse choice of California wines. And don't miss dessert. Fried pancake with red-bean paste is like a hot, crunchy Chinese crêpe, not too sweet and very voluptuous. Dinner for two, with wine, costs about $70.
Open Mon.-Fri. 11 a.m.-2:30 p.m. & 5:30 p.m.-10 p.m., Sat. & Sun. 10:30 a.m.-2:30 p.m. & 5:30 p.m.-10 p.m. Cards: AE, MC, V.

Yamato
717 California St.,
Nob Hill
• 397-3456
JAPANESE

12/20

Yamato has been one of San Francisco's best Japanese restaurant for decades and has been honored with many awards—though lately, with more fashionable (and expensive) competitors on the scene, Yamato is overlooked, at least by reviewers. But its adoring fans, both Oriental and Occidental, know the truth—Yamato is still a very good restaurant. We are among the fans of this elegant house atop Nob Hill, with its lovely Japanese decor, remarkably gracious service and traditional but well-prepared cuisine. Sushi and sashimi are admirable, and the quality of the tempuras, teriyakis and sukiyakis is beyond reproach. Seafood fans must have the appetizer of steamed clams, a huge pot of just-barely cooked, exceptionally fine clams. Wines are reasonably priced. An à la carte dinner for two, with sake, will run about $55.
Open Tues.-Fri. 11:45 a.m.-2 p.m., Tues.-Sun. 5 p.m.-10 p.m. All major cards.

Yaya Cuisine
397 1/2 8th St.,
South of Market
• 255-0909
MIDDLE EASTERN/
CALIFORNIAN

It's about time the intense, engaging chef Yahya Salih had his own restaurant. After years of backing up culinary stars (most recently, Jeremiah Tower at Stars), Yahya is finally in a position to present his personal cuisine to a clamoring public. There is plenty of clamoring, too—reservations are a must for this tiny, noisy, utterly charming South of Market eatery. The logic is simple: Yahya combines his own assemblage of Middle Eastern cuisines with a California attitude toward fresh local ingredients used creatively, with frequent resort to a grill. The results are lovely to look at, heaven to eat. Elliptical plates bear fat, fragrant sausages of chicken

and lamb, nutty pilaf, lightly sautéed fresh vegetables, garlicky eggplant, tangy tabouli, olive-oily hummus. The rice soaks up all kind of savory juices. The clientele is true to the neighborhood, ranging from bohemian artists to buttoned-down young male executives with diamond studs in their ears. Short but well-matched wine list. Dinner with wine comes in at about $40 for two.
Open daily 5:30 p.m.-10:30 p.m. All major cards.

Yuet Lee
1300 Stockton St.,
Chinatown
• 982-6020
CHINESE

12/20

In spite of the tragic loss of former master chef Michael Yu several years ago, followers of this quirky restaurant have not felt a slip in quality here. Yuet Lee still serves several near-flawless Hong Kong–style Cantonese seafood dishes, albeit in an ambience best described as grim: a dank downstairs dungeon outfitted with tables, an upstairs room next to the open kitchen (definitely the preferred seating, but you'll wait forever for a table here) and a garish green-and-orange Formica dining room. But the dinginess is quickly forgiven after a taste of the Maine lobster or Dungeness crab, two of Yuet Lee's best dishes. Either crustacean is netted from a murky fish tank and quickly stir-fried to a gleaming perfection with black beans and chilis or with ginger. The best dishes are those that are expensive or odd; anything whole is also good—poached chicken, steamed sand dab or catfish. Everyone orders the crunchy, fried "salt and pepper" squid, one of the best squid dishes we have tasted. Vegetable dishes, particularly a water spinach called "long green" cooked with either garlic or fermented bean curd, are also a good bet. To add to the physical discomfort, no beer or wine is served, but both can be brought in from a narrow grocery two doors north on Stockton Street, which apparently makes a living off thirsty Yuet Lee customers. A seafood dinner for two, with tea, will run about $50.
Open Wed.-Mon. 11 a.m.-3 a.m. No cards.

Zola's
395 Hayes St.,
Civic Center
• 864-4824
FRENCH

In June of 1989, Zola's, one of our favorite French restaurants in the city, took a big step: co-owners Larry Bains and Catherine Pantsios moved from their small Sacramento Street locale to larger quarters near Davies Hall. And since then, this exemplary French country restaurant has matured into a truly stellar establishment. We always loved the simple elegance of the original Zola's (where Acquerello is now located), and in the new Zola's, the partners have, again, given their design sense full play in the handsome, understated decor: walls painted in a quirky pastel, beautifully crafted Italian lights, and flower arrangements that look like studies for the Dutch masters create a serene effect. This is one place where the decor never distracts from the food. Further, Larry Bains has mastered the art of making you feel welcome and comfortable. It's so rare to receive a truly personal welcome in San Francisco restaurants that this always feels special—and may be one reason why Zola's is among the most French of the French restaurants in the Bay Area. It's also among the most civilized. As soon as you sit down, you are served crisp, crusty dinner rolls and a plate of olives scented with Provençal herbs.

Zola's hard-working chefs, Catherine Pantsios and Rachel Gardner, both have a strong commitment to flavor and tradition, and at Zola's they show off their love of earthy French regional cooking. It's a fairly small menu with daily specials (when it changes seasonally, the new menu is sent out to regular customers on lovely pastel notecards). Zola's scope has given these chefs the chance to cook their hearts out, and as a result you can find dishes here that are increasingly rare elsewhere. Confit de canard has always been one of the house specialties, and nobody in San Francisco does it better. Though confit is usually an autumn or winter dish, in spring Pantsios might accompany the meltingly tender duck with baby artichokes. One of her best quail dishes also has a Southwest France emphasis: quails stuffed with sausage and Armagnac-soaked prunes. Among the best starters are tapenade tart with mesclun and baby greens; tomato tart perfumed with basil; and sautéed sweetbreads in a hazelnut-and-blood-orange vinaigrette. Look for the infrequent special regional menus, which through the years have featured the food of not only France but Spain and Italy as well. It's smart to reserve well in advance for these dinners because they attract a flock of faithful regulars. The wine list will impress you with its regional favorites. Two can dine (with wine) for about $80.
Open Mon.-Sat. 5:30 p.m.-11 p.m. All major cards.

Zuni Cafe
1658 Market St.,
Civic Center
• 552-2522
CALIFORNIAN/
INTERNATIONAL

When you're driving down Market Street late at night, Zuni is a cheering sight, with the big windows steamed over, the crowd at the bar seen in fuzzy outline, and the oystermen at their post out front. Since Judy Rodgers has taken the kitchen in hand, there's always a crowd at the door waiting for the unreserved tables. But you can happily settle for the bar menu if you can't get a table—feast on a platter of freshly shucked oysters (and order them one by one, by variety) or a mixed seafood platter set up on stilts, a superlative hamburger with roasted peppers or a bowl of warming soup. Other good bets: polenta with dollops of Mascarpone; fritto misto of catfish, fennel, and radicchio; and the terrific sandwiches.

Rodgers cooks to feed you—and feed you well. We don't know of any other menu in town where we find so many hearty and satisfying dishes. There's the roast chicken for two, which comes out of the wood-fired oven a deep-mahogany gold. And there are the ribs baked in a brick oven, and the quail on a bed of wilted greens. . . Rodgers's secret is that she keeps it simple and uncomplicated. This is real food, not a concept, which is why you see so many people from the wine and food worlds eating here. The wine list, printed each day on the back of the throwaway menu, is well considered. Among the treasures here are Domaine Tempier's Bandol Rose, Bruno Giacosa's Arneis, Gerard Chave's Hermitage Blanc, Calera Pinot Noir, and Castello di Rampolla's Chianti Classico. Even more unusual than the wine list: the cheese course is given some attention here. You can order St. Nectaire with apples, mountain Gorgonzola with orange honey and walnuts, or fresh goat cheese with olives. And for after dinner, there's a nice list of dessert wines, brandies and liqueurs. A meal for two, with wine, will cost about $85.

Open Tues.-Sat. 7:30 a.m.-midnight, Sun. 7:30 a.m.-11 p.m. Cards: AE, MC, V.

QUICK BITES

ASIAN

B & M Mei Sing
62 2nd St.,
South of Market
• 777-9530

This is no place for intimacy. You place your order at the counter, take a numbered plastic disk, join strangers at a huge table and wait until a caterwauling waitress walks by with your plate. The sumptuous noodle dishes make the ordeal well worth it, which is why thousands of downtown businesspeople flock here daily for lunch. Delectable mein or fun noodles serve as a base for beef, pork, duck, shrimp, chicken or fish balls, and you can ask that wontons—incredibly delicate and smashingly seasoned—be thrown in as well. Our favorite is the gon lo mein with duck, a gigantic platter of thin noodles with tender duck in a rich, satiny sauce. To avoid crowds, arrive before noon or after 1:30 p.m. Lunch for two, with a beer each, will run just $12 or so.
Open Mon.-Fri. 10:30 a.m.-3:30 p.m., Sat. 10:30 a.m.-2:45 p.m. No cards.

Golden Dragon
833 Washington St.,
Chinatown
• 398-4550

Sheer heaven for carbo-loaders, Golden Dragon serves every variation of Chinese noodle dish. Tangles of mein and fun noodles are topped with all manner of savory sauces, meats, fish and vegetables, and they're all good. Try the mein noodles with tomato and beef, the braised noodles with barbecued pork and cabbage or the mein with shrimp and Chinese greens. The Formica-clad dining room is authentically chaotic. A mere $12 to $14 for two, with beer.
Open daily 8 a.m.-1 a.m. No cards.

Hong Kong Tea House
835 Pacific Ave.,
Chinatown
• 391-6365

For traditional no-frills dim sum, the Hong Kong Tea House sets the standard. Crowds form early outside this huge dining hall to sample the many "little hearts"—everything from sweet black-bean-paste dumplings to braised fried chicken feet, which is not for the faint of palate. What we can unreservedly recommend are the rice-flour balls filled with pork, but there's really nothing here you'll regret ordering. Two will feast for $18.
Open daily 9 a.m.-3 p.m. No cards.

Mifune
1737 Post St.,
Japantown
• 922-0337

This pleasant and comfortable café serves comfort food, Japanese style: wonderful bowls of steaming soup noodles that will take the chill out of the foggiest day. Though Mifune offers adequate, inexpensive and well-presented

sashimi and tempura dinners, noodles are the thing to get: soba, thin buckwheat-flour noodles, or udon, thick white noodles, typically served with miso soup and different combinations of meat and vegetables. We prefer the soba noodles served with either the marvelously crisp and light shrimp-and-vegetable tempura or the beef and egg. On warm days, the cold-noodle dishes are deliciously satisfying. Service is exceptionally prompt. About $17 for a noodle lunch for two, with sake.
Open daily 11 a.m.-9:30 p.m. All major cards.

Yank Sing
427 Battery St.,
Financial District
• 495-4510

Yank Sing's shrewd owners saw the potential in marketing dim sum to a largely non-Asian business-lunch crowd, and they have realized that potential beautifully. Both downtown branches are crowded, but less so than the typical dim sum house (and less frenzied as well). Attention is paid to service and presentation, and the quality is uniformly outstanding. True, you'll have less choice and a higher tab than at a Chinatown teahouse. The tables, however, are set with linen and flowers, and the dumplings and sweet and savory dishes are all heavenly. Lunch for two, with beer, will run as much as $25.
Open Mon.-Fri. 11 a.m.-3 p.m., Sat.-Sun. 10 a.m.-4 p.m. All major cards.

BARBECUE

Blackburn's Pit Barbeque
1338 Ocean Ave.,
Ingleside
• 239-7115

What makes trekking out to this relatively remote neighborhood unquestionably worthwhile is the oak-burning stove, which yields magnificently smoked meats and chicken. When topped with one of Blackburn's sauces (though the hot is not quite hot enough), the barbecue boasts a certain *je ne sais quoi* that puts this place in a league with the Bay Area's heavy hitters (Flint's and Everett & Jones). The hot links are superb, and the baked beans—redolent of smoky bacon—are like none we've ever tasted. A slab of beef or pork ribs, some beans and a soft drink will send two people on their merry way for $20 or less.
Open Mon.-Tues. 3 p.m.-10 p.m., Wed.-Thurs. noon-10 p.m., Fri.-Sat. noon-midnight. Cards: MC, V.

Everett & Jones Barbeque
5130 3rd St.,
Bayview
• 822-7728

This rather seedy branch of the acclaimed Berkeley barbecue house is almost as good as Oakland's Flint's, which is saying a lot. Out of the brick oven emerge outstanding chicken and hot links bathed in a fiery, soul-satisfying sauce. Only the overly chewy ribs keep Everett & Jones from stealing Flint's barbecue crown. Eat here or, better yet, take a heap of chicken and links home for about $16 for two.
Open Sun.-Thurs. 11 a.m.-midnight, Fri.-Sat. 11 a.m.-2 a.m. No cards.

Leon's Bar-B-Q
1911 Fillmore St.,
Upper Fillmore
• 922-2436

In a city not known for good barbecue, Leon's serves unusually tender and juicy ribs, chicken and fiery hot links. The rich sauce isn't the best in town, but it tastes just fine when you've a craving for spicy and authentic Southern barbecue. Accompaniments (cornbread, coleslaw, potato salad, baked beans) are ordinary—neither good nor bad. Skip the homemade desserts, which can be dreadful, and instead wander up Fillmore Street for an ice cream cone. About $25 for two, with beer.
Open Mon.-Sat. 11 a.m.-10 p.m., Sun. 1 p.m.-9 p.m. No cards.

San Francisco Bar-B-Q
1328 18th St.,
Potrero Hill
• 431-8956

Thai cuisine, with its fresh, vivacious tastes, has rapidly become dear to the hearts of many gourmands. But few realize that the Thais have also mastered the art of barbecue. Once you've sampled the grilled ribs or chicken—imbued with garlic and Thai spices—at San Francisco Bar-B-Q, you may never go back to American barbecue. The meats here are cooked to perfection, and the flavors seemingly explode in your mouth. (They're so well spiced, in fact, that you can feel free to skip the treacly dipping sauce.) The food is as inexpensive as it is exquisite: just $7.48 for a whole chicken. And though we couldn't possibly envision a better complement to the food than an ice-cold bottle of Thai Singha beer, the owners offer a small but tasteful selection of California wines. Crowds gather quickly to fill the tiny, unappointed dining room, so arrive early or order takeout—or bring your food next door to Bloom's Tavern. Dinner for two, with beer, will run $15 or so.
Open Tues.-Sat. 11 a.m.-2 p.m. & 4:30 p.m.-9:30 p.m., Sun. 3 p.m.-9 p.m. No cards.

CAFES & DINERS

Brain Wash
1122 Folsom St.,
South of Market
• 861-3663

We're certainly not the only ones who have often wondered, "Why doesn't someone open a fun, spiffy laundromat with a café and bar?" Finally someone was brainy enough to follow through on the idea. Just as we went to press, former party planner Susan Schindler was about to unveil her new Brain Wash, SOMA's latest entrant in the hip parade. We haven't been able to taste the food, but we can tell you that the concept is promising for those with dirty laundry *and* an appetite: a slick, high-tech laundromat separated by a glass wall from a SOMA-industrial café, featuring an oldies-stocked jukebox, a casual atmosphere, beer and wine, espresso and simple but chic snack food, from chili to sandwiches to all-American desserts. Plan on $1.25 a load to wash and about $8 a head for a simple meal, with beer.
Open Sun.-Thurs. 7:30 a.m.-11 p.m., Fri.-Sat. 7:30 a.m.-2 a.m. Cards: MC, V.

Café Latte
100 Bush St. (2nd Fl.),
Financial District
• 989-2233

With its fresh ingredients, Italian basics and Californian cuisine influence, Café Latte is one of the stars of the downtown lunch scene. Homemade pastas hang drying in view, soon to be incorporated into splendid salads with grilled marinated chicken, prawns or other fresh seafood. Other courses, ranging from marinated eggplant to fruit-and-cheese platters, are inspired, as are the homemade cakes and tarts. Expect a line during the lunch rush, but also expect gracious service once you're seated. Lunch for two, with house wine, will run about $22.
Open Mon.-Fri. 7 a.m.-10:30 a.m. & 11:30 a.m.-3 p.m. All major cards.

Caffè Trieste
609 Vallejo St.,
North Beach
• 392-6739

A North Beach survivor of the Beat era, Caffè Trieste was the espresso bar of choice for Jack Kerouac and Allen Ginsberg. Not much has changed since then—Trieste is still a good, cozy spot for conversation and a cappuccino or an apéritif. Come here on a Saturday night to hear opera or on a lazy weekday afternoon to wax philosophical with a friend.

About $12 for a sandwich and a glass of Chianti for two. *Open Sun.-Thurs. 7 a.m.-11:30 p.m., Fri.-Sat. 7 a.m.-12:30 a.m. No cards.*

Cha Cha Cha
1805 Haight St.,
Haight-Ashbury
• 386-5758

For the first few months of its short life, this eclectic, noisy little café was undiscovered and sleepy. But then the critics descended, and the lines have been long ever since. Thankfully, the sudden popularity didn't cause a drop in Cha Cha Cha's quality, and the American/Latin/trendy tapas are as tasty as ever. There are nice pastas with seafood, good grills (a choice New York steak with roasted sweet peppers is a bargain at $9) and a remarkable Cuban black-bean soup. While you wait for one of the few tables, amuse yourself by watching the crowd, a happy mix of diehard flower children and clean-cut yuppies. Dinner for two, with wine, will run about $28.
Open Mon.-Thurs. 11 a.m.-3 p.m. & 5 p.m.-11:30 p.m., Fri. 11 a.m.-3 p.m. & 5:30 p.m.-midnight, Sat. noon-3 p.m. & 5:30 p.m.-midnight, Sun. noon-3 p.m. & 5 p.m.-11 p.m. No cards.

Doidge's
2217 Union St.,
Cow Hollow
• 921-2149

Poached-egg fanciers are fussy people. They like them just so, and consequently are usually disappointed when they order them out. This is why Doidge's has such a loyal following—its fans know their poached eggs, whether plain or Benedict style, will be cooked with precision, arriving on the table with just the right amount of runniness. The same goes for the delicious baked eggs. This attention to eggy detail is evidence enough of the quality in this all-American café, which is charmingly decorated in an urban farmhouse sort of style. Though lunches and dinners are fresh and good, breakfast is the time to visit Doidge's (so many do that you should make reservations a few days in advance). Omelets are fluffy and perfectly cooked, french toast is heavenly, and fruit is vibrantly fresh. Bring your own wine at lunch or dinner, and expect to pay about $15 for breakfast for two.
Open Mon.-Wed. 8 a.m.-2 p.m., Thurs.-Fri. 8:30 a.m.-9 p.m., Sat.-Sun. 8 a.m.-3 p.m. Cards: MC, V.

Eagle Café
Pier 39 (2nd Fl.),
Fisherman's Wharf
• 433-3689

Although Pier 39 has rapidly become a tourist trap and teen hangout, the venerable Eagle Café is a refreshing breath of old San Francisco, serving hearty breakfasts and robust lunches to fishermen and dock workers. In an oaky, salty, manly setting, regulars put away fluffy, buttery hotcakes, eggs and the Eagle's signature corned beef hash. Lunch is

similarly proletarian and satisfying, with he-man-size steaks and dense soups thick with meat. The drinks are strong, the bar honest, and the Bay view sweeping. About $12 for breakfast or lunch for two, without drinks.
Open Mon.-Thurs. 7 a.m.-2:30 p.m. & 5 p.m.-9:30 p.m., Fri. 7 a.m.-2:30 p.m. & 5 p.m.-2 a.m., Sat.-Sun. 7 a.m.-3 p.m. & 5 p.m.-2 a.m. No cards.

Geva's
482A Hayes St.,
Civic Center
• 863-1220

Geva's fulfills two important roles in San Francisco: it checks in as a heavy hitter in the somewhat cuisine-arid opera/symphony neighborhood, and, more important, it's the city's first high-class Jamaican restaurant. With a formula that combines roots and elegance, Geva's gracefully delivers rich, dusky wonders. Start with the cod fritters. Crispy on the outside, they melt in your mouth but haunt the tongue with Jamaican spices, mysterious and fiery. There's certainly no need for the mundane Mexican-style salsa fresca that accompanies them. A puréed black-bean soup, flavored unlike any we've ever had, is also a taste-bud shocker, and after these two you'll scarcely have room for anything else. Still, there's the goat stew and the Caribbean fish stew—each wondrously satisfying in its own way. The wine list is impressive, and the sweet-potato pone, a pudding of yams, raisins and walnuts topped with whipped cream, is magnificent. Be sure to make reservations; the yuppies have been flocking here lately. About $40 for dinner for two, with wine.
Open Mon. 5:30 p.m.-9 p.m., Tues.-Thurs. 11:30 a.m.-2:30 p.m. & 5:30 p.m.-9 p.m., Fri. 11:30 a.m.-2:30 p.m. & 5:30 p.m.-10:30 p.m., Sat. 5:30 p.m.-10:30 p.m., Sun. 9:30 a.m.-3 p.m. & 5:30 p.m.-9 p.m. All major cards.

Mario's Bohemian Cigar Store
556 Columbus Ave.,
North Beach
• 362-0536

Don't you believe it when cynics proclaim the death of North Beach. It may not be as unspoiled as it was in the '50s, but as long as the Bohemian Cigar Store survives, the spirit of North Beach will carry on. Just across the street from Washington Square, Mario's is a true locals' hangout and the quintessential North Beach coffeehouse. Wonderful cappuccinos, delicious focaccia sandwiches and a lemony ricotta cheesecake (made by the owner's wife) are served at the bar or at one of the small tables in this bustling, homey hole-in-the-wall. About $7 for a sandwich and a cappuccino.
Open Mon. 10 a.m.-11 p.m., Tues.-Thurs. 10 a.m.-midnight, Fri.-Sat. 10 a.m.-1 a.m., Sun. 10 a.m.-6 p.m. No cards.

Pork Store Café

1451 Haight St.,
Haight-Ashbury
• 864-6981
372 5th St.,
South of Market
• 495-5956

The hearty American breakfast is raised to an art form in these crowded little coffee shops. Everything is wonderful, from the coffee to the grits, but we have our favorites: the perfect corned beef hash with poached eggs, the homemade biscuits and the incredible record-album-size pancakes cooked with berries, bananas or apples. About $12 or so for breakfast for two.
Open Mon.-Fri. 7 a.m.-3 p.m., Sat.-Sun. 8 a.m.-4 p.m. No cards.

Ruby's

489 3rd St.,
South of Market
• 541-0795

Following in the footsteps of Vicolo Pizzeria, upscale pizza places are descending on the city like so much well-drizzled olive oil. This is a welcome trend, because there isn't a good slice of New York–style pizza to be found in the entire Bay Area. One of the original owners of Vicolo opened Ruby's, a bustling, bright oasis on a grungy South of Market strip. The pizzas feature cornmeal in the crust and such toppings as leek, fennel sausage and other rarefied accoutrements. We haven't been let down yet. What keeps Ruby's from being a Vicolo clone is a wider menu, offering a couple of pastas a day (the tortellini with lemon-chive cream was impressive) and creative sandwiches. The slice-and-salad lunch special is a bargain. Two people will spend $18, with wine.
Open Mon.-Thurs. 11:30 a.m.-10:30 p.m., Fri.-Sat. 11:30 a.m.-11:30 p.m., Sun. 3 p.m.-10 p.m. All major cards.

Spuntino Italian Express

524 Van Ness Ave.,
Civic Center
• 861-7772

Spectrum Foods has done it again with Spuntino, a bustling café and bakery next to Harry's Bar, the jewel in Spectrum's crown. Spuntino was designed to attract local office workers, Civic Center employees and patrons of the opera, symphony and theater, and attract them it does. This bright, well-appointed café offers irresistible Italian fast food: antipasti salads, sandwiches made on freshly baked Italian breads (including focaccia), beautiful little pizzas, homemade pastries and rich gelati. It's all fresh, simple, tasty and reasonably priced: about $18 for lunch for two, with a glass of wine.
Open Mon. 7 a.m.-10 p.m., Tues.-Thurs. 7 a.m.-11 p.m., Fri. 7 a.m.-midnight, Sat. 10 a.m.-midnight, Sun. 10 a.m.-9 p.m. All major cards.

Squid's Café

96 McAllister St.,
Civic Center
• 861-0100

When it opened several years ago, Squid's seemed like an idea that couldn't go wrong, at least for calamari fanciers, with squid prepared expertly in a variety of cross-ethnic ways and served in a loud, new-wave environment. But since new wave became old and new owners took over,

Squid's lost some of its spark, and some of its once-great dishes are now merely good. But there is still some fine food here, especially the soul-satisfying calamari Elena—squid drowned in a bowl of spicy tomato sauce—and the frangione—a sandwich of grilled squid, superb Italian sausages (from Danny's), melted cheese and marinara sauce. Start with the deep-fried artichoke hearts, accompanied by house-made aïoli, and wash it all down with an Anchor Steam beer. The daily fresh-fish and pasta specials are hit or miss, but on request the spunky, punk waitpeople will steer you away from the failures. Dinner for two, with beer or wine, is about $25.
Open Mon.-Fri. 11:30 a.m.-11:30 p.m., Sat. 5:30 p.m.-11:30 p.m. All major cards.

Stars Cafe
555 Golden Gate Ave.,
Civic Center
• 861-8521

You'd think running one of the top restaurants in the city (Stars) and looking smug in those Dewar's Profile ads would be enough for Jeremiah Tower, but the man's ambition seems to know no bounds. A couple of years ago he opened Starfish, a now-defunct lunchtime eatery that served superb fish-and-chips. Next came Stars Cafe, a real melting pot of a joint, and now there's also 690 (see the Restaurants chapter), where Tower goes omni-ethnic trendy. At Stars Cafe, Tower tries to do a little bit of everything, with mixed results. There's everything from tapas (great) to minestrone (thin, uninspired) to chicken sandwiches (fine) to artichoke-mushroom risotto (bland) and more. Breakfast features the standard fare done with flair. Since the place is always crowded and reservations aren't taken, an early supper of tapas is a good way to go. As always with Tower, desserts are nonpareil. About $15 for two at breakfast and $26 for two at dinner, with beer or wine.
Open Mon.-Fri. 7:30 a.m.-10 p.m., Sat.-Sun. 10 a.m.-10 p.m. All major cards.

Stoyanof's
1240 9th Ave.,
Sunset District
• 664-3664

This lively, noisy, family-run café near Golden Gate Park is well known for its very good Greek dinners, but we especially like it for lunch, when you may order (self-service) delicious phyllo pastries filled with spinach, tender lamb or one of several cheeses, and sit in the lovely garden patio in back. The phyllo is especially fine and flaky. There are also good stuffed grape leaves and an interesting assortment of homemade desserts (apple strudel, Sachertortes). On a warm day, a Greek salad, a glass of wine and a plate of fresh fruit make for a lovely lunch. At dinner, expect aromatic

roast leg of lamb, perfect moussaka, baked chicken with a tomato-herb sauce, and baklava, all served in the hectic but charmingly decorated dining room. About $14 for a light lunch for two, with a glass of wine.
Open Tues.-Thurs. 10 a.m.-9:30 p.m., Fri.-Sat. 10 a.m.-10 p.m., Sun. 4:30 p.m.-9 p.m. All major cards (at dinner only).

Swan Oyster Depot
1517 Polk St.,
Polk Gulch
• 673-1101

Let the tourists line up at Fisherman's Wharf for overpriced, banal seafood cocktails—we'll be here at Swan's, pulling a stool up to the marble counter and reveling in the combination seafood salad (bay shrimp, prawns, crab, sometimes a bit of lobster), a different-every-day concoction that is one of our favorite San Francisco lunches. Also terrific are the rich New England–style clam chowder, the oysters and the freshly smoked salmon, especially when washed down with a glass of good, reasonably priced white wine. Swan's is first and foremost a retail fishmonger, so seating is limited to the counter and the amenities are basic—but the fish is heavenly. About $30 for a seafood lunch for two, with wine.
Open Mon.-Fri. 8 a.m.-5:30 p.m., Sat. 8 a.m.-5 p.m. No cards.

Tad's Steak
120 Powell St.,
Union Square
• 982-1718

The steaks are probably the worst reason to come here, though if you are desperate for a complete steak dinner for $4.99, you're in the right place. A much better reason to visit Tad's is the outstanding marinated roast chicken and the good homemade blue cheese dressing on the crisp green salads. Beer and a quite good house wine are inexpensive, and charming host Don Levin's madcap sense of humor lightens the atmosphere. This place is wildly popular with locals and tourists, both those on a tight budget and those who can afford to eat wherever they please but love a bargain. A mere $15 for dinner for two, with a glass of wine.
Open daily 7 a.m.-11:30 p.m. No cards.

Tommy's Joynt
1101 Geary St.,
Van Ness
• 775-4216

This garish sports-lovers' pub is to be commended for three things: its collection of more than 90 great beers from around the world; its old-style rathskeller atmosphere; and the fact that you can be fed here after midnight. The sandwiches of turkey, beef brisket and the like are inevitably dry and tough, if hefty, and the more ambitious dishes (usually Italian or Mexican) and the acclaimed buffalo stew look better than they taste. About $12 for a sandwich-and-beer meal for two.
Open daily 11 a.m.-2 a.m. No cards.

Trio Café
1870 Fillmore St.,
Upper Fillmore
• 563-2248

No proper Upper Fillmore shopping/browsing trip should begin without breakfast at Trio, a most civilized café owned by three enthusiastic, cheerful women. Have a bowl of caffè latte at the stand-up counter, or take one of the few tables in this pretty little white room and indulge in the lovely scones, the crisp toast with homemade jam, and the fresh-squeezed juices. Lunch runs to beautiful fruit-and-cheese platters, simple sandwiches and creative salads. Breakfast or lunch for two will be $9 to $17, with a glass of wine.
Open Tues.-Sat. 8 a.m.-6 p.m., Sun. 10 a.m.-4 p.m. No cards.

Vicolo Pizzeria
201 Ivy St.,
Civic Center
• 863-2382

Ever since the tiny, recherché Vicolo opened in this hidden alley, ravenous opera and symphony patrons have had to stop complaining about the lack of good neighborhood cafés. Cynics call this type of fare "yuppie pizza," meaning that the crust is puffy and the toppings include such things as capers, Gorgonzola and sun-dried tomatoes. But we find the pizza to be delicious and more Italian than most, as do the many who line up here daily. About $22 for a pizza meal for two, with wine.
Open Mon.-Sat. 11:30 a.m.-11:30 p.m., Sun. 2 p.m.-10 p.m. No cards.

Vivande Porta Via
2125 Fillmore St.,
Upper Fillmore
• 346-4430

Our favorite café in town, Vivande is a gourmand's paradise. Slick shelving and glass deli cases are packed with vegetable and pasta salads, tortas, pâtés, cheeses, sausages, pastries, wines and gourmet groceries. In the open kitchen behind the counters the industrious staff sautés pasta sauces, steams cappuccinos and arranges lovely plates of antipasti. That owner Carlo Middione, a cooking teacher and caterer, loves food is evident; that you will love his food will be evident with your first bite. To start, try the assorted cold plate, which can include such delights as caponata; wonderful whole roasted onions in balsamic vinegar; a salad of cannellini beans, caviar and onion, and another of celery, mushrooms and sweet red peppers; or any of several rich pâtés. The homemade pastas—with steamed mussels, savory sausage, carbonara or pesto sauces, and more—are all delicious, and the desserts, especially the lemon tart and the exquisite chocolate-nut roll, are incomparable. To avoid the lines that invariably form at lunch, arrive before 12:15. And make sure to stop here when you're stocking your next picnic basket. About $35 to $40 for a pasta-and-pastry lunch for two, with a glass of good wine.
Deli: open Mon.-Fri. 10 a.m.-7 p.m., Sat. 11 a.m.-6 p.m., Sun. 11 a.m.-5 p.m.; caf : open daily 11:30 a.m.-4 p.m. All major cards.

DELIS

Acropolis Bakery and Delicatessen

5217 Geary Blvd.,
Richmond District
• 751-9661

The ethnicity of the Acropolis is a bit confusing. Though its name is Greek, the current owners are Chinese, and the cooks and most of the regulars are Russian. The food, however, shares none of this confusion—it's all Russian and it's all exquisite. Everything is freshly made and delicious: homemade breads, meat pastries and pies, stuffed cabbage, splendid chicken cutlets, myriad salads and hearty desserts. Since Acropolis has been "discovered," the old Russian women who have been coming to this off-the-beaten-path (and mundane) section of the city for years now have to share their corner of the world with food-wise tourists and locals. Expect leisurely service, expect to share a table (perhaps with several of the old Russian women) and expect to pay about $12 for lunch for two.
Open Tues.-Sat. 10:30 a.m.-8 p.m., Sun. 11 a.m.-7 p.m. Cards: MC, V.

Max's Opera Café

601 Van Ness Ave.,
Civic Center
• 771-7300

Max's looks about as much like a real deli as the pop star Madonna looks like the Virgin Mary. In a room filled with a slick bar and stylish furniture, Broadway-bound waiters and waitresses, all smiles and good cheer, leave their serving stations at the drop of a matzo ball to hop on the piano and belt out a show tune or an aria. It's all great fun, but is it deli? As a Catskills comedian would say, "Take the food— *Please*." Max's serves huge portions of food that is either inedible (Max's still serves the worst lox on earth), barely edible (gigantic sandwiches of poor- to mediocre-quality meats) or rather decent (there is a fine smoked chicken breast and a few nice salads). The desserts (cheescake, chocolate cake, fruit cobblers) cover entire platters— they're gargantuan in size but lilliputian in quality. Nonetheless, long lines form every night to sample the indignities. About $30 for two, with wine.
Open Mon. 11:30 a.m.-10 p.m., Tues.-Thurs. 11:30 a.m.-midnight, Fri.-Sat. 11:30 a.m.-1 a.m., Sun. 11:30 a.m.-11 p.m. All major cards.

HAMBURGERS

Bill's Place
2315 Clement St.,
Richmond District
• 221-5262

There's usually a long wait here for a table or a counter seat, but the people-watching on eclectic Clement Street (lined with singles' bars, ethnic restaurants and interesting shops) will keep you amused. Not a place for the health-conscious, Bill's fries hamburgers that are among the messiest in town, a grease-lover's dream come true. Also greasy, but much less edible, are the french fries. But the milk shakes are great, the service is friendly and prompt, and the atmosphere is pleasant. About $20 for two, with beer or milk shakes. *Open Mon.-Thurs. 11 a.m.-10 p.m., Fri.-Sun. 11 a.m.-11 p.m. No cards.*

Clown Alley
42 Columbus Ave.,
North Beach
• 421-2540

This classic burger stand serves the best stand hamburger in town. Open until 2:45 a.m., Clown Alley is a favorite late-night stop for cabbies and partiers, as well as a favorite lunch spot for local businesspeople. The fries and shakes are no more than ordinary, but the juicy grilled burgers are great, especially when accompanied by a bottle of beer, something rarely found at burger stands. A burger and a beer will run about $6. *Open daily 6 a.m.-2:45 a.m. No cards.*

The Grubstake
1525 Pine St.,
Van Ness
• 673-8268

The burgers here are no more than decent, but they taste just fine at 4 a.m., when San Francisco's dining options are limited in the extreme. The Grubstake's house burger is large and cooked as ordered, topped with bacon and cheese, and the fries are among the best in town. Also worthwhile are the salads and breakfasts. This place is just off the most decadent part of Polk Street, which means the clientele ranges from prostitutes of either sex to cab drivers and bank presidents. About $15 for two. *Open daily 7 a.m.-5 a.m. No cards.*

Hamburger Mary's Organic Grill
1582 Folsom St.,
South of Market
• 626-5767

Hamburger Mary's is an absolute madhouse. At any given moment, the clientele may include yuppies casually attired, yuppies in business attire, transvestites, men in black leather and a suburban housewife or two, all suffering interminable waits for a table or a seat at the counter. Popular for years, this mental asylum serves some fairly good hamburgers (the

Meaty Mushroom is especially tasty), salads and omelets. Heartier fare—steaks, grilled fresh fish and a daily special or two—is also offered. The noise level is excruciating, and the waiters (young men in skin-tight clothing) often seem to be from another planet, but all in the name of fun. Not a place for Aunt Fanny from Des Moines! About $22 for two. *Open Mon.-Fri. 11 a.m.-2 a.m., Sat.-Sun. 10 a.m.-2 a.m. All major cards.*

Hard Rock Café

1699 Van Ness Ave.,
Van Ness
• 885-1699

Although this immense junk-food emporium was fashioned from an old automobile showroom, it is actually more reminiscent of another sort of transportation: a huge train station at rush hour. The noise level is so torturous that you'll have to carry on conversations in sign language, and only high school yell leaders will be able to transmit their orders to the young, attractive, free-as-a-breeze (but efficient) waitresses. As evidenced by the huge bar, the loud classic rock, the wild rock-memorabilia decor, the finned Cadillac emerging from a wall and the constant crush of trendy teens, the scene is the thing, not the food. That's just as well, because the otherwise tasty hamburgers are sometimes overcooked on the too-hot mesquite grill, and the barbecued chicken and ribs are cloyingly sweet. But the chili is tasty, and the desserts (strawberry shortcake, hot fudge sundaes, apple pie and chocolate cake) are all excellent. There's always a wait, much to the benefit of the bar's cash flow. From $20 to $30 for two, with beer or wine. *Open Sun.-Thurs. 11:30 a.m.-11:30 p.m., Fri.-Sat. 11:30 a.m.-midnight. All major cards.*

Mo's

1322 Grant Ave.,
North Beach
• 788-3779

With the continuing de-ethnicizing of North Beach, you'd think a new American café would be frowned upon. But locals of Italian descent have a soft spot for burgers, and Mo's delivers the goods. Made of fresh ground beef formed into a patty on the spot, the quarter-pound burger is cooked over lava rocks and served with house-made mayonnaise on a light, crispy bun. It's a classic treatment, as opposed to the ground-sirloin-on-scooped-out-French-bread approach of other local Italian haunts. A mountain of skinny, greasy french fries accompanies the sandwich. Mo's also serves a spicy and tasty, if somewhat dry, Thai-style breast of chicken on a bun, along with the requisite milk shakes. From $12 to $18 for two, with beer. *Open Sun.-Thurs. 11:30 a.m.-10:30 p.m., Fri.-Sat. 11:30 a.m.-11:30 p.m. No cards.*

MEXICAN & CENTRAL AMERICAN

La Cumbre
515 Valencia St.,
Mission District
• 863-8205

In the heart of San Francisco's Hispanic district, La Cumbre serves the best carne asada (marinated grilled beef) burritos in town. With guacamole and sour cream added, these huge burritos will satisfy the biggest hunger—but then you'd have to pass up the incredible quesadillas. The assortment of good Mexican beers is very reasonably priced. Not much more than $10 for two, with beer.
Open Mon.-Sat. 11 a.m.-10 p.m., Sun. noon-9 p.m. No cards.

Los Panchos
3206 Mission St.,
Mission District
• 285-1033

Aficionados of the gordito should consider graduating to its Salvadoran counterpart, the pupusa. A seasoned flour patty that is literally pumped up with cheese and grilled, then (optionally) topped with a spicy coleslaw, the pupusa can serve as a wonderful meal in itself, especially when complemented with a side order of fried plántanos (plantains) and sour cream. Or try a pupusa as an appetizer to preface a dish from Los Panchos's comprehensive and excellent menu of Mexican and Salvadoran food. A couple of pupusas per person, some plántanos and beer will cost about $14 for two.
Open daily 11 a.m.-4 a.m. No cards.

La Taquería
2889 Mission St.,
Mission District
• 285-7117

Most taquerías around these parts follow the dictum "Bigger Is Better." This means overstuffed burritos the size of toddlers. La Taquería breaks the rule, and the lines inevitably flowing out of this modest establishment prove that quality counts as much as quantity, even concerning the lowly burrito. La Taquería shuns rice, offering a lean-and-mean burrito composed of perfectly grilled meats, whole beans and a sprinkling of cilantro. The taco al pastor—two corn tortillas graced with cheese, well-seasoned pork and sprightly salsa—is a gem as well. From $7 to $10 for two with agua (fresh-fruit water) or beer.
Open daily 11 a.m.-8 p.m. No cards.

Taquería San Jose
2830 Mission St.,
Mission District
• 282-0203
3274 24th St.,
Mission District
• 282-7018

Picking the best Mission District burrito house is a highly subjective game, but Taquería San Jose is definitely in the running. The atmosphere may be strictly plastic and florescence, but you can sample burritos stuffed with whole beans, fresh salsa and such unusual but authentic ingredients as lengua (tongue) and meat from the cabeza (head).

For the less adventurous there are the usual ingredients, in ample dosage and handled with care. Also delicious are the small meat sandwiches called tortas. Burritos and beer for two will run about $10.
Open daily 8 a.m.-2 a.m. No cards.

El Tazumal Taquería
3530 20th St.,
Mission District
• 550-1928

Many of the fine Salvadoran and Mexican dishes served at El Tazumal Restaurant next door (see Restaurants) can be sampled at this convenient little taquería. Each of the many regulars has his or her own passionate favorite—ours is the robustly delicious chile relleno burrito. About $10 for two, with a beer.
Open Mon.-Fri. 9 a.m.-8 p.m., Sat. 9 a.m.-7:30 p.m. No cards.

NIGHTLIFE

INTRODUCTION

THE CITY AT NIGHT

"The city that knows how" knows, above all, how to have a good time at night. Concentrated in vibrant pockets throughout the many ethnically, culturally and economically diverse neighborhoods, from the Marina to the outer Mission, the waterfront to the Sunset, San Francisco's nightlife is as rich and eclectic as the city's population. As one of the world's great bar towns, San Francisco has more classy saloons, cozy pubs, boisterous taverns, colorful watering holes and seedy dives than even the natives can fully appreciate. Similarly, a wide variety of nightclubs spans both the hilly geography and the spectrums of music and comedy. But the entertainment clubs don't have an exclusive hold on rock, jazz or humor: many of the city's bars offer live performances. For specific monthly and weekly listings, consult the *Bay Guardian*, *S.F. Weekly*, the *San Francisco Chronicle*'s "Datebook," the *Oakland Tribune*'s "Calendar" and *San Francisco*, *Frisko* and *Focus* magazines.

BARS

Abbey Tavern
4100 Geary Blvd.,
Richmond District
• 221-7767

On any given weekend night, the Abbey Tavern is bursting with a young and boisterous crowd bellying up to the horseshoe-shaped bar for frothy pints of Guinness on tap (kept at basement temperature in true Irish fashion). One of the most popular Irish pubs in the city, the Abbey calms down to a friendly neighborhood pace during the week, when you can actually make conversation or play a casual game of darts. Prepare to stand in line on St. Patrick's Day. *Open daily 11 a.m.-2 a.m. No cards.*

The Albion Club
3139 16th St.,
Mission District
• 621-9213

As with many of San Francisco's classic neighborhood watering holes, the Albion maintains a low profile during the week, with locals splitting time between the bar, the pool table and the jukebox in the corner. This is a perfect place to pause while roaming the Mission. On weekends, expect to see hordes of young, collegiate-looking swells; you can retreat to The Back Room to hear local mavens of

the growing "new acoustic" folk-music and alternative-cabaret scenes.
Open daily 2 p.m.-2 a.m. No cards.

Balboa Café

3199 Fillmore St.,
Marina District
• 921-3944

Everything at the Balboa oozes calculation, from the deliberately nostalgic exterior to the classic fern-bar interior and the yupped-out, late-night cruisers in designer clothes. Tourists can't resist this narrow café and bar, which specializes in hamburgers, nouvelle lunches, coffee and snow-cone drinks. Nor can shoppers from the upscale Union Street boutiques. It's worth the wait for tongue-in-chic people-watching.
Open daily 11 a.m.-2 a.m. All major cards.

The Blue Lamp

516 Geary St.,
Union Square
• 885-1464

The faded satin wall coverings, the cast-off piano bar (with no piano) and the tattered tables and chairs signal a once-grand watering hole gone to seed. Aptly, the early-evening clientele, drawn from the nearby Tenderloin area, has seen better times as well. But on certain nights, The Blue Lamp flickers back to life, as one or another of the musical acts, ranging from oldies rock and blues to "way hip" neocabaret, attracts a young, black-leather-jacketed crowd from South of Market (SOMA) or the Haight. They go elbow-to-elbow against the regulars. If you happen in when Connie Champagne and Her Tiny Bubbles or some other such camp act is holding down the tiny stage, you're in for one of those only-in-San Francisco experiences.
Open daily 10 a.m.-2 a.m. No cards.

The Boondocks

The Embarcadero & Spear
St. (Pier 28),
South of Market
• 777-1588

When the new wave of socially conscious journalists deserted the long-standing Press Club for, among other things, its sexist membership policies, it swept into The Boondocks, going mano-a-mano with the declining population of longshoremen from the nearby docks. The mix at this alternative press club and working-class bar is as refreshing as the salty, foggy breeze blowing in off the Bay.
Open Mon.-Fri. 11 a.m.-9 p.m., Sat. 10:30 a.m.-6 p.m. Cards: MC, V.

Bouncer's Bar

64 Townsend St.,
South of Market
• 397-2480

One of the oldest waterfront bars in the city, Bouncer's retains its blue-collar flavor, even as dockworkers and longshoremen are displaced from the shipping industry by containerized cargo and automation. On weekends, this convivial joint takes on new life with funky live music by such hardworking denizens of the local blues, country and

rock scenes as Lisa Kindred, Twist Turner and Freeway Frank.
Open Sun.-Wed. 11 a.m.-9 p.m., Thurs.-Sat. 11 a.m.-2 a.m. Music Fri.-Sat. 9 p.m., Sun. 3 p.m.-7 p.m. No cards.

Buena Vista
2765 Hyde St.,
North Beach
• 474-5044

Legend has it that the ever-crowded "Bee Vee" introduced Irish coffee to San Francisco in 1953. Now, it reputedly serves 1,700 of the drinks a day to the tourists who jam the round oak tables and crowd up to the old mahogany bar. Overlooking the Bay, close to Ghirardelli Square, the Cannery and Fisherman's Wharf, this plainly decorated, turn-of-the-century café is as much a tourist attraction as it is a bar, so expect the resultant hubbub.
Open Mon.-Fri. 9 a.m.-2 p.m., Sat.-Sun. 8 a.m.-2 a.m. No cards.

Carnelian Room
Bank of America Bldg.,
555 California St.,
Financial District
• 433-7500

As long as height limits are maintained on new construction, no bar will challenge the panoramic view from the Carnelian Room. From an elevation of 780 feet (53 floors), the vistas are so breathtaking that it might take you a while to notice the spectacular interior decor of European art and antiques. The prices of everything, especially the food, are as sky-high as the setting; dress codes (jackets and ties for men) are enforced in the evening. But there's no better way to see the Golden Gate Bridge, the Pacific Ocean, the Marin hills and the city itself while sipping a cocktail.
Open Mon.-Fri. 3 p.m.-12:30 a.m., Sat. 4 p.m.-1:30 a.m., Sun. 10 a.m.-12:30 a.m. Cards: AE, MC, V.

Deluxe
1511 Haight St.,
Haight-Ashbury
• 552-6949

The gentrification of Haight-Ashbury might be symbolized by the sleek, sculpted metal doors of the Deluxe. Deco-consciousness abounds, from the streamlined exterior to the black-and-silver interior. And the clientele is dominated by the most recent émigrés to the former hippie haven—young, well-heeled trendoids. It adds up to a visually intriguing alternative to the run-of-the-gin-mill neighborhood bar.
Open daily 2 p.m.-2 a.m. No cards.

Dovre Club
3541 18th St.,
Mission District
• 552-0074

Without losing its neighborhood flavor, the Dovre offers a heady brew of politics—Irish Republican, feminist, local radical—and a forgettable decor. Journalist Warren Hinckle said of the Dovre, "It smells the way a bar ought to smell—like a toilet." You don't have to raise your glass to "Patrick's Irish Toast" posted above the door ("Let's drink to the final defeat of the British army in Northern Ireland")

to enjoy this unpretentious hangout. Not everyone talks politics; you can shoot pool with friendly folks or take a turn at Irish step dancing. Drinks are good and reasonably priced.
Open daily 8 a.m.-2 a.m. No cards.

Eagle Café
Pier 39, #201,
Fisherman's Wharf
• 433-3689

A small miracle of redevelopment along the Embarcadero was the preservation of the Eagle Café, since 1928 the best real saloon on the waterfront. Sure, they had to move it across the street and replant it amid the plastic tourist schlock of Pier 39, but the interior remains unchanged and the prices are shockingly fair. Among the cafeteria-style breakfast and lunch dishes, the corned beef hash is legendary. Outdoor seating brings the Bay view into your lap, and there are still plenty of old salts around to bend your ear with tall tales from the sea.
Open Mon.-Thurs. 7 a.m.-2:30 p.m. & 5 p.m.-9:30 p.m., Fri. 7 a.m.-2:30 p.m. & 5 p.m.-2 a.m., Sat.-Sun. 7 a.m.-3 p.m. & 5 p.m.-2 a.m. No cards.

Edinburgh Castle
950 Geary Blvd.,
Union Square
• 885-4074

Delicious fish and chips that the waiter orders for you from the Old Chelsea around the corner arrives wrapped in newspaper. Malt vinegar stands in bottles on the tables. Darts are thrown perpetually on the back mezzanine. Bartenders pull rich drafts of Bass, Watney's, John Courage, Guinness and the local favorite, half & half (ale and stout). Unblended single-malt whiskies are available. The convivial, countryside pub atmosphere is accented by old, heavy wooden tables, beamed ceilings, intimate balconies, Scottish knickknacks and British memorabilia. The jukebox is thick with music from the British Isles. And the tavern is large enough to accommodate hearty crowds. It all adds up to one of the most delightful and relatively untouristed establishments in the Bay Area.
Open Mon.-Fri. 5 p.m.-2 a.m., Sat. 4:30 p.m.-2 a.m., Sun. 4:30 p.m.-1 a.m. No cards.

L'Etoile
Huntington Hotel,
1075 California St.,
Nob Hill
• 771-1529

A meeting place for the rich and famous, this subterranean bar in the posh Huntington Hotel is an extension of the equally famous and social restaurant. The safari motif and the stiff prices are a bit much, but the music of brilliant cocktail pianist Peter Mintun and the chance to hobnob with high society more than compensate. One could not overdress for L'Etoile.
Open Mon.-Sat. 5:30 p.m.-midnight. All major cards.

Harrington's Bar & Grill
245 Front St.,
Financial District
• 392-7595

Not to be confused with similarly named Irish bars (Herrington's on Jones and Harrington's Harry Pub on Larkin), this large, two-room, two-bar watering hole is mobbed at 5 p.m., and the singles action is heavy in the early evening. Despite the Financial District location, the clientele includes plenty of casually dressed folk, and when the after-work crowd thins, Harrington's becomes an easy-going hangout where the Irish whisky flows generously. *Open Mon.-Tues. 9 a.m.-10 p.m., Wed.-Thurs. 9 a.m.-11 p.m., Fri. 9 a.m.-1 a.m., Sat. 11:30 a.m.-7:30 p.m. No cards.*

House of Shields
39 New Montgomery St.,
Financial District
• 392-7732

When director Wim Wenders wanted to shoot in a bar that would pass as John's Grill in the film *Hammett*, he eschewed the original, which still exists, in favor of the House of Shields. Indeed, you get the feeling that you're stepping back into the 1920s or '30s, or even earlier, when you toddle into this classic drinking spot. The setting is comfortingly reminiscent of a bygone golden era: large curved booths and ornate light fixtures, waiters in formal wear who don't introduce themselves with "Hi, I'm Chuck and I'll be serving you tonight," stuffed big-game heads, a replica of the old Comstock Bar from the nearby Palace Hotel, even spittoons. One comes here to sip and sit leisurely (but not on bar stools, as there are none) and to chat amicably (not to watch TV, as there is none). *Open Mon.-Fri. 9 a.m.-10 p.m. Cards: AE, MC, V.*

Ireland's 32
3920 Geary Blvd.,
Richmond District
• 386-6173

If northern and southern Ireland were reunited, there would be 32 counties, which explains the name of this popular Irish pub, and gives a good indication of the strong IRA tilt. It also indicates that the crowd is a no-frills assemblage of neighborhood folk and Irish devotees who will cross the city for a pint of Guinness and good conversation. *Open daily 11 a.m.-2 a.m. Cards: AE, DC.*

Jay 'n' Bee
2736 20th St.,
Mission District
• 648-0518

Looking for a slice of down-to-earth neighborhood life in a San Francisco bar? You'll find it at this bustling, unadorned tavern—in its crowded, narrow tables, ample breakfasts, hearty lunches and boisterous crowd of neighborhood workers, cops on the beat and journalists from the alternative weekly newspaper, the *Bay Guardian*, which is around the corner. Once people start hanging out here, they tend to remain loyal, but the atmosphere welcomes

ABSOLUT
SAN FRANCISCO.

GAULT MILLAU
BOLD, SOPHISTICATED GUIDES
TO THE BEST OF THE VERY BEST

Titles Available:

THE BEST OF CHICAGO
THE BEST OF NEW ENGLAND
THE BEST OF FRANCE
THE BEST OF HAWAII
THE BEST OF HONG KONG
THE BEST OF ITALY
THE BEST OF LONDON
THE BEST OF LOS ANGELES
THE BEST OF NEW ORLEANS
THE BEST OF NEW YORK
THE BEST OF PARIS
THE BEST OF SAN FRANCISCO
THE BEST OF WASHINGTON, D.C.

newcomers.
Open Mon.-Fri. 6 a.m.-10 p.m., Sat. 7 a.m.-9 p.m., Sun. 8 a.m.-7 p.m. No cards.

Lascaux
248 Sutter St.,
Union Square
• 391-1555

Although both sides of the Bay offer plenty of first-rate, all-star jazz, such intimate venues as Lascaux allow gifted local talents to keep bread on the table. (Fine lunches and dinners are served here.) Perhaps the most remarkable feature of this fine bar and rotisserie is the nightly rotation of pianists, guitarists, reed players and singers. Such names as Tee Carson, Dick Conte, Mark Levine, Eddie Duran and Joyce Cooling may not mean much to most tourists, but without them the pulse of San Francisco jazz would disappear.
Open Mon.-Fri. 11:30 a.m.-midnight, Sat. 5 p.m.-midnight. Cards: AE, MC, V.

The Little Shamrock
807 Lincoln Way,
Sunset District
• 661-0060

The Great Earthquake of 1906 took down walls here in the Sunset District, but The Little Shamrock cashed in a bit of its Irish luck and stood its ground. This genuine survivor has been in the same location since 1893. The oldtime decor includes a clock that stopped ticking during the earthquake, along with the original bar and back bar. On weekend afternoons, athletic types spill in from the softball fields and bicycle paths in Golden Gate Park, but it's still easy to find a quiet nook in which to play backgammon, dice or darts, or to simply sink into a reverie on one of the living room couches in the alcove.
Open daily 3 p.m.-2 a.m. No cards.

Mission Rock Resort
817 China Basin St.,
China Basin
• 621-5538

Hardly a bar that you would run across by accident, the Mission Rock is tucked among the piers and dry docks south of the Bay Bridge, far removed from the tourist traps of Fisherman's Wharf and Pier 39. Here you'll find an assortment of fishermen, longshoremen, shipbuilders and anyone with a good nose for a great waterfront hangout. From the two outdoor decks, better sheltered from the breezes than points north, you can look out across the Bay or down along the docks and watch a working waterfront, not a Disneylandish replica.
Downstairs bar: open daily 7 a.m.-7 p.m. (closing time varies); upstairs bar: open daily 8 a.m.-2 a.m. Cards: AE, MC, V.

Le Montmartre

2125 Lombard St.,
Marina District
• 563-4618

This attractive Marina bistro combines a romantically French environment with seductive live Brazilian music played by several of the Bay Area's splendid Latin jazz and pop bands. Attracting a wonderfully international crowd of Europeans and South Americans—and, of course, French sailors when their ships are in port—Le Montmartre is decorated with Parisian dioramas and features a jukebox stocked with the dreamy vocals of Edith Piaf, Charles Aznavour and others.
Open nightly 4 p.m.-2 a.m. No cards.

Lefty O'Doul's

333 Geary Blvd.,
Union Square
• 982-8900

Before the Giants moved here from New York, the home-town baseball team was the minor league Seals, and Frank J. "Lefty" O'Doul was one of the city's great sports heroes. This old-fashioned bar and cafeteria, suitable for the entire family, is rife with baseball lore and memorabilia, including fascinating photographs of Lefty—with Dizzy Dean, Joe DiMaggio, Gen. Douglas MacArthur—and other legends. Hof brau–style sandwiches and generous hot dishes complete the homey atmosphere.
Open daily 8 a.m.-2 a.m. No cards.

Pat O'Shea's Mad Hatter

3754 Geary Blvd.,
Richmond District
• 752-3148

With three satellite dishes, nine 25-inch televisions and sports memorabilia galore, Pat O'Shea's is one of San Francisco's premier sports bars, impossibly crowded when the 49ers are on the tube. But football jocks aren't the only patrons. In the evening, University of San Francisco students make this a regular hangout; at lunchtime, it fills up with neighborhood workers drawn by the cheap pints of brew and outstanding corned beef sandwiches; several nights a week local blues and rock bands play for dancing.
Open daily 10 a.m.-1:30 a.m. No cards.

Paradise Lounge

11th & Folsom,
South of Market
• 861-6906

As the South of Market (SOMA) area remakes itself into a self-important haven of hipness, the folks at the Paradise refuse to take the scene too seriously. The young crowd, spinning off the neighborhood's burgeoning new music scene, sport ultra-cool fashions and geometric haircuts. But the nightly no-cover-charge entertainment (Sunday through Thursday nights)—including jazz, pop cabaret and tap dancing—adds an offbeat lounge-lizard touch. The hors d'oeuvres are free, and the drinks come in chilled glasses. On Fridays and Saturdays, the cover is $3, and the performers leap from the city's huge reservoir of rising stars. The Paradise has been a primary hotbed of the neofolk music scene. Hey, if Paradise isn't lofty enough for you,

more music and spoken-word acts are offered upstairs in Above Paradise.
Open daily 1 p.m.-2 a.m. Cover varies Fri.-Sat. No cards.

Paul's Saloon

3251 Scott St.,
Marina District
• 922-2456

Paul's is the only bluegrass bar in the city. It features a cozy and unpretentious bar with a fireplace and a friendly, casually dressed clientele. Banjos, guitars, mandolins and fiddles send their jittery, swinging sounds into the air, inspiring infectious grins and uninhibited foot stomping. There's no need to dress up—just come ready to absorb some of the best locally produced "high lonesome" harmonies and down-home pickin'.
Open daily 3 p.m.-2 a.m. Shows nightly 9 p.m.-12:30 a.m. No cards.

Perry's

1944 Union St.,
Pacific Heights/
Marina District
• 922-9022

Because it's famous for several reasons, this bar and restaurant is always jammed. Recommended in the original *Preppy Handbook* as a premier pickup spot, Perry's is crawling with upscale singles in the evening, some of whom come to spot the politicos and celebrities in action. Others are drawn by the rather expensive, but reliably good, American food—breakfasts and brunches, burgers, chicken, soups—in the back dining room. Unlike the city's most famous fern bars, Henry Africa's (on Van Ness) and Lord Jim's (on Broadway), Perry's has a broad-based appeal—thus the constant crush.
Open daily 9 a.m.-midnight. Cards: AE, MC, V.

Persian Aub Zam Zam

1633 Haight St.,
Haight-Ashbury
• 861-2545

Don't tell Bruno that you heard about his splendid oasis from a guidebook. Don't be in a rush, and don't flop down on the couches in the cozy back alcove and expect gracious service. But appreciate the Persian Aub Zam Zam for what it is, and you'll experience one of the most perfect bars in San Francisco. His father opened the place more than 40 years ago, and as he will tell you in his curmudgeonly commentaries, Bruno has seen the Haight-Ashbury neighborhood evolve (or disintegrate) around him ever since. His specialty is the martini (although he can't get his favorite British Plymouth gin anymore), and he looks down on "Madison Avenue" brands and frilly concoctions. The dimly lit decor is softly soothing, and the jukebox is full of sweet, swinging music from the big-band era. The entire windowless bar, from the arched doorways and tiered liquor shelves to the romantic mural behind the bar and Bruno

himself, is a classic.
Open Mon., Wed., Fri. & Sat. 4 p.m.-2 a.m. (Closing time varies.) No cards.

The Plough and Stars
116 Clement St.,
Richmond District
• 751-1122

No Irish pub crawl would be complete without a stop at this no-frills, no-nonsense, music-oriented bar. The crowd is an unpretentious mix of Irish nationalists, serious drinkers from the old country and blue-jeaned young folk from the neighborhood. The biggest attraction is the evocative live and recorded Irish music—the best airs, reels and jigs in the city, for listening or dancing.
Open daily noon-2 a.m. No cards.

Redwood Room
Four Seasons Clift Hotel,
495 Geary St.,
Union Square
• 775-4700

Located in the grand old Clift Hotel, this elegantly appointed room is a classic. The high ceilings, the gorgeous dark wood, the art deco lighting fixtures and furnishings, the majestic paintings, the brass railings and the beveled glass all come together to create an aura of impeccable class. Union Square conventioneers, elderly women dressed up for the afternoon, hotel guests and tourists fill up the comfortable chairs and soak in the grand style.
Open daily 11 a.m.-3 p.m. & 4:30 p.m.-1 a.m. All major cards.

The Rite Spot
2099 Folsom,
Mission District
• 552-6066

Ask around and you'll find that The Rite Spot is one of the favorite bars of the most unlikely people, and thus the clientele is diverse and unpredictable. The afternoon regulars play liars' dice with the bartender. The weeknight crowd includes folks dispersing from the Mission District clubs and theaters. On weekends, the few designer-attired suburbanoids who've discovered this art bar come by, hoping to absorb some of its bohemian flavor. But The Rite Spot's hipness is its lack of deliberate hipness. Now and then the jukebox yields to live music at the piano.
Open Mon.-Fri. 1:30 p.m.-2 a.m., Sat.-Sun. 7 p.m.-2 a.m. No cards.

La Rocca's Corner Tavern
957 Columbus Ave.,
North Beach
• 441-9260

While the original charm of North Beach corrodes under new coats of pastel paint, while old Italian family businesses are displaced by franchise ice cream, cookie and pizza joints, and while the characters who are the human face of that charm lose ground to lawyers, accountants and real-estate developers, La Rocca's remains a holdout for neighborhood integrity. Art Institute students clad in black hang out with old North Beachers, and tourists weave through without upsetting the balance. The delicate equilibrium is main-

tained by an earnest atmosphere, timeworn decor and a jukebox that appeals to all ages and tastes. People have even been seen dancing cheek-to-cheek here.
Open Sun.-Thurs. noon-midnight, Fri.-Sat. noon-2 a.m. No cards.

Roland's
3309 Fillmore St.,
Marina District
• 567-1063

Something more than a bar, and yet not quite a full-fledged jazz club, Roland's fills a unique niche in the city. The music is always live, played by an array of Bay Area artists often accompanied by versatile saxophonist Jules Broussard. From bebop to pop fusion, salsa to soul, the music is always bright and swinging, occasionally spelled by stand-up comedy. The crowd is lively.
Open nightly 4 p.m.-2 a.m. Cover $6 Thurs.-Sat. Cards: AE.

Saloon
1232 Grant Ave.,
North Beach
• 989-7666

Sometimes called the 1232, this venerable North Beach institution has become a haven for hippie holdovers, where musicians from the golden era of San Francisco rock bands (Quicksilver Messenger Service, Country Joe and the Fish, Big Brother and the Holding Company) can work out with new bands in front of fans who knew them when. The musical mainstay is blues, just as gritty and raw as the setting dictates. The bar itself is even more of a survivor than the clientele, having been around since 1861. It doesn't quite look every year of its age, but it has a distinct Beat and pre-Beat character.
Open Mon.-Sat. 9 p.m.-2 a.m., Sun. 4 p.m.-2 a.m. No cards.

Specs' Twelve Adler Museum Café
12 Adler St.,
North Beach
• 421-4112

In recent years, a few stalwarts have attempted to re-create the golden age of jazz in North Beach, and Specs' has been one of the most successful attempts. Not that this colorful little off-Columbus bar needs bebop jam sessions to add any character—the locals and regulars supply plenty of that. Brick walls slanting narrowly off the alley are practically hidden beneath humorous signs and arcane memorabilia from Barbary Coast days, and old black-and-white photographs capture the images of the neighborhood's heyday. Once you've settled into this comfortable, salty, sometimes loud and rowdy dive, you'll feel the modern era fade away.
Open Mon.-Fri. 4:30 p.m.-2 a.m., Sat.-Sun. 5 p.m.-2 a.m. No cards.

Tommy's Joynt
1101 Geary Blvd.,
Van Ness
• 775-4216

You can spot Tommy's Joynt from three blocks away, so bold and tasteless is the giant lettering splashed across the outside walls. But for all its tourist-trap trappings and precious bric-a-brac, Tommy's is a funky and genuine hof

brau with a terrific selection of more than 90 beers and a hearty menu famous for buffalo stew, bean 'n' beer soup and thick sandwiches.
Open daily 10 a.m.-2 a.m. No cards.

Tosca Café
242 Columbus Ave.,
North Beach
• 986-9651

Sometimes on weekends, when the place is hopping, the dance-beat thumps from the disco downstairs obliterate the grand sounds from Tosca's famous jukebox. The opera records add one more element of old-world charm to this classic North Beach hangout. Weeknights are quieter and therefore better for a casual drop-in. Slide into one of the old leather booths and settle in for a legendary cappuccino, made here with chocolate, steamed milk and brandy. Or design your own coffee drink and see what name the friendly waiter gives it.
Open nightly 7 p.m.-2 a.m. No cards.

Vesuvio Café
255 Columbus Ave.,
North Beach
• 362-3370

Although North Beach boasts precious few reminders of the Beat era, when Kerouac, Ginsberg, Corso and others scrawled or read their poetry in the bookstores and cafés, the Vesuvio has hardly changed since it opened in 1949. Located near Lawrence Ferlinghetti's City Lights Bookstore, this delightfully casual bar is appropriately dark and cozy, with a balcony for people-watchers and an abundance of nooks where you can settle in for a long, comfortable stay. Poets and chess players are always in evidence, and tourist fascination with the authentic bohemianism seems to have subsided.
Open daily 6 a.m.-2 a.m. No cards.

Washington Square Bar & Grill
1707 Powell St.,
North Beach
• 982-8123

Ed Moose's famed restaurant, just off picturesque Washington Square, is notable for its solid and dependable Italian menu, but the bar is legendary for the steady clientele of writers, reporters, lawyers and politicians. The "Washbag" is typically packed with this neatly attired professional crowd, standing around the long bar, which is hosted by especially friendly barkeeps. But even more rewarding than the celebrity-gazing is the music supplied by a rotating crew of superb pianists, particularly Norma Teagarden, rollicking keyboard sister of the late, great trombonist Jack, and Harlem stride specialist Mike Lipskin, the city's finest saloon pianist, who re-creates the sounds and aura of the 1920s and '30s through music inspired by Fats Waller and James P. Johnson.
Open Mon.-Fri. 11:30 a.m.-midnight, Sat. 11:30 a.m.-2 a.m., Sun. 10 a.m.-midnight. All major cards.

CABARET

Cirque Room
950 Mason St.,
Fairmont Hotel,
Nob Hill
• 772-5163

With the demise of the legendary Venetian Room, squeezed out by changing demographics and more cost-efficient jazz and rock clubs, the Cirque remains the Fairmont's contribution to the city's cabaret scene. Mostly local performers of jazz and pop standards, along with occasional comic repartee, are featured in the cocktail hour and after-dinner shows.
Shows Mon.-Sat. 5:30 p.m. & 9 p.m. No cover. All major cards.

Club Fugazi
678 Green St.,
North Beach
• 421-4222

In its sixteenth year and its umpteenth incarnation, Steve Silver's "Beach Blanket Babylon" is still wowing the tourists and the local repeats who can't get enough of the high-camp song-and-dance routines. First it went "Bananas," then "To the Moon," and now BBB "Goes Around the World," featuring zany tunes, outrageous costumes and world-record-breaking hats. The Fugazi is an old North Beach Italian music hall that has retained its cozy charm amid the frenetic off-off-off-Broadway antics of the talented Babylon cast. Minors are admitted to the Sunday matinee only.
Shows Wed.-Thurs. 8 p.m., Fri.-Sat. 8 p.m. & 10:30 p.m., Sun. 3 p.m. & 7:30 p.m. Tickets $12-$25. Cards: MC, V.

Finocchio's
506 Broadway,
North Beach
• 982-9388

Long before San Francisco's gay population burst out of the closet, the female impersonators at Finocchio's were all the rage. And even though the novelty of cross-dressing has worn off with the jaded citizenry, and campy stage drag has been raised almost to the level of art by Charles Pierce, Finocchio's is still a prime nightlife attraction, especially for busloads of voyeuristic tourists. Don't expect to be ignored when the "ladies" start flapping through the house. There's no drink minimum.
Open Tues. & Thurs.-Sun. 8 p.m.-1:30 a.m. Shows Tues. & Thurs.-Sun. 9 p.m., 10:20 p.m. & 11:40 p.m. Cover $10. No cards.

Plush Room
York Hotel, 940 Sutter St.,
Union Square
• 885-6800

For all of San Francisco's vaunted sophistication, cabaret is a risky business here. Just look at the checkered career of the lovely and appropriately named Plush Room. Tucked into the small, understated elegance of the York Hotel, this true cabaret was up and down in the '80s, but as it heads into the '90s it holds on to the belief that an audience exists for the type of cool, intelligent entertainment it presents. If the stream of New York singers specializing in Gershwin, Porter, Coward, Berlin and Sondheim dries up, San Francisco can supply such fine and sensitive vocalists as the remarkable Weslia Whitfield. There's a two-drink minimum.

Shows Tues.-Thurs. 8:30 p.m., Fri.-Sat. 8 p.m. & 10:30 p.m., Sun. 8 p.m. Cover varies. All major cards.

Zephyr Theatre
25 Van Ness Ave.,
Civic Center
• 861-6895

For more than three years, a lively company of four has been making light of bachelors and bachelorettes through the delightful melodies and incisive lyrics of songwriter Morris Bobrow. The revue is called "Party of One," and in a city where the single life is sometimes elevated to a world view, this cockeyed celebration of unwedded bliss is particularly appropriate.

Shows Fri. 8 p.m., Sat. 7 p.m. & 9 p.m. Cards: MC, V.

COMEDY

San Francisco has long been a hotbed of stand-up comedy, from the North Beach days of Lenny Bruce, Mort Sahl, the Smothers Brothers and others through the meteoric rise of Robin Williams and Whoopi Goldberg. Although there are only a few pure comedy clubs, many bars and music clubs include comics in their bookings. So you can choose whether to see a novice get his or her stage feet in an out-of-the-way bar or be entertained by a TV-ready comic with loads of confidence. Also, the annual San Francisco Comedy Competition, a springboard to national attention, runs for several months at various venues throughout the summer and fall season; check newspaper listings for details.

Cobb's Comedy Club
The Cannery, 2801 Leavenworth St.,
Fisherman's Wharf
• 928-4320

The Monday night showcase at this simple, 200-seat club is one of the best places to hear San Francisco's aspiring comics. For only five bucks you get ten to twelve comedians in a genuine hybrid of styles that steer pretty clear of the sophomoric anatomical standbys of all too many stand-ups. National headliners are featured the rest of week, with strong opening and middle supporting acts. The bar is located far enough away from the stage so the show takes precedence. A nonsmoking section is available, and a sepa-

rate restaurant, Cafe Zero, is accessible before the shows and serves food in the club as well.
Shows Mon. 8 p.m., Tues.-Thurs. & Sun. 9 p.m., Fri. 9 p.m. & 11 p.m., Sat. 7 p.m., 9 p.m. & 11 p.m. Cover varies. Cards: MC, V.

Holy City Zoo
408 Clement St.,
Richmond District
• 386-4242

In the guise of a homey neighborhood bar, woody and informal, the Zoo functions as a breeding and training ground for the city's immense brood of stand-up comics. You can't expect Robin Williams to show up unannounced and improvise for half an hour (although it's not out of the realm of possibility), but you can count on witty material being worked out by a variety of crazy characters. In addition to regular showcases, the Zoo hosts the Tuesday open-mike night, the Monday night "Talk Show" and the best students from its own stand-up workshop. There's usually a two-drink minimum.
Shows Sun.-Thurs. 9 p.m., Fri.-Sat. 9 p.m. & 11 p.m. Cover $2-$7. Cards: MC, V.

Improv
401 Mason St.,
Nob Hill
• 441-7787

Although it is stamped out of a national mold like a franchise restaurant, the Improv, billing itself as "America's Original Comedy Showcase," has become a valuable addition to the local comedy scene. Located in the basement of the old City Cabaret, it is plugged firmly into the national circuit, featuring higher-profile, TV-exposed comics four nights week. On Mondays, up-and-coming locals take their turn in front of the plain brick wall and the slashing neon "Improv" sign. The local showcase is a notch or two above the open-mike approach, which often leaves both performer and audience embarrassed. You can expect solid performances in an intimate setting.
Shows Mon. 8 p.m., Tues., Thurs. & Sun. 9 p.m., Fri.-Sat. 9 p.m. & 11 p.m. Cards: AE, MC, V.

Punch Line
444 Battery St.,
Financial District
• 397-7573

As local comics climb the ladder of success, they pass through the Punch Line, San Francisco's most "professional" comedy club. Part of entertainment baron Bill Graham's nightlife empire, the slick, brick-walled, comfortable club presents some of San Francisco's most polished performers, along with amateur showcases, an open-mike night on Sundays and a "Comedy Underground Night." It is also one of the regular sites for the annual Comedy Competition. Mexican food, pizza, deli sandwiches and snacks are available, and there's a two-drink minimum.

Open Tues.-Sun. 7:45 p.m.-1:30 a.m. Shows Tues.-Thurs. &
Sun. 9 p.m., Fri.-Sat. 9 p.m. & 11 p.m. Cover $4-$8. Cards:
MC, V.

Rose and Thistle Upstairs
1624 California St.,
Polk Gulch
• 771-3866

For a closer look at the grass roots of Bay Area comedy, drop into this rather barn-like, weekend-only club, where the mix of borderline professionals and talented improvisors keeps the comedy quotient unpredictable. Some of the performers are greener than the hills of Ireland, but many of the theme shows are right on the mark. The emphasis is on improvisational comedy, anchored by the Improv Irregulars and others, and an element of surprise is ensured by the drop-in local showcase. There's a two-drink minimum, and you must be 21 or older.
Shows Fri.-Sat. 7 p.m. & 9 p.m. Cover $5. No cards.

DANCING

Bahia
1600 Market St.,
Civic Center
• 861-8657

The latest wave of world-beat music to wash across the Bay Area is Brazilian, hence the rise of this authentic "Tropical Brazilian Club," where the music is live and the emphasis is on sultry movement. Such persuasively polyrhythmic performers as Viva Brasil and Celia Malherios create the mesmerizing sambas, breathy ballads and lilting Brazilian jazz that lift patrons off their seats and propel them to the dance floor.
Open daily 4 p.m.-2 a.m.; live music Sun.-Thurs. 9 p.m.-1 a.m., Fri.-Sat. 9:30 p.m.-1:30 a.m. Cover varies. Cards: MC, V.

Cesar's Palace
3140 Mission St.,
Mission District
• 648-6611

This large, lively club in the city's predominantly Hispanic outer Mission District offers a spacious dance floor, a colorfully mixed crowd and the best Latin music in the Bay Area. Cesar's Latin All-Stars, the brassy house band of master musicians, churns out a variety of Afro-Cuban polyrhythmic dance beats. Once in a while, great salsa and Latin jazz artists from New York appear.
Open Thurs. 8 p.m.-2 a.m., Fri.-Sun. 9 p.m.-6 a.m. Cover $6. Sunday tea dances noon-5 p.m. (free for seniors). No cards.

City Nights
715 Harrison St.,
South of Market
• 546-7774

This large, splashy and highly popular SOMA disco attracts all kinds of dancers for specialized nights of classic and up-to-the-minute (but sometimes less-than-cutting-edge) music, often designed and sponsored by the city's big FM radio stations. KMEL hosts modern rock; KSOL puts on a "Night at the Apollo." More mainstream than some of the other trendy spots, but still demanding hip dress, City Nights devotes other evenings to funk and Top 40. The Sunday feature is the "Dreamland" gay tea dance. *Open Wed.-Sun. 6:30 p.m.-6 a.m. No cards.*

Club Metropolis
1484 Market St.,
South of Market
• 621-5001

A sparkling addition to the uncontrollably burgeoning South of Market scene, this large complex is aimed slightly above the middle of the road—"casually elegant attire required"—but does not aspire to being a clone of the hipper-than-thou arty nightspots that triggered the SOMA movement. It features a very big dance floor, large booths for lounging, excellent loud sound and a young crowd that follows the dress code. *Open Mon.-Fri. 11 a.m.-2 a.m., Sat. 8 p.m.-2 a.m. Cover $5 Fri.-Sat. Cards: MC, V.*

Firehouse 7
3160 16th St.,
Mission District
• 621-1617

A long, narrow, high-ceilinged club that indeed was once a neighborhood fire station, Firehouse 7 pioneered the Bay Area's early world-beat scene by featuring an international dance mix of reggae, calypso, soca, Brazilian and African pop. The same cosmopolitan vision continues to break down barriers between national music styles, combining soul, funk and postmodern rock/reggae into the steaming stew that keeps folks hopping and the spirits congenial. *Open daily noon-2 a.m.; dancing begins at 9:30 p.m. Cover $2 Sun. No cards.*

I-Beam
1748 Haight St.,
Haight-Ashbury
• 668-6006

When it's not the live showcase for cutting-edge rock bands from around the world (see "Music Clubs" in this chapter), the Beam is San Francisco's premier new-wave dance club, with the emphasis on *new*. Deejays throughout the city thrive on one-upmanship, and here they pride themselves on playing the latest discs from the underground. The music is ultra-modern, from industrial to acid house and whatever comes next. The sound is loud and steely, consistent with the dizzying laser and light shows, flashing videos and silver-and-black industrial decor. The crowd is young, hip, dressed in black and sometimes as concerned with haircuts as with music. *Open Tues.-Sat. 9 p.m.-2 a.m., Sun. 5 p.m.-2 a.m. Cover varies; students admitted free Wed.-Thurs. No cards.*

Kennel Club

628 Divisadero St.,
Golden Gate Panhandle
• 931-1914

When it's not hosting underground or college-radio rock bands, this minimally decorated box-like club throbs with hot tracks for hip dancers. On Fridays and Sundays Doug Wendt, the Bay Area's foremost reggae deejay, shows unusual videos and spins current and classic discs from Jamaica, New Orleans, Trinidad, Nigeria, Zaire, Algeria and other sources of world beat. On Fridays and Sundays, the Kennel Club becomes The Box, a gay disco pulsating to funk and soul.
Open Tues.-Sun. 9 p.m.-2 a.m. Cover varies. No cards.

New Orleans Room

Fairmont Hotel,
California & Mason sts.,
Nob Hill
• 772-5259

Once home to the legendary San Francisco trombonist and bandleader Turk Murphy, the New Orleans Room now showcases Don Neely's Royal Society Sextet, which swings its way through classic dance arrangements of old-time Crescent City jazz from the 1920s and 1930s. Patronized by upscale tourists who can afford the steep Nob Hill drink tabs, along with unrepentant fans of pre-Depression sounds, the New Orleans Room is a class joint for Prohibition-era hoofers.
Open Tues.-Sat. 6 p.m.-2 a.m. Shows 9:30 p.m.-1:30 a.m. Cover $3. All major cards.

Oasis

278 11th St. (at Folsom St.),
South of Market
• 621-8119

One of the pioneering ventures of the SOMA renaissance, the Oasis is a former motel transformed into a new-wave entertainment and dining complex. During the warm season, the Plexiglas dance floor is taken off the swimming pool for Friday afternoon "Weekend Warm-Ups." At night, the fairly funky (with aspirations toward industrial chic) multiroom club hosts a young, hip dancing and drinking crowd, with a soundtrack of new rock, urban funk and Top-100 dance hits. Wednesday nights are especially worthwhile: roots rock and blues bands shake the sliding glass doors for free. There's a two-drink minimum.
Open for dancing Tues.-Sun. 8 p.m.-3 a.m.; open for lunch Mon.-Fri. 11 a.m.-3 p.m. Cover $3 after 9 p.m. No cards.

Palladium

1031 Kearny,
North Beach
• 434-1308

When the urge to dance strikes you late at night in North Beach, head for the Palladium, which offers loud Top 40, alternative dance, funk, soul and rock tunes until dawn. A holdover from the disco era, this garish, thumping club attracts young suburbanites and tourists, feeding them a constant diet of surging rhythms and flashing videos.
Open Wed.-Sun. 9 p.m.-6 a.m. Cover $7. No cards.

Rockin' Robin's

1840 Haight St.,
Haight-Ashbury
• 221-1960

Particularly popular with the *Big Chill*dren of the baby-boom era, this casual and funky Haight-Ashbury club has live deejays spinning old platters from the golden age of rock and roll. Specializing in '50s and '60s oldies, they play rockabilly, Motown, R & B, soul and vintage rock. In addition to videos, pinball machines, free shuffleboard and tequila nights on Sundays, the amusements include dancing bartenders. (A downtown branch has been added at 133 Beale Street.)
Open daily noon-2 a.m. Cover $1-$3 (after 9 p.m.). No cards.

The Stone

412 Broadway,
North Beach
• 391-8282[Stone]

After the live heavy metal, hard-rock and new-wave shows are over, young devotees of all of the above head for "Club 412" at The Stone, an after-hours dance club that showcases very loud deejay rock and a bright panorama of videos. Its once-seedy decor has been transformed by lots of black paint. There's a small bar in the back corner, tiered tables for taking a breather and a large dance floor for bouncing around to the latest sounds.
Open for dancing Sat. 11:15 p.m.-6 a.m. Cover $8. No cards.

JAZZ

Bajones

1062 Valencia St.,
Mission District
• 282-2522

John Bajones has made his popular neighborhood bar something of a chameleon on the local jazz scene by vacillating in his booking policy between pop-oriented dance bands and straight-ahead acoustic jazz. Located just a heartbeat away from the center of the city's Mission District, Bajones is roomy and neighborly, with good sound and a vibrant, ethnically mixed clientele. Live Latin music, rock, blues and funk are the commercial mainstays, but top-flight jazz musicians appear on an irregular basis.
Open nightly 6 p.m.-2 a.m. Shows 9:30 p.m. Cover $4-$5. No cards.

Kimball's

300 Grove St.,
Civic Center
• 861-5555

When the near-legendary Keystone Korner closed in the early '80s, Jane and Kimball Allen turned their restaurant into the city's premier jazz club. The economics of jazz have occasionally reeked havoc with bookings, but the Allens have persevered, moving the listening room upstairs and sticking to a policy of three- to five-night runs of mid- to

top-flight acts, as well as supporting the local jazz community with special nights organized by the grass-roots Jazz in Flight and Bright Moments Music Club organizations. The blockbuster shows have been shifted to the magnificent Kimball's East (see review following). Hoping to draw in the jazz crowd while not alienating the toney clientele that drops in after the opera, ballet or symphony around the corner, Kimball's offers mostly mainstream jazz in a Californian cuisine setting of blond wood and decently priced drinks. Artfully presented dinners and snacks from the oyster bar are available.
Open Tues.-Sat. 11:30 a.m.-1 a.m. & occasionally Sun.-Mon. for lunch or music. Cards: AE, MC, V.

Kimball's East
5800 Shellmound Ave.,
Emeryville
• 658-2555

The foundation of Jane and Kimball Allen's enterprise is the Real Foods natural grocery, and when they were setting up shop in the burgeoning Emeryville Public Market, Kimball discovered an upstairs space that seemed perfect for a jazz club. The result is one of the finest jazz showcases not just in the Bay Area but in the world. Nearly 400 people can fit comfortably in the tiered seating of this beautiful room with unobstructed sightlines. A high-tech sound system (by the same company that services Carnegie Hall) is tuned to the precise characteristics of the club. Amplified live music rarely sounds this good. For five or six nights a week, the biggest names in jazz and popular music hold forth, often inspired to brilliant performances by the elegant but unpretentious surroundings. The stage has hosted big bands, Latin orchestras and tap dancers. A "Happenin' Hour," Tuesday through Saturday from 5 to 8 p.m., features a rotating roster of superb Bay Area pianists. Chef Robert Mott oversees an excellent, eclectic menu of Californian, Southwestern and Cajun/Creole cuisine for full dinners or late-night snacks, making Kimball's East the rare jazz club that gets high marks from restaurant reviewers. If jazz is going upscale, this is the way it should be.
Open Tues.-Sun. 5 p.m. Showtimes, closing times & cover vary. Cards: MC, V.

Koncepts Cultural Gallery
480 3rd St.,
Oakland
• 763-0682

Even San Francisco's excellent network of jazz nightclubs is not enough to accommodate the full range of sounds on the scene. Several years ago, a dedicated collective of music-lovers established this music/poetry/art gallery as an East Bay alternative. When it moved into a former Santa Fe railroad station in downtown Oakland, Koncepts improved its position as the finest nonclub public listening space for jazz and related musical styles. The most exciting creative

musicians from New York, Los Angeles, Chicago and Europe (and their Bay Area peers) love to play in this comfortable room, where listeners are attentive and juices, teas and sodas are served in lieu of alcohol. The programming is irregular, but something is usually going on every weekend, ranging from avant-garde saxophone or Trinidadian steel drum sounds to swinging big bands, Latin ensembles or gritty soul/jazz.
Concert times & ticket prices vary. No cards.

Milestones
376 5th St.,
South of Market
• 777-9997

The gracious and mellifluous Sonny Buxton oversaw the design of this nightspot in his image—radiating natty elegance. A SOMA hole-in-the-wall became a classy bar, with polished brass gleaming against muted earth tones and pastels, and an intimate (read undersize) listening area for first-rate jazz. Buxton has slipped the scene, however, and the recent jazz fare has been less impressive than during the club's first few auspicious years. Although the priority is "drinking jazz" rather than "listening jazz," the drinks are overpriced, the service sometimes intrusive, and the sound system just fine. Milestones showcases local talent almost exclusively these days; touring bands are the exception. The crowd comprises black and white businessfolk stopping in after work, journalists (including columnist Herb Caen) from the newspaper buildings down the street and jazzophiles hungry for a bebop fix.
Open Mon.-Fri. 4 p.m.-2 a.m., Sat. 6 p.m.-2 a.m., Sun. 5 p.m.-1 a.m. Showtimes & cover vary. No cards.

Pasand Restaurant and Lounge
1875 Union St.,
Marina District
• 922-4498

By day, Pasand is a fine restaurant serving southern Indian cuisine. By night, the pace picks up as one of three fine house bands fills the lounge with pleasant jazz. A half dozen of the city's many jazz vocalists rotate with the bands, singing bebop, blues, pop and Latin standards to a casually dapper crowd. Dinner is served until 10 p.m., but good burgers and delicious appetizers are available until 1 a.m.
Open daily 11:30 a.m.-2 a.m. Shows 8:30 p.m.-12:30 a.m. No cover. Cards: AE, MC, V.

Yoshi's Restaurant & Nightspot
6030 Claremont Ave.,
Oakland
• 652-9200

Gertrude Stein's alleged dictum that "there is no there there" aside, San Francisco's best jazz club is in Oakland. Just a 25-minute ride from the city (by BART or by car across the Bay Bridge), Yoshi's boasts the loveliest listening space and the best jazz bookings in the Bay Area. The 200-plus-seat room adjoins a fine Japanese restaurant and shares the same tasteful, airy decor. The high, slanted ceiling creates a refreshingly open feeling and bounces the sound neatly into the upstairs balcony. Hosts graciously turn off the blenders and espresso machines and discourage audiences from talking during the music. Since the restaurant's liquor license doesn't apply to the showroom, only nonalcoholic drinks are served, but you can slip out to the "real" bar upstairs in between sets and tipple to the accompaniment of vintage jazz videos. Two or three nights a week, local pianists, vocalists and combos hold forth in the relaxed fashion of an upscale neighborhood bar. But the rest of the time, large, racially and generationally diverse crowds pack in for the fine, internationally famous jazz artists who play four- and five-night runs.

Open nightly 7 p.m.-1 a.m. Shows Sun.-Thurs. 8 p.m. & 10 p.m., Fri.-Sat. 9 p.m. & 11 p.m. Cover varies. Cards: AE, MC, V.

MUSIC CLUBS

There has never been a shortage of rock and roll in San Francisco. Since the heyday of the great acid-rock bands that played for free in Golden Gate Park, a vital underground rock scene has been part of the city's rich cultural character. Those days are kept alive (or embalmed, depending on your point of view) by a recently reunited Jefferson Airplane and a 25-year-old-and-still-truckin' Grateful Dead. Sometimes the struggling local bands are overshadowed by the megagroups, and a lot of attention is given to major touring bands playing such concert venues as the Warfield Theatre, the Fillmore (closed due to earthquake damage but scheduled to reopen sometime in 1990), the Cow Palace, Shoreline Amphitheatre, the suburban Concord Pavilion and the Greek Theatre in Berkeley. But the best grass-roots music, peppered with hot out-of-town acts, can be found at the clubs listed below.

Club DV8
540 Howard St.,
South of Market
• 957-1730

As you approach DV8, through back alleys and deserted parking lots beneath the concrete maze of criss-crossing freeways and Bay Bridge on- and off-ramps, you might instinctively start snapping your fingers, like some refugee from *West Side Story*. Once inside the foreboding, bouncer-guarded warehouse door, you could cut the hipper-than-thou atmosphere with a switchblade. Faux marble columns and other ultra-cool Greco-Roman decorations abound. "Underground dancing" and art installations—iguanas in sand pits, pop sculptures—are mainstays of this trendy South of Market club, along with the young, posing crowd dressed in black. Punk chic notwithstanding, the crowds for the live rock shows, featuring the latest new-wave band from Minneapolis or synth-pop pretenders from Europe, can be tamely middle-of-the-road, like the celluloid heroes of *West Side Story*.

Hours, showtimes & cover vary. Cards: AE, V inside club; no cards at the door.

Covered Wagon Saloon
917 Folsom St.,
South of Market
• 974-1585

As rock generations sort themselves out and new bands burst out of the garage to entertain kids whose parents writhed to the Beatles, Rolling Stones and Motown, new clubs spring up to accommodate the sound and the fury. The Covered Wagon set up camp in SOMA, the territory that's experiencing a new gold rush of music-hungry prospectors. Dancing goes on every night, but it's Thursday and Saturday when the guitars come out and the youthful (but over-21) crowd jams into the small joint for loud doses of the lastest alternative music, from thrashing hard rock to new-wave country, blues, R & B and postmodern dance grooves.

Open daily 8 a.m.-2 a.m. Shows Thurs.-Sat. 9 p.m. Cover varies. No cards.

DNA Lounge
375 11th St.,
South of Market
• 626-1409

Warehouse chic is the predominant theme in San Francisco's burgeoning South of Market area, where industrial buildings are remodeled with postmodern disregard for stylistic coherence. Although the club-goers sometimes wear the detached look of fashion models, they are twitching with the underlying anxiety common to scenemakers. With its large bar, planted smack in the middle of the main floor, and its room-circling balcony, DNA is an ideal club for observing the genetic code of the evolving SOMA subspecies. The music is loud and booming, and bookings favor up-and-coming local bands that play original, offbeat rock and roll, which makes DNA one of the best spots to hear early rumblings of the Bay Area's next big thing in pop.

Open Mon.-Sat. 9 p.m.-2 a.m. Showtimes & cover vary. No cards.

Full Moon Saloon
1725 Haight St.,
Haight-Ashbury
• 668-6190

If you aren't concerned with the latest trends in synth-pop, hard-core punk, hairstyles and attitudes, the Full Moon offers a down-home alternative to the cutting-edginess of the hip SOMA nightspots. The decor is funky, the dress casual, and the clientele relaxed, befitting the lingering posthippie ethos that the club preserves in legendary Haight-Ashbury. Summer of Love holdouts and baby

boomers on a bender hang out to hear dinosaurs from the acid-rock era. But the main fare is a revolving schedule of local reggae, rhythm and blues and good ol' rock and roll intended for dancing. Occasional headliners include visiting Chicago blues musicians and Motown-era revival acts.
Open nightly 8:30 p.m.-2 a.m. Shows 9:30 p.m. Cover varies Thurs.-Sat. Cards: MC, V.

Great American Music Hall

859 O'Farrell St.,
Union Square
• 880-0750

San Francisco's most eclectic music club is indeed a beautifully maintained turn-of-the-century music hall, complete with Corinthian pillars, ornate red-and-gold rococo trim and a U-shaped balcony overlooking the stage and main floor. Although it has the standard nightclub small round tables and cane-back chairs (usually jammed together for maximum seating), the Great American Music Hall is the most comfortable spot in town to see the greatest variety of music. The most popular Bay Area dance bands hold forth with '60s soul and R & B on nights when out-of-town headliners aren't booked. The music swings from straight-ahead jazz through country, bluegrass, folk, new age, Latin jazz, blues, soul, funk and fusion, and the promoters aren't afraid to take a commercial risk when they know the music is of a high artistic and adventurous quality. Everybody should be able to find something of interest in any given week. Good sandwiches, burgers and salads are available from the kitchen at relatively reasonable prices.
Open 1 hour before early show (usually 8 p.m. or 8:30 p.m.). Closing time & cover vary. No cards.

I-Beam

1748 Haight St.,
Haight-Ashbury
• 668-6006

You won't want to frequent the Beam if you're allergic to styling mousse or if you develop a nervous reaction to the color black. You'll have to put your aversions aside if you want to see the hottest underground rock bands from the U.S. and the U.K. Before they break through to mainstream audiences or sign with major record labels, or during their noncommercial careers as cult bands heard only on college radio, "new music" groups play this venerable neoindustrial nightclub. If the wave is new—whether it's punk, garage-band thrash, neopsychedelic, nouveau-folk or electric noise—it's bound to break at the Beam. Amid giant I-beams and drill bits, strobe lights and lasers flash while avant-garde videos are projected on the walls and incredibly loud music batters the crowd. You can retreat to the lobby or one of the two bars for a respite before hurling yourself back into the throng. Headliners don't usually take the stage before midnight on Mondays (the Tuesday sets are earlier), and the shows are standing- , dancing- or slam-

ming-room only.
Open Mon.-Sat. 9 p.m.-2 a.m., Sun. 5 p.m.-2 a.m. Live shows Mon.-Tues. Showtimes & cover vary. No cards.

Kennel Club
628 Divisadero St.,
Golden Gate Panhandle
• 931-1914

This boxy little club changed names and orientations several times in the '80s but seems to have settled into its current identity as a showcase for alternative rock and world-beat sounds. A handful of booths run along the walls; a large, square bar and a pool table take up chunks of the floor. The live music presented several nights a week features the Bay Area's up-and-coming postpunk bands playing everything from thrash and industrial funk to gentler neofolk and reggae. T-shirts, jeans and black leather are the informal dress code of the college-age crowd. On three or four nights deejays spin discs for dancers; world-beat maven Doug Wendt plays reggae, African and other international rhythms. Two other nights the club becomes a gay disco called The Box. Vital signs at the Kennel Club include packed crowds, thick heat and loud music.
Open Tues.-Sun. 9 p.m.-2 a.m. Cover varies. No cards.

Last Day Saloon
406 Clement St.,
Richmond District
• 387-6343

One of the least pretentious rock clubs in the city, the Last Day is an old standby. Pop styles may come and go, but as long as there are audiences for earnest rock, blues and reggae, this solid nightspot will be packing them in. The dance floor is small, surrounded by tables, with a walk-up bar and a rear room for overflow seating. In addition to local favorites who churn out a multitude of boogie grooves, often for no cover, the Last Day books top blues, rock and R & B artists from around the country. The club appeals to the rowdier side of the Big Chill generation, and is frequented by rough-hewn regulars from the Sunset and Richmond districts.
Open daily 2 p.m.-2 a.m. Showtimes & cover vary. No cards.

Lou's Pier 47
300 Jefferson St.,
Fisherman's Wharf
• 771-0377

Right in the heart of the tourist mecca, Lou's retains a bit of Barbary Coast flavor largely through the gritty sounds of the live music booked nightly. The blues-and-roots music revival of recent years has been buoyed by bars such as this, willing to employ local musicians and to offer patrons down-home accompaniment to the drinks and the view. Ron Hacker and the Hacksaws, Ron Thompson and the Resistors, Brenda Boykin, Chris Cobb and Mark Naftalin are among the powerhouse performers.
Open daily noon-2 a.m. Showtimes vary. Cover $2-$4. Cards: MC, V.

Nightbreak

1821 Haight St.,
Haight-Ashbury
• 221-9008

The decor, dress and clientele are casual funk, the scene is '80s eclectic, and the bands are among the best local offbeat rockers who haven't yet broken into the bigger clubs. Thrashing garage pop with idiosyncratic twists is the specialty several nights a week; when bands aren't booked, rock deejays get the crowd moving.

Open daily 1 p.m.-2 a.m. Showtimes & cover vary. No cards.

Noe Valley Ministry

1021 Sanchez St.,
Noe Valley
• 282-2317

Borrowing the sanctuary of an actual Sanctuary Movement church, the Noe Valley Ministry Music Series presents an eclectic mix of folk, jazz, new-age and experimental music. Nearly every weekend, some nationally known troubadour, local stalwart or adventurous music group takes the small stage and makes good use of the room's intimate seating and fine acoustics. Avant-garde jazz musicians, performance artists, storytellers, folksingers, blues pickers and unclassifiable pioneers show up at one time or another. Pop star Bobby McFerrin, who lives in the area, has often worked on his act here. The volunteer staff sells homemade refreshments before the early-starting shows and between sets, which adds to the casual, homey feel.

Shows Sat. (Fri. occasionally) 8:15 p.m. Ticket prices vary. No cards.

Slim's

333 11th St.,
South of Market
• 621-3330

It was the dream of San Francisco pop star Boz Scaggs to own an old-fashioned, Texas-style rhythm-and-blues juke joint. With the help of several partners, including the manager of Huey Lewis and the News, he's realized that ideal in a revamped SOMA warehouse. While the sometimes trendy and upscale clientele gives Slim's something less than a roadhouse feel, and the booking is not all blues by a long shot, the brick-walled club has established itself as the city's most dependable stage for roots music, with exceptionally good sound. Promoter Harry Duncan defines the sound with R & B, soul, country, neofolk, jazz, rockabilly, Cajun and zydeco, and he brings in a brilliant array of historically important and aspiring artists. Slim's has also become a stop for modern rockers who want to play to more intimate crowds. The house band, the Solid Senders, churns out vintage blues and R & B, often joined by Scaggs in his blues-guitarist persona, Presidio Slim. The kitchen turns out the best club food in the city: a crisp Californian/Southwestern cuisine of pizzas, pastas, chicken, sandwiches, salads and snacks. But for most shows, only early-arriving patrons secure tables, and it's SRO the rest of the night.

Open 1 hour before early show. Showtimes & cover vary. Cards: AE, MC, V.

The Stone

412 Broadway,
North Beach
• 391-8282

The Broadway strip has been beleaguered for years by topless joints and more recently by antagonism between teen cruisers and the cops, but The Stone has held its ground as a mainstream rock showcase and after-hours dance club. The broad, spacious room features a large dance floor and table seating on two terraced levels. Security folk can be brusque with overindulgent patrons, and the drink service is sometimes spotty, but the atmosphere is fairly loose. The college-age crowd changes according to the music being performed, which includes hard rock, underground pop and trendy new wave, but leans toward the latest variations of heavy metal.

Open Sun.-Thurs. 8 p.m.-2 a.m., Fri.-Sat. 7 p.m.-6 a.m. Shows Sun.-Thurs. 9 p.m., Fri.-Sat. 8 p.m. Cover varies. No cards.

HOTELS

INTRODUCTION

For all the other things it's got, San Francisco is also a hotel mecca. How many honeymooners have watched the fog roll in over the Bay from their hotel room? Plenty. How many businesspeople, for that matter, have thanked their lucky expense accounts that this trip was to San Francisco and not to Oshkosh when they checked in to their Nob Hill or Union Square hotel? No matter what your taste, in San Francisco you'll be able to find your style of accommodations. But remember, the secret is out, so book well in advance of your visit to get exactly what you want. Our selection ranges from sumptuous suites to far humbler lodgings, but note that some hoteliers put as high a price on charm or modern facilities as others do on pure luxury. In other words, don't assume that "charming" means "cheap." Conversely, don't assume that hotels falling under the "Luxurious" heading are truly luxurious: the place may position and price itself as a luxury hotel, but that doesn't mean it delivers the goods. Hotels are listed in four categories: Luxurious, Small & Charming, Large & Modern and Airport. The prices quoted include taxes and service. Bellhop!

SYMBOLS & ABBREVIATIONS

Our opinion of the comfort level and appeal of each hotel is expressed in the following ranking system:

 Very luxurious

 Luxurious

 Very comfortable

 Comfortable

Symbols in red denote charm.

Credit Cards
  AE: American Express
  DC: Diners Club
  MC: MasterCard
  V: VISA

LUXURIOUS

Campton Place Hotel

340 Stockton St.,
Union Square, 94102
• 781-5555,
Fax 955-8536

Campton Place was a hit from the beginning, as much for its acclaimed restaurant as for its supremely elegant rooms. Opened in 1983 after $18 million in renovations, Campton Place doesn't have the old–San Francisco aura of some of the city's other great hotels, such as the St. Francis or the Clift, but the location is great—just off Union Square—and the ambience is refined and discreet. With just 126 rooms, Campton Place is never overrun with conventioneers or large tour groups. The lobby, lounges, guest rooms and large suites are exceptionally attractive and comfortable, with a skillful mix of rich colors, antique and contemporary furnishings, plush carpets and fresh flowers. Service is stressed: there are intelligent concierges, promp room service, a brigade of business and secretarial services and valet parking ($19 a day). The restaurant is almost as good as its reputation; the bar is a nice spot for a quiet drink.
Singles & doubles: $180-$300; suites: $450-$750.

The Donatello

501 Post St.,
Union Square, 94102
• 441-7100,
Fax 885-8842

Just off the chaos of Union Square sits The Donatello, a most refined hotel that belongs to the prestigious Relais et Châteaux chain. The affiliation is deserved—this is a very attractive, friendly and discreet hostelry. The lobby and bar lounge areas are opulent without being fussy and cluttered; everything, with the exception of the highball-glass chandelier, is in solid good taste. Rooms are spacious and quiet; some may seem to have been decorated by Aunt Martha, but they're all more than comfortable. Amenities include a quiet bar, an acclaimed Italian restaurant, valet parking ($16 a day), afternoon tea, complimentary *Wall Street Journal*s and terry robes. Reception, valet and concierge services are exceptionally helpful.
Singles & doubles: $140-$165; suites: $280-$315.

Fairmont Hotel

950 Mason St.,
Nob Hill, 94108
• 772-5000,
Fax 772-5026

This Nob Hill oldtimer gained even more fame after a several-year run as the St. Gregory on the TV series *Hotel*. Being a famous TV facade alone is reason enough to stay away from the Fairmont, unless you don't mind large (albeit relatively prosperous) tour groups. The massive lobby is dramatically ornate but uninspired; it's easy to feel lost. The views, however, from the tower addition (notable for its forgettable exterior) are spectacular. Rooms are large and

well appointed, and the service is good. There are seven restaurants, including one smack on top of the tower; another remains open 24 hours a day. The Venetian Room is a supper club that headlines big-name singers.
Singles: $145-$250; doubles: $175-$280; suites: $450-$5,000.

Four Seasons Clift Hotel

495 Geary St.,
Union Square, 94102
• 775-4700,
Fax 441-4621

Unquestionably the finest of San Francisco's grand old hotels, the Clift is perhaps best known for its atmospheric Redwood Room bar, featuring polished redwood paneling and beautiful art deco light fixtures. The adjoining restaurant, the French Room, is an old-fashioned delight, with gleaming chandeliers, painted woodwork and good food; the lobby is appropriately dramatic. A recent $18 million renovation included marbling in the bathrooms and a new safety system. The Four Seasons management is making a concerted effort to woo the business traveler who is tired of the sterility and impersonality of the glass-tower hotels; there is a full-time business concierge, as well as secretaries, conference rooms and such high-tech amenities as computer modems and fax machines. Guests can use the Nikko fitness center for $20 per day.
Singles: $145-$205; doubles: $145-$225; suites: $375-$700. Weekend & theater packages also available.

The Mark Hopkins Inter-Continental

1 Nob Hill (California &
Mason sts.),
Nob Hill, 94108
• 392-3434,
Fax 421-3302

The Mark Hopkins is a longtime favorite of conservative, middle-aged couples who favor Lincoln-Continentals and Cadillacs over Porsches and BMWs. The lobby is elegant in an outdated way: crystal chandeliers, lots of mirrored walls, '70s-style contemporary furniture (tufted leather couches, glass-and-brass coffee tables) and sweeping drapes. The large rooms and suites have recently been redecorated with alternating color schemes of either silver-gray or khaki and gold, thick carpeting and Regency-style writing desks. Service is bright and friendly. The Top of the Mark, the hotel's rooftop bar, is a must-visit on a clear night.
Singles: $165-$225; doubles: $195-$255; suites: $375-$1,500. Weekend packages available.

Huntington Hotel

1075 California St.,
Nob Hill, 94108
• 474-5400,
Fax 474-6227

The Huntington's quiet refinement makes it our favorite Nob Hill hotel. Its regulars have included such prosperous people as Calvin Klein, Robert Redford and Leontyne Price, all of whom care more about discretion and the quality of their rooms than about passing through a gigantic, dramatic lobby. Though certainly attractive (white woodwork, deep-red carpets and upholstery), the Huntington's teeny lobby is anything but ostentatious. The

rooms, however, boast a high degree of comfort and opulent but tasteful (with the occasional lapse) furnishings. Personal service is stressed, as is the individuality of the rooms, which are furnished with antiques, objets d'art and paintings. With only 140 rooms (containing huge, newly remodeled baths), the Huntington gives you the feeling of staying in one of Europe's fine old hotels. There's a complete range of business services as well as an excellent concierge. L'Etoile remains an admirable (and expensive) classical French restaurant, and The Big Four, an extremely handsome tribute to San Francisco's Victorian-era railroad magnates. Here's a welcome bonus: the price of your room includes a full American breakfast at The Big Four.
Singles: $160-$245; doubles: $180-$245; suites: $310-$430.

The Mandarin Oriental Hotel

222 Sansome St.,
Financial District, 94111
• 885-0999,
Fax 433-0289

If you've been looking for Asian-style service in America, you'll want to plan a trip immediately to the Mandarin Oriental. Part of a hotel group of Bangkok and Hong Hong fame, The Mandarin Oriental landed with a bang a few years back in an area not known for upscale hotels. In what may be the oddest configuration in town, the Mandarin Oriental occupies the top eleven floors of a commercial building smack in the heart of the Financial District. Those floors are numbered 37 through 48, which places guests above most of the surrounding high-rises, and even occasionally above the fog that swirls through the concrete jungle on summer evenings. The rest of the year, the 160 lavish rooms and suites feature unobstructed views of the city and portions of the Bay. You'll pay steep prices for the privilege of being surrounded by furnishings worthy of a Park Avenue penthouse, but for quality, service and business convenience, these accommodations are hard to beat. Business services and the outstanding Silks restaurant (see Restaurants chapter) are located off the lobby. Valet parking is $17.50 a day.
Singles & doubles: $230-$370; suites: $450-$900. Weekend package: $170.

Portman Hotel

500 Post St.,
Union Square, 94102
• 771-8600,
Fax 398-0267

Architect-developer John Portman, for whom the 21-story Portman Hotel is named, may not have to worry about guests stealing the plush terrycloth robes, but perhaps he should fret that someone might walk off with one of the valets that help make a sojourn here so enjoyable. This level of personal service—one valet for every seven of the hotel's 330 rooms and suites—is a direct lift from the Asian philosophy of hospitality. (The hotel is a joint venture with the Peninsula Group of Hong Kong.) Despite its size, the Portman has an intimate atmosphere, once you get past the

first three floors of public spaces. Smallish rooms echo some of the contempo-classical architectural details of the exterior, with lots of arches, recesses and expanses of marble. Elegantly decorated with custom-designed furniture, they have built-in storage cabinets and spacious desks. Nearly as large are the bathrooms, with all-marble surfaces and the separate tub-shower arrangement favored in Asia. Extensive business services are available in the four-suite Executive Conference Center. Guests who must travel to meetings or the airport can hop into one of a fleet of Rolls-Royces. Valet parking is $18 a day. The cuisine of southern France is a hallmark of the open-air Portman Grill.
Singles: $170-$350; suites: $475-$1,200.

Sheraton-Palace Hotel
639 Market St.,
Union Square, 94102
• 392-8600

As we went to press, this grand old dowager was in the throes of a massive renovation, and the hotel's doors are closed until the summer of 1990, perhaps even later. It's too early to tell what the renovation will bring, or what the style of the place will be. We just hope they don't tamper with the Pied Piper Room, the old hotel's clubby, wood-paneled restaurant and bar with the wonderful Maxfield Parrish mural of the same name, or the Garden Court, a breathtaking room of marble columns, crystal chandeliers and rich carpeting, all underneath a remarkable leaded-glass dome. (Once the hotel's carriage entrance, the Garden Court had become a Sunday brunch hot spot.) We hope that the remodeling won't spoil the atmosphere here.

The Sherman House
2160 Green St.,
Pacific Heights, 94123
• 563-3600,
Fax 563-1882

Northern California is full of enterprising people who are converting charming old houses into homey inns—but none have created an inn as luxurious and opulent as The Sherman House. Built in 1876 by Leander Sherman, the owner of the Sherman Clay Music Company and a devoted opera buff, the house boasts a three-story recital hall where turn-of-the-century musicians performed. In 1980 Manou Mobedshahi and his young wife bought the old mansion and spent four years and a considerable fortune restoring the buildings and extensive gardens, originally laid out by Thomas Church. The main house has twelve rooms and the carriage house, six; all are straight out of the pages of *Architectural Digest*. Every one is large and furnished with exceptionally fine antiques and rugs, and most have canopied beds, down comforters, marble fireplaces, modernized black-granite bathrooms, wet bars, whirlpool tubs, color TVs and stereo systems. Some have such extras as a private garden or rooftop deck; a few rooms and the restaurant have Bay views. The personal service is exemplary: maids will unpack your luggage; chauffeurs will pick you up from the airport in a Rolls or a '62 Jaguar; the skilled Swiss chef will prepare a refined snack or full-blown feast any time of the day or night. The Sherman House is located away from all the other top hotels in Union Square, Nob Hill and the Financial District, which does not recommend it to the dine-and-disco set. But it is a perfect stop for those who value old-world refinement, crave a taste of bygone San Francisco and don't mind paying through the nose. Valet parking is $10 a day.

Singles & doubles: $210-$350; suites: $500-$700.

Sir Francis Drake
450 Powell St.,
Union Square, 94102
• 392-7755,
Fax 391-8719

Though hardly luxurious, the Sir Francis Drake is one of the better known of the old–San Francisco hotels. Hordes of middle-American clientele love the doormen dressed up like Renaissance artisans, the Union Square location and the ornate lobby and lounges. But we don't get it. We find this aged Englishman to be too touristy and crowded, with ordinary rooms and disappointing restaurants (the Starlite Roof and Crusty's Sourdough Café, places no local would dream of visiting). Still, the staff is friendly, the location is bull's-eye, and the prices altogether palatable. Parking is $17 a day. We'll let you footsore Union Square shoppers in on a secret: on the mezzanine level you'll fine huge, beautiful public restrooms.

Singles: $120-$180; doubles: $160-$200; suites: $265-$430. Weekend package: $119.

Stouffer's Stanford Court
905 California St.,
Nob Hill, 94108
• 989-3500,
Fax 391-0513

The Stanford Court eschews the more vulgar ostentation of the neighboring Fairmont, opting instead to project an image of refined luxury. The "Court" in the name refers to the courtyard automobile entrance, which flaunts a large stained-glass dome over a fountain. The smallish lobby is homey and inviting, and the rooms are large and quite comfortable, though the furnishings are a bit dated. Make sure to request a room with a view—not all have them. Many longtime guests swear by the Stanford Court, but we find the place lacking the cachet that makes a hotel great. And we've experienced some lapses in the service in recent years. Public facilities include a beautiful ballroom, a lovely bar and several restaurants, including the famed (but disappointing) Fournou's Ovens. Valet parking is $17 a day, with in-and-out privileges.

Singles: $180-$230; doubles: $210-$260; suites: $410-$800.

Westin St. Francis

335 Powell St.,
Union Square, 94102
• 397-7000,
Fax 774-0124

We do love visiting the St. Francis, one of San Francisco's most famous grand old hotels, just to see the exceptional rosewood-paneled lobby and to have a drink in the evocative lobby bar. But we have not enjoyed staying here since the construction of the modern tower some years ago, which brought the room total up to an excessive 1,166 and overran the place with tourists. The location is ideal in some ways—facing Union Square—but it is a little *too* close to the action; lower-level rooms can be noisy. Although recently purchased by Japanese investors, Westin still runs the show. Valet parking is $15 a day.
Singles: $145-$305; doubles: $180-$305; suites: $300-$2,000.

SMALL & CHARMING

The Abigail

246 McAllister St.,
Civic Center, 94102
• 861-9728

Bargain hunters who don't mind being away from Union Square and downtown—or want to be near the Civic Center and the Opera House—call up The Abigail immediately to make a reservation. You can't beat the charm, friendliness and comfort for the price. "Haute hunt" describes the decor at this British-owned hotel: moose heads peer over the small lobby, with its black-and-white tile floors and homey clutter; prints of sporting dogs and hunting scenes line the walls. The rooms are small and not completely immune to street noise, but they are comfortable. Each is equipped with surprisingly handsome antiques, an aging color TV, a phone and a private bath that is clean and large enough, if not especially modernized. As of this writing, a new restaurant is expected, but no one seems confident enough to give a date. There's no parking, so you'll have to use a local garage.
Singles: $62; doubles: $72; suites: $150.

The Albion House

135 Gough St.,
Civic Center, 94102
• 621-0896

An eight-room bed-and-breakfast that is neither especially cheap nor especially luxurious, in a neighborhood that is neither chic nor shabby. Not far from the Opera House and Symphony Hall, the Albion counts many small cafés and galleries as its neighbors. It lacks the fussy charm of the city's more Victorian-style inns, but the large, redwood-beamed living room and the small, comfortable rooms (seven with private bath) are attractively decorated nonetheless. If you are sensitive to street noise, ask for a room toward the back.

No hotel parking, but spaces are easy to find in the neighborhood, and the lots are inexpensive.
Singles & doubles: $65-$85; suites: $110.

The Amsterdam
749 Taylor St.,
Nob Hill, 94108
• 673-3277

There are few amenities—no valet parking, no concierge, no restaurant, no room service, no elevator—but this frumpy little hotel is a find for the frugal. The location is swell, just above the Sutter Street shops and galleries on the south slope of Nob Hill. The Amsterdam has 27 small, plain rooms on three floors, some with private baths. The accommodations are clean and comfortable; all are equipped with phones and small black-and-white TVs. Complimentary Continental breakfast is served in the folksy lobby.
Singles: $38 (sharing bath), $52 (private bath); doubles: $42 (sharing bath), $56 (private bath).

The Archbishop's Mansion
1000 Fulton St.,
Civic Center, 94107
• 563-7872

No ordinary parson's quarters are these. Built in 1904, this bed-and-breakfast is a resplendent example of old–San Francisco wealth, though it was built not for some captain of industry, but for the city's archbishop. The three-story mansion facing historic Alamo Square (near the Opera House and the Civic Center) has been lovingly restored to its original beauty: rich, polished woodwork, thick carpets, vaulted ceilings, crystal chandeliers and a lovely stained-glass dome over the staircase. Fifteen large rooms feature queen-size beds, nineteenth-century French antiques, fine linens and silks and private baths; many have fireplaces or Jacuzzi baths. Amenities include a good breakfast served in your room, limousine service to the nearby Opera House or Symphony Hall and an accommodating staff. Another plus: free parking.
Rooms: $100-$159; suites: $189-$265.

Galleria Park Hotel
191 Sutter St.,
Union Square, 94104
• 781-3060,
Fax 433-4409

A creation of developer Bill Kimpton and interior designer Nan Rosenblatt, the Galleria Park originally opened in 1911, and was restored and reopened a few years ago. The lobby is an art nouveau vision, with a crystal skylight, etched glass and a sculpted fireplace. There are 177 rooms and suites; rooms are small but exceptionally attractive, and suites are lovely and well designed, with soothing colors, fireplaces, stereos and large TVs. Like the Bedford, this hotel stresses comfort, style and economy over service. Though the staff is friendly, there is neither a doorman nor a concierge (but the bellman can be trusted for advice). Amenities include a short outdoor jogging track, well-appointed conference rooms and two restaurants: Brasserie

Chambord and Bentley's Restaurant and Oyster Bar. The latter is a split-level affair with an upstairs dining room, flanked with a balcony, that overlooks the piano bar near the entrance. Parking is a reasonable $12 a day.
Singles & doubles: $120; suites: $145-$275.

Hotel Bedford
761 Post St.,
Union Square, 94109
• 673-6040,
Fax 563-6739

The Bedford, a member of the Kimco hotel chain, offers one of the best deals in the area. All singles and doubles, even those with king-size beds and good views, are just $94. The old hotel was renovated skillfully and tastefully, if not opulently (though it's elegant for the price). The lobby is cheerful; it opens onto the walnut-paneled Wedgwood Bar and the new Café Champagne (owned by the people who run Brasserie Chambord). Rooms are compact, clean and comfortable, with minirefrigerators, small color TVs, pastel walls and floral fabrics; bathrooms are old-fashioned but not rickety. The small staff is friendly. Located three blocks west of Union Square, the Bedford is close enough for convenience but far enough away to be out of earshot of the clanging cable cars. Valet parking is $14 a night.
Singles & doubles: $94; suites: $155.

Hotel Diva
440 Geary St.,
Union Square, 94102
• 885-0200,
Fax 346-6613

If Eurostyle is your style, you'll feel right at home at Hotel Diva, one of the newest additions to the moderately sized and priced Union Square hotels. True, the entrance and postage-stamp-size lobby (stainless steel and glass, with four large TV monitors tuned to the same movie) make the Diva look a bit like a bank. But the small rooms are as well equipped and cleverly designed as can be, featuring high-tech TVs with VCRs, minibars, comfortable beds with down comforters and contemporary streamlined Italian furniture. Unfortunately, the views are mostly of neighboring brick walls, but that helps ensure quiet. Forget a restaurant or room service, but there are some slick conference and meeting rooms and an accommodating staff. If you can't abide noise, request a room on an upper floor.
Singles & doubles: $119; suites: $139.

Hotel Griffon
155 Steuart St.,
Embarcadero, 94105
• 495-2100,
Fax 495-3522

Hard by the Embarcadero, the 63-room Hotel Griffon stretches five stories, high enough to afford some views of the downtown skyline. Opened in the spring of 1989, it has small rooms and suites, the latter with petite redwood balconies. The high ceilings and sandblasted brick walls give away the structure's origin as a waterfront hotel—it was built just after the 1906 earthquake. Mahogany headboards sport images of the legendary taloned griffon; the same wood is used generously for desks and occasional tables. Decorated with tweedy rugs, good-looking Italian alabaster light fixtures and such subdued color schemes as cream and blue, the accommodations are handsome, if simple. It's a great location for doing business in the nearby Financial District, but not the kind of place to spend a lot of time in your room. Amenities include room service, honor bars and complimentary Continental breakfast; valet parking is $15 a night. Bistro Rôti is popular for its oven-roasted meat and game dishes (see Restaurants chapter).

Singles: $105; doubles: $115-$125; suites: $135-$170. Weekend packages available.

Hotel Majestic

1500 Sutter St.,
Western Addition, 94109
• 441-1100,
Fax 673-7331

Tassled pillows, lace curtains and four-poster beds announce the Hotel Majestic's turn-of-the-century heritage. All the rooms in this five-story Edwardian structure are color-coordinated with almost-matching fabrics, rugs and patterned wallpaper. Unfortunately, the overall effect is a tad threadbare. Period antiques and various nooks and crannies imbue the place with a cozy, guest-home ambience. The lobby in particular exudes an old-manor feel appropriate to the residential neighborhood. The adjacent restaurant and bar, Café Majestic, specializes in Californian cuisine and some updated San Francisco classics.

Singles & doubles: $95-$145; suites: $175-$200.

Hotel Union Square

114 Powell St.,
Union Square, 94102
• 397-3000,
Fax 885-3268

Tremendously popular, no doubt because of its good location and low prices, the Union Square won't wow you with its service; nor is it as sophisticated as its sister hotels, Hotel Diva and Kensington Park. Rooms are old and vaguely musty, and the Continental breakfast includes coffee served in environmentally incompatible cups. Most doubles are just $99, however, so one can't be too fussy—unless one needs to park a car, at $15 per day. Avoid the rooms facing the street; the nearby cable-car line ensures constant noise.

Singles & doubles: $99-$139; suites: $280.

Hotel Vintage Court

650 Bush St.,
Union Square, 94108
• 392-4666,
Fax same

Designer Nan Rosenblatt has left her distinctive touch on yet another reasonably priced San Francisco hotel, the Vintage Court—perhaps the best-looking hotel she has designed. Located just far enough away from Union Square to avoid excessive noise, the Vintage Court is a very good value: just $97 for any room. All the rooms are quiet and homey, with comfortable king-size beds, stocked minibars, cable TVs, nifty furnishings and Rosenblatt's trademark floral fabrics. (Reserve early to get one of the larger rooms.)

The lobby is welcoming and calm, and the staff is charming, if minimal (like others in this small chain, the Vintage Court has neither valet parking nor a concierge). Curiously, this modestly priced hotel is home to Masa's, the incredibly expensive (and excellent) French restaurant.
Singles & doubles: $97.

Inn at the Opera
333 Fulton St.,
Civic Center, 94102
• 863-8400,
Fax 861-0821

This marvelous five-story inn has many things going for it: history (built in 1927 to house opera stars), location (a few steps from the Opera House and Symphony Hall), decor (shades of peach, lots of fresh flowers, tasteful artworks and objets d'art) and ambience (luxuriously low-key). Plus, the service is first-rate: because of its connections, the Inn can get its guests choice seats for ballet, opera and symphony performances. There are, however, a few minor drawbacks, namely smallish rooms and noise from the nearby freeway. Rooms are well equipped (wet bars, minirefrigerators, microwaves, terry robes); all have queen-size beds. The Act IV Lounge features a pianist in the evening and a late supper, served until 1:30 a.m.
Singles & doubles: $105-$195; suites: $155-$195.

The Inn at Union Square
440 Post St.,
Union Square, 94102
• 397-3510,
Fax 989-0529

A small European-style hotel, The Inn at Union Square could almost be considered a bed-and-breakfast. In good B & B fashion, Continental breakfast and afternoon tea are served in the small parlors on each floor. Here's the gravy— the place offers a level of service that most B & Bs don't, including a 24-hour concierge, valet parking and complimentary newspapers. The rooms are inviting, if a bit fussy, with lots of florals and Georgian furniture; most have king-size beds and down pillows, and there's a penthouse suite with a fireplace, bar, sauna and whirlpool tub. The suites face Post Street and can therefore be a bit noisy; some of the rooms look onto neighboring brick walls, which provide noise insulation.
Singles & doubles: $105-$170; suites: $170-$300.

Kensington Park Hotel
450 Post St.,
Union Square, 94102
• 788-6400,
Fax 346-6613

A handsome but eccentric little hotel near Union Square, the Kensington Park has adopted a British style. The small, attractive lobby (shared with neighbor Theater on the Square) is on the ground floor, but the hotel's rooms don't start until the fifth floor—the Elks Club's dining, meeting and exercise rooms occupying the interim. Rooms are small but not cramped, with English furnishings in shades of blue, green and rose. Complimentary coffee, tea and crumpets are served each morning in the foyers; during the afternoon,

guests gather around the lobby piano for tea and sherry. The staff makes an effort to make each guest feel welcome. Valet parking is $16 a day.
Singles & doubles: $110-$120; suites: $350.

The Mansion Hotel

2220 Sacramento St.,
Pacific Heights, 94115
• 929-9444

Those who expect cable TV, coffee shops and convention facilities from a hostelry will not enjoy the Mansion, a posh bed-and-breakfast that reeks of refinement and old-world charm. The 1887 Queen Anne house near Lafayette Park has nineteen guest rooms—and no TVs, thank you very much. Some rooms have marble fireplaces or private terraces. All are furnished with beautiful antiques. Breakfast is served in bed, and you can hear nightly performances of classical music in the parlor. The hotel restaurant serves Californian cuisine Tuesday through Saturday night at a prix fixe of $25 weekdays, $35 weekends. Tennis players will enjoy the proximity to Lafayette Park's courts. Parking is available nearby for $10 a day.
Singles: $119-$139; doubles: $134-$154.

The Orchard Hotel

562 Sutter St.,
Union Square, 94102
• 433-4434,
Fax 433-3695

Here's a decent stop for Union Square shoppers who expect comfort but would rather spend their money at Gump's or Saks than on a pretentious hotel. The Orchard sits on relatively quiet Sutter Street, which houses all sorts of wonderful shops. The lobby, done in shades of rose and green, is as inviting and comfortable as it is attractive. Guests and visitors alike may enjoy a drink in the lobby bar or a blend of Continental and Californian food in the adjacent restaurant, Sutter Garden. The 96 compact rooms are homey and rather ordinary, with aging but spotless bathrooms and the obligatory minibars.
Singles & doubles: $99-$120; suites: $195.

Petite Auberge

863 Bush St.,
Union Square, 94108
• 928-6000,
Fax 775-5717

There is no more cozy inn in all of San Francisco (except for the neighboring White Swan, owned by the same good people). A romanticized interpretation of the French country look has been skillfully assembled here: earthy paver-tile floors, delicately flowered wallpaper, country furnishings and French windows and doors. "Darling" is probably the best word for this place. (We must take exception, however, to the abundance of embarrassingly cute stuffed teddy bears.) The basement level comprises a breakfast room with French doors opening onto a small garden, and a lounge/bar area, where good California wines and tea are served in the afternoon. The upper floors are taken up by 26 small and adorable rooms, all with aging (but perfectly fine) bathrooms and queen-size beds, many with fireplaces. The suite has both a private entrance and its own patio. The Bush Street location is a short walk to Union Square, yet away from the throng of tourists. Valet parking is $15 a day. *Singles & doubles: $105-$155; suites: $195.*

The Prescott Hotel

545 Post St.,
Union Square, 94102
• 563-0303,
Fax 563-6831

Opened in 1989 in conjunction with Wolfgang Puck's Postrio restaurant on the lower floors, the Prescott is another project of omnipresent hotelier Bill Kimpton. Cherry-wood furnishings and a color scheme of hunter green and deep red with flashes of gold suit the decor, which is a blend of neoclassical and Empire. There's a men's-club feeling to the 109 smallish rooms and suites, all outfitted with the requisite armoires and marble-clad baths. The theme is underscored in the "living-room-style" lobby, complete with wood-burning fireplace and overstuffed furniture. The extensive remodeling job hasn't entirely done away with the hotel's slightly claustrophobic feel, but an extremely handsome interior design, coupled with a first-rate location (and a leg up on reservations at Postrio), makes the Prescott a very good Union Square choice. *Singles & doubles: $139; suites: $189.*

The Queen Anne

1590 Sutter St.,
Civic Center, 94109
• 441-2828,
Fax 775-5212

This large (49-room) bed-and-breakfast sits north of the Civic Center, not far from prestigious Pacific Heights and within walking distance of Japantown. The four-story, authentically restored Queen Anne–style mansion has a plush parlor, a majestic mahogany staircase, two conference rooms and—*mon dieu*—free parking. Rooms range in size from small to spacious; they all have high ceilings, antique furnishings, telephones and remote-control TVs. The better rooms have fireplaces, wet bars and bay windows. Wake up to Continental breakfast served in your room; relax with afternoon tea and sherry in the parlor. A perfect marriage of bed-and-breakfast charm and modern convenience. *Singles & doubles: $94-$125; suites: $125.*

Stanyan Park Hotel

750 Stanyan St.,
Golden Gate Park, 94117
• 751-1000,
Fax 668-5454

Built in 1905 and restored in 1983, the Stanyan Park is on the National Register of Historic Places. Just across the street from Golden Gate Park and around the corner from funky Haight Street, its location attracts fans of the great park and doctors visiting nearby U.C. Medical Center. Both comfort and period ambience are maintained here: bathrooms have been reasonably modernized, and antique furnishings are simple and homey. For a larger group or an extended stay, consider one of the two-bedroom suites,

which sleep six and include kitchens, dining rooms and four-poster beds. The room rate includes a decent Continental breakfast and friendly service. Weekend visitors should be prepared for daytime noise from the many park visitors.
Singles: $68-$88; doubles: $78-$88; suites: $110-$160.

Villa Florence
225 Powell St.,
Union Square, 94102
• 397-7700,
Fax 397-1006

Villa Florence is another old hotel that has been skillfully spruced up for a clientele that doesn't want to spend much more than $100 for a Union Square location. This particular location is a little tawdry, but it is ideally situated for a Union Square shopping spree. The Italianate lobby is unusually attractive, with a fireplace, plush seating and a lovely fresco of Florence. To one side is the popular Italian restaurant, Kuleto's. The rooms combine simple, modern dressers and armoires (which, of course, hide TVs) with flowery chintz bedspreads, drapes and overstuffed chairs. A good home-away-from-home for the price.
Singles & doubles: $109; suites: $125-$175.

The Washington Square Inn
1660 Stockton St.,
North Beach, 94133
• 981-4220

Those enamored with the old-world charm of North Beach and Washington Square will be pleased to find this friendly, pleasant hideaway. The fifteen-room bed-and-breakfast faces onto the park; the two most expensive rooms have bay windows overlooking the square. The rooms are predictably homey and cozy (and often small), and they are as quiet as can be expected of a Washington Square location. Most have private baths and some have king-size beds. Prices include breakfast as well as the tea and very nice scones served in the afternoon by the personable staff. You'll never find parking in North Beach, so be prepared to pay $17 a day to stash your car.
Singles & doubles: $65-$150.

White Swan Inn
845 Bush St.,
Union Square, 94108
• 775-1755,
Fax 775-5717

Without a doubt our favorite B&B–style inn in San Francisco. The White Swan, sister to the Petite Auberge, makes large and modern hotels seem like gulags. Though officially a bed-and-breakfast, the White Swan has none of the problems that keep some people away from B&Bs. Each of the 27 rooms is roomy, boasting a fireplace, refrigerator, phone, color TV and decent-size (if a bit dated) bathroom, and the inn offers such amenities as valet parking, concierge and secretarial services. The English-country look has been created with remarkable skill; every inch of the place is attractive and inviting. The lower level houses a large breakfast room (with doors opening onto a small garden),

a lounge and a cozy library, all with fireplaces. The breakfast is more than generous, as are the afternoon hors d'oeuvres, tea and wine. Add $15 a day for parking.
Singles & doubles: $145-$160; suites: $250.

LARGE & MODERN

Cathedral Hill Hotel
1101 Van Ness Ave.,
Civic Center, 94109
• 776-8200,
Fax 441-2841

This remodeled-but-still-boxy hotel may not have the most attractive interior in town (too much green for our taste), but it is not without advantages. For one, it has free parking, a big bonus in car-clogged San Francisco. For another, you can get all the big-hotel amenities, including a swimming pool, in-room movies, conference and banquet facilities and the Hilltop Club, the hotel's full-service concierge floor with deluxe rooms. The standard rooms are average in size and equipped with comfortable but generic hotel furniture.
Singles & doubles: $95-$180; suites: $350-$650. Weekend packages available.

Hotel Nikko
222 Mason St.,
Union Square, 94102
• 394-1111,
Fax 394-1106

All of San Francisco's new downtown hotels seem to be counting on a hefty percentage of foreign trade, but none more so than the Hotel Nikko. The lower levels of this 25-story tower (which euphemistically describes its location as Union Square West) are devoted to restaurants, public rooms, the Japan Airlines ticketing counter and the Executive Assistance Center, complete with televisions, VCRs and a multilingual staff. But the best amenity is the health club, with its workout room, sauna, deep Japanese baths and full-size heated indoor swimming pool, covered by an arch of glass. Rooms and suites are minimalist; the sleek, contemporary furnishings and understated color schemes may seem severe by Western standards. The Nikko is a good bet for business travelers keen on Japanese high-tech savvy, but it's lacking in charm for vacationers seeking deluxe accommodations. For a touch of the Orient, book one of the Japanese suites, or have a multicourse kaiseki dinner in Benkay, the excellent penthouse restaurant. Valet parking is $17 a day.
Singles: $150-$190; doubles: $175-$215; suites: $325-$1,150.

Hyatt Regency San Francisco

5 Embarcadero Center,
Financial District, 94111
• 788-1234,
Fax 398-2567

This Financial District monster sits at one end of the sprawling Embarcadero Center, which makes it a good location for visiting businesspeople. There are more than 800 rooms, plus large meeting facilities, so expect to see a lot of people milling around the huge, often-photographed atrium-style lobby, which soars twenty stories overhead and might be the largest in the country. Rooms are spacious and tastefully furnished, though rather bland and corporate; upper rooms can have fine vistas of the north Bay. Visit the revolving rooftop bar (avoid the restaurant) for a dizzying sight. The daily tab for on-site parking is $17.
Singles: $195; doubles: $225-$268; suites: $350-$995.

The Meridien Hotel

50 3rd St.,
Union Square, 94103
• 974-6400,
Fax 543-8268

This sterile (from the outside, that is) tower is located just south of Market Street, not far from Union Square and the Moscone Center. Part of the international chain owned by the French government, the Meridien is to be commended for its personal attention, its attractive, comfortable rooms and its superb French restaurant, Pierre. The rooms feature well-stocked minibars (good wines, mineral waters, European chocolates and biscuits) and dramatic views. Service is unusually friendly and helpful. The weekend packages include excellent bargains on suites as well as rooms.
Singles: $162-$202; doubles: $188-$228; suites: $650-$1,400. Weekend packages available.

Miyako Hotel

1625 Post St.,
Japantown, 94115
• 922-3200,
Fax 921-0417

With 205 rooms, the Miyako is one of the smallest of San Francisco's modern hotels, and certainly one of the most pleasant. We prefer the simple, handsome Japanese-style rooms (tatami mats, futon-style beds and deep soaking tubs) over the Western-style rooms, though they still have such Japanese touches as shoji screens and wood-block prints. Overstressed businesspeople should request one of the twelve rooms or suites with private redwood saunas. The service is lovely; the Garden Bar is a peaceful spot. Parking is $15 a day.
Singles: $95-$160; doubles: $115-$180; suites: $250-$750.

San Francisco Hilton & Tower

333 O'Farrell St.,
Union Square, 94102
• 771-1400,
Fax 771-6807

Business must be booming at the Hilton, because it continues to expand like mad. The current room count is a staggering 2,090—making this the largest hotel in Northern California. If you don't mind staying in a hotel bigger than most farm towns, you'll enjoy the Hilton. The tower rooms are large, quiet and comfortable, the location is convenient to Union Square shopping and downtown office buildings, and the views can be wonderful. Expect to see stampeding hordes of conventioneers, and plan on

getting lost now and then. On-site parking costs $16 per day.
Singles: $145-$205; doubles: $170-$230; suites: $250-$2,000.

San Francisco Marriott Fisherman's Wharf

1250 Columbus Ave.,
Fisherman's Wharf, 94133
• 775-7555,
Fax 474-2099

Although it aggressively woos the business traveler, the Marriott is not exactly convenient to downtown and the Financial District. Nor is it convenient to good restaurants, since Fisherman's Wharf is an enclave of overpriced tourist traps. But it is an attractive, quiet hotel with 256 well-appointed rooms and friendly service. Business travelers can take advantage of the complimentary morning limousine to the Financial District, and enjoy a room on the top-floor Executive Level, a private-club floor that features Continental breakfast, complimentary newspapers and other bonuses. Valet parking is $14 a day, with in-and-out privileges.
Singles & doubles: $182-$212; suites: $235-$250.

Sheraton at Fisherman's Wharf

2500 Mason St.,
Fisherman's Wharf, 94133
• 362-5500,
Fax 956-5275

A tourist hotel in the heart of San Francisco's tourist mecca, Fisherman's Wharf. But the business traveler is not neglected: there's a shuttle service to downtown and an in-house business center. The 525 rooms are standard-issue Sheraton, which is to say modern, quiet and comfortably appointed, if less than inspirational in decor. The hotel's several restaurants are no better than the nearby Fisherman's Wharf seafood houses. Parking is a meager $9 a day, with in-and-out privileges.
Singles & doubles: $145-$220; suites: $375. Packages available on an irregular basis.

AIRPORT

San Francisco Airport Hilton

San Francisco International Airport, 94128
• 589-0770,
Fax 489-4696

It may look like another terminal, but, no, it's the Airport Hilton—the only hotel with the dubious distinction of being located on the airport's grounds. The decor is dreadful, and there's nothing to do but sit by the pool and watch planes roar by overhead. But if you need to be right at the airport (perhaps for an early-morning departure), you can expect reasonable comfort. Buses run every ten minutes to all the airline terminals, and parking is free.
Singles: $125-$145; doubles: $140-$160; suites: $250-$440.

CHANEL

CHANEL BOUTIQUE: 155 MAIDEN LANE,

SAN FRANCISCO   (415) 981-1550

©T&CO. 1990

©T&CO.

TIFFANY & CO.

Seven ways to say three words.
Diamond, emerald, ruby and sapphire
rings from Tiffany. Available at Tiffany & Co.,
252 Grant Avenue, San Francisco,
415-781-7000.

TIFFANY & CO.

SHOPS

INTRODUCTION

TO MARKET, TO MARKET

Like all great cities, San Francisco is a classic market town. Even with the proliferation of suburban shopping malls, the city continues to draw shoppers from all over the Bay Area, even from all over the West (we know many Angelenos who come to San Francisco every December to do their Christmas shopping). The lure of San Francisco's shops is irresistible. You can pamper yourself on a Magnin's or Neiman's spree (facial, lunch, shopping), you can admire Union Square's jewels and designer clothes, you can wander such great neighborhood shopping streets as Union and Sacramento, where mixed in with the upscale chains and lively restaurants are terrific one-of-a-kind boutiques. Oh, the malls have struck the city, too—the San Francisco Centre with its gargantuan Nordstrom; tourist-mobbed Ghirardelli Square and Pier 39; Stonestown; and such chain-store collections as Embarcadero Center and Crocker Center Galleria—but these places have little to do with San Francisco's standing as a great shopping town. It's the city's creative mix that makes it such a powerful credit-card magnet. Since its founding, San Francisco has been an eccentric town, a strange collaboration between the conservative and the crazy. It's this mix that gives San Francisco's shopping scene its character. No matter what you're seeking—from the trendy to the staid, the classic to the bizarre—you'll find it here.

San Francisco's best shops, with a few exceptions, are clustered together in one of several great neighborhood shopping districts. Here are our favorites:

UNION SQUARE - This is the most famous of San Francisco's shopping districts. The downtown region centers on a one-block spot of greenery of the same name. Aside from the department stores and big-money boutiques adjacent to Union Square, make sure to wander Sutter Street and Maiden Lane.

JACKSON SQUARE - If words like Chippendale, Regency and French provincial are music to your ears, head for the Jackson Square area of the Financial District. Roughly bordered by Pacific, Montgomery, Washington and Sansome, this spot is home to many fine antiques dealers.

UNION STREET - The young and the upscale have made Union Street in historic old Cow Hollow the city's premier shopping street. Start at Van Ness and head west about ten blocks or so, and you'll pass through a shopper's paradise. There are plenty of cafés and bars along the way to keep your spirits up.

UPPER FILLMORE STREET - One of the city's newest shopping districts is on upper Fillmore Street, from Sutter to Pacific. Vivande and Trio, two of our favorite city cafés, can be found here, along with a couple of dozen unique and worthwhile shops.

SACRAMENTO STREET - Farther west in prosperous Presidio Heights is a several-block-long stretch of Sacramento Street lined with shops that would also be at home on trendy Union Street.

HAIGHT STREET - For a look at how the times have been a changin', head over to Haight Street in the Haight-Ashbury, the locus of flower power in the '60s. The baby boomers have moved up in the world, and mixed in among the remaining street people and diehard hippies are smartly dressed yuppies taking time out from restoring their Victorian houses to spend some money in the very '80s and '90s shops that have sprung up here.

In general, we have limited our reporting on San Francisco's best shops to those found within the city limits. A few exceptions were made, however, most notably in the "Food" section—several food shops in the East Bay and Marin are among the best in the country and are worth a trip from San Francisco.

ANTIQUES

Along with poking into the scattered, idiosyncratic collection of shops listed in this section, antiques aficionados should make a pilgrimage to the Jackson Square area of the Financial District, on Jackson Street near Montgomery. This officially declared Historic District is rife with such fine antiques merchants as Norman Shepherd and John Doughty, both of whom sell seventeenth-, eighteenth- and nineteenth-century French and English pieces; Hunt Antiques, dealers in Jacobean, Georgian and Regency furniture and art; Carpets of the Inner Circle, which sells, appraises and restores antique rugs; and Robert Domergue, who specializes in French provincial and Italian furniture.

Argentum
1750 Union St.,
Cow Hollow
• 673-7509

Glass cases of fine silver of the eighteenth and nineteenth centuries, including silverware, candlesticks, vases, some American arts-and-crafts pieces and affordable silver seals, line the walls of this lovely store, located at the back of an alley off Union Street.
Open Mon.-Sat. 11 a.m.-5:30 p.m.

Artiques
2167 Union St.,
Cow Hollow
• 929-6969

Billing itself as "affordable art," Artiques is a major dealer of Icart- and Maxfield Parrish–vintage lithographs. There's also a varied assemblage of seventeenth- to early-twentieth-century etchings, lithographs and oils. Neither the art nor the prices are blue chip, but there are some very good pieces. If you poke around a bit, you're sure to find something you not only love but can afford.
Open daily 10 a.m.-6 p.m.

Bauer Antiques
1878 Union St.,
Cow Hollow
• 921-7656

Eighteenth-century French antiques are sold at reasonable prices. The basement contains English and French country furniture and some prints; these pieces pale beside what's available upstairs, but the occasional find surfaces.
Open Mon.-Sat. 11 a.m.-5 p.m.

Bizen
3314 Sacramento St.,
Presidio Heights
• 346-3933

Although just large enough to step inside of and turn around, this tiny shop is floor-to-ceiling with antique Japanese treasures. Among them is a respectable collection of Imari ware, both the hand-painted sometsuke and the stenciled inban. Especially elegant and affordable are the eighteenth-century woven and lacquered flower baskets from Kyoto.
Open Tues.-Sat. 11 a.m.-4 p.m.

Hawley Bragg
3364 Sacramento St.,
Presidio Heights
• 563-8122

Hawley Bragg specializes in French antiques, but it certainly keeps an eye out for other interesting objects, and there are quality items in a good range of prices—from $3,000 for a spectacular pair of nickel silver chairs crowned with rams' heads, made in India for the English during the Raj, to $85 for framed hand-colored etchings. Interior design services are also available.
Open Mon.-Sat. 10 a.m.-5:30 p.m.

Edward Davidson
1714 Union St.,
Cow Hollow
• 563-2404

Some of the most arresting items in this collection of silver and antiques are the pieces of antique silver jewelry, and the silver napkin rings would make nice, unusual gifts. The rest of the collection is made up of various antiques, primarily vintage English, American and San Francisco silver.
Open Tues.-Sun. 11:30 a.m.-5:30 p.m.

Paris 1925
1954 Union St.,
Cow Hollow
• 567-1925

There are more reproductions and art deco–inspired furniture and objects than vintage pieces here. Only the watches would be of any interest to the serious deco collector.
Open Mon.-Sat. 11 a.m.-7 p.m., Sun. 11 a.m.-6 p.m.

Seven Seas Ltd.
1909 Union St.,
Cow Hollow
• 921-7090

This unprepossessing shop boasts a noteworthy assortment of folk art, textiles and kimonos from Indonesia, Thailand and Japan, respectively. The kimonos, all silk, are 30 to 40 years old, in good condition and in the $90-to-$300 price range. Among the handcrafts, standouts are the tightly woven baskets from the island of Lombok, just off the coast of Bali; the Indonesian wood carvings; and the marvelous wayang, the intricately carved shadow puppets.
Open Mon.-Sat. 10 a.m.-6 p.m., Sun. 11 a.m.-5 p.m.

Therien & Co.
411 Vermont St.,
South of Market
• 956-8850

Serenely existing in the shadow of the 101 Freeway, Therien's civilized shop features old Sheffield plates and antique porcelain, much of which is beautifully displayed on seventeenth- and eighteenth-century furniture. There are some especially lovely silver pieces, including a few contemporary tea services and serving utensils. Since the Sutter Street shop has closed, the inventory here has increased and the volume of turnover is high.
Open Mon.-Fri. 9:30 a.m.-5 p.m.

West of the Moon
3464 Sacramento St.,
Presidio Heights
• 922-4650

Established fifteen years ago as a folk-art gallery, West of the Moon is now actually three separate concerns at the same address: Lost Art, which deals in artifacts of Africa, the Americas and Oceania; New World Antiquities, which features pre-Columbian and especially Mayan pieces; and West of the Moon, which now focuses on native North American work.
Open Wed.-Sat. 1 p.m.-4:30 p.m., or by appt.

BEAUTY

BEAUTY PRODUCTS

Agraria
1156 Taylor St.,
Nob Hill
• 771-5922

Agraria's house blend of potpourri, redolent of roses and Provence, is as appealing as the romantic shop. Your sense of smell will be agreeably assaulted by the sachets, potpourris, candles and Floris of London soaps, oils and fragrances.
Open Mon.-Sat. 10 a.m.-5 p.m.

The Body Shop
2072 Union St.,
Cow Hollow
• 922-4076

Seventeen years ago in Berkeley, The Body Shop made its mark in the world of toiletries by opening a small shop selling quality handmade soaps—in all sorts of traditional and exotic fragrances—that were cut, wrapped and labeled right there. It also initiated the practice of recycling containers and customizing scents. Consistent high quality and an interesting variety of products ensured its success; there are now five shops in the Bay Area, one in New York and a mail-order business. The long, narrow Union Street shop is filled with temptations for self-indulgence—the entire Body Shop line of bath oils, bubble baths, lotions, soaps,

shampoos, masks, creams, cleansers and those intoxicating oils that range from Canton rose to frankincense to muguet. A few imported toiletries are also stocked, along with Mason Pearson and Altesse brushes, Karina combs, perfume bottles, soap dishes, natural sponges and so much more.
Open Mon.-Sat. 10:30 a.m.-6 p.m., Sun. 11 a.m.-6 p.m.

Crabtree & Evelyn
Crocker Center Galleria,
50 Post St.,
Financial District
• 392-6111

Whimsy and nostalgic romance are the watchwords of this renowned English fragrance company. We are especially fond of the Alice in Wonderland and Babar soaps and tins, as well as the sweet little baskets, which make wonderful hostess gifts. Also noteworthy are Crabtree's scented bath oils, sculpted soaps, rosewood brushes and attractively packaged teas and jams. There are several branches in San Francisco and the Bay Area.
Open Mon.-Sat. 9:30 a.m.-6 p.m.

L'Essential
1728 Union St.,
Cow Hollow
• 928-4483

Take three steps down from the sidewalk, close your eyes and breathe. You'll either start sneezing violently or think you've been transported to a linen closet somewhere in the south of France. The walls in this lovely wood-paneled shop are festooned with romantic bunches of dried flowers, and there are baskets, wooden boxes and glass vases replete with handmade scented soaps and potpourris of various blends from Provence. This charming shop has also started carrying European facial and skin products; it will soon be offering facials using a special volcanic mud. Also stocked in abundance are spices and teas.
Open Mon.-Sat. 10:30 a.m.-7 p.m., Sun. 10:30 a.m.-6 p.m.

Sutro Bath Cosmetics
1980 Union St.,
Cow Hollow
• 563-7624

Like The Body Shop, Sutro Bath carries its own line of toiletries—it's just not as extensive. Sutro also stocks the complete lines of English toiletries made by Potter & Moore and Taylor of London, along with a variety of bath accessories.
Open daily 11 a.m.-6 p.m.

BODY SHOPS

Elizabeth Arden
230 Post St.,
Union Square
• 982-3755

There's nothing like walking through this famous red door for a steam and a facial to make you forget your cares—and a couple of years, too. The rich and the severely stressed should try the five-plus-hour head-to-toe beauty treatment, which runs $200 and includes a light lunch; two other package deals, both of which cost $175 and also include

lunch, combine facials, hair styling, manicures, eyebrow shaping and makeup application. Arden's complete line of makeup and skin- and hair-care products are also sold here (at full retail price).
Open Mon.-Sat. 9 a.m.-4 p.m.

The Beauty Terrace
Neiman-Marcus,
150 Stockton St.,
Union Square
• 362-3900

Urban life got you down? Then visit Neiman's for a "Day of Pampering." You'll decompress via an hour-long body massage, an hour-long facial, a hair cut and styling, a light lunch (wine included) in the lovely Rotunda restaurant, a manicure, a pedicure and a makeup job. You'll emerge $165 poorer, but you'll certainly feel like a queen for a day. For those with less time and money, The Beauty Terrace offers each service separately. Its technicians are skilled and friendly.
Open Mon.-Wed. & Sat. 10 a.m.-6 p.m., Thurs.-Fri. 10 a.m.-8 p.m.

Mary Oei's About Face
629 Taylor St.,
Union Square
• 775-9452

Mary Oei and her staff are patient, thorough facial experts who see each client's face as a new and different challenge. Depending on your skin type and your specific problems, they will use one of seven different lines of professional European skin-care products. A facial, which mainly consists of a deep pore cleaning and peeling, costs $60 with Mary or $52 with one of her associates. The salon also offers waxing, manicures and pedicures, and stocks a good selection of cosmetics and European body creams.
Open Mon.-Sat. 9 a.m.-5 p.m.

Spa Nordstrom
San Francisco Centre,
865 Market St.,
Union Square
• 978-5102

Way up on the fifth floor of this wit-addling department store is an oasis of luxurious calm, the Spa Nordstrom. If you can afford to fork over $195, you'll enjoy six hours of healthy self-indulgence: the "Day Spa," an aromatic body shower, thalasso therapy, herbal body treatment, full body massage, aromatic scalp treatment, a facial and nail care, and a "spa cuisine" lunch. Short of this, there are the individual services: theraputic facials ($45 for one hour), massages, herbal body treatments, nail care and waxing. The emphasis is on creating a luxurious, rejuvenating experience, and all the products used are plant derivatives, sea extracts and natural clays. Spa Nordstrom sells a complete line of these creams, cleansers, balms and masks, plus nail colors and spa accessories.
Open Mon.-Wed. 9:30 a.m.-8 p.m., Thurs.-Fri. 9:30 a.m.-9 p.m., Sat. 9:30 a.m.-7 p.m., Sun. 11 a.m.-6 p.m.

HAIR SALONS

Cutting Corner
I. Magnin, Stockton & Geary sts.,
Union Square
• 362-2100

A good, basic hair salon for men and women on I. Magnin's sixth floor. Don't come here for the latest haircut that's making the SOMA nightclub rounds, but do make an appointment if you want a cut that is stylish but won't draw too much attention to yourself. Men's cuts are a reasonable $23, and women's are $35; weaving, perms and the like are also offered.
Open Mon. & Thurs.-Fri. 9:30 a.m.-8 p.m., Tues.-Wed. & Sat. 9:30 a.m.-6 p.m., Sun. noon-5 p.m.

Masa's Hair Salon
2536 California St.,
Presidio Heights
• 921-4033

The six stylists at Masa's are adept at chic but not overly trendy haircuts. A basic cut and styling for men ranges from $28 to $35; for women, $30 to $35, with extra charges for coloring, special moisturizing treatments and so on. Most of the stylists will stay late to give you an after-work cut. There is neither a manicurist nor a makeup person on staff.
Open Mon.-Sat. 9 a.m.-5 p.m. (hours may vary).

Transitions
166 Grant Ave.,
Union Square
• 433-7174

This longtime downtown salon has about twenty stylists, all of whom can provide you with a fashionable cut that suits your face and lifestyle. Cuts range from $25 to $40, depending on the stylist. Every conceivable hair service is provided, along with complete facial and beauty treatments.
Open Tues.-Wed. & Fri.-Sat. 9 a.m.-6 p.m., Thurs. 9 a.m.-7 p.m.

BOOKS & STATIONERY

BOOKS

Acorn Books
740 Polk St.,
Civic Center
• 563-1736

A virtual emporium of used and out-of-print titles. The rare books are beautifully displayed, and the store as a whole is well organized and clean—a rarity in the rare-book business.
Open Mon.-Sat. 10:30 a.m.-8 p.m., Sun. noon-7 p.m.

Argonaut Book Shop
786 Sutter St.,
Union Square
• 474-9067

A simple, uncluttered, quiet shop stocked with rare and out-of-print books, prints, maps and manuscripts. Owner Robert Haines has an especially fine collection of books and maps of early California, including the Gold Rush days, along with some lovely prints of old San Francisco. A must for the California history buff.
Open Mon.-Fri. 9 a.m.-5 p.m., Sat. 9 a.m.-4 p.m.

Austin Books
1687 Haight St.,
Haight-Ashbury
• 552-4122

You're sure to walk out with a couple of finds after visiting this clean, well-organized shop, formerly known as Charing Cross Road, which boasts an intriguing collection of used hardcover and paperback books. Prices are very fair, and the friendly owners will be happy to try to fill any special requests for hard-to-find books.
Open daily 11 a.m.-6 p.m.

Books Inc./Tro Harper
140 Powell St.,
Union Square
• 397-1555

This large, well-stocked general bookstore has something for everyone. Especially noteworthy are the cookbooks. Its weeknight hours make Books Inc. a good spot for browsing after work.
Open Mon.-Fri. 9:30 a.m.-9:30 p.m., Sat. 9:30 a.m.-7:30 p.m., Sun. 10 a.m.-6 p.m.

The Booksmith
1644 Haight St.,
Haight-Ashbury
• 863-8688

One of the signs of this neighborhood's gentrification, The Booksmith is spacious, attractive, organized and stocked with a well-rounded selection of new books and magazines. The collections of fiction (especially oversize paperbacks), mysteries, cookbooks, photography and architecture books are commendable.
Open Mon.-Sat. 10 a.m.-9 p.m., Sun. 10 a.m.-6 p.m.

Brentano's
San Francisco Centre,
865 Market St.,
Financial District
• 543-0933

This is a good, general bookstore with a respectable selection of coffee-table and travel books. Handsome and well organized, the store carries a decent assortment of paperbacks and the latest hardcover best-sellers, a well-stocked magazine rack, postcards and local maps—exactly what a bookstore in an upscale shopping mall should have.
Open Mon.-Wed. 9:30 a.m.-8 p.m., Thurs.-Fri. 9:30 a.m.-9 p.m., Sat. 9:30 a.m.-7 p.m., Sun. 11 a.m.-6 p.m.

Browser Books
2195 Fillmore St.,
Upper Fillmore
• 567-8027

Although the location has changed and the books are carefully organized on attractive wooden shelves, Browser still has that cozy bookwormish atmosphere, filled with books of every kind. The selection continues to be strong in contemporary and classic fiction, and unusual travel books, but space limitations have put an end to the used

books. You can still help yourself to a cup of coffee and plop down for a lengthy appraisal of your selection before committing to a purchase, but within five minutes of embarking on this pleasant diversion, we found ourselves faint from a decided lack of ventilation and staggered, gasping, to the door.
Open Mon.-Sat. 10 a.m.-10 p.m., Sun. 9 a.m.-10 p.m.

City Lights Books
261 Columbus Ave.,
North Beach
• 362-8193

A cultural mecca since 1953, City Lights is synonymous with the literary life of the city. Through its door have passed the movers and shakers in every branch of the arts from the Beat Era to the present. Still going strong, the bookstore has expanded—a former Italian travel agency next door is now a room devoted entirely to poetry—and boasts possibly the best selection of periodicals and books in town. Each member of the staff has a particular area of expertise, be it film or music or nineteenth-century French poetry, and keeps the inventory in that area up-to-date. Stop here to while away an hour or two checking out the latest small-press publications, then buy the latest novel by that 23-year-old literary prodigy and saunter down the street for an espresso at the Puccini.
Open daily 10 a.m.-midnight.

A Clean Well-Lighted Place for Books
601 Van Ness Ave.,
Civic Center
• 441-6670

The name, taken from a Hemingway short story, is very apt. This place is not only clean and well lighted, it also boasts a nicely chosen poetry and contemporary fiction section, a well-stocked mystery section, and a titillating selection of biographies and travel books. The shop frequently hosts book signings and offers a pleasant hour's distraction while you kill time before the next showing of that foreign film at the Opera Plaza Cinema.
Open Sun.-Thurs. 10 a.m.-11 p.m., Fri.-Sat. 10 a.m.-midnight

Cookbook Corner
620 Sutter St.,
Union Square
• 673-6281

Tucked away in the YMCA building is this fine collection of new, used and out-of-print cookbooks from all over the world, as well as wine books and regional charity cookbooks.
Open Mon.-Sat. 9:30 a.m.-6 p.m.

B. Dalton
Embarcadero Center,
Financial District
• 982-4278

One of the large chains that proliferate throughout the country, this branch surely carries all of the current, popular books that anyone might need. Besides, it's wonderfully anonymous. The only other B. Dalton in the city is at 200

Kearny Street near Union Square (956-2850).
Open Mon.-Fri. 9:30 a.m-6:30 p.m., Sat. 10 a.m.-6 p.m., Sun. noon-5 p.m.

Gourmet Guides
2801 Leavenworth St.,
North Beach
• 391-5903

Recently relocated to spacious new digs at the Cannery, Gourmet Guides sells virtually every cookbook, wine book and travel guide in print, including back issues of *Gourmet* from the '50s and '60s. Its roomy new quarters have allowed it to spread out, widen the selection a bit (including some attractive food-related posters and greeting cards) and organize everything well. Mail order is a big part of its business, so if it doesn't have what you're looking for, it'll get it for you—it ships all over the country. A must-visit for amateur cooks, dedicated gourmets and armchair travelers. Be sure to get on its mailing list to receive the list of the latest titles.
Open Mon.-Wed. 10 a.m.-8 p.m., Thurs.-Sat. 10 a.m.-8 p.m., Sun. 11 a.m.-5 p.m.

Green Apple Bookstore
506 Clement St.,
Richmond District
• 387-2272

Green Apple is a favorite of the city's bibliophiles. The shop stocks new titles, but of more interest are the stacks of used literature way in the back. Large numbers of used books—poetry, filmmaking, and pyschology—are mixed in with the new titles on the second floor.
Open Sun.-Thurs. 10 a.m.-10 p.m., Fri.-Sat. 10 a.m.-midnight.

Hunter's Bargain Bookstore
151 Powell St.,
Union Square
• 397-5955

An offshoot of Books Inc., Hunter's is a large, cluttered outlet for discount books, primarily publishers' closeouts. Most tend to be underwhelming specialty books, but you can almost always find at least one worthwhile bargain.
Open Mon.-Fri. 9:30 a.m.-9:30 p.m., Sat. 9:30 a.m.-7:30 p.m., Sun. 10 a.m.-6 p.m.

Paperback Traffic
1501 Polk St.,
Polk Gulch
• 661-8848

Good for contemporary fiction and art, Paperback Traffic also carries hardcover titles and an interesting selection of magazines.
Open daily 10 a.m.-10 p.m.

Sierra Club Bookstore
730 Polk St.,
Civic Center
• 923-5600

Naturalists, environmentalists and outdoors enthusiasts should hike over to this small, friendly bookstore stocked with books and maps on the Bay Area, the Sierra, Alaska and the Wild West. Hunters, real estate developers and hopeless urbanites won't feel at home here.
Open Mon.-Fri. 10 a.m.-5:30 p.m., Sat. 10 a.m.-5 p.m.

Solar Lights

2068 Union St.,
Cow Hollow
• 567-3206

The discount tables displayed a few steps below street level always lure us into this comfortable, unpretentious shop. The fiction section is kept up-to-date, and there are lots of just-released-titles in general. A good place for a brief respite during a day's shopping on Union Street.
Open Mon.-Thurs. 10 a.m.-10 p.m., Fri.-Sat. 10 a.m.-11 p.m., Sun. 11 a.m.-7 p.m.

William Stout Architectural Books

804 Montgomery St.,
Financial District
• 391-6757

Unlike at the Sierra Club Bookstore, artificial structures are the things of beauty here. An outstanding collection of new and rare architectural books for both the scholar and the layman is well displayed on shelves and tables. A must for the architect, designer, landscaper and dedicated home-owner.
Open Mon.-Wed. & Fri.-Sat. 10 a.m.-5:30 p.m., Thurs. 10 a.m.-9 p.m.

Waldenbooks

2169 Chestnut St.,
Cow Hollow
• 563-1658

This popular chain has three outlets in the city. The staff at this one is particularly fond of the fiction section, which will wear out the fingertips of even the most avid browser.
Open Mon.-Fri. 10 a.m.-8 p.m., Sat. 10 a.m.-6 p.m., Sun 11 a.m.-6 p.m.

STATIONERY

Desk Set

3252 Sacramento St.,
Presidio Heights
• 921-9575

One of life's little pleasures is good stationery and desk accessories. This is understood at Desk Set, which stocks elegant stationery and cards that can be imprinted with whatever you want right there on the premises. Tempting knickknacks include picture frames, blank books bound in leather and cloth, letter openers, metal seals with sealing wax, stacks of agendas and smart address books, French Elysée fountain pens and even personalized computer paper.
Open Mon.-Fri. 10 a.m.-6 p.m., Sat. 10 a.m.-5 p.m.

Gump's

250 Post St.,
Union Square
• 982-1616

When young women from wealthy San Francisco families become engaged, they hurry over to Gump's to order impeccable engraved invitations on Crane paper. (While there, they also register for china and crystal.) The stationery department in this San Francisco shopping landmark is nonpareil, with exquisite stationery, striking desk accessories, silver letter openers and picture frames. The level of service is as high as the prices.
Open Mon.-Sat. 9:30 a.m.-5:30 p.m.

Oggetti

1846 Union St.,
Cow Hollow
• 346-0631

Oggetti's hand-marbled stationery from Florence is perfect for *billets-doux,* thoughtful thank-yous and wonderful gifts. Marbling clearly must be a major industry in Florence, since virtually everything in this charming eighteenth-century-style shop—from the notebooks to the bookmarks to the pencils—is covered in it, which robs it of some of its cachet. Out of the context of the shop, however, these items are perfectly lovely and romantic. We would be pleased as punch to receive a gift of the stationery with illuminated and gilded initials at the top.
Open Mon.-Thurs. & Sat. 10 a.m.-6 p.m., Fri. 10 a.m.-8 p.m., Sun. 11 a.m.-6 p.m.

Quantity Postcards

1441 Grant Ave.,
North Beach
• 986-8866

Not only does Quantity Postcards sell thousands of strange, outlandish and hilarious postcards, it publishes them, too. You'll find all of its wacky cards here, along with boxes of vintage postcards and some put out by other publishers. Bring your sense of humor and plenty of stamps.
Open daily noon-11 p.m. (hours may vary).

Union Street Papery

2162 Union St.,
Cow Hollow
• 563-0200

High-quality announcements, invitations and personal stationery are the specialty here, and the selection will occupy you for a while. The large assortment of greeting cards in this split-level shop includes some one-of-a-kind cards of handmade paper folded into fanciful shapes, and among the wrapping papers are some beautiful examples of hand marbling.
Open Mon.-Sat. 10 a.m.-6 p.m., Sun. 11 a.m.-5 p.m.

CHILDREN

BOOKS

Qimbys

3411 California St.,
Laurel Heights
• 751-7727

A most organized and well-stocked bookstore for children, this shop will both supply all your child's cultural necessities and create some new ones. Books are arranged according to subject—folklore, myths, art history, poetry—and all the classics are here, even in foreign languages. There's a mind-boggling array of video and audio cassettes, the latter both spoken and music. Some sensible toys and an art-supplies department are at the rear. On Wednesday mornings story readings are held and on Saturday mornings, creative activ-

ities. A day late for the latter, we exited with a French edition of *Babar* to enjoy over a café au lait a couple doors away at Peet's Coffee.
Open Mon.-Sat. 9:30 a.m.-6 p.m., Sun. 11 a.m.-5 p.m.

CLOTHES

Benetton 012
450 Powell St.,
Union Square
• 391-4146

The very same wool sweaters and cotton shirts and pants that adorn seemingly every teenager in the western world are now made to fit children under the age of 12. If your third-grader is fashion-conscious, he'll talk you into spending far more than you should (even though the prices are not unreasonable).
Open Mon.-Sat. 10 a.m.-6:30 p.m., Sun. noon-6 p.m.

Dottie Doolittle
3680 Sacramento St.,
Presidio Heights
• 563-3244

When the 6-year-old little darling stamped her little patent-leather-shod foot and sobbed that she would have only the black velvet dress with the hand-embroidered smocking ($165), we knew we were in the right place. This pleasant, spacious shop is supply central for Daddy's little princesses, from age 4 to 14 (and considering the prices, let's hope Daddy is royalty of some sort). There's stylish sportswear by Nini Bam Bini and Up, Up & Away, as well as a multitude of classic pretty dresses. Fetching, beautifully made infant wear is divided up into pink and blue at the rear of the store, where you'll also find exquisite silk and linen christening gowns.
Open Mon.-Sat. 9:30 a.m.-5 p.m., Sun. noon-5 p.m.

Familiar
1828 Union St.,
Cow Hollow
• 563-0777

The first U.S. location for this Japanese chain, this large shop is stocked for the infant and toddler. The bulk of the bright, well-made and pricey clothing is produced under the store label. Highlights include the good selection of first shoes—Weeboks and Trotty among them—and the comprehensive Beatrix Potter area, featuring all of her little creatures in books, clothes, toys and dishes. And to entertain restless shopping companions, there's a backyard with a wooden-house maze and a goldfish pond.
Open Mon.-Fri. 10 a.m.-6 p.m., Sat. 11 a.m.-6 p.m., Sun. 11 a.m.-5 p.m.

Kids Only
1415 Haight St.,
Haight-Ashbury
• 552-5445

If you can't abide clutter, stay out of this shop. But if you're looking for attractive, practical, fairly priced clothing for infants and children, you will have come to the right place. No $150 designer playsuits here, just fun, well-wearing

clothes, with a particular emphasis on Osh Kosh. Kids Only is also a must-visit for clothing historians and lifelong hippies—it stocks tiny tie-dyed T-shirts in psychedelic colors.
Open Mon.-Sat. 10 a.m.-6 p.m., Sun. noon-5 p.m.

Kinder Sport
3566 Sacramento St.,
Presidio Heights
• 563-7778

Apparently, it's never too soon to take sports seriously, judging by the success of this ski-clothing shop for children from 8 to 18. Eschewing animal prints, French ski wear manufacturers, such as Killy and Boy, have simply miniaturized their adult lines for the small but earnest skier.
Open Mon.-Sat. 10 a.m.-6 p.m.

Mudpie
1699 Union St.,
Cow Hollow
• 771-9262

Running the gamut from Osh Kosh to Jean Bourget and Dior, this moderately upscale shop has a few surprises. How can you resist red-watermelon rompers with little black seeds, complete with a hat fashioned to resemble half a watermelon to crown your little tot?
Open Mon.-Sat. 10:30 a.m.-6 p.m., Sun. noon-5 p.m.

Sheridan-Flynn
3462 Sacramento St.,
Presidio Heights
• 921-5961

Any shop that bills itself as an "infant clothier" is most likely going to involve a major fiscal and cultural experience. And, yes, this place is not only expensive, but the help is pretty darn huffy. Our innocent note-taking goaded one tight-lipped matron into asking us to leave. To be fair, however, we must admit that this "clothier" does carry some very smart imported duds—Tartine de Chocolat is just one of the standouts—and its own line of precious silk christening gowns.
Open Mon.-Sat. 10 a.m.-6 p.m.

Thursday's Child
1980 Union St.,
Cow Hollow
• 346-1666

Why are so many childrens' clothing shops, even expensive ones, such pandemonium? Is the clothing too small to organize? There are some great finds in this packed basement shop, such as Monkey Wear—imaginative, pricey all-cotton playclothes—if you have the patience to sort through the stacks on tables and shelves, and all the merchandise hanging from the ceiling and walls.
Open Mon.-Sat. 10 a.m.-6 p.m., Sun. 11 a.m.-5 p.m.

Trumpette
2506 Sacramento St.,
Upper Fillmore
• 931-7900

A bold star is the leitmotif for the imaginatively designed clothing for children sold in this shop. Trumpette, from San Francisco, designs clothing for children from 6 months to 8 years. In bright primary colors and buffalo plaids, the snap-bottom pants and T-shirts are simple and ingenious. We were delighted by the high-waisted, snap-bottom pants

with wide black elastic suspenders and the rich-hued hand-knit little sweaters. If we were ten months old, we'd refuse to be seen in anything else.
Open Mon.-Sat. 10 a.m.-6 p.m., Sun. noon-5 p.m.

Young Man's Fancy
3527 California St.,
Laurel Heights
• 221-4230

This San Francisco institution is where boys and young men are outfitted in the traditional prep-school look. There are button-down oxford cloth shirts, shetland sweaters and tweed jackets galore by such makers as Boston Trader and Polo University. The wide selection includes tennis, golf and ski attire, and Young Man's Fancy's own well-made, well-priced label.
Open Mon.-Sat. 9:30 a.m.-6 p.m.

Yountville
2416 Fillmore St.,
Upper Fillmore
• 922-5050

In this bright little shop you'll discover a well-rounded selection of clothes and accessories for newborns to 5-year-olds, with a few things for older children. Fabrics are cotton, and the makers range from Absorba to such trendy-tot outfitters as Malima, Baby Guess and Ton Sur Ton. There are also a few Brio and Ambi toys.
Open Mon.-Sat. 10 a.m.-6 p.m., Sun. noon-4 p.m.

FURNITURE

Jonathan-Kaye
3548 Sacramento St.,
Presidio Heights
• 563-0773

Literally spilling out the door onto the sidewalk, unfinished pine furniture for children is the principal merchandise here. There are bunk beds and dressers, chairs and desks, all well made, reasonably priced and just waiting for the stroke of the paintbrush. Jammed in with the furniture are some high-quality toys by Brio and Gund, a respectable assortment of Paddington bears and a good selection of books.
Open Mon.-Fri. 10 a.m.-6 p.m., Sat. 10 a.m.-5:30 p.m., Sun. noon-5 p.m.

TOYS

FAO Schwarz
48 Stockton St.,
Union Square
• 394-8700

Though nationally famous, this acclaimed toy store (which recently moved a few blocks to this location) from New York seems unremarkable now that fine children's stores are proliferating. True, there are captivating train sets, Steiff and Trupa stuffed animals and extravagant child-size race cars, but most of the merchandise can be found at any decent toy store, in many cases for less money. Still, no child

will object to an FAO Schwarz outing.
Open Mon.-Fri. 10 a.m.-6 p.m., Sat. 10 a.m.-5:30 p.m., Sun. noon-5 p.m.

Game Gallery of Carmel
1 Embarcadero Center,
Financial District
• 433-4263

Need some exercise for your excess intellect? Come here and pick up an elaborate chess set, or intricate computer puzzles and word games, or seemingly every element ever conceived for Dungeons and Dragons. A new and curious twist on the latter is the role-playing games with titles like "Macho Women with Guns" and its sequels "Batwing Renegade Girls" and "Renegade Nuns on Wheels." The sales staff is always prepared to talk turkey about combat strategies.
Open Mon.-Fri. 10 a.m.-6 p.m., Sat. 10 a.m.-5 p.m., Sun. noon-5 p.m.

Heffalump
1694 Union St.,
Cow Hollow
• 928-4300

This sunny Victorian shop is an orderly cornucopia of educational toys and books—and it even has a lot of things that kids really go for, like the fluorescent-blue rubberish, creepy rope-thing that can be stretched to unbelievable lengths only to snap back to its original size. This makes an interesting contrast to the veritable menagerie of Steiff stuffed animals and oversize, hand-carved and -painted Pinocchios mounted on the walls, slated for heirloomdom. You might have some trouble dragging your child out of here; ten minutes past closing time we were asked politely to please leave.
Open Mon.-Wed. 10 a.m.-6 p.m., Thurs.-Fri. 10 a.m.-6:30 p.m., Sun. 11 a.m.-5 p.m.

Imaginarium
3535 California St.,
Laurel Heights
• 387-9885

Like Alice, we wanted to go through the little door, next to the regular one, but it was too small. We could have crawled through on our hands and knees, we guess, but one has to maintain one's dignity. No matter, once we got in we threw dignity to the winds. After all, the slogan of this delightful store is "A Store Kids Can Handle," meaning that kids can actually play with the toys, and we meant to put the staff to the test. In addition to the usual educational toys by Play Skool, Ambi and Brio, there are Slinkys, wind-up dinosaurs, super string (which we'll refrain from describing) and elaborate plush hand puppets by Gund. Equally enchanting are the dolls—Madame Alexander's Storybook Dolls; Carolle dolls from France, which are geared to the age of the child and behave accordingly; dolls by Pauline, with porcelain-colored flesh and realistic hair; and those perennial favorites, Raggedy Ann and Andy.

There are many books and cassettes. Check out the minerals for the budding geologist.
Open Mon.-Sat. 9:30 a.m.-6 p.m., Sun. noon-5 p.m.

Jeffrey's
445 Sutter St.,
Union Square
• 982-3320

An all-purpose toy store with a representative collection of contemporary kids' toys. Dolls range from Madame Alexander to Barbie, and you can find everything from Care Bears to Laser Tag to intelligent educational toys. Two other shops can be found in the Embarcadero Center (397-8838) and Ghirardelli Square (776-6780).
Open Mon.-Sat. 9:30 a.m.-6 p.m., Sun. noon-5 p.m.

The Littlest Mouse
3484 Sacramento St.,
Presidio Heights
• 567-5121

Can't afford the down payment on that Victorian dream house? Then work out some of your frustration in a small way by having the skilled and accommodating staff here build you (or even your child) a doll-house replica, correct down to the Chippendale dining set, the chintz curtains and the (electrically wired) chandelier. They understand obsession here—it goes with the territory. They'll copy any house, or build one for you from their selection of kits, or sell you a kit to build your own. You can then fill it with furniture made to order or from the selection of miniature accoutrements available here, which is both sizable and choice (ask to see the hooked rugs painstakingly rendered in needlepoint). There's a wide range of options and prices, and this is one house-building experience that won't end in a life-and-death struggle with a contractor.
Open Tues.-Sat. 11 a.m.-5 p.m., or by appt.

CLOTHES

ACCESSORIES

Brava Strada
3247 Sacramento St.,
Presidio Heights
• 657-5757

All roughened concrete and smooth marble, Brava Strada offers an eclectic sampling of Italian leather handbags, art jewelry and various accessories in an oh-so-postmodern environment. From the spare, bleached first floor, where art jewelry by both local and East Coast designers is displayed in long glass cases, and attractive leather goods by Italian designer Desmo slouch against the rough walls, you

ascend a brief flight of marble steps to the next level, where a large transparent case holding drawers of sweaters, sunglasses, gloves and belts awaits. Emphasis is on accessories, but the store also carries three lines of knitwear: Kay Cosserat from Britain, Franco Guare from Los Angeles and Braeda & Huran from the Bay Area. Wardrobe consultation and personal shopping services are also available.
Open Mon.-Sat. 11 a.m.-6 p.m.

Eyes in Disguise
2189 Union St.,
Cow Hollow
• 474-5321

As everyone knows, sunglasses are *the* necessary accessory for both the terminally and the wannabe hip, the budding *vedette* and the incurable night owl, forced at times to scurry around during daylight hours, and this is the place to get the right pair. On wavy cement shelves set into the walls are just about every look and make of sunglasses that anyone could possibly be interested in, including sports styles. Specs designed by Jean Paul Gaultier, L.A. Eyeworks, Oliver's People, Alain Mikli, La Roche, Armani, Wayfarer, plus sports styles by Vaurnet, Gargoyle and others, are well displayed in this small shop.
Open Mon.-Sat. 11 a.m.-7 p.m., Sun. noon-5 p.m.

Hermès
212 Stockton St.,
Union Square
• 986-6184

Once a small boutique tucked away in I. Magnin, this French firm, originally known for the best in equestrian gear, now has its own premises on Union Square. This tastefully appointed two-story boutique is a sort of House of Hermès *manqué* in that it stocks mainly Hermès's greatest hits—the illustrated silk scarves, the ties, the belts, the address books and a saddle or two—to appeal to tourists. The selection represents a fraction of what's available from this designer and none of the hardcore France-interprets-the-English-dandy stuff that put this place on the map (on the Faubourg du St.-Honoré, that is), but the items available are still pretty wonderful. The silver flasks, watches and leather goods are all very well made and, for the most part, exceptionally handsome—both chic and classic at the same time—*and* appropriately expensive. The salespeople are almost disappointingly courteous and attentive.
Open Mon.-Sat. 10 a.m.-6 p.m., Sun. noon-5 p.m.

Kicks
1951 Union St.,
Cow Hollow
• 567-5580

There are mainly socks here, and in good supply. Hot Sox, Leggale, Hue come in a riot of colors and patterns, trimmed or plain, bulky or delicate, pretty or outrageous. There's also a small selection of panties and stockings.
Open Mon.-Thurs. 10 a.m.-7 p.m., Fri. 10 a.m.-7:30 p.m., Sat. 10 a.m.-7 p.m., Sun. 11 a.m.-6 p.m.

Swaine Adeney

434 Post St.,
Union Square
• 781-4949

Before you toddle over to the club, pop by Swaine Adeney with your gentleman's gentleman and have him pick out a few trifles for you. While he selects some valises for your next big-game jaunt, visit the room stocked with jolly fine rifles, all handmade in England by Westley Richards. Then have him choose a silk umbrella and a few pairs of leather gloves that will complement your tweeds on city strolls. It's no wonder Swaine Adeney is the umbrella maker to the Queen Mother—they are beautifully made and proportioned, constructed of the finest woods, leathers, silks and nylons in a plethora of colors and patterns, all supremely tasteful. The leather products—belts, briefcases, wallets, luggage—are equally well made and discreetly handsome, as is the riding gear upstairs. The prices limit the clientele to the landed gentry.
Open Mon.-Fri. 9:30 a.m.-6 p.m., Sat. 10 a.m.-6 p.m.

CASUAL

Aca Joe

295 Geary St.,
Union Square
• 788-8780

Like The Gap and The Limited, Aca Joe stores have spread faster than wildfire. And also like The Gap and The Limited, Aca Joe sells fun, colorful sportswear made of sturdy cottons, at prices that are more than fair. The unisex line is limited to T-shirts, sweatshirts, cotton sweaters, cotton jackets, striped shirts, chinos and elastic-waist shorts and trousers, many of which feature Aca Joe's logo. The logos we could live without, but we do like the simple styles and loose, comfortable cuts. There are several other branches, including one in Ghirardelli Square (474-6960).
Open Mon.-Thurs. 9:30 a.m.-9 p.m., Fri.-Sat. 9:30 a.m.-10 p.m., Sun. 11 a.m.-7 p.m.

Banana Republic

224 Grant Ave.,
Union Square
• 788-3087

Although there's no disputing the high quality and good cut of these khaki and natural-tone cotton ensembles, we wouldn't be caught dead wearing them abroad, especially in Africa or India. There's nothing like a logo-printed Banana Republic T-shirt to advertise your tourist status. But we cannot fault the chinos, mesh T-shirts, unadorned polo shirts, military-style shorts, bomber jackets and striped cotton shirts for stateside casual wearing, and we would gladly take the overpriced but well-designed and rugged luggage around the world. Visiting these safari-crazy stores is as fun as going on the Jungleland Cruise at Disneyland. Devotees should make the trek up to Mill Valley (59 Throckmorton Street, 383-4900), where the Banana Republic craze started. There's another city branch at 2253

Polk Street (474-9711).
Open Mon.-Wed. 9:30 a.m.-7 p.m., Thurs.-Fri. 9:30 a.m.-9 p.m., Sat. 9:30 a.m.-6:30 p.m., Sun. noon-5 p.m.

Benetton
457 Powell St.,
Union Square
• 398-4494

These bright Italian boutiques are becoming as common as McDonald's in American (and European) cities, San Francisco among them. Benetton's forte is the sweater; its wool and cotton pullovers and cardigans are almost always great-looking and are almost reasonably priced. There are also some unisex cotton shirts, wool and cotton trousers and a few jackets. Despite being a chain, Benetton has managed to stay fashionable and young—though its ubiquitousness means your chic outfits will hardly be one of a kind. You'll find other Benettons in the Embarcadero Center (982-2609) and at 1969 Union Street in Cow Hollow (931-4347).
Open Mon.-Sat. 10 a.m.-6:30 p.m., Sun. noon-6 p.m.

Bolla
1903 Fillmore St.,
Upper Fillmore
• 346-3131
1764 Haight St.,
Haight-Ashbury
• 386-3290

Contemporary, casual sportswear for young-in-spirit men and women from such makers as Girbaud, Paris Blues and Renaissance. T-shirts, cotton trousers, chic miniskirts, some great rayon separates, funny English shoes and an array of good-looking sunglasses make up Bolla's fashionable (but not extreme-cutting-edge) look. The selection is small but quite reasonably priced.
Open Mon.-Sat. 11 a.m.-6 p.m., Sun. 11 a.m.-5:30 p.m.

Button Down
3640 Sacramento St.,
Presidio Heights
• 563-6715

Yet another Ralph Lauren clone, this cozy shop carries primarily its own handsome line of traditional, outdoors-oriented clothing for men and women. There are great swashbuckling raincoats, thick hand-knit sweaters, manly robes and luxurious yet practical separates for career women. Accessories are displayed in handsome wood cases with glass doors, and there's some very nice leather luggage laying about.
Open Mon.-Sat. 10 a.m.-6 p.m.

California
2343 Market St.,
Castro District
• 864-1534

This stark, white, architecturally crude space is an apt venue for the fanciful, weird and currently bright creations of California's daring style-makers. Among them rank Roberto Robledo—represented here by his brilliantly colored Lycra and cotton knit dresses—and menswear designers Joseph Domingo, Jajo, Hank Ford and K. Kohberger, whose "Cocktail Dress from Hell," a little orange satin spandex number trimmed with matching tassels, left us with our jaws agape. Our equilibrium was restored by the sight

of a couple of piles of intricately tie-dyed T-shirts—something we could immediately relate to. And as in virtually every boutique in San Francisco, there are handmade earrings and hats, in this case both rather pointedly odd. It is precisely this unbridled experimental quality about the fashions here, however, that makes California such an exciting shop.
Open daily 11 a.m.-7 p.m.

Carnevale
2206 Union St.,
Cow Hollow
• 931-0669

Richly embroidered jackets and vests in muted tones by Zelda, Street Life's shaped cotton and lyrca separates, the Madcap Milliner's floral-printed chapeaus with velvet bands and cool shirts by Studio Tokyo are some of the small but very hip assortment of men's and women's fashions by fledgling designers available in this bright, spare little shop.
Open Mon.-Sat. 11 a.m.-7 p.m., Sun. noon-6 p.m.

C P Shades
2121 Fillmore St.,
Upper Fillmore
• 923-0544

Comfort is the statement here, not high fashion. C P Shades's baggy cotton-jersey T-shirts, cardigans, sweaters and elastic-waist skirts, pants and shorts for women are so comfortable that they'd make fine pajamas. The look is rumpled, beachy and oh-so-California, and the prices are within reach, if a bit high given the clothing's simplicity. Soon, you will have to come here for this clothing, since at press time C P Shades had closed its discount store and the line will no longer be available in department stores.
Open Mon.-Wed. & Fri. 11 a.m.-7 p.m., Thurs. 11 a.m.-9 p.m., Sat. noon-6 p.m., Sun. noon-5 p.m.

Ralph Davies
77 Maiden Ln.,
Union Square
• 397-3200

Your basic postmodern industrial couture emporium, Ralph Davies offers possibly San Francisco's vastest assortment of creative contemporary clothing for men and women by such ne plus ultra designers as Thierry Mugler, Yojhi Yamamoto, Byblos and Issey Miyake. Filed along the cement walls are wrap dresses by Romeo Gigli, Jean Paul Gaultier morning coats, Jean-Charles de Castelbajac teddy bear coats and Moschino's marionette jacket trimmed with a couple of place settings of gold flatware. There are strange-hued, exaggerated hats that truly look designed by a mad hatter—Jacques Le Corre in this case—and very *recherché* accessories: wonderful jewelry, sunglasses, belts and handbags. From the entry level you can either climb a flight of zigzag stairs to the Armani room above or head downstairs to peruse the off-season specials or venture into Comme des Garçons, formerly a separate boutique entered from Geary and now an adjunct to Ralph Davies. The clothing in this *endroit*, designed by Rei Kawakubo, requires commitments on the part of the wearer—both a considerable financial commitment and a serious commitment to setting yourself apart from the ordinary buttoned-down hordes. If you have the wherewithal to spend $100 on a T-shirt and $1,000 on a sportcoat, come on down! *Open Mon.-Sat. 10:30 a.m.-6:30 p.m.*

Flying Colors Cotton Company
1872 Union St.,
Cow Hollow
• 563-0440

T-shirt clothing for women in a riot of colors and styles is the main attraction. You can mix and match these mostly cotton, inexpensive separates to wear for aerobics, jogging, going to a go-go or just hanging out. A small investment in bright socks, black leggings or a red sweatshirt is a thrifty way to add panache to a tired wardrobe—and not just for the under-30 crowd. Many locations in San Francisco and the Bay Area.
Open daily 10 a.m.-8 p.m.

The Gap
1485 Haight St.,
Haight-Ashbury
• 431-6336
934 Market St.,
Union Square
• 397-2266

The Gap offers the best bargains in attractive American casual wear today, especially for men. The cotton shirts, trousers, polo shirts, denim jackets and jeans are similar in design and quality to the classic sportswear made by Ralph Lauren and Calvin Klein, at half the price: $30 for pleated cotton chinos, $32 for a white button-down shirt, $40 for an oversize cotton sweater. The women's line (cotton trousers, skirts, blouses, shorts and sweaters) is also fun, well fitting and low-priced. And, of course, there are Levi's of every size and style. The Haight store is a sign of how times have changed—it sells its preppy clothing on the acclaimed corner of Haight and Ashbury, where patched jeans and tie-dye once reigned supreme. There are many other stores, including one on Polk, one on Chestnut and one on Market in the Castro.
Open Mon.-Fri. 10 a.m.-8 p.m., Sat. 11 a.m.-7 p.m., Sun. 11 a.m.-6 p.m.

Marithé & Francois Girbaud
17 Stockton St.,
Union Square
• 391-0120

This place is too hip. Gray, spare industrial interior with tiny dressing rooms—what a shower would have looked like, had one appeared in *The Cabinet of Dr. Caligari*—constructed by placing large, odd-shaped frosted glass doors across a couple of corners: not much space to maneuver. On the ground floor are men's and women's sportswear, including Girbaud's great-fitting jeans and khakis, which are still $55 to $69 (and considerably less than anything else here). It's all very understated and sexy, and we were

particularly lusting after the trenchcoats. A staircase ascends to a mezzanine where sale items can be found.
Open Mon.-Sat. 10 a.m.-7 p.m., Sun. noon-6 p.m.

M.A.C.
814 Post St.,
Union Square
• 775-2515

Who says you can't judge a book by its cover? That's precisely why one shops here. Not only does this clothing imply what one is about, some of it literally spells it out, like Katharine Hamnet's eccentric T-shirt couture, boldly lettered with political slogans. Or make your statement with avant-garde clothing by Texan Todd Oldham and San Francisco's own brilliant Hank Ford, who has a room devoted to her creations. Just making any purchase here will make a statement—about your financial status.
Open Mon.-Sat. 11 a.m.-7 p.m., Sun. noon-5 p.m.

JEWELRY

Cartier
231 Post St.,
Union Square
• 397-3180

This large branch of the acclaimed Parisian jeweler and watchmaker is an opulently serene establishment, with glass cases glowing from the wealth inside. Naturally, you'll want to inspect the justly famous watches and the extravagant jewels, but don't neglect the fabulous—and not terribly overpriced—displays of silver. The staff is content to let you browse.
Open Mon.-Sat. 10 a.m.-5:30 p.m.

Di Lelio's
1739A Union St.,
Cow Hollow
• 771-8445

Not only is the antique silver and gold jewelry here worth a visit, but the vintage costume jewelry is some of the best we've found. Inspired abstract brooches from the '40s and chunky link bracelets from the '50s compose part of this choice, reasonably priced selection. And, as in every notable shop like this, the owner's enthusiasm for the merchandise overrides her interest in making a sale. A good place to visit periodically to see what marvels have come in. Hours vary.
Open Mon. & Thurs.-Sat. noon-5:30 p.m.

Gump's
250 Post St.,
Union Square
• 982-1616

The choicest pearls and jade and the finest gold and silver are crafted into exquisitely simple pieces with price tags that will send you reeling. Equally attractive are the necklaces, earrings, brooches and rings made of such stones as tourmaline and lapis lazuli. Because Gump's combs the world for the finest raw materials and designs and manufactures these pieces itself, you can be assured of their quality. But you'll pay dearly for that assurance.
Open Mon.-Sat. 9:30 a.m.-5:30 p.m.; jewelry dept. open until 5 p.m.

Jest Jewels

2049 Union St.,
Cow Hollow
• 563-8839

A pricier, adult version of the five-and-dime. You could walk out of here with a jewelry collection to rival the late Duchess of Windsor's in style if not in cost. The selection runs the gamut from faux baroque pearls to bits of anodized engine parts, and what an assortment of watches!—cheap tickers to handsome quartz knockoffs of serious timepieces. Also worth a visit are the sunglasses with miniature tableaux of California scenes recreated on the frames.
Open Mon.-Fri. 11 a.m.-8 p.m., Sat. 10 a.m.-10 p.m., Sun. 11 a.m.-7 p.m.

Laykin et Cie

I. Magnin,
Stockton & Geary sts.,
Union Square
• 362-2100

You can be assured that these baubles, while made of impeccable emeralds, rubies, diamonds and sapphires, will not make *too* much of a statement. As befits its longstanding relationship with I. Magnin, San Francisco's oldest old-money merchant, Laykin et Cie sells refined, elegant but not too ostentatious jewelry at appropriately high prices. The watch collection is lovely.
Open Mon. & Thurs.-Fri. 9:30 a.m.-8 p.m., Tues.-Wed. & Sat. 9:30 a.m.-6 p.m., Sun. noon-5 p.m.

St. Eligius

1748 Union St.,
Cow Hollow
• 771-2282

Reminiscent in spirit of the work of Tiffany's famous designer, Jean Schlumberger, precious stones are used as clever accents in the gold jewelry made here. The eye of the pheasant is a ruby; the dewdrops on the leaf are diamonds. A marked art deco influence is expressed in many of the pieces, but most of it is interesting in its own right. Along with gem appraisal and brokerage, St. Eligius is linked to a computer network that can locate that flawless, marquise-cut emerald you've been searching for.
Open Tues.-Fri. 10 a.m.-6 p.m., Sat. 10:30 a.m.-5 p.m.

Shreve & Co.

200 Post St.,
Union Square
• 421-2600

An old San Francisco jeweler in an old building that survived the great earthquake and last year's version, Shreve & Co. is a bastion of conservative good taste. The window displays are always a treat, and the silver pieces are especially lovely. There's also a full range of crystal and fine gifts.
Open Mon.-Sat. 9:30 a.m.-5:30 p.m.

Tiffany & Co.

252 Grant Ave.,
Union Square
• 781-7000

Even the least materialistic among us delights in receiving one of these famous little blue boxes—for inside will surely be something wonderful. Whether exorbitant or modest, a gift from Tiffany is almost always beautiful. We especially like Elsa Peretti's modern silver pieces, Jean Schlumberger's classic designs for gold and gems, and the timeless silver gift items, from teething rings to picture frames. Elegant brides register here for Tiffany's own sterling and china. Service is friendly, if slow, and the ambience is conducive to browsing. *Open Mon.-Sat. 10 a.m.-5:15 p.m.*

Tom Wing & Sons
190 Post St.,
Union Square
• 956-4700

Gump's isn't the only place in town for jade. Fans of the beloved gem of the Orient should visit Wing's elegant shop to inspect the unusual collection of striking lavender, apple-green and emerald-green jade. Asian antiques complement the jade, and diamonds, pearls and watches round out the jewelry selection.
Open Mon.-Sat. 9 a.m.-5 p.m.

Union Street Goldsmith
1763 Union St.,
Cow Hollow
• 776-8048

Specializing in gold jewelry and custom design, Union Street Goldsmith handles the work of a few well-known artisans whose designs are contemporary. Some pearls and silver jewelry are also showcased.
Open Mon.-Sat. 11 a.m.-5:45 p.m., Sun. noon-4:45 p.m.

MENSWEAR

Ariston
349 Sutter St.,
Union Square
• 421-2830

This open, attractive store sells the clothing of just three designers: Armani, Ungaro and Hugo Boss. You'll cut a European figure in these slick, well-cut suits and separates. Service can be less than helpful.
Open Mon.-Sat. 9:30 a.m.-6 p.m.

Brooks Brothers
201 Post St.,
Union Square
• 397-4500

You won't turn any heads in these square duds, but neither will you find yourself next year with a closetful of dated clothes. Designed for the man who likes to be part of the crowd—and doesn't like to part with too much money—Brooks Brothers' clothes are well made of mostly natural fabrics, with cuts that are impervious to fashion's passing fancies. We find the suits, ties and shoes dreadfully dull, though they work well as Financial District uniforms. The cotton button-down shirts, invented by Brooks several decades back, are very good buys, and some of the sports-wear does have a hint of flair.
Open Mon.-Sat. 9:30 a.m.-6 p.m., Sun. noon-5 p.m.

Bucks
2033 Fillmore St.,
Upper Fillmore
• 673-0360

There ain't a lot here, but what there is, is choice (to borrow a phrase from Spencer Tracy in *Pat and Mike*). Simple, handsome rayon shirts by Bill Robinson, Italian designer line cotton shirts, well-tailored suits and smooth leather jackets by Robert Comstock are standouts in this small men's boutique that makes a half-hearted attempt at the ubiquitous postmodern industrial interior design treatment. Among the accessories are some uninteresting hand-painted-looking ties and some very interesting watches by Barrington. The general look here is more sohphisticated than rugged.

Open Mon.-Fri. 11:30 a.m.-7 p.m., Sat. noon-7 p.m., Sun. noon-6 p.m.

Bullock & Jones
340 Post St.,
Union Square
• 392-4243

This 135-year-old San Francisco institution is a bastion of maleness, a favorite of the conservatively dressed business-man. Inside the handsome three-story building you'll find Hickey-Freeman and Oxxford suits, Cole Haan, Church's and Bally shoes, Pringle cashmere sweaters and Bullock & Jones's own shirts, ties, pajamas, sportswear and undergarments. Some of the more bold attempts at fashion—the checked silk sportcoats, polka-dot sport shirts, matching beach sets and pseudo-suede jackets—are dismal failures, but the classic pima-cotton dress shirts, paisley ties, linen and wool trousers, Cole Haan loafers and cotton sweatsuits are all eminently wearable.

Open Mon.-Fri. 9:30 a.m.-6 p.m.

Casanova
1977B Union St.,
Cow Hollow
• 929-7600

For men who like to look seriously turned-out, Casanova purveys mostly French and Italian menswear, highly tailored in fine wools and linens. Its clientele probably thinks Brooks Brothers is an investment firm.

Open Mon.-Sat. 10:30 a.m.-6:30 p.m., Sun. noon-6 p.m.

The Hound
111 Sutter St.,
Union Square
• 989-0429
3 Embarcadero Center,
Financial District
• 982-1578

The outstanding virtue of this shop is that you can get shirts made to order here (minimum order of two) for a reasonable sum ($44 to $80) in a standard variety of good-quality fabrics, with a choice of collar and cuff styles, in six to eight weeks. As the name implies, the shop affects the atmosphere of an English haberdashery, and it does carry some English goods, such as Alan Paine sweaters, but the the suits, all featuring a natural shoulder, are American-made by designers such as Norman Hilton, Chaps, Oak Loom and Free-burg of Boston.

Sutter St. branch: open Mon.-Fri. 9:30 a.m.-6 p.m., Sat. 10 a.m.-5:30 p.m. Embarcadero Center branch: open Mon.-Fri. 10 a.m.-6 p.m., Sat. 10 a.m.-5 p.m.

Macy's
120 Stockton St.,
Union Square
• 397-3333

Across the street from the main store, this five-story edifice devotes three floors to men's clothing. Virtually every men's designer is represented, from Girbaud and Ralph Lauren to Giorgio Armani and Issey Miyake. The merchan-

dise is well organized, the price range is fairly wide (nothing is cheap), the selection is staggering, and there are two restaurants to retreat to if you become overwhelmed. During holiday shopping, the store posts someone at the door fully versed and able to direct you to which of the five floors will suit your needs.
Open Mon.-Fri. 9:30 a.m.-9 p.m., Sat. 9:30 a.m.-6:30 p.m., Sun. 11 a.m.-6 p.m.

M. Menswear
1977A Union St.,
Cow Hollow
• 563-2777

Fine European menswear that is casual and trendy for the most part, featuring such brands as Spencer, Shanghai and Kitkit.
Open Mon.-Sat. 10:30 a.m.-6:30 p.m., Sun. noon-6 p.m.

Polo/Ralph Lauren
90 Post St.,
Financial District
• 567-7656

Ralph Lauren's old-rich clothing strikes a perfect balance between high fashion and conservative good taste—his dress and casual lines are infinitely more interesting than Brooks Brothers', though they'll still look at home on Wall Street or a world-class yacht. The suits, sportcoats and shirts have an American cut, and the sportswear has an American sense of color and preppiness, yet all the clothing has a touch of European sophistication. Though the fabrics and construction are very good, we still find the prices a bit excessive.
Open Mon.-Sat. 10 a.m.-6 p.m.

Swaine Adeney
434 Post St.,
Union Square
• 781-4949

Along with a marvelous array of fine umbrellas and leather goods, Swaine Adeney sells properly stodgy business suits and tweeds, all sturdily made in Britain. Of note are the shoes, leather belts, gloves and discreet ties.
Open Mon.-Fri. 9:30 a.m.-6 p.m., Sat. 10 a.m.-6 p.m.

Syaal
1864 Union St.,
Cow Hollow
• 929-1864

We're not sure what "Men's Fashions With A Woman's Point Of View" means (unless it's clothing a woman would like her husband or boyfriend to buy so he'll look right standing next to her), but that's the motto here. Given the merchandise displayed, which is mostly fine Italian sweaters and shirts and an amazing stock of socks, we don't think many men would object.
Open Mon.-Fri. 11 a.m.-7 p.m., Sat. 11 a.m.-6 p.m., Sun. noon-5 p.m.

Think Tank
149 Gough St.,
Civic Center
• 255-9313

A combination art gallery and boutique, Lat Naylor's spacious, designed-down-to-the-hangers shop features the menswear he designs, small art exhibitions and theme installations that change seasonally, such as German Expres-

sionism, a fairly tortured affair with twisted humanoid figures displayed across one wall behind chicken wire. If the art doesn't appeal, the clothing certainly does. The small number of pieces—a basic jacket, trousers, overcoat and three styles of white shirts—are cunningly cut and beautifully made in muted tones.
Open Mon.-Sat. 11 a.m.-7 p.m.

Gianni Versace
Crocker Center Galleria,
50 Post St.,
Financial District
• 956-7957

Very chic, very Italian and very expensive. The line changes with each season; at our last visit to this minimalist shop (in summer) we admired a small collection of mostly black and white suits, sportcoats, trousers and shirts in linen and cotton. One particular black linen jacket that caught our eye was in the $800 range. The Italian salespeople will try to pounce on you, but give them one well-timed withering look, and they'll let you browse in peace.
Open Mon.-Fri. 10 a.m.-6 p.m., Sat. 10 a.m.-5:30 p.m.

Wilkes Bashford
375 Sutter St.,
Union Square
• 986-4380

A veritable supermarket of clothing for the fashionable man. Wilkes Bashford recently moved across the street to an even larger space; it now has six floors of suits, sportcoats, tuxedoes, shoes, shirts, overcoats and accessories—cutting-edge fashion for men who want more than a basic button-down. Valentino, Brioni, Matsuda, Armani—it's all here, and it's all expensive. The third floor (men's suits and jackets) keeps shoppers' spirits up with a bar, and the selection and quality of the clothing are exceptional. We especially like Wilkes Bashford's own line of shoes. Womenswear and jewelry are also sold.
Open Mon.-Wed. & Fri.-Sat. 10 a.m.-6 p.m., Thurs. 10 a.m.-8 p.m.

LARGE & SMALL SIZES

Rochester for the Special Man
Mission & 3rd sts.,
South of Market
• 982-6455

Rochester is a lifesaver for the fashion-conscious large or small man. The well-established store has an especially good selection of business wear—suits, sportcoats and trousers from the likes of Chaps, Hickey-Freeman, Lanvin, and Hart, Schaffner & Marx—along with Cole Haan and Bally shoes up to size 16, and sportswear from a variety of makers. Several locations in the Bay Area.
Open Mon.-Wed. & Fri.-Sat. 9 a.m.-6 p.m., Thurs. 9 a.m.-8 p.m., Sun. noon-5 p.m., or by appt.

RECYCLED CLOTHING

Aaardvark's Odd Ark
1501 Haight St.,
Haight-Ashbury
• 621-3141

This musty shop, one of a chain of six scattered about the West, isn't as good as it once was; perhaps the competition has become more fierce for old military uniforms, '50s party dresses and vintage tweed sportcoats. But the selection of antique Hawaiian shirts remains good.
Open Mon.-Thurs. & Sat. 11 a.m.-7 p.m., Fri. 11 a.m.-8 p.m., Sun. noon-6 p.m.

Masquerade
2237 Union St.,
Cow Hollow
• 567-5677

Although the selection is small, the vintage clothing and jewelry sold here were chosen with a discerning eye. Shirts are the shop's specialty, with soft gabardine numbers that could have been found in Gary Cooper's closet and the most exotic Hawaiian shirts we've ever seen. They're all interesting and in good condition, but also fairly expensive, with the Hawaiian shirts going for around $150. Unusual gifts can be found among the accessories, like the hand-painted ties and Bakelite bangles. Definitely worth a visit.
Open Mon.-Sat. noon-7 p.m., Sun. noon-6 p.m.

Old Vogue
1412 Grant Ave.,
North Beach
• 392-1522

The previously worn leather jackets, tuxedoes, shirts, khaki trousers, Hawaiian shirts, party dresses and lots of denim in this cheerful shop are clean, moderately priced and in good condition. No priceless classics, but a better-than-average selection of popular recycled clothing.
Open Mon. 11 a.m.-7 p.m., Tues.-Thurs. 11 a.m.-10 p.m., Fri.-Sat. 11 a.m.-11 p.m., Sun. noon-8 p.m.

La Rosa
1711 Haight St.,
Haight-Ashbury
• 668-3744

An unusual store that both rents new tuxedoes and vintage evening gowns and sells used clothing, La Rosa has an excellent selection of near-perfect used overcoats, sportcoats, leather jackets and vintage tuxedoes and dinner jackets. Prices aren't rock-bottom, but they're justified by the quality.
Open Mon.-Sat. 10 a.m.-7 p.m., Sun. 11 a.m.-6 p.m.

The Way We Were
2238 Fillmore St.,
Upper Fillmore
• 346-1386

No recycled junk here: The Way We Were is home to a lovely collection of clothing from the last 100 years. Come here for a one-of-a-kind formal dress in perfect condition, with period shoes, gloves and jewelry to match; marvelous hats from the '20s, '30s and '40s; fluffy party frocks; and exceptionally beautiful white tuxedo shirts, many from the days of detached collars and some with fine detailing. Owner Doris Raymond loves her merchandise and will steer you to the best buys. Our favorite vintage clothing store in the city.

Open daily 11 a.m.-7 p.m., Sun. noon-5 p.m.

SHOES

Avventura
San Francisco Centre,
865 Market St.,
Financial District
• 546-1600

As the name suggests, the shoes here are made in Italy, mostly for the Avventura label, but also for Nancy Knox and Banfi. The styles range from decidedly Eurostyle to classic English, and many are fashioned from exotic skins, such as ostrich, crocodile, lizard and baby alligator. Prices begin at $160, which is reasonable considering the quality. Fine leather wallets and belts by De Vecchi and wonderful cotton and wool socks, all hand-finished in Italy, are also here to tempt you.

Open Mon.-Wed. 9:30 a.m.-8 p.m., Thurs.-Fri. 9:30 a.m.-9 p.m., Sat. 9:30 a.m.-7 p.m., Sun. 11 a.m.-6 p.m.

Bally of Switzerland
238 Stockton St.,
Union Square
• 398-7463

Supple leathers and skilled craftsmanship combine to make shoes that are boring and, in some cases, downright ugly. We don't object too strenuously to the sensible women's models, and the men's dress shoes with laces are quite wearable, but the famous loafers, many with little gold doodads on the vamp, remind us of leisure suits. Nonetheless, their quality is legendary and their prices are high.

Open Mon.-Fri. 9:30 a.m.-6:30 p.m., Sat. 10 a.m.-5:30 p.m., Sun. noon-5 p.m.

Kenneth Cole
2078 Union St.,
Cow Hollow
• 346-2161

Kenneth Cole has certainly carved out an enviable niche in the *chaussures* trade. Like his witty, politically correct print ads, his shoes are well designed, well made and economically feasible. For men, his styles are just hip enough and his man-tailored women's shoes are quite sexy, as is his wry interpretation of the ubiquitous Louis XIV heeled pump— just the right degree of exaggeration in tapestry or black satin with baroque yellow embroidery. In addition to men's and women's shoes in this rather spare space are a few attractive accessories—handbags, socks, belts and sunglasses. The sales staff is admirable—attentive and helpful without being overbearing.

Open Mon.-Sat. 10 a.m.-8 p.m., Sun. 11 a.m.-6:30 p.m.

The Dinostore
1553 Haight St.,
Haight-Ashbury
• 961-3933

Shoes for the rebel angel in us all. This *punkesque* little boutique features only black shoes, by a maker aptly called Slang, in the heavy oxford and paramilitary styles still so popular among disenchanted youth. There are a number of

variations on this basic theme, some of which—the short lace-up boots—we could imagine ourselves wearing, given the correct ensemble, say a motorcycle jacket, garishly printed cotton leggings and T-shirts, sold here as well.
Open Mon.-Sat. 11 a.m.-7 p.m., Sun. noon-6 p.m.

Maud Frizon
249 Grant Ave.,
Union Square
• 398-1311

Frizon's fanciful, extravagant shoes, especially the women's, are among our very favorites, though our net worth is not yet sufficient to allow us to actually purchase a pair. Anyone interested in shoe fashion must visit this ultracool gallery dedicated to the shoe as an objet d'art.
Open Mon.-Fri. 10 a.m.-6 p.m., Sat. 10:30 a.m.-5:30 p.m.

Gimme Shoes
868 Post St.,
Union Square
• 928-6677

After you've picked out a new ensemble at MAC (see "Casual Clothes") for a party at the hottest of the SOMA clubs, stop into this tragically hip store for a pair of the latest shoe sensations from Europe. Gimme's men's and women's shoes are le dernier cri in shoe design for the monied nightclub set.
Open Mon.-Sat. 11 a.m.-7 p.m.

Joan & David
172 Geary St.,
Union Square
• 397-1958

Designer stairs seem to be a popular architectural motif in San Francisco boutiques these days (since, we suppose, the only directions available are either up or down) and this little shop has a fairly treacherous set. All transparent acrylic with a shiny chrome bannister, it descends not far from the entrance, against a mirrored wall—a somewhat confusing arrangement that almost sent us plunging headlong into the sale section downstairs without even having to pretend to examine the new merchandise on the main floor first. And there are always a few attractive pairs on sale, almost bringing them into our price range. Although expensive ($129 seems to be the basic starting price), Joan & David shoes are all beautifully made in Italy and manage to successfully combine the sensible with the imaginative. We had hoped to revel in an emporium of the stuff, now that the enterprise has established an independent venue, but the selection is eclectic. The staircase aside, the shop is nicely done up with wooden shelves and black-leather settees, and boasts a sales staff that can be described as committed.
Open Mon.-Wed. & Fri.-Sat. 10 a.m.-6 p.m., Thurs. 10 a.m.-7 p.m., Sun. noon-5 p.m.

Macy's
170 O'Farrell St.,
Union Square
• 397-3333

Macy's boasts about the most astounding shoe collection we've ever seen. From Sperry Topsiders to Pfister pumps, Keds tennies to Polo loafers, every shoe imaginable can be found in this multilevel, intelligently organized shoe department. Highlights include Macy's own Charter Club line of stylish, reasonably priced women's shoes for wide, narrow and large sizes. Cole Haan, Anne Klein, Bruno Magli, Reebok, Van Eli, Joan & David, Timberland, Amalfi . . . you name it, it's here.
Open Mon.-Fri. 9:30 a.m.-9 p.m., Sat. 9:30 a.m.-6 p.m., Sun. 11 a.m.-6 p.m.

Bruno Magli
285 Geary St.,
Union Square
• 421-0356

Magli attracts an older, conservative crowd that can afford the prices and appreciate classic lines and quality Italian construction. Investment dressers put their money into these reassuringly classic shoes. Some of the men's models are especially handsome.
Open Mon.-Wed. 9:30 a.m.-6:30 p.m., Thurs.-Fri. 9:30 a.m.-7 p.m., Sat. 9:30 a.m.-6 p.m., Sun. 11:30 a.m.-5:30 p.m.

Nordstrom
San Francisco Centre,
865 Market St.,
Union Square
• 243-8500

Nordstrom is giving Macy's a serious run for its money in the shoe department, which, at the San Francisco Centre location, is staggering. Even Cinderella could be shod here. There are five different shoe departments: women's, men's, Brass Plum for young women, salon shoes and children's shoes, which carry just about every brand you've ever heard of. Add to the scope of the selection the sales staff's attentive zeal and you come up with a shoe department that makes further research unnecessary.
Open Mon.-Wed. 9:30 a.m.-8 p.m., Thurs.-Fri. 9:30 a.m.-9 p.m., Sat. 9:30 a.m.-7 p.m., Sun. 11 a.m.-6 p.m.

Raana
2134 Fillmore St.,
Upper Fillmore
• 563-3828
1796 Union St.,
Cow Hollow
• 885-4440

A small shop with a choice selection of European designer shoes for men and women. Mario Valentino's shoes and handbags are the main attraction, but there are also fetching creations by Jean Paul Gaultier, Stéphane Kelian (and her other line, Mosquito), and both Claude and Tony Montana (no relation). The other shop on Union also carries women's clothing by Thierry Mugler, Genny and Max Mara.
Fillmore St. branch: open Mon.-Sat. 11 a.m.-7 p.m., Sun. noon-7 p.m. Union St. branch: open Mon.-Sat. 10 a.m.-7:30 p.m., Sun. noon-6:30 p.m.

Shaw

2001 Union St.,
Cow Hollow
• 922-5676

Shoe fetishists have their own map of the city, and Shaw is on it. The boot selection is ample, and the women's shoes range from Via Spiga to Anne Klein to Shaw's own good-looking line.
Open Mon.-Sat. 11 a.m.-7 p.m., Sun. 12:30 p.m.-5:30 p.m.

22 Steps

280 Sutter St.,
Union Square
• 398-7797

Exactly twenty-two steps down a sort of Neo-Geo staircase you find yourself in a pinto-carpeted den of astounding shoes: inspired examples from Michael Perry, Robert Clergerie and Stéphane Kelian, not to mention the odd, painted and bulbous-toed curiosities by Free Lance that sport the disclaimer: "Free Lance shoes are designed for those of a robust personality. We do not accept responsibility for injury or death due to harassment." Actually, the most response they would probably elicit would be a giggle, since they look like something only the village idiot would wear. A better choice is a pair of the shoes handmade in England by Paul Harnden—costly at $400, but extraordinary. Also worth noting are the exquisite earrings made by Gabriela: miniature putti holding aloft a single pearl and languid hands releasing a perfect coral teardrop, both designs executed in gold, and regular or anodized silver.
Open Mon.-Sat. 10 a.m.-6 p.m.

Enzo Valenti

2117 Union St.,
Cow Hollow
• 346-5111

This boutique offers the imaginative footwear of Maud Frizon, Andrea Carrera and, of course, Enzo Valenti, among others. There are also a few items of clothing by comparable designers at comparable prices, and a large selection of men's shoes. Valenti's former shop on Grant Avenue is now part of Maude Frizon (249 Grant Avenue).
Open Mon.-Fri. 11 a.m.-7 p.m., Sat. 11 a.m.-6:30 p.m.

WOMENSWEAR

Ambiance

1458 Haight St.,
Haight-Ashbury
• 552-5095

One of our favorite boutiques in town, this split-level shop houses an array of young-in-spirit sportswear, dresses, costume jewelry and accessories—some trendy, some discreet, most falling somewhere in between. We love Ambience's own cotton knit separates and felt hats, the '40s-style rayon separates by Cartoon and the delicate, embroidered cotton underwear—T-shirts and panties—by Mary Beth. Among the pieces of jewelry were marvelous silver charm bracelets with tiny ballet slippers and commedia dell' arte masks.
Open Mon.-Thurs. & Sat. 10 a.m.-7 p.m., Fri. 10 a.m.-8 p.m., Sun. noon-7 p.m.

Laura Ashley

253 Post St.,
Union Square
• 788-0190
1827 Union St.,
Cow Hollow
• 922-7200

Now a virtual emporium for the English country look, Laura Ashley can provide you with the wherewithal to dress yourself up like Little Bo Peep, then fling yourself down on a matching settee in a room wallpapered in the same little print. As with Ralph Lauren, there's a Laura Ashley product for just about every aspect of life, except paper towels, which we expect are in the works. Within the confines of the original concept, the clothing, linens and housewares are well designed and well made. The sallies into more contemporary-looking clothing, however, are ill conceived. These new quarters on Post Street, also accessible from Maiden Lane, have provided the room to expand the store of household goods and to add a separate department for children's attire.
Post St. branch: open Mon.-Sat. 10 a.m.-6 p.m. Union St. branch: open Mon.-Sat. 10:30 a.m.-6:30 p.m., Sun. 11 a.m.-5 p.m.

Bebe

1954 Union St.,
Cow Hollow
• 563-6661

A women's annex to the men's shop M. Menswear, Bebe caters to the European taste for tight leather skirts, large leather jackets and black fitted wool dresses. Kitkit, ABS, Sarah Sturgeon and Jersey are just a few of the labels you'll find here, along with some pretty impressive sequined bustiers.
Open Mon.-Sat. 10:30 a.m.-6:30 p.m., Sun. noon-6 p.m.

Donna East/West

1424 Grant Ave.,
North Beach
• 397-4447

The setting is unimpressive, but there are some nice things to be found here. Donna's look is loose, unconstructed and natural, with linens, cottons and knits in attractive earth tones. The sensual and costly Go Silk line is here, as are the dark modern ensembles of Roberto Robledo and Selwyn Peck. Handbags are from Johnny Farah.
Open Mon.-Sat. 11 a.m.-7 p.m., Sun. noon-6 p.m.

Dosa

2063 Union St.,
Cow Hollow
• 931-9939

Yet another small white boutique, this one features marvelous hand-knit sweaters under the Dosa label, crisp white cotton and silk shirts by Equipment, and rayon georgette pull-on skirts, tightly pleated and brilliantly colored. The inventory is small but the level of taste is high.
Open Mon.-Sat. 10 a.m.-6 p.m., Sun. noon-6 p.m.

Earthly Goods

1918 Union St.,
Cow Hollow
• 922-0606

The racks and racks of natural-fiber clothing almost cause gridlock in this busy and very popular shop. At earthly prices, it offers a staggering choice of mostly cotton items by Esprit, Axis, Cotton Cruise, O.K. Sam and Shadows, a line of beautifully cut, slightly faded separates. As if this weren't enough, there are racks of sale clothing in the back room. A few lines of moderately priced shoes are sold here, too: Zodiac, 9 West, Nina and Unisa.
Open Mon.-Sat. 10 a.m.-6:30 p.m., Sun. noon-6 p.m.

Futur Ancien

1801 Union St.,
Cow Hollow
• 921-0140

Helmut Newton's models could stop here to outfit themselves on the way to a photo session. The starkly chic creations of Kansai and the eveningwear by Christopher Morganstern, Patricia Kline, Joan Vass, Stephen Sprouse and Michele Lamy are featured in this glittery little boutique. It's all very Eurostyle and very costly, down to the ultracool shades by Alain Mikli.
Open Mon.-Thurs. & Sat. 11 a.m.-6:30 p.m., Fri. 11 a.m.-7:30 p.m., Sun. 11 a.m.-6 p.m.

Susan Griffin

170 Sutter St.,
Union Square
• 433-4800

Want to throw your image into a little relief against the legions of no-nonsense career women striding onward in muted two-piece suits and one-inch heels, eyes fixed on the horizon, briefcases clutched to their breasts? Have a look in this elegant shop, where the choices run from Perry Ellis to the almost bohemian Lycra and cotton separates by Street Life. With a little help from Kamosho, Pearl C. and Emil Rutenberg, you can emerge looking both sexy and serious. Priced for the executive budget.
Open Mon.-Fri. 10 a.m.-6:30 p.m., Sat. noon-5:30 p.m.

Nancy Heller

San Francisco Centre,
865 Market St.,
Financial District
• 227-0300

A small boutique on the street level of the gargantuan San Francisco Centre, Nancy Heller serves up the usual fare of little girl's undershirt T-shirts, as one would expect, and, as one wouldn't, a lot of tailored leather in black and autumn colors, some styles decidedly Western. One section of wall space is devoted to Molton Brown English toiletries, and most attractive are the accessories—the costly jewelry, watches and handbags chosen by Nancy Heller to compliment her designs.
Open Mon.-Wed. 9:30 p.m.-8 p.m., Thurs.-Fri. 9:30 a.m.-9 p.m., Sat. 9:30 a.m.-7 p.m., Sun. 11 a.m.-6 p.m.

JLC Designs

2124 Union St.,
Cow Hollow
• 346-0343

Definitely not for the SOMA crowd, sophisticated ensembles by the likes of Basco Collector, Nicole Miller and Kymio are sold here. There are also hats, jewelry and good

handbags to put together a total look, and upstairs in this split-level boutique is a sizable collection of gleaming leather jackets and skirts.
Open Mon.-Sat. 11 a.m.-6 p.m.

Jim Elle
2237 Fillmore St.,
Upper Fillmore
• 567-9500

"Clothes for the Fashion Confident" is Jim Elle's motto, and if you're confident enough to shell out several hundred bucks for a Romeo Gigli outfit, you'll fall in love with the place. It's all crisply modern and tasteful, and not everything is expensive. Don't miss the belt collection.
Open Mon.-Sat. 11 a.m.-7 p.m., Sun. noon-6 p.m.

Betsy Johnson
2031 Fillmore St.,
Upper Fillmore
• 567-2726

If you've never left the '60s or are seeking to recreate that spirit, you'll be in your element here. It also helps if you're under 30 and have the figure to wear skin-tight black cotton minidresses and second-skin pullovers. In addition to possibly being the city's headquarters for black stretchy dresses, this place is also supply central for stretchy separates in bold flower prints, bright plaids and stripes. Definitely night-on-the-town stuff and a bit pricey for the simplicity of the concept and construction.
Open Mon.-Sat. noon-7 p.m., Sun. noon-6 p.m.

Kalf
1971 Sutter St.,
Upper Fillmore
• 563-6788

Now this is what we call minimal. In a small, bare, stark white room, on four poles extending from one wall, are hung sixteen different items of clothing (four on each pole), all black and white, all designed by Japanese couturier Fumio Tanuma. Also in the room are a single low table, on which lie three folded shirts (exquisite), and a desk, behind which sits an engaging saleslady, eager to be of help in spite of a less than complete command of English. As if this were not intriguing enough, she leads one to a room in back where the high-tech yet rather handmade-looking lamps and tables by Alan Skaramsky are for sale. The galvanized steel torchère lamps exhibit an odd grace and are more successful than the wooden tables topped with stainless steel under a thick laminate of resin.
Open Tues.-Sat. 11 a.m.-6:30 p.m., Sun. noon-5 p.m.

Khyber Crossing
2259 Fillmore St.,
Upper Fillmore
• 563-2933

If you've seen *Gunga Din* six times, hie yourself to Khyber Crossing, a wonderfully romantic store that will have you looking like an English noblewoman in no time at all. The range is complete, from hardy khakis to fine linen blouses to lacy dresses perfect for bridesmaids or garden parties, by such designers as Ralph Lauren, Ruff Hewn and Nancy Johnson. Completing the picture are discreetly helpful

saleswomen and a spacious, uncluttered store accented with steamer trunks and British colonial touches.
Open Mon.-Fri. 11 a.m.-6:30 p.m., Sat. 10 a.m.-6 p.m., Sun. noon-6 p.m.

Knitz
1429 Grant Ave.,
North Beach
• 391-3480

A minuscule, one-of-a-kind shop that's a must for any woman who loves knits. Anna Martin and Anna Katharina, a shy but friendly mother-and-daughter team, design and knit these sweaters and outfits themselves. A few ready-to-wear sweaters are available, but most of the outfits are custom-made—you pick from the selection of beautiful yarns and classic styles, and your ensemble is knitted to fit. The prices are fair given the quality and handwork.
Open Mon.-Sat. 11 a.m.-7 p.m., Sun. noon-5 p.m.

Ted Lapidus
156 Geary St.,
Union Square
• 362-2660

The styles are ho-hum, the prices are frightening and the Isuzu-esque salesmen aren't nearly as funny as Joe. You can do much better elsewhere in Union Square.
Open Mon.-Sat. 9:30 a.m.-6 p.m.

Janice Lee
1998 Union St.,
Cow Hollow
• 922-0253

Janice Lee's own sophisticated, fairly classic designs, those of her ex-husband under the Char label, and a smattering of some Joanie Char creations fill the racks in this sizable boutique, catering to the woman who can afford it. Belts, scarves and costume jewelry are within easy reach to correctly accessorize her look.
Open Mon.-Fri. noon-8 p.m., Sun. 11 a.m.-6 p.m.

The Limited
Crocker Center Galleria,
50 Post St.,
Financial District
• 788-3201

This spacious store is the nicest Limited we've been in—a handsome showcase for mass-market clothes, with a pianist to keep the mood serene. It's not mere kismet that The Limited is one of Wall Street's biggest success stories—these people know how to design, price and market clothes. You won't be the only woman on your block wearing Forenza's youthful sweaters and jeans, Krizia's chic black-and-white ensembles and Outback Red's urban-farmgirl khakis and chambrays, but you'll find the price-to-quality ratio hard to resist. The socks, overcoats, watches and belts are also great buys. At press time, a deluxe new store with a Limited Express downstairs (with an awesome Watteau-inspired mural at the entrance) was being completed on the corner of O'Farrell and Stocton streets, across the street from Macy's. Many other branches.
Open Mon.-Fri. 9:30 a.m.-6 p.m., Sun. 10 a.m.-5 p.m.

Madrigal

590 Sutter St.,
Union Square
• 989-3478

Classic clothes for the traditional woman. Madrigal's own line of bright, preppy sportswear and cruisewear is only mildly overpriced and is guaranteed to keep you looking solidly Republican. There's also some sportswear by Ruff Hewn and shoes by Cole Haan.
Open Mon.-Sat. 10 a.m.-6 p.m.

Jessica McClintock

353 Sutter St.,
Union Square
• 397-0987

Upstairs are a few racks of hyper-romantic "designer" silk and lace dresses, some of which make lovely wedding dresses or elegant eveningwear. Downstairs are a few racks of "off-the-rack" silk and lace dresses, which make just as lovely wedding or evening dresses and cost half as much, along with less formal cotton dresses. All of Jessica McClintock's dresses are ultrafeminine and most are old-fashioned in spirit. Don't judge them on the hanger—they'll look better on you.
Open Mon.-Sat. 10 a.m.-6 p.m.

Mondi

Crocker Center Galleria,
50 Post St.,
Financial District
• 781-4604

Mondi's chic, colorful, moderately expensive sportswear is European in tone and is neither dully traditional nor annoyingly trendy. The sweaters and knit ensembles are particularly winning.
Open Mon.-Sat. 10 a.m.-6 p.m.

North Beach Leather

190 Geary St.,
Union Square
• 362-8300
1365 Columbus Ave.,
Fisherman's Wharf
• 441-3208

Apparently seeking to shed its image as one-stop shopping for your basic female rock star, North Beach Leather is now ensconced in a lovely wood-paneled shop right on Union Square. Michael Hoban, the featured designer, has sought to add a touch of bourgeois chic to the current line, but there's still definitely something fetishistic about these skin-tight leather dresses and miniskirts. For men, there are leather jackets in many styles, ranging from distressed bomber to blazer. The original store, which opened in North Beach and then moved down to the Fisherman's Wharf area, still boasts the type of leatherwear that the shop is known for. The bondage-like vestments, many in shades of hot pink and purple, require both a good supply of the green and crinkly ($400-$600 for a dress, a *small* dress) and a certain level of fitness, not only to look good in them but to muster the strength to zip them up. Eventually this branch will be an outlet for sale merchandise only.
Geary St. branch: open Mon.-Sat. 10 a.m.-7 p.m., Sun. noon-5 p.m. Columbus Ave. branch: open Mon.-Sat. 9:45 a.m.-8 p.m., Sun. 11 a.m.-7 p.m.

Obiko

794 Sutter St.,
Union Square
• 775-2882

One of the advance guard in the art-as-clothing movement, Obiko is still going strong. The truly unique shop, a cluttered little hole-in-the-wall, represents about 100 clothing designers and milliners who create fantasies in printed silks, ethnic-looking, richly textured weaves, deeply hued velvets and felts. We sighed over the silk, rainbow-colored cobweb atop gossamer shifts, and lost our hearts to a little green-felt Robin Hood hat stuck with two saucy pheasant plumes.
Open Mon.-Fri. 10 a.m.-6 p.m., Sat. 10 a.m.-5 p.m.

Q's

3349 Sacramento St.,
Presidio Heights
• 346-7481
3603 Sacramento St.,
Presidio Heights
• 931-1899
101 Spear St.,
Financial District
• 243-9339

Q's emphasis is on designer sportswear. Silk Club, Dorthée Bis, Bowman Traders, Reminisence and others of that ilk are all represented with their various renditions in silk, rayon and cotton.
Open Mon.-Fri. 10:30 a.m.-6:30 p.m., Sat. 10 a.m.-6 p.m., Sun. noon-4 p.m.

Talbots

2 Embarcadero Center,
Financial District
• 781-2128

We've always suspected that Diane Feinstein sends a personal shopper here. Silk bows at the throats of suit-clad women bound for success while clasping smart briefcases come immediately to mind upon entering this shop. The clothing is well made and moderate to expensive in price, and Talbots's rapid expansion from a mail-order business to a burgeoning chain verifies its strong following. Although now under the same management as Ann Taylor, Talbots's tailored, no-nonsense style does not seem to have been affected.
Open Mon.-Fri. 10 a.m.-6 p.m., Sat. 10 a.m.-5 p.m.

Ann Taylor

441 Sutter St.,
Union Square
• 989-5381

Although in the last year or so the clothing seems to have lost just a little of its sophistication, we still love Ann Taylor and always find several items worth buying. As the years have passed, more of the clothing has become Ann Taylor's own label, which is designed for young-in-spirit urban women who may have just graduated from Esprit's hip-student look. Always worthy are the leather jackets and belts, pleated trousers in seasonal linens or wools, white silk and cotton blouses, Girbaud-style cotton pants, beautiful Joan & David shoes and city-slicker dresses that can go from the office to the evening. Prices vary wildly—one little cotton blouse may be $90 and another may be $45. In back are a couple of permanent sale racks that frequently include something of interest. Other Ann Taylors can be found in

Ghirardelli Square (775-2872) and the Embarcadero Center (989-5355).
Open Mon.-Sat. 10 a.m.-6 p.m.

Three Bags Full
2181 Union St.,
Cow Hollow
• 567-5753
500 Sutter St.,
Union Square
• 398-7987

Known for its high-quality wool sweaters, many of which are hand-knit, for women, men and children, Three Bags Full also stocks special soaps for wool and an astounding variety of socks. Occasionally it'll have a few interesting separates to complement the sweaters, as well as a few wonderful Il Bisonte handbags.
Union St. branch: open Mon.-Sat. 11 a.m.-6 p.m., Sun. noon-5 p.m. Sutter St. branch: open Mon.-Sat. 10 a.m.-6 p.m.

Trellis
1932 Fillmore St.,
Upper Fillmore
• 928-4606

Sister store to Ambience (see above) in the Haight-Ashbury, Trellis stocks some of the same merchandise (such as Ambience cotton-knit separates), but the look is a bit more cool, to wit the rayon shirts in various modern prints by Café and the paperbag-waisted khakis by UFO. We sighed over the black suede bomber jacket and the natural-colored leather handbags, of which there are numerous styles. A worthwhile stop during a day spent poking around on Fillmore Street.
Open Mon. 10 a.m.-8 p.m., Tues.-Thurs. 10 a.m.-9 p.m., Fri.-Sat. 10 a.m.-8 p.m., Sun. 11 a.m.-6 p.m.

Trend
3 Embarcadero Center,
Financial District
• 362-0799

Not everything here is wonderful—in fact, some of the clothing looks cheap—but generally there are good buys. You'll find E.J. Harper linens and Jane Singer dresses, all at prices that bordered on the discount. Worth a look.
Open Mon.-Thurs. 10 a.m.-6 p.m., Fri. 10 a.m.-6:30 p.m., Sat. 10 a.m.-5:30 p.m., Sun. noon-5 p.m.

Uko
2166 Union St.,
Cow Hollow
• 563-0330

Just getting to the threshold of Uko is an accomplishment; first you steal through a plant-lined alley, then trudge up a very steep (45-degree grade?) black ramp to the second-floor shop. (This must make for great spectator sport when it rains.) Once inside, you are treated to a small, select array of Japanese designer wear: wonderful, very tailored white cotton shirts for men and women, and linen trousers, skirts, jackets and dresses, most of them by Emico, a designer who has a chain of shops in Japan. Although high, the prices won't bring on the cardiac arrest you expect from most Japanese designer clothing. (What will bring on cardiac arrest is that ramp.) The shop itself is spare, elegant and

nicely lit, and the sales personnel are pleasant; unfortunately, not everyone will be fit enough to make it inside.
Open Mon.-Sat. 11 a.m.-7 p.m., Sun. noon-6 p.m.

Gianni Versace
70 Post St.,
Financial District
• 956-7977

Attractive, dramatic haute couture for women who like to make a statement and like to make it in black. The shockingly costly black party frocks are especially lovely. Bring your man along to pick out an ensemble at the men's boutique next door—the two of you will make a terribly chic matched set.
Open Mon.-Fri. 10 a.m.-6 p.m., Sun. 10 a.m.-5:30 p.m.

Adrienne Vittadini
San Francisco Centre,
865 Market St.,
Financial District
• 777-3440

Smooth and elegant, Adrienne Vittadini's boutique glows with blond satin wood and mirrors, punctuated by small TV monitors endlessly and silently playing looped tapes of fashion shows. Featured here are Vittadini's signature knits, bold-patterned sweaters, many of which are heavily beaded, and her current line of separates. On the expensive side.
Open Mon.-Fri. 9:30 a.m.-8 p.m., Sat. 9:30 a.m.-8 p.m., Sun. 10:30 a.m.-6 p.m.

Eileen West
33 Grant Ave.,
Union Square
• 982-2275

Eileen West's trademark is the pretty cotton-linen-lace dress that seems especially well suited to sorority girls and young society matrons. The fabrics are feminine but not as annoyingly ditsy as Laura Ashley's, and the cuts are stylish in a restrained manner; the drop waist has been particularly popular here these last couple of years. Less interesting than the dresses are the separates, but we are fond of the cotton nightgowns and robes, which make good gifts. On the first floor, with its lovely wrought-iron arch entryway, are Eileen West's pale, delicate linens and sundry knickknacks, such as ornate pewter and silver picture frames, French glassware by Luminarc and all the necessities for a cozy breakfast in bed: English-looking, fussy tea sets, trays, napkins—just don one of the lacy cotton nightgowns and hop in.
Open Mon.-Sat. 10 a.m.-6 p.m.

White Duck
517 Sutter St.,
Union Square
• 433-6249

If Talbots is too square and MAC too strange, and you don't want to look like everyone who shops at the middle-of-the-road chain stores, come to White Duck. It sells only clothing of its own design—classic pieces in linen, cotton, silk and wool that will appeal to the woman who has a sense of style but who doesn't live on the sartorial edge. The knits are especially attractive, and all the pieces coordinate beautifully and travel well.
Open Mon.-Sat. 10 a.m.-5:30 p.m.

Zoe
2400 Fillmore St.,
Upper Fillmore
• 929-0441

There isn't much to this spare, chic shop, but what is there is pretty nice. The collection changes with the season, but expect to see a lot of Nancy Heller and Joan Vass and, in the spring and summer, some smart linens. There are a very few choice accessories, mainly belts.
Open Mon.-Fri. 11 a.m.-6:30 p.m., Sun. noon-5 p.m.

DISCOUNT

Burlington Coat Factory
5th St. & Howard,
South of Market
• 495-7234

One of the really worthwhile discount shops, this one is also huge. The brand names of clothing for men, women and children are names you'll recognize from department stores, and the styles are fairly current. Outerwear, however, is the real attraction here. Take the escalator to the second floor to find yourself in an acre of coats of every description: classic Chesterfields by name designers, short wool coats, rain coats, fur coats. There's also a good-size linens-and-bedding department. Discounts vary from 20 to 60 percent, designer items being less discounted.
Open Mon.-Sat. 9:30 a.m.-3 p.m., Sun. 11 a.m.-6 p.m.

Esprit Factory Store
499 Illinois St.,
South of Market
• 957-2550

A high-tech warehouse with an immense, constantly changing array of Esprit clothing, shoes and accessories at 30 to 35 percent off and often up to 50 percent on items that have been marked down again. Grab a supermarket-style shopping cart and load up on Esprit's lively, youthful sportswear, dresses and hip-young-professional separates. You'll have to do a little digging and elbow your way through the throngs, and the quality of the selection is not consistent, but there are almost always good bargains.
Open Mon.-Fri. 10 a.m.-9 p.m., Sat. 10 a.m.-5 p.m., Sun. 11 a.m.-5 p.m.

LARGE & SMALL SIZES

The Company Store
1913 Fillmore St.,
Upper Fillmore
• 921-0365

Fashionable sportswear and dressy dresses for women size 8 to 24 are poorly displayed on cluttered racks. But there are some nice finds that make digging through the mess worthwhile.
Open Mon.-Fri. 11 a.m.-7 p.m., Sat. 10 a.m.-6 p.m., Sun. noon-5 p.m.

Especially Petites

Crocker Center Galleria,
50 Post St.,
Financial District
• 781-0351

We have a hard time mustering sympathy for the size 2 who complains of a shortage of clothing that fits, but we will admit that her plight is a real one. For small women who are sick of sleeves that go to their fingertips and suit jackets that go to their knees, Especially Petites stocks a solid, middle-of-the-road selection of small-size professional clothing and sportswear.
Open Mon.-Fri. 9:30 a.m.-6 p.m., Sat. 10 a.m.-5 p.m.

LINGERIE

Aricie

Crocker Center Galleria,
50 Post St.,
Financial District
• 989-0261

Such European makers as Gemma, Ronsard, Valentino, Arrete and Adagio are well represented here, as well as Wacoal from Japan and such American standards as Poiret and Jezebel. There are tons of frilly foundations and drop-dead loungewear, including some hand-painted silk gowns. Not only is the merchandise expensive, tasteful and seriously sexy, but there are always a lot of well-heeled gentlemen buying it. They must be either loving husbands or big-spending philanderers, or maybe they're parading around in it under their pin-striped suits.
Open Mon.-Fri. 9:30 a.m.-6 p.m., Sat. 10 a.m.-5 p.m.

Toujours

2484 Sacramento St.,
Presidio Heights
• 346-3988

Everywhere you turn in this tiny lavender-scented shop your eye is greeted with pastel silks, fragile lace and fine cottons. The shop is run by Beverly Weinkauf, who has collected the prettiest natural-fiber lingerie made by various European and Bay Area designers. From Europe there are Calida, Hanro and Valentina; from the Bay Area, Treesha, Cinzia and Underwriters, with their witty cotton nighties and underthings. The pièces de résistance, however, are the finely woven straw hats—by local designer Laura Fenenga—that collapse so prettily on one's head.
Open Mon.-Fri. 11 a.m.-7 p.m., Sat. 11 a.m.-6 p.m.

Victoria's Secret

395 Sutter St.,
Union Square
• 397-0521

Anyone who's ever ordered from the Victoria's Secret catalog probably receives about 25 issues a year and, consequently, has little interest in actually setting foot in the shops—but they're worth a visit, since the merchandise is somewhat different from what's offered by mail. It's nice to see that these stores carry something other than lace garter belts and push-up bras. There are more cotton items, menswear-styled underthings, such as silk boxers and cotton T-shirts (it also carries these for men), sachets and cuddly chenille robes. There are several other locations.
Open Mon.-Sat. 10 a.m.-6 p.m., Sun. noon-5 p.m.

MATERNITY

Expecting ... the Best
1905 Fillmore St.,
Upper Fillmore
• 931-1010

No big bows at the throat and puffed sleeves here. This nationwide chain offers sophisticated maternity wear under its own label and others such as Monday's Child, Pink & Blue and Isis. Fabrics range from natural to synthetics and the styles tend to be conservative—very appropriate for the career mom-to-be.
Open Mon.-Sat. 11 a.m.-6 p.m., Sun. noon-5 p.m.

Japanese Weekend
864 Post St.,
Union Square
• 775-1529

Not your traditional maternity wear by any means, this line was created by a choreographer who has some very precise ideas about how maternity clothing should look and feel. Japanese Weekend is known for the invention of the Obi-Katsurogi (O.K.) waistband, which allows garments to rest comfortably on the hips. Flip It, the designer's popular cotton and Lycra underwear, also features the O.K. waistband. The pants, tunics, skirts and nursing tops, all cotton interlock, are stylish and contemporary.
Open Mon.-Sat. 10 a.m.-6 p.m.

DEPARTMENT STORES

Emporium-Capwell
835 Market St.,
Financial District
• 764-2222

Housed in an ornate old building that dates back to before the 1906 earthquake, Emporium-Capwell is a solid, functional all-purpose department store whose merchandise is neither frumpy nor elegant. It stocks major mass-market brands of clothing, housewares, furniture, shoes and accessories—the standard lines from Liz Claiborne, Calvin Klein, Evan Picone, Generra and the like. The basement level is occupied by Market on Market, a large gourmet department with pleasant espresso and gelato bars, along with a decent deli, wine shop and sweet shop.
Open Mon.-Fri. 9:30 a.m.-8 p.m., Sat. 9:30 a.m.-6 p.m., Sun. noon-6 p.m.

Macy's
Stockton & O'Farrell sts.,
Union Square
• 397-3333

What Bloomingdale's is to New York, Macy's is to San Francisco. It's a jangling, chaotic, big-city department store, with everything from discount racks to haute couture, along with a continual crush of tourists, locals and shoppers from the suburbs. The main building takes up an entire city block, and there's a huge five-floor annex just for menswear and children's clothing. We find Macy's headache-inducing, though we do love the fabulous women's shoe department, with shoes from seemingly every designer on Earth and plenty of styles for the hard-to-fit woman. Otherwise, expect a larger-than-usual range of department-store housewares, clothing, cosmetics and so on. *Open Mon.-Fri. 9:30 a.m.-9 p.m., Sat. 9:30 a.m.-6:30 p.m., Sun. 11 a.m.-6 p.m.*

I. Magnin
135 Stockton St.,
Union Square
• 362-2100

Elegant, refined and a tad stuffy, I. Magnin caters to the San Francisco woman who wants well-made, stylish (but not too trendy) clothing. Though womenswear is the focus, there's more: an exceptionally well-rounded gourmet store, a good beauty salon, a superb collection of baby and children's clothing, a very fine stationery department and a branch of Laykin et Cie that is well stocked with conservatively dazzling gems. Magnin began as a lingerie merchant, and it still carries some exquisite handmade lingerie. The cosmetics department is also notable, both for its selection and service. Old money will feel right at home in this old-line store, founded right here in San Francisco in 1876. *Open Mon. & Thurs.-Fri. 9:30 a.m.-8 p.m., Tues.-Wed. & Sat. 9:30 a.m.-6 p.m., Sun. noon-6 p.m.*

Neiman-Marcus
150 Stockton St.,
Union Square
• 362-3900

Neiman's Texas nouveau-riche roots are disguised under San Francisco's old City of Paris dome, but the merchandise selection still betrays a certain flash and ostentatiousness. Not all, however, is overdone; there are some wonderfully luxurious departments, especially lingerie, gourmet foods, women's and men's couture, and cosmetics. And one of our very favorite downtown lunch spots is the Rotunda restaurant on the top floor under the beautiful dome—the setting is fabulous, the sophisticated salads and light entrées are delicious, and the service is exemplary. *Open Mon. & Thurs.-Fri. 10 a.m.-8 p.m., Tues.-Wed. 10 a.m.-6 p.m., Sat. 10 a.m.-6 p.m., Sun. noon-6 p.m.*

Nordstrom
San Francisco Centre,
865 Market St.,
Union Square
• 243-8500
285 Winston Dr.,
Stonestown
• 753-1344

Nordstrom has finally arrived in San Francisco, the anchor in a large, rather hideous airport-like mall, the San Francisco Centre. The grandest Nordstrom anywhere, this one has five floors, four restaurants and a spa, all accessed by a huge, circular, central escalator well, which descends to the other shops (mostly chain stores) in the lower depths of the mall. When you enter the store by elevator, you'll come upon the concierge's desk, where you can secure a map of the store (you'll need it) and details about and/or reservations for one of the restaurants. If you can make it past the shoe

department, an ocean of shoes, you might lose yourself for
an hour or so in the twinkling, siren-like counters of the
cosmetics department. With a great effort of will, you can
tear yourself free and ride victoriously up the escalator, only
to sink in the quicksand of the designer sportswear, and so
on, through the menswear, the teenwear, the childwear, all
to the tinkling tunes of a semipro at the grand piano. After
about an hour our eyes glazed over and we headed, with
the aid of our trusty map, for one of the restaurants to
restore ourselves. From our experience here, we can offer
the following advice: know what you want before you enter
(you'll find it), don't miss the restrooms (palatial) and don't
come alone.
*San Francisco Centre branch: open Mon.-Wed. 9:30 a.m.-8
p.m., Thurs.-Fri. 9:30 a.m-9 p.m., Sat. 9:30 a.m.-7 p.m., Sun.
11 a.m.-6 p.m. Stonestown branch: open Mon.-Fri. 10 a.m.-
9:30 p.m., Sat. 10 a.m.-9 p.m., Sun. 11 a.m.-6:30 p.m.*

Saks Fifth Avenue
384 Post St.,
Union Square
• 986-4300

This lovely West Coast sister of the classic New York society
department store has a well-rounded selection of upscale
merchandise. The sales are perhaps the best in town; other
strong suits include a good beauty salon, exceptional furs
at Revillon and sophisticated careerwear for women. Soli-
tary shoppers should note the restaurant and cappuccino
bar on the top floor, a good lunch spot for those dining
alone.
*Open Mon. & Thurs.-Fri. 10 a.m.-8 p.m., Tues.-Wed. & Sat.
10 a.m.-6 p.m., Sun. noon-5 p.m.*

FLOWERS

Bed of Roses
2274 Union St.,
Cow Hollow
• 922-5150

The smell of damp earth and cut greens will lure you into
this lovely, darkish little shop. In addition to a healthy array
of cut flowers, the store boasts walls lined with interesting
old—and just old-looking—baskets and vases, along with
wonderful reproductions of antique garden ornaments,
including the heads of pouting putti. You can even bring in
your favorite vase or pickle jar, and the very agreeable staff
will creatively fill it.
Open Mon.-Fri. 9:30 a.m.-5:30 p.m., Sat. 10 a.m.-6 p.m.

Bloomers

2975 Washington St.,
Pacific Heights
• 563-3266

Stacked on the towering shelves against tall white walls is every conceivable type of vase, basket or ribbon to complement the armful of lovely cut flowers you've snatched up here. The best idea, however, is to let the pros here design a bouquet for you. It's well known locally that they create some of the most creative and soulful arrangements anywhere.

Open Mon.-Fri. 10 a.m.-6 p.m., Sat. 10 a.m.-5 p.m.

Fleurtations

1880 Fillmore St.,
Upper Fillmore
• 923-1070

A small but choice selection of fresh flowers, including some you don't see at most florists. Stacks of baskets greet you on the sidewalk; inside, even more baskets hang from the ceiling and walls and sit on the floor, many filled with a panoply of beautiful silk and dried flowers. The pleasant staff and piped-in classical music keep the mood mellow.

Open Tues.-Fri. 11 a.m.-7 p.m., Sat. 10 a.m.-6 p.m., Sun noon-5 p.m.

Podesta Baldocchi

2525 California St.,
Pacific Heights
• 346-1300

This long-established San Francisco megaflorist does it all: small bouquets, huge parties, balloon bouquets, plant rentals, plant maintenance, fruit baskets, you name it. The selection of fresh stems and indoor plants is complete, and the designs can be stunning. Podesta Baldocchi also delivers.

Open Mon.-Sat. 8 a.m.-6 p.m.

FOOD

BAKERIES

Acme Bread Co.

1601 San Pablo Ave.,
Berkeley
• 524-1327

Steve Sullivan worked as the bread baker at Chez Panisse for three years before leaving to open Acme Bread Company. He still supplies breads to Chez Panisse and a slew of other Bay Area restaurants, but you can also buy his breads at the bakery. Displayed in baskets beneath a vintage poster from Marcel Pagnol's film *La Femme du Boulanger* are sweet-and-sour baguettes; smaller bâtards made from the same dough; the ladder-shape fougasse of Provence, flavored with rosemary and olive oil—sometimes with walnut or mint and olive oil; smooth ovals of country-style sourdough rye made with beer; and rounds of rustic sourdough pain du levain. Each of the sourdough breads has its own

unique starter. For instance, to develop the starter for the pain du levain, Sullivan allowed grapes from his father's vineyard (with the wild yeasts present on the grape skins) to ferment with whole-wheat flour. The same starter is replenished and used repeatedly to make just that particular bread. You'll also find a lighter mixed-grain loaf dubbed "upstairs bread" after Chez Panisse's upstairs café, where it is served, and a whole-wheat sourdough with walnuts. Most days, breads are sold out by midafternoon, so plan an early trip—and include a late-morning café au lait next door at Alice Waters's Café Fanny, which features toast and sandwiches made from Acme bread. Acme bread is also available at the Singer & Foy wine store in North Beach.
Open Mon. 9 a.m.-1 p.m., Tues.-Fri. 9 a.m.-about 4 p.m., depending on bread availability, Sat. 10 a.m.-about 4 p.m.

The Bagelry
2134 Polk St.,
Polk Gulch
•441-3003

The Bagelry bakes more than a dozen varieties of bagels, as well as bialys, which are made from the same dough but without the initial water boil. Weekends, try the Streusel made with brown sugar, fresh apples and sweet butter.
Open Mon.-Tues. & Thurs.-Sat. 7 a.m.-6:30 p.m., Wed. 7 a.m.-noon, Sun. 7 a.m.-4 p.m.

Bette's Bakeshop
1926 Shattuck Ave.,
Berkeley
• 841-0773

A spinoff of Bette's Oceanview Diner, this bakeshop does a great job with spiraled morning buns freckled with cinnamon, currant-studded scones and delicious muffins, including the Bay Area's best bran muffin. Look for such old-fashioned pies as rhubarb-strawberry and Boston cream, along with classic angelfood and devil's food cakes. Sandwiches and espresso, too, can be enjoyed at a few sidewalk tables.
Open Mon.-Fri. 7 a.m.-7 p.m., Sat. 8 a.m.-7 p.m., Sun. 9 a.m.-5 p.m.

Boudin Bakery at the Wharf
156 Jefferson St.,
Fisherman's Wharf
• 928-1849

The San Francisco sourdough here is made only from sourdough starter (no yeast, no preservatives). And any day from 8 a.m. to 2 p.m. you can watch the entire process through a window that looks into the baking room. Boudin will also ship loaves out of state on request.
Open daily 7 a.m.-8 p.m.

Casa Sanchez
2778 24th St.,
Mission District
• 282-2400

Fresh corn and flour tortillas are made all morning long. Casa Sanchez has every size, from miniature Mexico City–style rounds to giant fourteen-inch flour tortillas to wrap a substantial Americano burrito.
Open Mon.-Sat. 8 a.m.-6 p.m.

The Cheese Board
1504 Shattuck Ave.,
Berkeley
• 549-3183

The Cheese Board, one of the oldest collectives in the nation, celebrated its 23rd birthday recently. Members of this worker-owned cheese shop not only know their cheese, they also produce baguettes—white or whole-wheat rye—that are indisputably the best in town for both texture and flavor. Leavened entirely with a lively sourdough "mother" that's kept in a big earthenware crock, the bread is made in small batches in the kitchen at the back of this excellent cheese store. The dark breads are wonderfully solid, moist loaves: try the sourdough beer rye, made with cracked rye and dark beer, or the sesame multigrain buckwheat. A tasty buttermilk-corn-Cheddar bread is made with both corn-meal and corn kernels. On Fridays they bake tender braided loaves of challah, and on weekends, Sunday bread, a hon-eyed sweet bread with raisins and nuts. And don't forget the wonderful, and sometimes eccentric, pizza. Anyone for brussels-sprouts pizza?
Open Tues.-Sat. 10 a.m.-6 p.m.

Cocolat
2119 Fillmore St.,
Upper Fillmore
• 567-1223
655 Montgomery St.,
Financial District
• 788-5778

Alice Medrich is best known for introducing chocolate truffles to the Bay Area. Her chocolate cakes, made with the same care and assurance, are just as divine. They're always elegant, never overdecorated, and sold by the slice as well as whole, so you can buy an assortment for a dinner party. They include a masterful rendition of reine de saba; the gâteau royal, which alternates layers of marzipan and raspberry preserves with chocolate cake; and the gâteau des îles, drenched in Curaçao and layered with apricot jam and coffee buttercream. Holidays are marked by the appearance of such inspired offerings as Medrich's Christmas pudding, raspberry Linzertorte, special Easter cakes and heart-shape sweets for Valentine's Day. Baking chocolate and a few distinguished dessert wines are also available. The original store, at 1481 Shattuck Avenue in Berkeley (843-3265), is still there, and there are additional stores in Oakland, Corte Madera, on 24th Street in Noe Valley and at the Stanford Court Shopping Center. Mail order, too.
Fillmore St. branch: open Mon.-Thurs. 10 a.m.-7 p.m., Fri.-Sat. 10 a.m.-8 p.m., Sun. 12:30 p.m.-5:30 p.m. Montgomery St. branch: open Mon.-Thurs. 8:30 a.m.-6:30 p.m.

Danilo
516 Green St.,
North Beach
• 989-1806

The display of baked goods in this venerable North Beach bakery changes throughout the day, as fresh batches of Italian bread, big, country-style loaves and thin sticks of grissini (hand-rolled breadsticks) emerge from the oven.

Danilo also has cialde (lacy anise-flavored cookies) and Genovese-style panettone.
Open daily 6:30 a.m.-6:30 p.m.

Dianda Italian American Pastry

2883 Mission St.,
Mission District
• 647-5469
Green St. & Columbus Ave.,
North Beach
• 989-7745

Elio Dianda, once pastry chef at Salza in Lucca, Italy, developed all the recipes for the Italian pastries at Dianda; his three sons carry on the tradition. They bake moist amaretti, delicate allumettes and other cookies, along with a classic torta de mandorle and a bevy of other sweets. The zabaglione that goes into the torta de zabaglione e rum and the zuppa inglese is still whisked by hand in a big copper bowl. The Diandas' chewy, subtly spiced panforte is dense with nuts and covered with a delicate wafer, and their tall panettone is a classic.
Mission St. branch: open Mon.-Sat. 7 a.m.-6:30 p.m., Sun. 7 a.m.-4:30 p.m. Green St. branch: open daily 8 a.m.-7 p.m.

Dominguez Bakery: Flor de Jalisco

2951 24th St.,
Mission District
• 821-1717

These panes (Hispanic breads) are very good and always fresh, baked several times a day. You'll find fresh egg bread, sweet crescent rolls and large, leaf-shape hojaldre, as well as panes dulces in dozens of fanciful shapes and various flavorings—anise, vanilla, lemon, pineapple—and miniature Central American pastries.
Open daily 8 a.m.-9 p.m.

The English Tea Shoppe: A Crumpet Bakery

511 Irving St.,
Sunset District
• 564-2255

Honeycombed with holes to catch sweet butter, the fresh crumpets made here are a sumptuous morning or tea-time treat. Eat one here with cream cheese, lemon curd, bitter-orange marmalade or any of a dozen or so toppings, or take them home in packages of six.
Open Tues.-Fri. 8 a.m.-5:30 p.m., Sat. 9 a.m.-5 p.m.

Fantasia Bakery

3465 California St.,
Presidio Heights
• 752-0825

German-born Ernst Weil trained at the Cordon Bleu before founding this European bakery years ago. Today, a small army of bakers in South San Francisco are kept busy producing cakes and pastries on a grand—perhaps too grand—scale. Small batches they're not, but many of the bakers are European-trained, and the quality is consistent despite the volume of production. Some of the desserts are too sweet for today's palate, but if you want napoleons, petits fours, Black Forest cake or Sachertorte, Fantasia may be the place. At Christmas, in addition to all sorts of German holiday cookies, they make Baumkuchen, a cake of Gypsy origin cooked on a spit over an open fire. The batter is poured onto the rotating spit and cooked layer by layer to resemble the rings of a tree, then glazed with sugar or chocolate. *Open Sun.-Mon. 8:30 a.m.-6 p.m., Tues.-Sat. 7:30 a.m.-6:45 p.m.*

Il Fornaio

2298 Union St.,
Cow Hollow
• 563-3400
Levi Plaza, 1265 Battery St.,
North Beach
• 986-0646

These attractive bakeries are related to the Il Fornaio chain in Italy, where each shop is a living museum of Italian regional breads and pastries. When the first shop opened on Union Street, bakers from Italy came over to train the staff. Though not always perfect translations, the breads and pastries were high in quality and fantastic in variety. Customer demand edited down the number of breads and, particularly, pastries that were baked daily. Still, almost everything turns up in the repertory once in a while: gnarled loaves of raisin bread; great wheels of pane pugliese; breads with peppers, potatoes, dates or even tomatoes worked into the dough; breads in whimsical shapes; and handy grissini (breadsticks). All are sold by the kilo, just as in Italy, so you can buy just part of a loaf if you like. The Battery Street shop is inside the dreamy Italian restaurant Il Fornaio, and while the selection is more limited, the complex also includes a posh little take-out shop where you can pick up roast chickens, pasta salads and heroic sandwiches to go. *Union St. branch: open Mon.-Sat. 7 a.m.-7 p.m., Sun. 7 a.m.-5 p.m. Battery St. branch: hours vary.*

Fran Gage
Pâtisserie Française

4690 18th St.,
Castro District
• 864-8428

The French flag flies in front of this blue-and-white gem of a bakery. To one side is an appealing baking room with scrubbed wooden tables and ovens at the back; to the other is a tiny retail shop with Fran Gage's beautiful bread arranged on trays behind the counter: torpedo-shape French country sourdough dusted with flour; round loaves of pain de seigle, a rye sourdough; and dainty mounds of her superlative walnut bread. Also on display are examples of ornate breads decorated with grape bunches or sheaves of wheat that she'll make on request. And in the pastry case are individual desserts, such as genoise layered with buttercream, rum-soaked chocolate hazelnut cake, tartettes and white-chocolate mousse. Gage honed her skills at Gaston Lenôtre's famous school outside Paris. Ornate wedding cakes have become a specialty here, too; demand is high, so be sure to sign up well ahead of time. *Open Mon.-Sat. 7:30 a.m.-7 p.m., Sun. 9 a.m.-5 p.m.*

House of Bagels

5030 Geary Blvd.,
Richmond District
• 752-6000
2427 Noriega St.,
Sunset District
• 661-2865

Eight kinds of bagels are sold in these two bakeries, plus a half dozen Eastern European breads, including egg twist, rye corn and pumpernickel.
Open daily 7 a.m.-5:30 p.m.

Just Desserts

248 Church St.,
Mission District
• 626-5774
836 Irving St.,
Sunset District
• 681-1277
3735 Buchanan St.,
Marina District
• 922-8675
3 Embarcadero Center,
Financial District
• 421-1609

Founded in 1974, Just Desserts is a wholesale bakery with four bakery/cafés throughout the city. All of them are comfy, low-key cafés where people come in to have a slice of banana-walnut cake or apple-crumb pie with their tea or coffee. Pastries are all homey and American, and everything is baked from scratch—from the New York–style cheesecake that launched the business to black-bottom cupcakes, blueberry muffins, danishes and even that relic of the '60s, carrot cake with cream-cheese frosting. It bakes dozens of lemon-buttermilk and poppyseed cakes, Southern pecan pies, plus fudge brownies, oversize cookies and shortbread. There's another branch in the Embarcadero Center (421-1609).
Church St. branch: open Mon.-Fri. 8 a.m.-11 p.m., Sat.-Sun. 9 a.m.-11 p.m. Other three branches: hours vary.

Liguria Bakery

1700 Stockton St.,
North Beach
• 421-3786

This venerable North Beach bakery is known for its delicious focaccia (Ligurian pizza bread). "That's all we make—we don't fool around," says the man behind the counter. Baked all morning long in the old brick-floored oven, it comes plain, seasoned with olive oil and salt or topped with scallions or tomato sauce. Also tempting are the panettone and thick, toasted biscotti made from dark anise bread.
Open Mon.-Sat. 8 a.m.-5 p.m., Sun. 7 a.m.-noon.

La Nouvelle Pâtisserie

2184 Union St.,
Cow Hollow
• 931-7655

Jean-Yves Duperret fills the shelves of this Union Street shop with beautifully crafted French pastries: feather-light palmiers, slender allumettes and buttery croissants. And his shimmering fruit tarts in the window stop passersby in their tracks. He also serves light luncheon fare, making La Nouvelle Pâtisserie as close as you can get to a Parisian *salon de thé*.
Open 6:30 a.m.-7 p.m., Fri.-Sat. 6:30 a.m.-11 p.m., Sun. 7 a.m.-6 p.m.

La Palma
Mexicatessan
2884 24th St.,
Mission District
• 647-1500

This place is a fine source of delicious, freshly made corn and flour tortillas baked on large iron griddles in back. Don't miss La Palma's tour de force, the thick hand-patted tortillas made by the skilled ladies in the kitchen. You can also stock up on bundles of dried chiles, beans, searing hot sauce and corn husks for tamales.
Open Mon.-Sat. 8 a.m.-6 p.m., Sun. 8 a.m.-5 p.m.

La Pâtisserie
397 Arguello Blvd.,
Richmond District
• 386-6633

Good croissants, but most of all, lovely cakes, such as the framboise, a génoise soaked in framboise liqueur, layered with raspberry jam and iced in pale pink.
Open daily 8 a.m.-6 p.m.

Sheherazade
Bakery
1935 Lawton St.,
Sunset District
• 681-8439

This bakery should be nominated as a city treasure. The Middle Eastern pastries sold here are all made with phyllo dough that is hand-stretched on the premises. Fresh and not preservative-adulterated, the phyllo is as supple and tender as a bolt of silk and can be easily folded into complex shapes. Take home some honey-sweetened baklava, or buy a roll of the phyllo to make your own. If you've ever had trouble working with phyllo dough, try again with this bakery's superlative product.
Open Mon.-Sat. 9 a.m.-5 p.m.

Sweet Things
1 Blackfield Dr.,
Tiburon
• 435-8583

Since Sharon Leach and Marsha Workman closed their Fillmore Street shop several years ago, customers have had to drive over the Golden Gate to the original bakery in Tiburon for the rich chocolate-mousse torte, which boasts a pound of bittersweet chocolate in every cake. You can also get wonderful coffee cakes in several varieties; the most sought after is the Hungarian sour-cream coffee cake swirled with cocoa, brown sugar, cinnamon and walnuts. And they've got such old-fashioned treats as snickerdoodles, sand tarts, homemade fudge, peanut butter cookies and chocolate-chocolate-chip cookies.
Open Mon.-Fri. 7:30 a.m.-7 p.m., Sat. 8:30 a.m.-6 p.m., Sun. 9:30 a.m.-6 p.m.

Tassajara Bread
Bakery
1000 Cole St.,
Haight-Ashbury
• 664-8947
Green's, Building A,
Fort Mason
• 771-6330

The Tassajara bakers, mostly students at the Zen Center, make bread with tender care; lately, however, the bread doesn't seem to be as consistent as it once was. At least a half dozen kinds are baked every day. Try the stone-ground whole wheat, the tender challah, the substantial sourdough corn rye and the excellent potato bread, moist with freshly grated potatoes. At Christmas they make panettone and stollen, both rich with glacéed fruits and nuts. And they

have tempting walnut-cranberry scones and morning pastries on the hefty side, along with oversize brownies, macaroons and chocolate. The bakery is a nice place to take a book and sit with some tea and pastries. Tassajara bread is also sold at lots of locations throughout the Bay Area.
Cole St. branch: open Mon.-Fri. 7 a.m.-9 p.m., Sat. 7 a.m.-7 p.m., Sun. 8 a.m.-2 p.m. Fort Mason branch: open Tues.-Sat. 10 a.m.-4:30 p.m.

True Confections
17 Madrona St.,
Mill Valley
• 383-3832

Morning pastries—croissants, pain au chocolat, scones and buttery apple turnovers—are the strong suit here. But the Black Forest cake and the classic tortes have passionate fans all over the Bay Area. During the summer glittering wheels of fresh-fruit tarts, silky lemon mousse and the strawberry cake—a light génoise soaked in kirsh, layered with meringue and filled with fresh berries and cream—are added to the list. Best of all are the pies: strawberry, rhubarb, blueberry and peach. During the holidays, look for sugar-dusted kugelhopf, wreaths of sweet Christmas bread and moist loaves of French pain d'épice (spice bread).
Open Mon.-Fri. 7 a.m.-6 p.m., Sat. 8 a.m.-6 p.m.

La Victoria
2937 24th St.,
Mission District
• 550-9292

The windows are filled with dozens of kinds of Mexican cookies and panes dulces glazed with sugar and baked in fantasy shapes. Go in, grab a tray and tongs and help yourself to a heap of these sweet treats. Great—and inexpensive—party fare.
Open daily 10:30 a.m.-10 p.m.

Victoria Pastry
1362 Stockton St.,
North Beach
• 781-2015

The cornetti made here are better than most you'll find in Italy. These large, plump crescents made from a tender brioche-like dough are perfect for dunking in your morning cappuccino. Traditionally a Christmas specialty, round loaves of panettone are baked here year-round. It's one of the things that thankfully haven't changed in North Beach.
Open Mon.-Sat. 7 a.m.-6 p.m., Sun. 8 a.m.-5 p.m.

Wood-Fire Bakery
958 San Leandro Ave.,
Mountain View
• 966-1022

All the flours are freshly milled and organically grown. And every label proclaims "no sugar, no fats or oils added." The Oat Bran Extra, made with unbleached wheat, whole wheat and rye sourdough, keeps especially well.
Open Mon.-Fri. 4 p.m.-6 p.m.

Yamada Seika Confectionery
1955 Sutter St.,
Japantown
• 922-3848

This tiny shop features traditional Japanese pastries made in elaborate shapes, such as manju (a sweet bean pastry) and yokan (candies jelled with agar-agar, a seaweed derivative). These may be something of an acquired taste, but the shop also sells lovely crackers.
Open Tues.-Sat. 9 a.m.-6 p.m., Sun. 9 a.m.-5 p.m.

BOOKS

Cookbook Corner
620 Sutter St.,
Union Square
• 673-6281

This sunny shop (inside the YMCA) is completely devoted to cookbooks. It's easy to spend the entire afternoon browsing through Taya Monfried's collection of English-language and foreign cookbooks, which includes just about everything currently in print, plus old and out-of-print books, wine books and regional charity cookbooks. Search service available.
Open Mon.-Sat. 11 a.m.-6 p.m.

Gourmet Guides
1767 The Cannery,
Beach & Leavenworth sts.,
Fisherman's Wharf
• 771-3671

Jean Bullock has two passionate interests, cooking and travel, and her charming bookstore (long a fixture in North Beach and just relocated to the Cannery) is stocked with books on these two subjects. The exuberant cookbook section includes books for novices, scholars and working chefs, as well as professional textbooks on cookery and pastry making. There's also a large collection of charity and Junior League cookbooks that contain regional recipes from all over the country. And armchair travelers can stock up on travel journals, all sorts of guidebooks, and maps to track down that restaurant you've been reading about. A mail-order service is also available; just ask to be put on the mailing list.
Open Mon.-Sat. 10 a.m.-6 p.m., Sun. 11 a.m.-5 p.m.

Household Words (Kay Caughran)
P.O. Box 7231,
Berkeley, CA 97407
• 524-8859

Former Berkeley librarian Kay Caughran deals in one-of-a-kind, out-of-print and hard-to-find books on cooking, eating, drinking and kindred subjects. Her annotated catalogs ($3), which list all the books she's collected in her wide-ranging searches, make interesting bedtime reading. Mail order only.

Wine Appreciation Guild
155 Connecticut St.,
Potrero Hill
• 864-1202

Although most of the business is wholesale, the guild's showroom is also open to the public. Along with corkscrews, wine buckets, wine racks, wine glasses and all kinds of accessories, it stocks an extensive collection of wine books

(ask for the catalog), including many from British publishers. Mail order is available, too. The catalog costs $2.
Open Mon.-Fri. 10 a.m.-5 p.m.

CHEESE

The Cheese Board
**1504 Shattuck Ave.,
Berkeley
• 549-3183**

One of the first and still the very best of the Bay Area's cheese shops, The Cheese Board has several great advantages. Because it is worker-owned, the people who wait on you really know the cheeses and may have been selling them for 10 years or more—even 22 years, since some of the original founders still work here. They're all experienced buyers, and they can describe each of the 300 or more cheeses as if they were friends of the family. Just as important: they take care of their cheeses. The store boasts a very good Italian cheese selection, including mozzarella di bufala, locally made mozzarella and ricotta and its own homemade Mascarpone. There's a strong showing of both French and Californian cheeses, plus several different feta cheeses, marvelous goat cheeses from all provenances, and The Cheese Board's own hearty fresh-baked breads, including the best baguette in the Bay Area.
Open Tues.-Sat. 10 a.m.-6 p.m.

Cheshire Cheese
**2213 Fillmore St.,
Upper Fillmore
• 567-4580**

Cheshire stocks more than 450 kinds of cheese, it's true, but most are precut, wrapped in plastic and crowded haphazardly onto the shelves. Cheddar, Gruyère and harder cheeses don't suffer, but you might want to buy more delicate cheeses elsewhere, or ask to taste before making a purchase.
Open Mon.-Fri. 7:30 a.m.-6:30 p.m., Sat. 8 a.m.-6:30 p.m., Sun. 9 a.m.-6 p.m.

Country Cheese
**415 Divisadero,
Castro District
• 621-8130**

This is a great place to buy such kitchen-staple cheeses as Gruyère and Cheddar. You'll find good prices on both imported and domestic cheeses, sold by the piece (usually not less than a pound). Watch for specials of Reggiano and other pricey cheeses used in cooking. And the store stocks Ferrante Cheese Company's locally made mozzarella, too. While you're there, you can stock up on flours, grains and nuts in bulk. There's a Country Cheese in Berkeley, too (841-0752).
Open Mon.-Sat. 10 a.m.-6 p.m.

Creighton's Cheese & Fine Foods
673 Portola Dr.,
Twin Peaks
• 753-0750

Creighton's has the same owners as the Sixth Avenue Cheese Shop, but with a much larger retail space, it stocks many more gourmet items and a broader range of bakery goods.
Open Mon.-Fri. 7:45 a.m.-7 p.m., Sat. 9:30 a.m.-7:30 p.m., Sun. 8:30 a.m.-6:30 p.m.

Laurel Wine & Cheese Center
Laurel Village,
3415 California St.,
Presidio Heights
• 751-4242

Laurel may not have the city's biggest selection of cheeses, but everything it does have is of top quality and in good condition: good Parmigiano, Romano, Cheddar, Stilton and Brie, for example, plus handsome pâtés, pasta from Fettuccine Brothers and a well-edited wine selection.
Open Mon.-Fri. 6:30 a.m.-6:30 p.m., Sat. 8:30 a.m.-5:30 p.m., Sun. 10:30 a.m.-5 p.m.

Say Cheese
856 Cole St.,
Haight-Ashbury
• 665-5020

Much of San Francisco learned about cheese after Bob Wiskotzil and George Kovatch opened this store in 1976. These days, under new owners, the store stocks 150 to 200 cheeses, depending on the season. Buy Swiss Raclette, and they'll rent you the machine and all the fixings. The shop often has unusual cheeses, perhaps sheep's milk Manchego from Spain or Montosio from the Veneto.
Open Mon.-Fri. 10 a.m.-7 p.m., Sat. 10 a.m.-6 p.m., Sun. 10 a.m.-5 p.m.

Sixth Avenue Cheese Shop
311 6th Ave.,
Richmond District
• 387-4192

The walls are covered with blackboards listing the 200 to 300 cheeses sold here during any given week. Where they are kept in this immaculate shop is anybody's guess. But the clerks know their cheeses (for once), and you can find excellent pâtés, caviar, a small selection of wines and special olive oils, vinegars and mustards. They've recently added their own bakery, too.
Open Mon.-Fri. 10 a.m.-7 p.m., Sat. 10 a.m.-6:30 p.m., Sun. noon-6 p.m.

COFFEE

Coffee, Tea & Spice
1630 Haight St.,
Haight-Ashbury
• 861-3958
4 Embarcadero Center,
Financial District
• 362-0585

This no-nonsense coffee store sells beans (which are roasted at the Haight Street store) by variety. You can also buy basic spices, including whole nutmeg with a little grater, aceto balsamico and imported chocolates. Coveted: the big slab of white chocolate from Switzerland. Prices on Nissan Thermoses, cobalt-blue teapots and all sorts of coffee-making equipment are some of the best in town.
Open Mon.-Fri. 7:30 a.m.-6 p.m., Sat. 10 a.m.-5 p.m.

Freed, Teller & Freed
1326 Polk St.,
Polk Gulch
• 673-0922

For almost 100 years, Freed, Teller & Freed has been quietly selling its own roasted coffees and imported teas to discriminating customers. Prices are very low, and this place really knows its business. The Darjeeling is exceptional, and if you ask the right questions, the staff can give you an education in tea. Also for sale: herbs and spices in bulk and well-chosen tea- and coffee-making implements, including sets of two tall copper pots with handles for pouring out your morning café au lait. Mail order is available.
Open Mon.-Sat. 9 a.m.-6 p.m.

Graffeo Coffee Roasting Co.
735 Columbus Ave.,
North Beach
• 986-2420

The seductive smell of roasting coffee will suck you right to the door of Graffeo in North Beach. A fixture in the neighborhood for 50 years, Graffeo has been tops in San Francisco for Italian-style—read espresso—coffee through three generations of the Repetto family. The Rube Goldberg–like roaster and rough burlap bags labeled Costa Rica, New Guinea, Java and Colombia take up most of the floor space. Just as in Italy, they keep it simple with just one Graffeo blend, roasted light or dark, and a single water-processed, 100 percent Colombian decaf. That means the coffee you buy is roasted that morning; by late afternoon, they're sometimes sold out. Mail order available. There's another store on 4th Street in San Rafael.
Open Mon.-Fri. 9 a.m.-6 p.m., Sat. 9 a.m.-5 p.m.

Mr. Espresso
1902 Encinal Ave.,
Alameda
• 865-3944

Carlo di Ruocco—otherwise known as Mr. Espresso—believes in roasting his beans over an oak fire. "Because the heat has some moisture in it," he explains, "it penetrates the bean evenly and roasts slower. That means more flavor." He's managed to convince Café Fanny, Square One, Modesto Lanzone and a slew of other restaurants that his espresso roast is the best in town. His stylish Viennese, dark French roast and straightforward mocha java are excellent, too, but it is the Neapolitan espresso that is winning fans among dedicated espresso drinkers. The selection of cappuccino machines is also terrific. Mr. Espresso is sold in some coffee stores, markets and bakeries around the Bay Area as well, and it can be purchased by mail order.
Open Wed.-Sat. 11 a.m.-5 p.m.

Peet's Coffee
1156 Chestnut St.,
Russian Hill
• 931-8302
3419 California St.
• 221-8506

Alfred Peet became the first to bring gourmet coffee to the Bay Area when he opened the first Peet's Coffee in Walnut Square in Berkeley in 1966. He grew up in the tea and coffee business in Holland and was an expert buyer and roaster. Unfortunately, since he left the business some years ago, the firm's penchant for very dark roasts has become even more pronounced, and many of the 30 or so coffees have a decidedly burnt taste—but that doesn't deter passionate fans. Best bets are the Garuda, Sulawesi-Kalossie and Major Dickason's blends. The tea selection continues to be superb. And Peet's has an outstanding selection (often at very good prices) of coffee grinders, espresso makers, coffee makers, teapots and the like. You can also buy Peet's coffees and teas at several branches in Berkeley, Menlo Park and Oakland, or through mail order.

Chestnut St. branch: open Mon.-Fri. 8 a.m.-7 p.m., Sat. 8 a.m.-6 p.m., Sun. 9 a.m.-6 p.m. California St. branch: open Mon.-Fri. 8 a.m.-7 p.m., Sat. 8 a.m.-6 p.m., Sun. 9 a.m.-6 p.m.

CONFECTIONS

The Candy Jar
210 Grant Ave.,
Union Square
• 391-5508

A Hungarian with a strong bent for perfectionism, Maria Stacho spent an entire year developing the recipe for the basic truffle she sells in her charming, minuscule Grant Avenue shop. She created dozens of variations on the theme, all of which appear in her repertoire from time to time. Best bets: the truffles filled with haunting fruit-flavored creams. Try the Grand Marnier truffle, too, with its center steeped in orange and then dipped in darkest chocolate. Bring in a silver basket from Tiffany's, an antique tin or even a plain paper bag, and The Candy Jar will fill it with an assortment of truffles and candies. You can also purchase Godiva chocolates here.

Open Mon.-Sat. 9:30 a.m.-6 p.m.

Chocolates from Chocolates
218 Church St.,
Mission District
• 431-3640

The heady scent of chocolate fills this bandbox of a shop that produces competent chocolate truffles in a dozen or so flavors, along with chocolate-covered graham crackers, Oreo cookies and even pretzels.

Open Mon.-Fri. 11:30 a.m.-7 p.m., Sat. 10 a.m.-6 p.m.

Cocolat
2119 Fillmore St.,
Upper Fillmore
• 567-1223
655 Montgomery St.,
Financial District
• 788-5778
4106 24th St.,
Noe Valley
• 647-3855

When Alice Medrich started fooling around with her Paris landlady's chocolate truffle recipe, one truffle led to another, and soon she was the undisputed truffle queen of California, if not the entire country. Her romantic Cocolat shops, with their nostalgic French decor and ravishing truffles and chocolate gâteaux, are responsible for turning countless chocolate-lovers into fanatics. Nobody makes better truffles maison. These are very dark, not too sweet and rolled in unsweetened cocoa to resemble the famous black truffle. Her dipped chocolate truffles are endlessly inventive (at last count her repertoire included more than 30), and you can count on any of them—hazelnut, chestnut, Grand Marnier, framboise, pistachio—to be remarkably good. Somehow you always end up buying far more than you intend—a few for a friend, a few for enjoying with your murder mystery, a few more for the movies. Life without Cocolat would be grim. The original store is at 1481 Shattuck Avenue in Berkeley (843-3265). Additional stores are in Oakland, Corte Madera and at the Stanford Court Shopping Center.

Fillmore St. branch: open Mon.-Thurs. 10 a.m.-7 p.m., Fri.-Sat. 10 a.m.-8 p.m., Sun. noon-8 p.m. Montgomery St. branch: open Mon.-Fri. 8:30 a.m.-6:30 p.m. 24th St. branch: open Mon.-Sat. 10 a.m.-7 p.m., Sun. noon-5 p.m.

Confetti le Chocolatier

4 Embarcadero Center,
Financial District
• 362-1706
The Cannery,
2801 Leavenworth St.,
Fisherman's Wharf
•474-7377

One of the prettiest chocolate stores we've ever seen, Confetti features Moreau chocolates from Switzerland. Made in a small family-owned factory with more than 100 years' experience in making fine chocolates, the Moreau chocolate "collection" comprises dozens of molded and filled confections, all shipped to San Francisco on the night flight from Geneva so they arrive as fresh as possible. It also has chocolates from Chocolatier Le Manon in Brussels, and local master chocolatier Joseph Schmidt's truffles and chocolates. Anyone for chocolate golf balls? An espresso bar in the corner serves cappuccino dusted with superior cocoa.

Open Mon.-Fri. 8 a.m.-6 p.m., Sat. 10 a.m.-5 p.m.

Findley's Fabulous Fudge

1035 Geary St.,
Van Ness
• 673-6655
397 Geary St.,
Union Square
• 434-3121

There are times when a chocolate truffle, however sophisticated, just doesn't do it. What you crave is fudge. Remember old-fashioned fudge—gooey, full of nuts, irresistible? Findley's has been turning out batch after 25-pound batch for decades now. Your best bets are the bags filled with one piece of each of the fifteen fudges made here. Then you can taste the classic walnut-studded fudge, the Chicago cream (no nuts), the almond fudge (with almonds instead of walnuts) and the rum du café, spiked with rum and dark coffee. You'll want to go on and on.

Van Ness branch: open Mon.-Fri. 10 a.m.-5 p.m., Sat. 11 a.m.-5 p.m. Union Square branch: open Mon.-Fri. 10 a.m.-10 p.m., Sat. 10 a.m.-11 p.m., Sun. 12:30 p.m.-8:30 p.m.

Godiva Chocolatier

Crocker Center Galleria,
50 Post St.,
Financial District
• 982-6798

As you would expect, here you'll find luxurious, sculpted chocolates from the renowned Belgium firm. Although we find homegrown Cocolat to be better, Godiva nonetheless sells lovely chocolates, and receiving one of those little gold

boxes is something akin to receiving one of Tiffany's little blue boxes. Branches in Corte Madera and the Stonestown Galleria.
Open Mon.-Fri. 9:30 a.m.-6 p.m., Sat. 10 a.m.-5 p.m.

House of Brussels Chocolates
2066 Chestnut St.,
Marina District
• 931-0661

Chocolates are handmade at this Marina District store using Callebaut chocolate imported from Belgium. The staff will put together all sorts of gift boxes of molded, filled chocolates, and for the less tradition-minded, they have chocolate baseballs (for the World Series), chocolate cameras and even a chocolate computer (IBM clone—Macintosh not yet available).
Open Mon.-Fri. 10 a.m.-7 p.m., Sat.-Sun. 10 a.m.-5 p.m.

Nob Hill Chocolates
1386 Pacific Ave.,
Nob Hill
• 474-6335

This small chocolate workshop will appeal to the child in everyone. You'll want to buy everything as soon as you breathe in the aroma of chocolate and candy making in the traditional Swiss style. The ingredients all come from Europe and are blended to make the chocolate right on the premises, including chocolate bars in six to ten flavors that are wrapped and labeled by hand. The dark-chocolate espresso bar and the cappuccino bar with milk chocolate walk out the door as fast as they are made. Much of the production of molded chocolates and truffles goes to restaurants. The candy makers here also design such popular gifts as chocolate champagne bottles filled with an assortment of chocolates.
Open by appt. only.

Joseph Schmidt Confections
3489 16th St.,
Mission District
• 861-8682

This is the most enchanting chocolate shop in the city, especially at Easter, when it practically bursts with chocolate bunnies, huge speckled white-chocolate eggs and demure little baskets filled with very realistic eggs and maybe a woodsy chocolate mushroom or two. Swiss-trained Joseph Schmidt is a master chocolatier, sufficiently confident of his craft to step outside tradition and come up with such wonderful, goofy creations as his chocolate spiny cactus and his dark- and white-chocolate saddle shoe. Schmidt's beautifully crafted truffles can be found not only here but in several specialty and chocolate shops in the Bay Area. The more than two dozen flavors include such knockouts as chocolate decadence, Hawaiian coconut, English walnut and white kirsch. He does a witty "cherry bomb" and a white-chocolate mushroom, too. And those miniature tennis balls, baseballs and golf balls with nougat fillings are really something—not to mention the white-chocolate

swan boats and the free-form chocolate bowls swirled with color (fill them with mousse or sorbet for an elegant dinner party). He also makes individual petal-shape cups.
Open Mon.-Sat. 10 a.m.-6:30 p.m.

Teuscher Chocolates of Switzerland
255 Grant Ave.,
Union Square
• 398-2700

This 50-year-old Swiss firm is best known to chocolate fanciers for its seductive Champagne truffle. That's all the more reason to try a small sampling of the other flavors, about a dozen in all, made with the same care and craftsmanship. Though all the truffles and molded chocolates are made in Switzerland, they're just as fresh as the locally made candies because they're flown in once a week from Zurich. *Open Mon.-Sat. 9 a.m.-7 p.m., Sun. 1 p.m.-5 p.m.*

ICE CREAM

Bravo Fono
99 Stanford
Shopping Center,
Palo Alto
• 322-4664

Now that the small Fono ice cream shop on Fillmore is closed, it's back to Palo Alto for the gelato many aficionados (including us) consider tops in the Bay Area. Paulette and Lazlo Fono didn't just amble into the ice cream business. They traveled extensively in Italy, stopping to work with master gelato makers, then returned to California, where they built each recipe from scratch, using American ingredients and Italian machines. Theirs is the definitive mocha and nocciola (hazelnut). The amaretto is gritty with crushed almonds, while the chocolate has an extraordinary balance of sweet and bitter. Don't miss the sorbetti, or ices, especially if you have the time to savor them under the big white umbrellas outside. These gelati are also sold at Euromarket in Berkeley.
Open Mon.-Sat. 11 a.m.-9:30 p.m., Sun. noon-9:30 p.m.

Double Rainbow
407 Castro St.,
Castro District
• 621-2350

As kids, Michael Sachar and Steven Fink spent their summers scooping ice cream on Coney Island. In 1977 they moved to San Francisco and opened their first ice cream parlor on Castro Street. Now they have their own line of superpremium ice cream and shops in many locations all over the Bay Area (and California). This is American-style ice cream, as rich and creamy as it comes. If you need to be convinced, taste the ultra-chocolate or the pistachio studded with whole nuts. Many other locations, including 3933 24th Street near Noe Valley (621-3420) and 1653 Polk Street in Polk Gulch (775-3220).
Open Sun.-Thurs. noon-11 p.m., Fri.-Sat. noon-midnight.

Gelato Classico Italian Ice Cream

2223 Chestnut St.,
Marina District
• 931-7251

The first of the new-wave gelaterias to charm San Francisco, Gelato Classico is still riding the gelato crest while other shops have closed their doors due to the more recent yogurt mania. Its ingredient for success? American flavors made in Italian machines, which gives the ice cream a dense, seductive texture without an overly exotic taste. There are many other locations, including Clement Street in the Richmond District, Post Street in Union Square, Union Street in North Beach and Parnassus Avenue near the Haight.
Open Mon.-Thurs. & Sun. noon-11 p.m., Fri.-Sat. noon-midnight.

Gino Gelateria

701 Columbus Ave.,
North Beach
• 981-4664

A popular North Beach spot for housemade gelato and sundae combinations.
Open daily 6:30 a.m.-10 p.m.

Latin Freeze

3338 24th St.,
Mission District
• 282-5033

Paletas are frozen-fruit bars made of puréed fresh fruits. Here they make them in such tropical flavors as mango and papaya. There's Jamaica (hibiscus flower), cacahuete (peanut) and fresh coconut, too. Have one or two on the spot and take home an assorted dozen for your freezer.
Open Mon.-Sat. noon-7 p.m., Sun. noon-4 p.m.

MARKETS

ETHNIC MARKETS

Bombay Bazaar

548 Valencia St.,
Mission District
• 621-1717

It's hard to walk into this enticing Indian grocery and not buy enough ingredients to cook Indian food for two years straight. It has unusual dhals, special flours for making Indian bread and all the spices that are so hard to find elsewhere. You'll even find tikka spice paste for grilled meats and poultry and, of course, an arsenal of pickles, chilis and chutneys, plus edible gold and silver leaf and Indian cooking implements. There's a second Berkeley location.
Open Tues.-Sat. 10 a.m.-6 p.m., Sun. 10 a.m.-5:30 p.m.

Casa Lucas Market

2934 24th St.,
Mission District
• 826-4334
3100 16th St.,
Mission District
• 431-8445

This is the place to get the ingredients you'll need to cook Caribbean, Central American and Latin American dishes. Hundreds of specialty items are stocked on the crowded shelves—everything from Brazilian palm oil and dried hominy to salt cod, Andean dried potatoes and tins of chorizo imported from Spain. The produce department displays

fresh tamarind, coconuts in the husk, mangoes, papayas and cherimoyas.
Open daily 8 a.m.-8:30 p.m.

Haig's Delicacies
642 Clement St.,
Richmond District
• 752-6283

Haig's carries a full line of Middle Eastern groceries, as well as spices and ingredients for Indian and Indonesian cooking. Stop here for wine-dark Kalamata olives, Greek olive oil, feta cheese in brine, phyllo dough from the Sheherazade bakery, soujouk (spicy beef sausages) and basturma (Armenian-style dried beef cloaked in a ruddy spice paste), plus green beans to roast for your Arabian-style coffee.
Open Mon.-Sat. 10 a.m.-6 p.m.

Lucca Delicatessen
2120 Chestnut St.,
Marina District
• 921-7873

After 60 years of roasting chickens, making salads and baking zucchini frittatas, the folks at Lucca Delicatessen have got it down. (And they weren't even fazed by the '89 earthquake that wreaked havoc on this neighborhood.) This is the most authentic of the city's neighborhood Italian delis, and a necessity for cooks in search of anchovies under salt, well-aged Parmesan, pancetta and polenta flour. Early morning twice a week, they make their own truly delicious ravioli, stuffed with finely chopped meat, Swiss chard and cheese. No machine here—the cooks use one of those old-fashioned wooden ravioli pins, then cut the plump little squares apart with a pastry wheel. Some of the other pasta places in town could use a lesson.
Open Mon. 10 a.m.-6:30 p.m., Tues.-Sat. 9 a.m.-6:30 p.m., Sun. 9 a.m.-6 p.m.

May Wah Trading Co.
1265 Stockton St.,
Chinatown
• 397-1527

In the midst of Chinatown, May Wah does a landmark business in Southeast Asian ingredients. The produce outside is exceptional: stalks of fresh lemon grass, tiny crimson chilis, young coconuts and fragrant Southeast Asian herbs grown locally. Inside, look for all the requisite fish sauces, chili sauces and pastes, rice papers, peanuts and more. Check the refrigerator case for Vietnamese pâtés wrapped in foil, rolls of rice-noodle dough studded with scallions and dried shrimp, and French baguettes.
Open daily 7:30 a.m.-6 p.m.

Metro Food Co.
641 Broadway,
Chinatown
• 982-1874

An emporium of Shanghai foodstuffs, Metro Food has a grand selection of ingredients for Chinese cooking: several grades of jellyfish in big crocks, dried Chinese mushrooms and other fungi, packaged spices, Szechuan vegetables and so forth. The refrigerator cases harbor fresh egg and rice

noodles, dumplings, fish cakes and rice cakes, as well as fresh bean-curd skin and fermented sweet rice pudding.
Open daily 9:30 a.m.-6 p.m.

Mi Rancho Market
464 7th St.,
Oakland
• 451-2393

Mi Rancho in downtown Oakland is both a tortilleria and a Mexican market. You can buy handmade corn and blue-corn tortillas still warm from the griddle, plus papery husked tomatillos, tortilla chips in bulk, myriad dried chiles and chile powders and hot sauces in a range of firepower. They've added a few tables in the corner where you can sit down to enjoy freshly made burritos and tamales.
Open Mon.-Sat. 8 a.m.-6 p.m.

Molinari Delicatessen
373 Columbus Ave.,
North Beach
• 421-2337

Heroic Italian sandwiches, dull Italian-American salads, a respectable array of cold cuts and cheeses and a mixed bag of Italian wines are the basic fare at this North Beach deli. But Italian cooks also can find baccalà (salt cod) and stock fish, musky porcini mushrooms, semolina, arborio rice, Tuscan olive oils and other imported goodies.
Open Mon.-Sat. 8 a.m.-5:30 p.m.

K. Sakai
1656 Post St.,
Japantown
• 921-0514

K. Sakai is a bustling Japantown supermarket with a well-groomed produce department and a busy fish counter. The meat counter stocks barbecued pork for your noodle dishes and paper-thin beef for sukiyaki and shabu-shabu. One refrigerator holds all the distinctly shaped fish cakes, another just the pickles. You'll find even the most esoteric Japanese ingredients somewhere on K. Sakai's shelves.
Open Mon.-Sat. 9 a.m.-6 p.m.

Hans Speckman
1550 Church St.,
Mission District
• 282-6850

A splendid array of wurstwaren awaits at this German deli, everything from Bratwurst and Liverwurst to paprika sausage and Westphalian ham, along with Swiss Bundnerfleisch (air-dried beef) and the house Leberkäse (a pork and veal meatloaf). You can buy German-style horseradish, plus the pumpernickel and rye breads the deli has collected from local Eastern European bakeries. And there are more than twenty German beers.
Open Mon.-Thurs. 11 a.m.-6:30 p.m., Fri.-Sat. 10 a.m.-7 p.m., Sun. noon-6 p.m.

Wee Wah Trading Co.
1248 Stockton St.,
Chinatown
• 434-2553

Across the street from the May Wah Trading Company is Wee Wah, which stocks a similar array of Southeast Asian spices and condiments, plus such produce as taro root, sugarcane and baby bok choy.
Open daily 7 a.m.-6:30 p.m.

GOURMET MARKETS

Edibles

Belgian chocolates, dainty crackers, imported shortbread and all the usual trappings of a department-store gourmet shop are here. But Edibles also has Narsai's pâtisserie, charcuterie and boulangerie at the back, where you can buy the TV cooking personality's signature pâtés, smoked fish and caviar, as well as freshly baked breads, croissants, miniature brioches and pastries. There's also a wonderful collection of jams, vinegars, relishes and other condiments under Narsai's label, including a fabulous hot fudge sauce, plus a number of other top-quality lines to round out the selection. And be sure to check out the superb collection of single-malt scotches and fine Armagnacs from the respected négociant Francis Darroze.
Open Tues.-Wed. & Sat. 9:30 a.m.-6 p.m., Mon. & Thurs.-Fri. 9:30 a.m.-8 p.m., Sun. noon-5 p.m.

Epicure

Neiman Marcus,
150 Stockton St.,
Union Square
• 362-3900

The best thing about Neiman Marcus's gourmet department is the Petrossian boutique tucked discreetly in one corner—and painted the same blue as the caviar purveyor's famous store on the boulevard de Latour-Maubourg in Paris. If you want to splurge and splurge big, this is the place to buy sevruga and beluga caviar, smoked eel, smoked salmon and cod roe. The truly exceptional quality justifies the high prices. Epicure's other strong points are the cart of biscotti and cookies from the DiCamillo bakery in Niagara Falls and the display of biscotti (almond or hazelnut, chocolate-dipped or plain) from the local La Tempesta bakery. You'll also find a few fashionable cheeses and cold cuts, some decent pâtés and rare roast beef. And if you really feel the need to have Neiman Marcus's own brand of West Texas mesquite, go right ahead.
Open Mon.-Wed. & Fri.-Sat. 10 a.m.-6 p.m., Thurs. 10 a.m.-9 p.m., Sun. noon-5 p.m.

Euromarket

1601 Martin Luther King St.,
Berkeley
• 841-7737
6309 College Ave.,
Oakland
• 652-4171

A great new entry into the gourmet market scene with two East Bay stores stocked with goodies. The larger Berkeley store has one of best selections of deli meats and pâtés around (think Bundnerfleisch, smoked breast of duck, pâté and Thai chicken sausages from Le Pique Nique), plus an attractive serve-yourself cheese case containing knowledgeably chosen and reasonably priced imported and domestic cheeses. Look for teas from the famous Marriage Frères in Paris, French cookies and Bravo Fono ice creams. Auntie Pasta shares the space at the Berkeley location. Euromarket

has an all-star list of East Bay breads, featuring all the contenders except breads from The Cheese Board.
Berkeley branch: open Mon.-Sat. 7 a.m.-7:30 p.m., Sun. 8:30 a.m.-7 p.m. Oakland branch: open Mon.-Sat. 9:30 a.m.-7 p.m., Sun. 10 a.m.-5:30 p.m.

The Oakville Grocery
7856 St. Helena Hwy., Oakville
• (707) 944-8802

Those of us who remember and miss San Francisco's Oakville Grocery can't resist paying a visit now and again to its country cousin, the original store in the Napa Valley. It's still lavishly stocked with Smithfield hams, country pâtés and terrines, olives in every hue and top-quality herbs and spices. If you're visiting the wine country, this is picnic heaven. Throw a baguette, some local goat cheese and whatever else appeals to you into a basket. You can buy the wine here, or from one of the wineries up the road.
Open daily 10 a.m.-6 p.m.

G.B. Ratto, International Grocers
821 Washington St., Oakland
• 832-6503

An unpretentious international grocer in the midst of downtown Oakland, G.B. Ratto stocks hard-to-find ingredients for a wide range of cuisines at very low prices. You can find the requisite dried beef and black beans for your feijoada, palm oil for your West Indian and African dishes, gumbo filé and andouille sausages for your gumbos, cracked green olives for your Moroccan tajine and leathery dried chiles for a chicken mole. Shop here for blue-corn polenta meal, dried fava and cannellini beans, top-quality basmati rice, cracked wheat and couscous in bulk. The bulk herb selection is one of the best in the Bay Area, and the cheese counter is no slouch, either. Look for bread from Acme, Metropolis and Semifreddi, plus Smithfield hams, superb bacon, Italian pancetta, Graffeo coffee and bulk baking chocolate. No matter how esoteric the ingredient, the people here will know what it is and will probably have stocked it at one time or another. Just twenty minutes across the Bay Bridge, Ratto makes a great rainy-day excursion— and it opens at 8 a.m., which is when you'll find caterers and professional cooks roaming the crowded aisles.
Open Mon.-Sat. 8 a.m.-5 p.m.

Trader Joe's
337 3rd St., San Rafael
• 454-9530
1975 Diamond Blvd., Concord
• 689-2990

L.A.'s immensely popular Trader Joe's chain of budget/gourmet stores has just opened two new Bay Area locations. And transplanted Angelenos have been making tracks to pick up terrific bargains in cheeses, nuts, crackers, wines, preservative-free (and often good) frozen foods, wild rice and a slew of other gourmet goodies. Best advice on the sometimes overwhelming selection of dirt-cheap international wines is to buy a bottle, try it and then come back for a case if it suits your palate. You can find good bargains in off-vintages and wines from little-known areas.

San Rafael branch: open daily 9 a.m.-10 p.m. Concord branch: open daily 9 a.m.-9 p.m.

Vasilio's Kitchen

Andronico's Park & Shop,
2655 Telegraph Ave.,
Berkeley
• 845-1062
Andronico's Park & Shop,
1850 Solano Ave.,
Berkeley
• 524-1673
Andronico's Park & Shop,
1414 University Ave.,
Berkeley
• 548-7061

Vasilio's is the high-tech gourmet delicatessen at the three Andronico's Park & Shop supermarkets in the East Bay. Daniel Strongin, former executive chef at the Claremont Resort Hotel and chef at the Ritz Boston, runs the kitchen, supervising the salads and take-out items, made here every day. Turnover is brisk, so everything looks well groomed and fresh—from the mozzarella sold in its brine, the locally made ricotta and the slew of imported and domestic cheeses to the unusual sausages made by Bruce Aidell and the broad selection of cold cuts, prosciutto and salami. There are breads from Acme, truffles from Joseph Schmidt, milk in glass bottles with the cream on top from Peninsula Creamery, gourmet coffees and an impressive meat counter staffed with real butchers.

Telegraph Ave. branch: open daily 8 a.m.-11 p.m. Solano Ave. branch: open daily 9 a.m.-11 p.m. University Ave. branch: open daily 8 a.m.-10 p.m.

Vivande Porta Via

2125 Fillmore St.,
Upper Fillmore
• 346-4430

Hands down the most beautiful food store in the city, Vivande celebrates Carlo Middione's love affair with Italian cooking. Author of several books on the subject (the most recent is *The Cooking of Southern Italy*), he's stocked his Fillmore Street salumeria with the best possible ingredients for cooking Italian, and he cooks antipasti and other dishes for taking home or taking out on a picnic (or eating in the café in back). The assembled goodies include prosciutto, pâtés, terrines, galantines, Italian cheeses, fresh sausages flavored with fennel and pepper, a profusion of fried sausages, various antipasti and salads, including one of pale-green fagioli with caviar, and homemade pastries and biscotti. Best bets are the pizza rustica and the torta milanese, a tall layering of spinach, cheese and red and yellow peperonata in a pastry crust. Anything from the rotisserie is great, especially the chicken roasted to a lovely mahogany color with rosemary and garlic or with lemon; on occasion there's quail, duck or pork loin. Sometimes there are charming little round loaves of panini di noce with walnuts and black pepper, and a simple but delicious version of focaccia topped with a bright marinara sauce and scattered with green onions. And for dessert, try the homemade amaretti or the terremoto (earthquake) cake. Shop for distinguished

Italian wines, Tuscan olive oils, arborio rice, dried porcini mushrooms and all manner of special Italian ingredients. *Open Mon.-Fri. 10 a.m.-7 p.m., Sat. 10 a.m.-6 p.m., Sun. 10 a.m.-5 p.m.*

MEAT, POULTRY & GAME

Andronico's Park & Shop
1200 Irving St.,
Sunset District
• 661-3220

This is one of a vanishing breed: a supermarket with quality meat, a remarkable selection of cuts, good specials and, what's more, real butchers behind the counter until closing—at the Telegraph Avenue store in Berkeley, that's 11 p.m. You want just half of a smoked shank or your veal liver sliced especially thin? No problem. Plus it's got great-looking veal, free-range chickens, fresh Cornish hens and freshly made sausages. This is where you'll meet late-night cooks buying pancetta, Bruce Aidell's New Orleans–style andouille sausages, a little Mascarpone and whatever else they need to whip up a late supper. The Berkeley markets are at 1850 Solano Avenue (524-1673), 2655 Telegraph Avenue (845-1062) and 1414 University Avenue (548-7061). *Open daily 7 a.m.-9 p.m.*

Antonelli & Sons
Cal Mart Super,
3585 California St.,
Presidio Heights
• 752-7413

This small counter offers the absolute freshest poultry, both free-range and organic. The staff will gladly bone your chicken breasts or order fresh game birds or poussin for a special dinner. The ranch eggs sold here are laid one day and sold the next. Also in Cal Mart Super is the fine Bryan's Quality Meats (see below). *Open Mon.-Sat. 8 a.m.-6:30 p.m.*

Bryan's Quality Meats
Cal Mart Super,
3585 California St.,
Presidio Heights
• 752-3430

The meat here is beautifully displayed in modest quantities, which means they cut it just as they need it. Steaks are labeled "prime" and "choice"—prime when they can get it, otherwise choice. But both are sold at the same price. The roasts are good-looking, too, and you'll see such old-fashioned cuts as flat-iron pot roast and cross-rib roast, plus handsome corned beef briskets, pale veal and corn-fed Eastern pork. Bryan senior no longer mans the counter, but he still buys the meat directly from the slaughterhouse, then brings it back to the store for aging. *Open Mon.-Sat. 8 a.m.-6:30 p.m.*

La Ferme Beaujolaise
2000 Hyde St.,
Nob Hill
• 441-6913

This French gourmet shop has taken over the space where Marcel & Henri once turned out the city's best pâtés and charcuterie. It's still a good source for smooth duck-liver pâtés, real country-style pork-laced pâtés, fresh sausages and cuts of veal and pork from the small butcher counter. Every night there's a different entrée. Don't miss the savvy collection of French wines and the Provençal herbs.
Open Mon.-Sat. 9 a.m.-7:30 p.m., Sun. 10 a.m.-6 p.m.

Harris'
2100 Van Ness Ave.,
Van Ness
• 673-1888

This highly regarded steakhouse serves only prime beef from Nebraska, aged 21 days before it hits the grill. You can buy the same meat served in the restaurant at the small counter just inside the entrance.
Open Mon.-Fri. 11:30 a.m.-9 p.m., Sat.-Sun. 2 p.m.-9 p.m.

R. Iacopi
1642 Grant Ave.,
North Beach
• 421-0757

This North Beach butcher shop dates from before the '06 quake—1896 to be precise—and it's still busy every morning making fresh and dried sausages for the Italian community. Iacopi turns out all kinds of regional sausages: hot Calabrese, sweet (not hot) Sicilian and garlicky Toscana, flavored with cloves, nutmeg and cinnamon. It makes its own pancetta and, even more unusual, cures its own prosciutto crudo. You can buy it sliced by the pound or whole (fifteen pounds) at considerable savings.
Open Mon.-Fri. 9 a.m.-7 p.m., Sat.-Sun. 10 a.m.-6 p.m.

Israel & Cohen Kosher Meat and Poultry
5621 Geary Blvd.,
Richmond District
• 752-3064

You'll find a good selection of both fresh and frozen kosher meat and poultry here, as well as canned and packaged Jewish foodstuffs.
Open Sun.-Fri. 7 a.m.-7 p.m.

Junmae Guey
1222 Stockton St.,
Chinatown
• 433-3981

Junmae Guey is an informal Chinese restaurant with Formica tables and a small deli where you can buy what may be the best roast pig in Chinatown. The roast duck and barbecued pork are also excellent. While you wait for your take-out order, sit down for a bowl of congee (Chinese rice gruel) to fortify you after braving the Chinatown crowds.
Open daily 8:30 a.m.-6 p.m.

Kwong Jow Sausage Manufacturing Co.
1157 Grant Ave.,
Chinatown
• 397-2562

The things to buy in this tiny Chinese sausage shop are hunks of chewy, dried lop cheong sausage, twists of bacon rind and slices of barbecued pork. The sausages are good sliced and steamed with rice for a quick, satisfying meal.
Open Mon.-Sat. 9 a.m.-6 p.m., Sun. 9 a.m.-5 p.m.

Little City Meats

1400 Stockton St.,
North Beach
• 986-2601

This longtime North Beach butcher shop specializes in locally raised veal, weighing in at just 60 to 70 pounds. Look for thick-cut veal chops, scaloppines, veal shoulder for stews and meaty veal shanks for osso buco. Sometimes the store has veal filet, and it always has breast of veal ready to stuff. Don't worry if you don't have a recipe—they're plastered all over the walls.
Open Mon.-Fri. 8 a.m.-6 p.m., Sat. 8 a.m.-5:30 p.m.

Magnani Poultry

6317 College Ave.,
Oakland
• 428-9496
1586 Hopkins St.,
Berkeley
• 528-6370

Magnani is a well-run store with top-quality, very fresh poultry. It sells Rocky Jr. free-range chickens as fast as hotcakes. Look for roasters, and small broilers as well as fresh Cornish game hens, chicken livers and as many backs as you can carry home for your stockpot. Or you can pick up one of the barbecued chickens. Duck livers and all sorts of fresh game birds are available by special request. This is also one of the few sources outside Chinatown for fresh, locally raised Peking duck, with head and feet intact.
Oakland branch: open Mon.-Fri. 9:30 a.m.-6:30 p.m., Sat. 9 a.m.-6 p.m. Berkeley branch: open Mon.-Sat. 10 a.m.-6 p.m.

Night Bird Game & Poultry Co.

650 San Mateo Ave.,
San Bruno
• 543-6508

Night Bird is a successful wholesaler of game and game poultry to restaurants and hotels. Home cooks can buy here, too, but since it takes about 45 minutes to process an invoice, it's a good idea to call your order in and pick it up later that day or the next. Tell the staff what you're looking for, and they'll tell you if they have it or can get it for you. This includes local quail, partridge, pheasant and squab, plus grouse, hare and red deer from Scotland. At one time Night Bird had caribou from Lapland, elk from Sweden and wild boar from Australia. A ranch in Texas raises elk and antelope for the firm.
Open Mon.-Fri. 7 a.m.-4 p.m.

Roberts Corned Meats

1030 Bryant St.
• 621-2624

Roberts went into business some 80 years ago, in 1910. Its renowned corned beef is cured from the inside out by directly injecting the beef with spice-laden brine rather than soaking the meat in brine. In addition to its unique curing method, owner Jim Dixon claims the San Francisco climate has something to do with the quality of the corned beef. This is also a good source for New York pastrami, hams, smoked or pickled tongue, pork hocks and bacon.
Open Mon.-Fri. 8 a.m.-11:30 p.m., 12:30 p.m.-3:30 p.m.

Sandy's
1040A Stockton St.,
Chinatown
• 989-0477

This tiny Chinese deli and café sells good roasted ducks, tender spareribs and tasty barbecued pork.
Open daily 8 a.m.-7 p.m.

Shew Wo Meat Co.
1151 Stockton St.,
Chinatown
• 982-7234

One of the many good Chinatown butcher shops, Shew Wo is the place for all manner of pork, impeccably fresh innards and such hard-to-find cuts as pigs' feet (fore or back), fresh pork belly (bacon) and pigs' ears and snouts. Prices are always very good, whether you're buying big slabs of ribs or a few pork chops for a barbecue.
Open daily 8:30 a.m.-6:30 p.m.

Sung Sang Market
1205 Stockton St.,
Chinatown
• 989-3060

Roasted foods are Sung Sang's strong suit: the main attractions are good roast pig, ducks roasted with anise and fresh coriander, and roast chickens and squab.
Open Mon.-Sat. 8:30 a.m.-5:30 p.m., Sun. 8 a.m.-5:30 p.m.

PASTA

Auntie Pasta
1501 Waller St.,
Haight-Ashbury
• 681-4242
741 Diamond St.,
Noe Valley
• 282-0738

From a single store in 1981, Auntie Pasta has become a Bay Area chain, successful because it has kept the concept simple: fresh pasta in many widths, shapes and flavors; sauces made every day; and just a few other essentials for preparing a pasta-based meal: olive oil, imported plum tomatoes, wine and great bread (in San Francisco, from Fran Gage's Pâtisserie Française, and in the East Bay, from Acme Bread Company). Expect to find a half dozen different pastas, flavored with roasted peppers, fresh garlic, red chile, beets or lemon. To top them, pick one of nine sauces, including a tomato-basil, a sweet red pepper and, for garlic-lovers, a cream sauce with roasted garlic and porcini mushrooms. The ravioli, however, could be more tender and supple. Numerous other locations include stores on 7th Avenue and McAllister near the Civic Center, 3101 Fillmore near the Marina and several in the East Bay.
Haight-Ashbury branch: open daily 11 a.m.-9 p.m., Sat. 11 a.m.-8 p.m., Sun. noon-8 p.m. Noe Valley branch: open Mon.-Fri. 11 a.m.-9 p.m., Sat.-Sun. 11 a.m.-8 p.m.

Fettuccine Brothers
2100 Larkin St.,
Russian Hill
• 441-2281

The fresh pasta in this charming little shop and café is made daily from durum and semolina flours, whole fresh eggs and filtered water, and comes in either plain egg or spinach versions. They'll cut it to whatever width you want and sell you some sauce if you don't have time to make your own.

The basics are marinara, a traditional bolognese sauce, a vongole (baby clam) sauce made with white wine, and a well-made pesto. But do try the northern Italian walnut sauce and, in warm weather, the primavera, lavished with the season's best fresh vegetables. The tortelloni stuffed with ricotta, Parmesan and spinach is a good bet, too. This excellent pasta is also available in some markets and delis. *Open Mon.-Sat. 11 a.m.-7 p.m., Sun. noon-7 p.m.*

New Hong Kong Noodle Co.
874 Pacific Ave., Chinatown
• 982-2715

Twenty-five sizes and types of Chinese noodles are produced by this Chinatown noodle company, including Shanghai-style noodles, very thick Hong Kong–style noodles and wide noodles. You'll also find several types of skins for wontons, potstickers and other dumplings. Prices are only slightly above wholesale.
Open Mon.-Sat. 8 a.m.-6 p.m., Sun. 10 a.m.-4 p.m.

The Pasta Shop
Rockridge Market Hall, 5655 College Ave., Oakland
• 547-4005

This Oakland shop makes some of the best pasta in the Bay Area (as quite a few restaurateurs will testify). Not only is the dough supple and fine, but it can be cut to any of six different widths—from angel hair up to pappardelle—or can be purchased by the sheet. The flavors are wonderful, too. Basics are egg, spinach, garlic and herb, whole wheat and tomato; specials include black pepper, buckwheat and saffron. The spa marinara sauce (no oil) and winter pesto (with arugula and Italian parsley) vie with the puttanesca sauce as customer favorites. Try the homemade ravioli with the squash, prosciutto and sage filling. The Pasta Shop also makes its own sausages and has a marvelous array of charcuterie and cheeses and a complete stock of Mediterranean groceries: olives and olive oils; flours for making your own pasta; imported dried pasta; vinegars; and hand-picked herbs from Greece. It also has some of the most daunting prices in the Bay Area.
Open Mon.-Fri. 10 a.m.-8 p.m., Sat. 10 a.m.-7 p.m., Sun. 10:30 a.m.-5 p.m.

Yuen Hop
824 Webster St., Oakland
• 451-2698

Yuen Hop sells fresh egg noodles "for chow mein," another type for soup; square and round wonton skins; egg roll skins and crispy noodles; and several kinds of tofu.
Open Mon.-Sat. 8 a.m.-6:30 p.m.

PRODUCE

Living Foods

149 Throckmorton Ave.,
Mill Valley
• 383-7121
222 Greenfield Ave.,
San Anselmo
• 258-0660
1581 University Ave.,
Berkeley
• 549-1714

This is a model natural-foods store with good-looking organic produce shrewdly supplemented by commercial produce when necessary. It stocks flavorful lettuces, wild mushrooms, blood oranges, lavender gem grapefruit and more, plus bulk nuts, grains, beans and flours, and spices and herbs sold by the ounce. It also has a great meat counter with free-range chickens, organic poultry and Niman-Schell naturally raised beef. Check the freezer section for frozen packs of organic chicken parts—perfect for making stock. The Berkeley store is the largest of the three.
Mill Valley branch: open Mon.-Fri. 9 a.m.-8 p.m., Sat. 9 a.m.-7 p.m., Sun. 10 a.m.-6 p.m. San Anselmo branch: open Mon.-Fri. 9 a.m.-8 p.m., Sat.-Sun. 10 a.m.-7 p.m. Berkeley branch: open Mon.-Fri. 9 a.m.-9 p.m., Sat. 9 a.m. -8 p.m., Sun. 10 a.m.-7 p.m.

Monterey Foods

1550 Hopkins St.,
Berkeley
• 526-6042

Monterey Foods is simply the best produce store in the Bay Area, if not in all of California. Whatever the season, there's always at least one New Yorker stopped dead in the aisles gasping at the low prices and all that gorgeous produce. There may be a few Southeast Asian herbs or vegetables you won't find, but Monterey has just about every other exotic item: fresh galangal and turmeric root, chiles in umpteen varieties, tamarind pods, Key limes, Spanish garlic, special pie apples and spectacular organic baby lettuces. Out front are bins overflowing with top-quality bargain produce, from mandarin oranges to sweet red pimientos, ripe avocados to slender young asparagus. In summer, look for giant strawberries and berries from small local growers, thumb-size pickling cucumbers, and melons galore.
Open Mon.-Sat. 9 a.m.-6 p.m.

Real Food Co.

1023 Stanyan St.,
Haight-Ashbury
• 564-2800

The produce here is both organic and commercial, but there's never any confusion, since everything is clearly marked and handsomely displayed in shallow baskets. The range of products is quite a bit broader than you'll find at other organic-produce stores. While you're here you can stock up on organic flours, polenta, whole grains, imported olive oils, raw milk cheeses, gourmet ice creams and more. Good bread selection, too. Other Real Food stores are

located on Polk Street, 24th Street, Sutter Street and in Sausalito and San Rafael.
Open daily 9 a.m.-8 p.m.

Rima's Green Valley
297 Page St.,
Haight-Ashbury
• 431-7250

This produce store may have changed its name from Green Gulch to Rima's Green Valley, but you can still find the same good selection of organic produce. In summer the shop stills get some of the Zen Center's Green Gulch farm overflow, but normally the mostly organic produce is purchased directly from truck farmers and farmer friends of the Zen Center. Breads from the Tassajara Bakery are also sold.
Open Mon.-Fri. 8 a.m.-8 p.m., Sat. 8 a.m.-7 p.m., Sun. 9 a.m.-3 p.m.

San Francisco Farmer's Market
100 Alemany Blvd.,
City South
• No phone

This outdoor farmer's market is such an old San Francisco tradition that it's just about as crowded on drizzly winter days as on sunny summer and spring mornings. Small truck farmers come in from outlying counties to set up their stalls and weigh out sweet oranges, fresh almonds and exotic greens. One stand sells garlands of chile peppers and garlic; another, baskets of beautiful berries. It's friendly, has pretty good bargains and is a fun place to shop, but come early—some of the stalls close by early afternoon.
Open Sat. 6 a.m.-late afternoon.

Wo Soon Produce Co.
1210 Stockton St.,
Chinatown
• 989-2350

Wo Soon is the best place in Chinatown for Chinese produce: fresh water chestnuts, baby bok choy, Chinese mustard and broccoli, handsome cabbage and watercress.
Open daily 7 a.m.-6 p.m.

SEAFOOD

Antonelli & Sons
Cal Mart Super,
3585 California St.,
Presidio Heights
• 752-7413

The Antonelli family has decades of experience with local seafood. They do their buying at the wharf in the early morning and bring everything back to the store for cleaning, scaling and cutting. It's great for thick, freshly cut fish steaks—halibut, swordfish and salmon—plus lots of whole fish, fresh filets and some shellfish. Live lobsters are available by request.
Open Mon.-Sat. 8 a.m.-6:30 p.m.

Canton Market
1135 Stockton St.,
Chinatown
• 982-8600

Canton is one of Chinatown's best poultry and fish markets, and its fish counter is popular with Chinese customers. Look for pristine scallops, giant squid, shrimp and whole

fish. Sometimes they'll even tell you the name of the fish, but don't count on it.
Open daily 8 a.m.-6 p.m.

Delta Crayfish
608 Hwy. 12,
Rio Vista
• (707) 374-6654

It's fun on the weekend to make an excursion to Delta Crayfish for enough of the little blue creatures to put on a real crayfish boil. Delta sells them to you live, just as it does to restaurants all over California. It's open only during crayfish season, and it's a good idea to call first.
May-Nov.: open daily 10 a.m.-5 p.m.

Flying Salmon
2512 Sacramento St.,
Upper Fillmore
• 567-4444

This spiffy shop, just off Fillmore Street, has a great caviar selection, everything from Russian beluga, osetra and sevruga to top-quality fresh Chinese caviar and domestic whitefish and salmon caviar. American sturgeon caviar is available by special request. There's a small fish counter as well.
Open Mon.-Sat. 10 a.m.-7 p.m.

Gulf Spray
609 Cole St.,
Haight-Ashbury
• 751-0473

Word is that Gulf Spray's buyer is at the wharf almost every morning choosing the best of the day's catch for this retail and wholesale business. Shellfish include locally raised Pacific oysters and mussels, Portuguese and Gulf oysters, fresh East Coast bay and sea scallops and blue crabs in season. The staff is generous with cooking advice, but buy only what looks freshest—which is what you should do at any fish market.
Open Mon.-Sat. 11 a.m.-7 p.m.

Monterey Fish Market
1582 Hopkins St.,
Berkeley
• 525-5600

Much of fishmonger Paul Johnson's business is supplying seafood restaurants with the best of what's available. A former chef and one of the authors of *The California Seafood Cookbook*, Johnson is an expert buyer; his small retail store is stocked with the same select fish he sells to restaurants—only what's fresh and in season—plus shellfish and some unusual specialties. Come here to see what a top-notch fish market should look like. The stuff is gorgeous.
Open Tues.-Sat. 10 a.m.-6 p.m.

La Rocca's Oyster Bar
3519 California St.,
Presidio Heights
• 387-4100

The window in front displays seafood to be cooked on-site or to take home and cook yourself. The selection is small enough and business brisk enough to assure you of impeccable freshness.
Open Mon.-Sat. 8 a.m.-5:30 p.m.

Sang Sang Market

1143 Stockton St.,
Chinatown
• 433-0403

Another popular Chinatown fish market, Sang Sang is a good place to find the requisite redfish for Cajun cooking, as well as loads of squid, clams and mussels and a great selection of whole fish. The store is long and narrow, and always impossibly crowded. Take a deep breath and plunge right in, waving like everybody else for the attention of the men behind the counter.
Open daily 8:30 a.m.-5:30 p.m.

Swan Oyster Depot

1517 Polk St.,
Polk Gulch
• 673-1101

The friendly staff at this decades-old café and fish market will sell you whatever oysters they're shucking for café customers that day, plus any of the fish they're serving: steelhead salmon, swordfish, ling cod, red snapper . . . whatever's available and fresh.
Open Mon.-Fri. 8:30 a.m.-5:30 p.m., Sat. 8:30 a.m.-5 p.m.

Wah Fat Fish Market

821 Pacific Ave.,
Chinatown
• 392-3837

This relatively new Chinatown fish market boasts five enormous tanks of live fish and crab. In front, you'll see boxes of live frogs, East Coast blue crabs and some very big turtles, which would crawl right out of their boxes if they could. The quality of the seafood at the counter is high. Most of the fish is sold in the round, but you can ask the vendors to scale and clean whatever you buy, and if you like, they'll quickly filet it.
Open daily 8 a.m.-6 p.m.

SPICES & HERBS

Bombay Bazaar

548 Valencia St.,
Mission District
• 621-1717

Stock up on all kinds of exotic flours, lentils and basmati rice before checking out the exceptional spice selection. You serve yourself from the rows of jars filled with everything from familiar coriander, mustard seed and turmeric to green or black cardamom in the pod—even the harder-to-find white variety. There's a wide range of spice mixes and spice pastes, too.
Open Mon.-Sat. 10 a.m.-6 p.m., Sun. 10 a.m.-5:30 p.m.

Buffalo Whole Food & Grain Co.

1058 Hyde St.,
Nob Hill
• 474-3053

Shop here for organic grains and flours milled at Giusto's in South San Francisco, and also for herbs and spices in bulk. Lined up alphabetically, the 180 jars of herbs, spices and teas make a study in color and texture. And at these prices, even the largest treasure trove of spices won't cost you all that much.
Open Mon.-Sat. 9 a.m.-9 p.m., Sun. 10 a.m.-8 p.m.

Haig's Delicacies

642 Clement St.,
Richmond District
• 752-6283

The best-known Middle Eastern food store in the city, Haig's is a great place for the innumerable spices used not only in Middle Eastern cooking but in Indian and Southeast Asian cooking as well. It buys in bulk and repackages in four-ounce quantities under its own label.
Open Mon.-Sat. 10 a.m.-6 p.m.

The Lhasa Karnak Herb Co.

2513 Telegraph Ave.,
Berkeley
• 548-0380
1938 Shattuck Ave.,
Berkeley
• 548-0380

Specialists in herbs and spices, Lhasa Karnak is a romanticist's idea of an herb store. Small and impeccably neat, the shop has dozens of gallon glass jars filled with herbs, spices, roots and seeds in all the colors of autumn and earth. The emphasis is medicinal, but the cook will find much of interest, too.
Open Mon.-Sat. 9:30 a.m.-7 p.m., Sun. 11 a.m.-6 p.m.

Nature's Herb Co.

281 Ellis St.,
Union Square
• 474-2756

Since 1915, Nature's Herb Company has been dispensing all manner of herbal remedies, custom tonics and culinary herbs and spices to generations of health-conscious San Franciscans. The old-fashioned store has hundreds of varieties of herbs, roots and seeds filed away in cabinets. For cooks, it has all the basics, plus such hard-to-find items as chicory root, galangal, mugwort, turmeric root and fragrant whole vanilla bean. All herbs are sold in leaf form, which maintains flavor longer than when ground or powdered. And there's no real minimum—clerks will sell you four ounces of this and that, if you like.
Open Mon.-Sat. 6:30 a.m.-3 p.m.

G.B. Ratto, International Grocers

821 Washington St.,
Oakland
• 832-6503

This old-fashioned store in the midst of downtown Oakland's Victoriana boasts an extensive serve-yourself spice section. Not only does it have dozens of familiar herbs and spices to scoop from gallon jars, but it also has the best sweet and hot paprika around, ground chiles labeled by variety, white poppy seeds and cream of tartar for grandma's recipes. The scent of the Greek hills pulls at you from bundles of wild oregano and thyme. Burlap sacks of dried red peppers and black peppercorns add their note, and the glorious mix of pink, green, black and white peppercorns belongs in everyone's arsenal of spices.
Open Mon.-Sat. 8 a.m.-5 p.m.

The Spice House

2343 Birch St.,
Palo Alto
• 326-8811

A wonderful resource for everything exotic, The Spice House stocks spices you've never even heard of, like cubeb pepper, used in classical recipes, and melagueta pepper, a relative of cardamom that is listed in some medieval recipes. Kalajeera, black cumin seeds and zubrovka, a grass used to

flavor vodka, are also in stock. This has to be the best herb and spice selection for ethnic cuisines in the Bay Area. And whenever possible, The Spice House stocks both the dried herb for your pantry and the healthy plant for your kitchen garden.
Open Mon.-Sat. 10 a.m.-5:30 p.m.

STAPLES

The Food Mill
3033 MacArthur Blvd.,
Oakland
• 482-3848

A favorite with cooks and bakers for the consistently high quality of flours, grains and cooking oils, The Food Mill sells almost all of its goods in bulk. To assure maximum freshness, it grinds all the whole-grain flours itself; you'll notice the difference immediately. Check here also for nut butters, cereals, dried fruit and nuts. Too bad it discontinued Friday night deliveries some years ago.
Open Mon.-Sat. 8:30 a.m.-6 p.m.

Ohs Fine Foods
2651 Mission St.,
Mission District
• No phone

Ohs has no telephone. That may be a bit eccentric, but never mind—the store is a good source for flours, grains, beans, nuts, dried fruits and spices, all displayed in open sacks in a store about as wide as your hand. At the front there's even birdseed for your parrot. You'll find very good prices on coffee, too, which Mr. Ohs roasts and distributes. Ohs is also known as the California Direct Importing Company.
Open Mon.-Sat. 9 a.m.-6 p.m.

WINE

Beltramo's
1540 El Camino Real,
Menlo Park
• 325-2806

Mecca for wine aficionados from all over the Bay Area, Beltramo's boasts a formidable collection of wines from every wine-growing region in the world.
Open Mon.-Thurs. 9 a.m.-9 p.m., Fri.-Sat. 9 a.m.-9:30 p.m., Sun. 9 a.m.-7 p.m.

California Wine Merchant
3237 Pierce St.,
Marina District
• 567-0646

The California Wine Merchant is true to its title: this tidy shop has what may be the widest selection of California wines in the city. That means a good stash of older California vintages, too.
Open Mon.-Sat. 11 a.m.-7 p.m.

Coit Liquors
585 Columbus Ave.,
North Beach
• 986-4036

Tony Giovanzana has managed to fit a remarkable selection of Italian, French and California wines into his corner liquor store in North Beach, along with a lot of good Champagne at some of the best prices in town. Customers buy steadily all day long, yet the shelves are always fully stocked. How does he do it? He has a huge cellar beneath the store. Be sure to check the grappa selection for such respected products as Gaja, Ceretto and Castello di Barbaresco.
Open daily 9 a.m.-midnight.

Connoisseur Wine Imports
462 Bryant St.,
South of Market
• 433-0825

Its warehouse space a maze of stacked wine crates, Connoisseur is the place to bone up on German wines and their intricate classification system. Connoisseur has fine examples of them all, from Spätlese to Trockenbeerenauslese, along with a staff that genuinely enjoys discussing these wines or any others in stock. It also has great old Bordeaux, a splendid collection of Sauternes of both recent and older vintages, fine Burgundies and gentlemanly vintage ports, plus a well-edited selection of California wines, many from wineries with limited production.
Open Tues.-Sat. 9:30 a.m.-5:30 p.m., Sat. 10 a.m.-5 p.m.

Corti Brothers
5770 Freeport Blvd.,
Sacramento
• (916) 391-0300

Yes, it's a long haul to Corti Brothers, but it's worth a drive to check out Darrell Corti's eclectic selection of old sherries, vintage Armagnacs, fragrant rums and spirits and fine wines. Luckily, you don't even have to drive, since Corti sells by mail order. While you're at it, you can order his extra-virgin olive oil from Catalonia, which in view of Italian olive oil prices is a remarkable bargain.
Open daily 9 a.m.-7 p.m.

Draper & Esquin
655 Davis St.,
Financial District
• 397-3797

When Draper & Esquin moved from the Vintner's Building on Sutter Street a few years ago, it lost a bit of its scholarly, decidedly old-world aura. No matter, it has kept its remarkable collection of old Bordeaux, quite good Burgundies, Champagnes, Sauternes and wonderful Italian wines. It's also one of the few stores in town with a stock of older California vintages as well as top-notch current releases. The annual catalog with snapshots of producers and notes on visits to the wine country makes for great bedtime reading. Another plus is free Bay Area delivery.
Open Mon.-Fri. 9 a.m.-6 p.m., Sat. 9 a.m.-5 p.m.

Enoteca Mastro
933 San Pablo Ave.,
Albany
• 524-4822

This small enoteca, or "wine library," is devoted entirely to Italian wines from Tuscany, Piedmont, Friuli, the Alto Adige and the Veneto. Owner Mark Anthony Mastro will

take you on a tour around the shop, describing the characteristics of each wine. And you can taste any of six different wines at the bar before you buy. Soon to open: a trattoria next door serving earthy regional Italian fare.
Open Tues.-Wed. 11 a.m.-6 p.m., Thurs.-Sat. 11 a.m.-6:30 p.m.

Liquor Barn
201 Bayshore Blvd.,
City South
• 282-0532

If you know your wines, you can find some extraordinary bargains here, mostly on imported wines. The California wine prices are competitive, but you can sometimes match or better them at other wine stores. But if you're up on wines from Tuscany, Piedmont, Alsace, the Rhône and Germany's Rheingau, stop in often for a quick browse. Wines appear and disappear with unseemly haste—and each Liquor Barn seems to have a slightly different stock of imported wines. Other stores are located in Alameda, Albany, Colma and San Mateo.
Open Mon.-Sat. 9 a.m.-9 p.m., Sun. 10 a.m.-8 p.m.

Kermit Lynch Wine Merchant
1605 San Pablo Ave.,
Berkeley
• 524-1524

Anyone who loves French wines, but must love them on a modest budget, is well acquainted with the wines of Kermit Lynch, wine merchant extraordinaire. Every wine he sells he has imported himself. He spends half the year in Europe revisiting his wine makers, tracking down properties he's heard about and discovering new producers. He has built his considerable reputation on what are known in Europe as "petits vins." And when he does buy from Bordeaux or Burgundy, he favors traditionally made wines at good prices. But since his producers almost all make wine in limited quantities and some have become stars, prices are inevitably going up. He has a special love, too, for the wines of the Côtes-du-Rhône and the Loire Valley. Look here for distinguished wines from Alsace, along with vintage Chiantis and other interesting Italian wines. Also tempting are the olive oils, jams and lavender honeys from wine producers. And you can taste a few of his wines at Alice Waters's Café Fanny next door.
Open Tues.-Sat. 11 a.m.-6:30 p.m.

Paul Marcus Wines
Rockridge Market Hall,
5655 College Ave.,
Oakland
• 420-1005

An expertly stocked little wine shop in Rockridge's exciting market hall, Marcus is a good place to look for the best from California, Italy and France.
Open Mon.-Fri. 10 a.m.-8 p.m., Sat. 10 a.m.-7 p.m., Sun. 10 a.m.-6 p.m.

Pacific Wine Co.
124 Spear St.,
Financial District
• 896-5200

The majority of the wines stocked in this Pacific Heights shop are personally selected in France by the buyer, Mike Lynch. You'll find wines from the Côtes-du-Rhône, the Loire and other wine regions, but the store's strength lies in its selection of Burgundies and Bordeaux. He's got Champagnes (more than 30), sumptuous dessert wines and a fine collection of Cognacs, Armagnacs and Calvados, plus a few dozen single-malt scotches.
Open Mon.-Fri. 10 a.m.-6 p.m., Sat. 10 a.m.-5 p.m.

Singer & Foy
1821 Powell St.,
North Beach
• 989-0396

A lovely sign hung from twined wrought-iron grape leaves marks this stylish North Beach wine bar and retail store. You'll find wines imported by Kermit Lynch, along with an astutely edited selection of older Bordeaux and Burgundies, some fabled California wines and the best of Oregon's Pinot Noirs. You can taste wines at the bar every day; special tastings are held on Friday and Saturday. Stop in, too, for marvelous breads from the Acme Bread Company in Berkeley.
Open Mon.-Sat. 11 a.m.-7 p.m.

Solano Cellars
1580 Solano Ave.,
Albany
• 525-0379

Offering an informed selection of California, French and Italian wines, plus good sherries and ports, Solano has a tasting bar that is open every day, and a bistro that serves food to accompany the wine at the bar. The atmosphere is companionable and the food quite good.
Open Mon.-Fri. 11:30 a.m.-8 p.m., Sat. 10 a.m.-8 p.m., Sun. noon-5 p.m.

John Walker & Co.
175 Sutter St.,
Union Square
• 986-2707

If you have a taste for legendary Bordeaux vintages or fine old Burgundies, you can find more than enough to keep you happy at John Walker. Surprisingly, even in this high-rent district, prices are sometimes just a touch lower than you might pay elsewhere. John Walker has kept some of these wines maturing in his warehouse for years—he didn't pay a fortune for them when they were young; he may charge you only a small one now.
Open Mon.-Fri. 9 a.m.-6 p.m., Sat. 9:30 a.m.-5 p.m.

The Wine House
535 Bryant St.,
South of Market
• 495-8486

John Carpenter is an importer who specializes in the wines of Bordeaux and Burgundy, although he has digressed into other, lesser-known French wine areas. Since his customers want to get a sense for older wines before they invest heavily in new ones, a good portion of his business is in older wines, both from Europe and California. Look here for rare

California vintages, noble Italian wines and vintage ports, Sauternes and Champagnes.
Open Mon.-Fri. 10 a.m.-6 p.m., Sat. 10 a.m.-4 p.m.

GIFTS

Aerial
The Cannery, 2801
Leavenworth,
Fisherman's Wharf
• 474-1555

"Active Lifestyles Artifacts and Waterbar" is how this place bills itself. We didn't see any signs of a waterbar but we did see plenty of other things that we were willing to go hopelessly into debt for. Finely crafted leather briefcases, unusual sunglasses, extraordinary watches—stop, pocket and wrist—overview maps of ancient Rome, sports shoes by Airwalk, genuine enameled French regiment pins, handmade paper, eclectic graphics books, handcrafted hats, strange and wonderful jewelry—all the objects of lust for the new-age, postmodern consumer. Shop to the modulated throbbing of Phillip Glass and a three-screen video of *Metropolis.*
Open Mon.-Wed. 10 a.m.-7 p.m., Thurs.-Sat. 10 a.m.-8:30 p.m., Sun. 11 a.m.-6 p.m.

Australia Fair
700 Sutter St.,
Union Square
• 441-5319

A cheery spot for rarely seen products from Down Under, many of which make good gifts. For children and animal-lovers, there are stuffed koalas; for rakish outdoorsmen, ranch coats and bush hats; for skiers, wool underblankets and lambskin rugs to decorate the cabin; and for gourmands, tins of Vegemite.
Open Mon.-Sat. 9:30 a.m.-5:30 p.m.

Virginia Breier
3091 Sacramento St.,
Presidio Heights
• 429-7173
Ghirardelli Square,
900 N. Point St.,
Fisherman's Wharf
• 474-5036

Looking for a really unusual gift? How about an iridescent little minnow pin, not a replica but the real thing covered in resin? Or a sculpture portraying the Earth emerging from a goat's back? Direct from Michigan, Virginia Breier brings you these marvels and much more in the arts and crafts vein. Venture past the pottery and furnishings in the front into the back, where all the weird and beautiful handcrafted jewelry is kept. Nothing here is what you could describe as inexpensive, but it certainly is one of a kind. Be sure to take a look at the demented, neofunk sculpture garden in the back.
Sacramento St. branch: open Mon.-Sat. 11 a.m.-6 p.m. Ghirardelli Square branch: open Mon.-Sat. 11 a.m.-6 p.m., Sun. noon-6 p.m.

H.P. Corwith Ltd.
1833 Union St.,
Cow Hollow
• 567-7252

There's a cool, art-gallery tone to this shop, with its white walls and glass cases, that quickly dissipates the minute you focus on the wacky stuff displayed. Along with some of the most winsome cloth vegetables we've ever seen are humorous dishes of fake food, miniatures of all kinds and handsome antique tools. Even people who have everything don't have most of the things sold here.
Open Mon.-Sat. 10 a.m.-6 p.m., Sun. 11 a.m.-6 p.m.

Dandelion
2877 California St.,
Laurel Heights
• 563-3100

One of our favorite rainy-day retreats, Dandelion exudes the dim, comfy atmosphere of an old country store. The dark floor-to-ceiling shelves hold a delightful assortment of imported soaps, cards, wrapping papers, candles, unusual children's playthings and fine fountain pens. Once you've decided on the right gift, not any easy task given the choices here, you can choose something appropriate to wrap it in. Among the housewares is a great selection of tablecloths in varied designs and fabrics, and at the back of the shop you can indulge your sweet tooth at the old-fashioned candy counter.
Open Mon.-Sat. 10 a.m.-6 p.m., Sun. noon-5 p.m.

Folk Art International Gallery
Ghirardelli Square,
900 North Point St.,
Fisherman's Wharf
• 441-6100

The showroom for the nonprofit Folk Art International group, this spacious shop on the second floor of the Cocoa Building offers a well-balanced selection of folk arts and crafts from around the world: masks from Mexico, South America and the Philippines; handwoven baskets from Africa; paintings from China, Ecuador and France; sculptures and artworks from as close as the Appalachians and as far as Sri Lanka; and antique bronzes, porcelains and ivory carvings from the Orient. You'll also find winsome toys, unusual furniture, Berber jewelry from Morocco's Atlas Mountains, and colorful clothing and textiles. Next door is the affiliated Xanadu Gallery (see below), now owned by Folk Art International, which specializes in tribal art.
Open Mon.-Thurs. 10 a.m.-6 p.m., Fri.-Sat. 10 a.m.-9 p.m., Sun. 11 a.m.-6 p.m.

Forma
1715 Haight St.,
Haight-Ashbury
• 751-0545

Forma sells gifts and objects for those who appreciate the bizarre side of life. In a stark faux-stone room are such modern-day necessities as troll dolls, Sea Monkeys, a statue of Bob Hope golfing, the Elvis Love Her Tender hair-care line, jars of human teeth and dishes festooned with black cats.
Open Mon.-Fri. noon-7 p.m., Sat. 11 a.m.-7 p.m., Sun. noon-6 p.m.

Fumiki

1894 Union St.,
Cow Hollow
• 922-0573

An eclectic array of antique and contemporary art objects and fine jewelry from Japan, China and Korea, including elegant silk obi (the sashes for kimonos) and a noteworthy group of ivory and wooden netsuke (the intricately carved toggles used to fasten small containers and obi).
Open Mon.-Sat. 10 a.m.-6 p.m., Sun. noon-5 p.m.

Goosebumps

Ghirardelli Square,
900 North Point St.,
Fisherman's Wharf
• 928-2112

Trendy, wacky and sometimes tacky, Goosebumps is also great fun. While TV theme songs play over the sound system, you can browse through the diverse selection of gifts, none of which are practical or essential: six-foot inflatable Bozo the Clown dolls, moronic joke books, outlandish T-shirts, plastic dinosaurs, liquid crystal jewelry, windup toys, see-through barbecue aprons and much, much more.
Open daily 10 a.m.-9 p.m.

Gump's

250 Post St.,
Union Square
• 982-1616

Like anything in one of those little blue boxes from Tiffany's, a gift from Gump's is always welcome. It helps to have a hefty net worth, though—the jade and pearl jewelry, crystal vases, silver frames, handsome desk accessories and exquisite Oriental antiques are breathtakingly expensive. Even if you don't want to buy, come here for a browse.
Open Mon.-Sat. 9:30 a.m.-5:30 p.m.

Margar's

1957 Union St.,
Cow Hollow
• 346-2719

Stashed in a little alley off Union Street, Margar's is basically a nice knickknack shop with a large candle selection, lots of marvelous ornamental mirrors in wood, brass and plaster, and an equal number of ornamental frames, which make the perfect gift for someone who'd like a nicely framed picture of you.
Open daily 10 a.m.-5:30 p.m.

The Nature Company

Ghirardelli Square,
900 North Point St.,
Fisherman's Wharf
• 776-0724

If you, like most good consumers, are regularly deluged with catalogs, chances are you're already familiar with The Nature Company. These very clever people sell an unusual collection of nature-related gifts for adults and children: animal posters, handsome moon-phase watches, geodes, wind chimes, stegosaurus T-shirts, globes (both inflatable and permanent), clever scientific toys and games, new-age records, tapes and compact discs, beautiful books, and posters featuring the work of such artists as Ansel Adams. A must-visit in Ghirardelli Square.
Open daily 10 a.m.-9 p.m.

SFO
1837 Union St.,
Cow Hollow
• 567-5913

Another T-shirt, sunglasses and plastic dinosaur store with a trendy edge. Definitely slanted toward teenagers.
Open Mon.-Fri. 10 a.m.-6:30 p.m., Sat. 10 a.m.-7 p.m., Sun. 11 a.m.-6:30 p.m.

The Sharper Image
532 Market St.,
Financial District
• 398-6472

The famous catalog come to life, with all kinds of fashionably useless items for the spoiled rich executive: household remote controls, space-age briefcases, suits of armor, radar detectors, miniature TVs, crossbows, air purifiers, elaborate exercise equipment, high-tech telephones and some incredibly boring jewelry. Several other locations.
Open Mon.-Sat. 10 a.m.-7 p.m., Sun. noon-5 p.m.

Techsis
Crocker Center Galleria,
50 Post St.,
Financial District
• 362-2777
5 Embarcadero Center,
Financial District
• 362-7655

Granted, these hologram watches won't put Cartier out of business, but they are unusual. Aside from the watches, Techsis sells similarly high-tech gifts, some of which are quite clever (the folding bikes and the games) and some of which are dreadful (the hologram jewelry).
Crocker Center branch: open Mon.-Fri. 9:30 a.m.-6 p.m., Sat. 10 a.m.-5 p.m. Embarcadero Center branch: open Mon.-Fri. 10 a.m.-6 p.m., Sat. 10 a.m.-5 p.m.

Xanadu
Ghirardelli Square,
900 North Point St.,
Fisherman's Wharf
• 441-5211

Next door to the Folk Art International Gallery (see above), which now owns it, Xanadu is a showcase for some remarkable tribal art and artifacts from Africa, Asia, Oceania and the Americas. From elaborate, expensive masks, intricately beaded animals and sculptures to moderately priced weavings to inexpensive elephant-hair jewelry (which brings the wearer good luck), the collection is chosen with a fine eye.
Open Mon.-Thurs. 10 a.m.-6 p.m., Fri.-Sat. 10 a.m.-9 p.m., Sun. 11 a.m.-6 p.m.

Yankee Doodle Dandy
1974 Union St.,
Cow Hollow
• 346-0346

The best items in this somewhat spurious Americana emporium are the genuine antique quilts, priced accordingly. The less wonderful things, and there are a lot, are the ersatz works of folk art—carved wooden pigs, cows and farm couples that are crudely rendered and painted. There's also a smattering of Native American giftware.
Open Mon.-Sat. 10:30 a.m.-5:30 p.m., Sun. noon-5 p.m.

Z Gallerie
2071 Union St.,
Cow Hollow
• 346-9000

High in design and low in price, Z Gallerie exhibits a strong predilection for high-tech—black calculators, black watches, black chairs and black tables set with black dishes and napkins. The merchandise is well selected, however, and will make the necessary statement without bankrupting you. At the back of the store are equally modern and

attractive housewares. The "gallerie" moniker is justified by the large stock of bathetic framed posters. There are Z Galleries in several other locations.
Open Mon.-Sat. 10 a.m.-9 p.m., Sun. 11 a.m.-6 p.m.

HOME

CHINA & CRYSTAL

Biondi Art Imports
412 Columbus Ave.,
North Beach
• 392-8096

A one-of-a-kind store filled with dazzlingly colorful Italian ceramics. The remarkable hand-painted dinnerware, vases, platters and objets d'art from several Italian manufacturers are Biondi's main draw, both in the store and through its large mail-order business, but there's more: espresso and cappuccino machines, authentic Italian cookware, pasta rollers and ornate Capodimonte china.
Open Mon.-Sat. 9:30 a.m.-6 p.m., Sun. noon-5 p.m.

Gump's
250 Post St.,
Union Square
• 982-1616

No trip to San Francisco can end without a visit to Gump's, the fabulous china/stationery/jewelry/gift store that opened its first downtown doors in 1862. Its stationery is refined and its jewelry is timeless, but the china and crystal departments are unequaled. There are more than 400 patterns from every fine maker in the world, including Waterford, Baccarat, Steuben, Limoges, Fitz & Floyd and Spode. As one would expect with such merchandise, the bridal registry, gift wrapping and shipping services are outstanding.
Open Mon.-Sat. 9:30 a.m.-5:30 p.m.

Wedgwood San Francisco
304 Stockton St.,
Union Square
• 391-5610

The entire range of Wedgwood's bone china and stoneware is available at this spacious store, which also stocks most Waterford crystal patterns. Our favorites from the Wedgwood line are the adorable Peter Rabbit china and the colorful Jasperware. Service is good.
Open Mon.-Sat. 9:30 a.m.-5:30 p.m.

FABRIC

Laura Ashley

253 Post St.,
Union Square
• 788-0190
1827 Union St.,
Cow Hollow
• 922-7200

Behind the racks of flouncy dresses, corduroy jumpers and cuter-than-cute little-girl clothes are shelves filled with Laura Ashley's English country fabrics. If used in moderation, these cotton prints can help create a lovely nursery or charming country cottage. If used excessively, the flowery patterns will make one long for the Bauhaus look. There's another store at 1827 Union Street in Cow Hollow.
Post St. branch: open Mon.-Sat. 10 a.m.-6 p.m. Union St. branch: open Mon.-Sat. 10:30 a.m.-6:30 p.m., Sun. 11 a.m.-5 p.m.

Britex Fabrics

146 Geary St.,
Union Square
• 392-2910

Traveling tailors and seamstresses head straight for Britex when they get into town—they know that few places in the world have such an extensive collection of fine fabrics, leathers, buttons and notions. From sea-island cotton to cashmere, couture knits to crêpe de chine, Britex has every kind of fabric imaginable. Get on the mailing list and you'll receive regular notices of the latest offerings. Though there's almost always a crowd, the staff is cheery and helpful.
Open Mon.-Wed. & Fri.-Sat. 9:30 a.m.-6 p.m., Thurs. 9:30 a.m.-8 p.m.

Marimekko

Crocker Center Galleria,
50 Post St.,
Financial District
• 392-1742

Once in the vanguard of modern Scandinavian fabric design in this country, Marimekko has brightened many a household with these bold, colorful fabrics and linens from Finland and is still going strong. The emphasis in this shop, however, has unfortunately shifted from the cheerful, contemporary cottons to simple cotton and wool clothing for men, women and children.
Open Mon.-Fri. 9:30 a.m.-6 p.m., Sat. 10 a.m.-5 p.m.

Pierre Deux

532 Sutter St.,
Union Square
• 788-6380

The front of this handsome French country store is filled with purses, cosmetic cases, pillows and notebooks covered with Pierre Deux's trademark fussy cotton prints. Those same fabrics—which we find attractive only in very small doses—are sold by the yard in the back.
Open Mon.-Sat. 9:30 a.m.-5:30 p.m.

FURNISHINGS

Bay Commercial Lighting Center
1140 Folsom St.,
South of Market
• 552-4110

Bay Lighting sells high-style and Eurostyle lighting fixtures—floor lamps, walls sconces, table lamps, hanging fixtures—from European and American designers. The selection of cutting-edge contemporary fixtures is exceptional. It's also a good place for well-made track and recessed lighting. The emphasis is on design and quality, not budget.
Open Mon.-Fri. 8 a.m.-5 p.m., Sat. 10 a.m.-2 p.m.

Cottonwood
3461 Sacramento St.,
Presido Heights
• 346-6020

Cottonwood showcases contemporary handcrafted furniture and accessories created by local, national and international artisans. The shop contains several spaces that are arranged as actual rooms, suggesting how the furnishings and tableware can be combined and incorporated into the room's decor. If the general style could be summed up, it might be described as post modern primitive. Many of the design motifs harken back to Frank Lloyd Wright furniture, Native American patterns, early American art glass. In one room, a wrought-iron table with Keith Haring–like designs cut out of the tabletop was set with thick, rich-hued glass dishes and what looked like rather crude wrought-iron flatware that the salesperson warmly assured us could be used to eat with (although our fillings cried out at the thought). There are some exceptional lamps with fragile paper shades and, as expected, a case of handmade jewelry in the same neoprimitive mode. Definitely a must.
Open Mon.-Fri. 10:30 a.m.-6:30 p.m., Sat. 10:30 a.m.-6 p.m., Sun. noon-5 p.m.

Crate & Barrel
125 Grant Ave.,
Union Square
• 986-4000

Just try to walk out of this huge, cheerful store without buying something—unless you have an iron will, you'll leave toting a Crate & Barrel bag filled with some intelligently designed, practical, inexpensive household item. Crate & Barrel's first West Coast store is a merchandising marvel, with three floors of great-looking household basics, from Adirondack chairs to terra-cotta dishes, storage systems to Champagne flutes—everything a fledgling yuppie needs to set up a first big-city apartment.
Open Mon.-Wed. & Sat. 10 a.m.-6 p.m., Thurs.-Fri. 10 a.m.-7 p.m., Sun. noon-5 p.m.

Fillamento

2185 Fillmore St.,
Upper Fillmore
• 931-2224

Young, modern and somewhat Eurostyle, Fillamento's merchandise is reminiscent of Conran's, the British home-furnishings giant. This is a good place for attractive dhurrie rugs, glassware, terra-cotta dishes, designer stainless flatware, dining room tables, folding chairs and clever storage systems. The staff is quite friendly.
Open Mon.-Wed. & Fri.-Sat. 10 a.m.-6 p.m., Thurs. 10 a.m.-8 p.m., Sun. noon-5 p.m.

Susan Howell Textiles

2200 Fillmore St.,
Upper Fillmore
• 567-3093

Recently relocated to larger quarters, Susan Howell carries some quite lovely rugs—some of her own making and some from the Navajo and the Orient. She also does a fine job of restoring worn or damaged rugs.
Open Mon.-Sat. 11 a.m.-6 p.m.

Japonesque

Crocker Center Galleria,
50 Post St.,
Financial District
• 398-8577

There's a timeless quality to the handcrafts, lanterns and furniture displayed in this quiet, modern shop. Some items are antiques, others new, but there is no break in continuity. Cases display small treasures, such as carved wooden "stones," eyeglass frames and netsuke. There are ukeoye, the woodblock prints from the turn of the century, and contemporary sculpture in stone and wood. Not hard-edged like many trendy Japanese designer shops.
Open Mon.-Fri. 11 a.m.-5:30 p.m., Sat. 11 a.m.-5:30 p.m.

Just Closets

3450 Sacramento St.,
Presidio Heights
• 563-6066

One of the better and more reasonably priced of the closet-organization companies that have sprung up in the last few years. Closets can be custom-designed and -installed, or you can create your own from the modular systems, baskets, shoe organizers and special hangers in the boutique. Some of these organizational systems are also great for home offices.
Open Mon.-Fri. 10 a.m.-6 p.m., Sat. 10:30 a.m.-5 p.m., Sun. noon-5 p.m.

Limn

457 Pacific Ave.,
Jackson Square
• 397-7474

Billing itself as "a continually changing display of furniture reflecting intriguing currents and lasting influences in contemporary design," Limn occupies a simple brick warehouse space—the perfect backdrop for its extraordinary tables, desks, chairs and couches. The artist- and architect-designed furniture, some of it created by owner Lee Friedlander, ranges from extreme to subtle. Radical and expensive lighting fixtures are sometimes carried here, and there's

usually an exhibition of painting or sculpture. A very exciting store.
Open Mon.-Fri. 9:30 a.m.-5:30 p.m., Sat. 11 a.m.-5:30 p.m.

Polo/Ralph Lauren
90 Post St.,
Financial District
• 567-7656

All it takes is many thousands of dollars and a few well-placed antique picture frames and, *voilà*, your entire house can instantly reek of old money. Ralph Lauren has tapped deep into America's new-found desire not to be crass and nouveau riche, first with his expensive classic clothing and now with his expensive classic furniture. These beds, linens, chairs, dressers, sofas, pillows and fabrics are elegant, tasteful, understated and well made, with designs that draw on the past instead of looking toward the future. Some of the fabrics—such as the plaids and hunting motifs—are tiresome, but most of Lauren's line is quite handsome in a solid, conservative way.
Open Mon.-Sat. 10 a.m.-6 p.m.

Revival of the Fittest
1701 Haight St.,
Haight-Ashbury
• 751-8857

Want a phone like the one Humphrey Bogart barked into in the old Sam Spade movies? How about a set of Fiestaware, or a streamlined Mixmaster that would have made Harriet Nelson proud? Then get on over to Revival of the Fittest, a cheerful store with well-displayed vintage and contemporary home and kitchen accessories. There's a small selection of choice furniture, along with great mantel and wall clocks, glassware, old-fashioned toasters, art deco lamps and antique jewelry.
Open Mon.-Sat. 11 a.m.-6 p.m., Sun. noon-6 p.m.

Santa Fe
3571 Sacramento St.,
Presidio Heights
• 346-0180

Oh no, not another Southwestern interior decoration shop, we sighed, entering this rustic-looking shop. And this turned out *not* to be just another of the above. It's a fairly serious shop, with a respectable selection of pre-1940s Navajo rugs and new knockoffs produced in Mexico, both contemporary and vintage kachinas, original Edward S. Curtis photogravures of noble-visaged Native Americans, and a few pieces of distressed furniture. The staff is knowledgeable and helpful, and a regular lecture series on various Southwestern topics is held.
Open Mon.-Sat. 10 a.m.-6 p.m.

Vignette
3625 Sacramento St.,
Presidio Heights
• 567-0174

Cleverly composed as a series of vignettes, this shop holds treasures in every tableau. One corner has an architectural theme, with handsome glass and wrought-iron tables (very reasonably priced) and leather items—diaries, boxes and an umbrella stand with stirrups on either side. A turn to your right and there's a tableau of black, high-tech table settings, lamps and Agnès B. sunglasses. In the opposite corner is a wrought-iron bed, plumped with white linens, draped with wispy mosquito netting, accented with an arrangement of dried flowers. A high level of taste and quality is very apparent here; even the postcard selection is extraordinary. *Open Mon.-Sat. 10 a.m.-6 p.m.*

La Ville du Soleil
444 Post St.,
Union Square
• 434-0657

We love this store, and although it has relocated, the atmosphere is quite the same. One could spend a whole afternoon here, roaming through the several rooms thick with antique French country furniture (marble bistro tables, huge pine dining tables, marvelous armoires and chests), fine linens, hand-painted china, unusual dolls, old signs from French bakeries, bars and cafés, French kitchenware and much, much more. La Ville du Soleil is an extremely romantic world unto itself, a kind of French country paradise. In one room, a life-size Alice and her friends are having a tea party on a lavishly set table; in another, you half expect a white-aproned waiter to come take your order for a tarte tatin and espresso. As in it's former quarters, upstairs you will find some remarkable new and antique linens, from christening gowns to Irish linen pillowcases. A must in any Union Square shopping trip. *Open Mon.-Sat. 9:30 a.m.-5:30 p.m.*

HOUSEWARES & KITCHEN ITEMS

Figoni Hardware Co.
1351 Grant Ave.,
North Beach
• 392-4765

A North Beach classic from another era. Friendly salesmen who've been here since the good old days bring down bulk nails, pipe fittings, wire, you name it from the old wooden shelves that climb all the way to the fifteen-foot ceiling. Figoni is worth a visit just for a look, since these old hardware stores are an almost-extinct breed. But it's also worth a visit if you're looking for sturdy, well-designed, inexpensive restaurant-quality glassware, dishes and cookware; simple home linens; stove-top espresso makers and kitchen gadgets; and even some sporting goods, including bocci balls and fishing tackle. It's like a visit to Lake Wobegone by way of Little Italy. *Open Mon.-Sat. 8 a.m.-5 p.m.*

Forrest Jones, Inc.

3274 Sacramento St.,
Presidio Heights
• 982-1577
151 Jackson St.,
Financial District
• 567-2483

There's something very traditional and familiar about Forrest Jones; it reminds one of those turn-of-the-century French shops photographed by Eugene Atget, with its wares hanging round the door and lining the entrance. Once you get past the baskets and leather shopping bags festooning this doorway, you can lose yourself in the maze of shelves filled with glasses, candles, napkins, napkin rings, travel accessories, cooking utensils and hand-painted Italian and French dishes. The staff is helpful, there are bargains to be found, and there's a great selection of Panama hats. *Sacramento St. branch: open Mon.-Sat. 10 a.m.-6 p.m., Sun. 11 a.m.-5 p.m. Jackson St. branch: open Mon.-Sat. 10 a.m.-6 p.m.*

Sue Fisher King

3067 Sacramento St.,
Presidio Heights
• 922-7276

You can realize any domestic fantasy in this elegant, densely packed shop. The walls are lined with fine linens, shower curtains, woolen blankets, pretty placemats and silver picture frames—items for the definitely upscale hope chest. *Open Mon.-Sat. 10 a.m.-6 p.m.*

Pic-Nic-Nac

2291 Pine St.,
Upper Fillmore
• 921-4800

Yes, this is a picnic shop, and as you might imagine, it's small and filled to the rafters with picnic paraphernalia. There's a variety of baskets, which can be custom-painted and -lined, plastic dishes, cups and utensils in varying quality, picnic sets—fancy baskets fitted with china dishes, glasses and metal utensils, tablecloths, napkins and barbecue supplies. This place could outfit any picnic, from Ascot to the teddy bears', and if yours is on Astroturf, don't worry, you can get plastic ants here to supply that natural touch. They also prepare gift baskets (we saw a smashing one lacquered in black for Chanel), and in November and December, the store is transformed into a Christmas boutique. *Open Wed.-Sat. 11 a.m.-5:30 p.m., Sun. noon-5 p.m.*

Whole Earth Access

401 Bayshore Blvd.,
City South
• 285-5244

This relatively new store is an offshoot of the very popular Marin and Berkeley stores, which are offshoots of the old Whole Earth Access catalog, a bible for the socially conscious early-'70s consumer. Today, Whole Earth is an appealing warehouse with unbeatable prices on high-quality computers, televisions, large and small appliances, cookware, dishes, kitchen supplies and some furniture. Don't buy without checking here first. *Open Sat.-Wed. 10 a.m.-6 p.m., Thurs.-Fri. 10 a.m.-8 p.m.*

Williams-Sonoma
150 Post St.,
Union Square
• 362-6904

Thousands of customers have made the Williams-Sonoma catalog immensely successful, and now residents of many American cities have a Williams-Sonoma of their very own. There are several in the Bay Area as well, but this branch, the company's headquarters, in its new location on Post Street, is the best of the bunch—several spacious rooms on two levels, done in white and green, filled but not crammed with the best kitchen products available. Dishes range from white classics to Italian charmers, cookware from copper to Calphalon, and appliances from cappuccino machines to Cuisinarts. We especially like the cotton table linens, colorful dishrags, copper cookware, cookbooks and gadgets. Heavy wooden chairs and tables and handsome outdoor furniture are displayed on the second level. Prices are on the high side of reasonable, though there are usually good special buys.
Open Mon.-Wed. 9:30 a.m.-5:30 p.m., Thurs.-Fri. 9:30 a.m.-7 p.m., Sat. 10 a.m.-6 p.m., Sun. noon-5 p.m.

LINENS

O'Plume
1764 Union St.,
Cow Hollow
• 771-6100

Oh, it's absolutely deluxe. With Italian silk sheets, Battenburg lace, plump goose-down comforters covered in fine Egyptian cotton and antique hand-embroidered pillowcases, tablecloths and handkerchiefs, this narrow street-level shop boasts the most exquisite linens imaginable. Its chubby down-filled pillows are guaranteed for ten years, and the store will custom-cover pillows and comforters. We had to fight the impulse to dive headlong into the snowy eiderdown displayed on an antique bed.
Open Mon.-Sat. 10 a.m.-6 p.m., Sun. noon-5 p.m.

Regina Linens
3369 Sacramento St.,
Presidio Heights
• 563-8158

Stacks of tablecloths, napkins, placemats, sheets and pillowcases surround you in this curious shop. The handiwork of China, Portugal and Belgium is represented in these stacks and on the walls. Prices are fair; at $3.95 the hand-embroidered linen handkerchiefs make charming gifts. One wall is devoted to an odd assortment of children's clothes.
Open Mon.-Sat. 11 a.m.-5:30 p.m.

Scandia Down Shops
1546 California St.,
Nob Hill
• 928-5111

Credit Scandia Down with bringing European-style down-comforter bedding to the American masses. These small shops sell good comforters, from the less-expensive feather down to the more expensive pure goose down, along with

down pillows, comforter covers and stylish cotton and cotton-blend sheets. Prices are fair.
Open Mon.-Fri. 10 a.m.-6 p.m., Sat. 10 a.m.-5 p.m.

IMAGE & SOUND

PHOTOGRAPHY

Brooks Cameras
45 Kearny St.,
Union Square
• 392-1900

Professionals and amateurs alike shop at Brooks, a large, solid, all-purpose camera store that sells cameras, accessories, film and darkroom supplies. It also rents and repairs cameras and has a good-quality overnight developing service. Prices are middle-of-the-road.
Open Mon.-Fri. 8:30 a.m.-6 p.m., Sat. 9:30 a.m.-5:30 p.m.

Adolph Gasser
181 2nd St.,
South of Market
• 495-3852

With a complete range of cameras, including the world's finest, Adolph Gasser caters to a professional clientele. You can also buy and rent video and movie cameras. The staff know their stuff.
Open Mon.-Fri. 8:30 a.m.-5:30 p.m., Sat. 9 a.m.-5 p.m.

Osaka-ya Camera
1581 Webster St.,
Japantown
• 567-1160

Steel yourself for impatient, almost rude service, and don't expect expert advice. But if you come to Osaka-ya knowing exactly which camera you want, Mr. Kim will sell it to you at the best price in town. Call first to see if he stocks the model you want.
Open Mon.-Sat. 10 a.m.-6 p.m., Sun. noon-5 p.m.

RECORDED MUSIC

Reckless Records
1401 Haight St.,
Haight-Ashbury
• 431-3434

Carefully graded used rock records are sorted by artist instead of stacked willy-nilly in bins, as is usually the practice at used record stores. Reckless guarantees its grades; if you buy a B-plus used copy of "Heartbreak Hotel" and find it to be a D-minus, you'll get your money back. Some new domestic and imported rock, too.
Open Mon.-Sat. 10 a.m.-11 p.m., Sun. 10 a.m.-8 p.m.

Recycled Records
1377 Haight St.,
Haight-Ashbury
• 626-4075

This crowded store recycles rock, jazz, blues and classical records, from recent releases to rarities. The records are well organized and fairly priced.
Open Mon.-Sat. 10 a.m.-8 p.m., Sun. 10 a.m.-7 p.m.

Streetlight Records
3979 24th St.,
Noe Valley
• 282-3550
2350 Market St.,
Castro District
• 282-8000

Two very good all-purpose record stores. Along with a complete range of new records in every category, Streetlight sells used, vintage, rare and out-of-print records. If you don't see it, ask for it.
24th St. branch: open Mon.-Sat. 10 a.m.-10 p.m., Sun. 11 a.m.-8 p.m. Market St. branch: open daily 11 a.m.-7 p.m.

Tower Records
2525 Jones St. (at Columbus
Ave. & Bay St.),
North Beach
• 885-0500

The best new-record store in the city, with virtually every new rock, pop, country, soul, jazz, blues and classical release on record, tape and compact disc. There's also a great collection of old rock and pop singles and classic rock and R&B. Hot new records are usually discounted. Tower puts such ordinary chains as Music Plus to shame.
Open daily 9 a.m.-12 midnight.

Village Music
9 E. Blithedale St.,
Mill Valley
• 388-7400

It may not have a big-city address, but Village Music is indubitably the best record store in the Bay Area—indeed, the best in the state. A veritable museum of music history, it boasts walls crammed with a priceless collection of gold records, photographs, autographs and memorabilia, and bins chockablock with a comprehensive collection of new, used, rare and obscure discs from every musical field, from rock and blues to soundtracks and opera. Every music fan should make a Marin pilgrimage to this outstanding store.
Open Mon.-Sat. 10 a.m.-6 p.m., Sun. noon-5 p.m.

STEREO & VIDEO

Audio Excellence
425 Washington St.,
Union Square
• 433-1335

When that workhorse Sony doesn't do it for you anymore, have a talk with one of the audiophile salesmen at this store. They'll have you listen to some of the finest sound components money can buy (and you need lots of money to buy here), from such makers as Thorens, Audio Research,

Michell and Kyocera. Naturally, you'll need a state-of-the-art video system to go along with your new stereo, so Audio Excellence carries the best from Proton, Thomson and NEC.
Open Mon.-Fri. 10:30 a.m.-5:30 p.m., Sat. 10 a.m.-5 p.m.

House of Music
2 Bryant St.,
Financial District
• 771-1962

Stereo components are treated as works of art here, with devoted, unusually knowledgeable salesmen singing the praises of exemplary but costly equipment from Mark Levenson, Bang & Olufsen, McIntosh and the like. The salesmen will steer you to the right pieces for your home, ear and budget without being pushy or pretentious. House of Music will also properly install, set up, maintain and fix your new equipment.
Open Tues.-Sat. 11 a.m.-6 p.m.

Whole Earth Access
401 Bayshore Blvd.,
City South
• 285-5244

If you're looking for good midrange stereo and video equipment, look no further than Whole Earth. Friendly, reasonably well-informed salesmen will sell you Sony (including the entire ES line), Aiwa, JVC, Harman-Kardon, Onkyo, Infinity, Mission and Boston Acoustics components at the lowest prices in town.
Open Mon.-Wed. 10 a.m.-6 p.m., Thurs.-Fri. 10 a.m.-8 p.m., Sat.-Sun. 10 a.m.-6 p.m.

LEATHER & LUGGAGE

Bottega Veneta
120 Geary St.,
Union Square
• 981-1700

A marvelous array of Italian leather goods is displayed on three floors in this fabled shop. The staff is friendly and unpretentious, and the luggage, briefcases, purses, belts and wallets are supple, handsome and unspoiled by logos or initials. But, of course, the prices are shocking (small, modest bags made of the signature woven leather *start* at $275).
Open Mon.-Sat. 10 a.m.-6 p.m

The Coach Store
164 Grant Ave.,
Union Square
• 392-1772

The styles may not be the most au courant, but the quality is undisputed. Many a woman is still carrying the Coach bag she bought five (or ten) years ago, a bit dirty perhaps, but still going strong. Since the hearty leather is crafted to last, the bags, belts, wallets and accessories are styled so they won't look foolishly dated in the years to come. But that's

not to say the merchandise is stodgy—many of these bags, especially the briefcases and drawstring purses—are beautiful. Recently some lovely Coach-label dark paisley and floral print scarves and ties have appeared in the shop.
Open Mon.-Sat. 10 a.m.-6 p.m., Sun. noon-5 p.m.

Mark Cross
170 Post St.,
Union Square
• 391-7770

These finely crafted leather products are worth their high price tags. Along with the supplest of calfskins and pigskins, the wallets, briefcases, purses and so on are handmade from such exotic hides as ostrich, alligator and lizard. Both the shop and the styles are elegant, timeless and refreshingly discreet.
Open Mon.-Sat. 10 a.m.-6 p.m.

Gucci
253 Post St.,
Union Square
• 772-2522

Snooty and touristy, Gucci appeals to those who like to advertise their supposed good taste. While it's true that these leather shoes, belts and coated-canvas-and-leather bags and wallets are well made (especially the shoes), we think the styles leave much to be desired. But if a bag plastered with Gs spells success to you, do hurry over.
Open Mon.-Sat. 10 a.m.-5:30 p.m.

Johnson's Leather Co.
1833 Polk St.,
Polk Gulch
• 775-7393

Now that motorcycle jackets are all the rage (or at least have been for some time), renewed interest has been taken in this vendor and manufacturer of leather clothing for men and women. For an entirely reasonable fee, you can have a motorcycle jacket made to order from the finest cowhide, with as many laces, studs, buckles and snaps as you wish, or a lovely lambskin blazer in your choice of colors with skins imported from England or Australia. Jackets tailor-made from the shop's existing models take about two weeks to complete; customized styles take three to four weeks and cost a bit more. Johnson's both wholesales to other stores and retails some labels, such as Greenwich, Mid Way, Mirage and Casablanca. The stock of jackets, pants, skirts and vests is sizable, and you can also have leather garments repaired, altered and cleaned here.
Open Mon.-Sat. 11 a.m.-6:30 p.m., Sun. noon-5 p.m.

Malm Luggage
222 Grant Ave.,
Union Square
• 392-0417
Crocker Center Galleria,
50 Post St.,
Financial District
• 391-5222

Exceptionally handsome luggage from fine manufacturers—Ghurka, Ralph Lauren, French, Hartmann—are sold here at prices that match the quality. Malm also carries Gold-Pfeil's purses, briefcases, wallets and leather accessories, which we find dowdy and overpriced.

Grant Ave. branch: open Mon.-Fri. 9:30 a.m.-6 p.m., Sat. noon-5 p.m. Crocker Center branch: open Mon.-Fri. 9:30 a.m.-6 p.m.

Overland Sheepskin Co.
21 Grant Ave.,
Union Square
• 296-9180

Originated in New Mexico, this shop's *raison d'être* is sheepskin—in a fairly wide range of basic styles for men and women. There are short jackets, long coats and examples of both in plush mouton, all made in New Mexico. The merchandise under the Overland Sheepskin Company label is supplemented by bright leather dresses and separates for women by Firenze of Santa Barbara and men's jackets by Robert Comstock and a few other makers. Accessories include tooled leather belts with silver buckles and tips, which you can buy separately for your own belts, and cuddly sheepskin booties.
Open Mon.-Sat. 9 a.m.-6 p.m.

Louis Vuitton
317 Sutter St.,
Union Square
• 391-6200

Although many consider Louis Vuitton's pieces major status symbols, we can't abide most of the line—specifically, the boring coated canvas bags and luggage covered in pretentious LVs. However, we are fond of the old steamer trunks and the initial-free all-leather pieces, especially the briefcases. Needless to say, if you have to ask, you can't afford it.
Open Mon.-Sat. 10 a.m.-5:30 p.m., Sun. noon-5 p.m.

SPORTING GOODS

Avenue Cyclery
756 Stanyan St.,
Haight-Ashbury
• 387-3155

Just across the street from Golden Gate Park, Avenue Cyclery sells impressive machines for the serious cyclist, including racing and mountain bikes from Klein, Cannondale, Biandi and Panasonic. But it also caters to the occasional park cruiser and rents three-speed, ten-speed and mountain bikes from Friday through Sunday for $2 to $4 an hour. There's also an in-house repair shop that is well stocked with parts.
Open daily 10 a.m.-6 p.m.

Eddie Bauer
220 Post St.,
Union Square
• 986-7600

Eddie Bauer caters to the rugged outdoorsman and outdoorswoman—even those who like to keep their activity limited to sitting in front of a roaring fire wearing a handsome flannel shirt. Most of the cotton and wool clothing for hiking, running, cycling and skiing carries the Eddie Bauer label, which ensures durability and fair prices; the same goes for the camping, fishing and other sports equipment sold here. The down jackets are especially good values. On the lower floor of this immense three-story shop are well-made shoes for walking, hiking and running. *Open Mon.-Wed. & Sat. 9 a.m.-6 p.m., Thurs.-Fri. 9 a.m.-7 p.m., Sun. 11:30 a.m.-5 p.m.*

Body Options
1858 Union St.,
Cow Hollow
• 563-4003

These shops stock enough aerobic wear to raise your pulse just looking through it all, not to mention wriggling in and out of it in the dressing rooms. You'll find leagues of swimsuits, leggings and leotards in Lycra and cotton by all the best makers: Gilda Marx, Dance France, Sexotard, Baryshnikov (to name a few), along with socks in every hue and attractive, simple cotton separates by Shadows. Items are reasonably priced. There are several other locations, including in Embarcadero Center, on upper Fillmore and on Chestnut in the Marina. *Open Mon.-Fri. 10 a.m.-7:30 p.m., Sat. 10 a.m.-6 p.m., Sun. 11 a.m.-6 p.m.*

City Cycle
3001 Steiner St.,
Cow Hollow
• 346-2242

For serious cyclists, the bicycles sold here are all hand-built and custom-made, using high-quality frames by Italian makers Inelli and Masi, Bertrand from Canada, Washington State's Gary Klein, and Fat Chance, an American trail-bike maker. The owners/operators are all experienced cyclists who will custom-build and -tailor your bike and keep it in perfect repair. This is the only distributor of Cinelli bikes—the Mercedes of the bike world—in San Francisco. Desiente apparel and some cycling accessories are also available. *Open Mon.-Tues. & Thurs. 10 a.m.-7 p.m., Fri. 10 a.m.-8 p.m., Sat. 9 a.m.-5 p.m., Sun. 10 a.m.-5 p.m.*

Copeland's Sports
901 Market St.,
Union Square
• 495-0928

This large, two-story paean to the active life sells just about everything for the athlete. The clothing selection is pedestrian, but the equipment—rowing machines, baseball bats, weights, camping gear—is first-rate. Service is friendly and informed. *Open Mon.-Sat. 9:30 a.m.-9 p.m., Sat. 9:30 a.m.-7 p.m.*

Ellesse
355 Sutter St.,
Union Square
• 421-6853

At these prices, you may not want to break a sweat, but you'll cut a good-looking figure on the tennis court or ski slope in your boldly colored matching ensembles. The active sportswear is limited to tennis and skiwear, and there's an equally expensive line of casual weekend wear. *Open Mon.-Sat. 9:30 a.m.-6:30 p.m., Sun. 10 a.m.-5 p.m.*

Fila
239 Grant Ave.,
Union Square
• 956-4170

There's no doubting that these tennis whites and ski colors are handsome and well made. You'll pay dearly, however, for the distinctive Fila logo splattered all over the tennis shirts, sweatsuits, headbands, socks and ski sweaters. *Open Mon.-Sat. 9:30 a.m.-6:30 p.m., Sun. 10 a.m.-5 p.m.*

First Step
216 Powell St.,
Union Square
• 989-9989

Athletic shoes of every size, color and logo are on display here: running shoes from New Balance, basketball shoes from Converse, tennis shoes from Nike, aerobics shoes from Reebok, walking shoes from Timberland and boat shoes from Sperry. Prices are in the middle. *Open Mon.-Sat. 9:30 a.m.-7:30 p.m.*

Hoy's Sports
1632 Haight St.,
Haight-Ashbury
• 861-4698

Here's a small general-purpose sporting goods store run by a gregarious and athletic young woman. The swimsuits, swim accessories, T-shirts, balls and weights are high in quality and reasonably priced. *Open Mon.-Sat. 10 a.m.-6 p.m., Sun. noon-5 p.m.*

Don Sherwood's Sport Shop
320 Grant Ave.,
Union Square
• 989-5000

A two-story, bustling emporium with a full inventory of golf and tennis equipment and fashions as well as maintenance services. The large, professional staff will put you on the right track, whether you need running shoes, aerobics ensembles or Mickey Mouse covers for your golf clubs. *Open daily 9:30 a.m.-6 p.m.*

Swiss Ski Sports
559 Clay St.,
Financial District
• 434-0322

An exceptionally friendly store devoted to all things ski. The selection of skis, boots, accessories and handsome clothing is broad and fairly priced, and there's also a good collection of tennis equipment and clothing. Snow reports and Tahoe ski information are always available. *Open Mon.-Fri. 10 a.m.-6 p.m., Sat. 10 a.m.-5 p.m., Sun. 11 a.m.-5 p.m.*

Tennis Shack
3375 Sacramento St.,
Presidio Heights
• 94118

The pleasant staff here will be pleased to show you Yamaha and Prince rackets, a variety of tennis clothing, mostly by Le Coq Sportif, and tennis shoes by Nike and Reebok, among other tennis paraphernalia. They'll also restring your racket.
Open Mon.-Fri. 10 a.m.-6 p.m., Sat. 9:30 a.m.-4:30 p.m., Sun. 11 a.m.-4 p.m.

TOBACCONISTS

Grant's Tobacconists
562 Market St.,
Financial District
• 981-1000

An aromatic shop with a well-rounded (but not inexpensive) selection of pipes, cigars, tobaccos, humidors and smoking accessories.
Open Mon.-Fri. 9 a.m.-5:30 p.m., Sat. 10 a.m.-5:30 p.m.

Jim Mate Pipe & Tobacco Shop
575 Geary St.,
Union Square
• 775-6634

This well-known tobacconist sells fine pipes from the likes of Sasieni, Dunhill and GBD, along with the world's finest cigars and tobaccos. Mate's house-blend tobacco is exceptional; also quite respectable are the five different house-brand cigars. The enthusiatic staff ships merchandise all over the States and to 46 foreign countries.
Open Mon.-Sat. 9 a.m.-5:30 p.m.

Sherlock's Haven
4 Embarcadero Center,
Financial District
• 362-1405

In a snug little corner of this large concrete mall sits this cozy, aromatic den. Frequented by the smoking outcasts of the world, cigarettes dangling from their lips and pipes clenched in their mouths, the shop offers a range of cigarettes from dizzying French Gitanes to smooth Virginia Plains, fine South American cigars, and the good standard French and English brands of pipes, plus gifts, such as attractive match strikers and ashtrays, for those whose bad habits you wish to indulge.
Open Mon.-Fri. 7:30 a.m.-6 p.m., Sat. 11:30 a.m.-6 p.m.

WHERE TO FIND . . .

A BABYSITTER

**Bay Area Baby
Sitters Agency**
• 991-7474

A state-licensed, extremely reliable agency that has been supplying San Francisco with mature babysitters for 40 years. Rates are $4 an hour with a four-hour minimum, plus an extra charge for transportation.

CLEANERS

**Brentwood
Cleaners**
1919 Fillmore St.,
Upper Fillmore
• 346-1919

This careful, full-service dry cleaner will pick up and deliver. It also offers good laundry and leather-cleaning services (neither of which is on the premises).
Open Mon.-Fri. 7:30 a.m.-6:30 p.m., Sat. 8 a.m.-5 p.m.

**Sagan Laundry &
Cleaners**
989 Post St.,
Union Square
• 775-8000

A large, well-located cleaner that also launders shirts on the premises. Laundry and shirts can be turned around in one day, and Sagan picks up and delivers to several downtown hotels.
Open Mon.-Fri. 7:30 a.m.-6:30 p.m., Sat. 8 a.m.-4 p.m.

A DATE

Great Expectations
2330 Marinship Way,
Sausalito
• 332-2353

Of the plethora of dating services that have sprouted in these lonely times, Great Expectations is probably the most successful. This branch has 2,700 members of all ages and from locations from Daly City to Santa Rosa, with a great many in the city. When you join, you are videotaped and a profile is kept on file; you then come in to inspect the videos and files of prospective mates (or at least, dates), and they will in turn study yours before a meeting is arranged. The staff is sales-oriented but friendly and unintimidating.
Open Mon.-Fri. 10 a.m.-8 p.m., Sat.-Sun. 10 a.m.-5 p.m.

A DRUGSTORE

Mandarin Pharmacy
895 Washington St.,
Chinatown
• 989-9292

This well-stocked pharmacy is notable for its friendly service and, most important, its free delivery.
Open Mon.-Fri. 10 a.m.-6:30 p.m., Sat. 10 a.m.-6 p.m.

Walgreen's Drugstore
135 Powell St.,
Union Square
• 391-7222

Though chaotic and rather drab, this Bay Area chain has everything a drugstore should have and is convenient for the downtown visitor.
Open Mon.-Sat. 8 a.m.-10 p.m., Sun. 9 a.m.-8 p.m.

A FIVE-AND-DIME

F. W. Woolworth Co.
898 Market St.,
Union Square
• 986-2164

A classic example of the classic American five-and-dime chain, complete with lunch counter. Socks, notions, candy, frying pans, greeting cards, wrapping paper . . . all the little necessities of everyday life are here. You might have to push past a few mumbling street people to gain entrance.
Open Mon. & Thurs.-Fri. 8:30 a.m.-8 p.m., Tues.-Wed. & Sat. 8:30 a.m.-6:30 p.m., Sun. noon-5 p.m.

A HARDWARE STORE

Figoni Hardware Co.
1351 Grant Ave.,
North Beach
• 392-4765

This store-out-of-time is a blast from North Beach's old Italian past. Worn wooden shelves stacked up to the high ceiling are filled with bulk nails, screws, chains and so on; the cheerful oldtimers who work here will climb a classic rolling ladder to get the supplies you need. These men also make keys, dispense advice and sell you inexpensive restaurant-quality dishes, glassware and kitchen supplies.
Open Mon.-Sat. 8 a.m.-5 p.m.

A LIMOUSINE

Luxury Limousine Service
824-6767

Here's an established firm that rents Lincoln and Cadillac limousines, complete with professional drivers, for $45 $55 an hour with a three-hour minimum.

A MESSENGER

Number 1 Special Delivery
974 Harrison St.,
South of Market
• 543-4285

Along with the usual letters and small packages, Number 1 will deliver unusually large objects—anything they can fit in their vans (up to 1,500 pounds). Consequently, Number 1 is the favorite delivery company of artists and galleries. They'll also deliver nights and weekends if arranged in advance. Rates are competitive.
Open Mon.-Fri. 8 a.m.-6 p.m.

A NEWSSTAND

Uptown News
14 Trinity Pl.,
Financial District
• 398-1641

Unfortunately, this all-purpose newsstand has limited hours. Fortunately, it has a good stock of out-of-town newspapers and foreign and unusual magazines, along with cigarettes, cigars and candy.
Open Mon.-Fri. 8 a.m.-5 p.m.

A PET HOTEL

Pet Express
Triple A Shipyard,
Bayview
• 822-7111

This popular kennel boards dogs and cats at reasonable rates ($10 a day for a retriever-size dog). And for an extra $10 each way, Pet Express will pick up and deliver your pooch. Book your pet as far in advance as possible to ensure a space, especially for the holidays. Grooming services are also available.

A PHOTO LAB

tom Hour
o
vell St.,
uare
'4

Bring your color shots of the cable cars here and they'll be ready for you to take home in an hour.
Open Mon.-Fri. 8:30 a.m.-6:30 p.m., Sat.-Sun. 9:30 a.m.-6 p.m.

hic Labs
ac
to

A good lab for careful developing and printing of black-and-white film. Though it'll cost you extra, Gamma will rush jobs.
Open Mon.-Fri. 9 a.m.-5 p.m.

A SECRETARY

Kelly Services
1 Post St.,
Financial District
• 982-2200

A large, long-established temp chain that will supply skilled typists, word processors, receptionists and general-purpose secretaries on an hourly, daily or monthly basis.
Open Mon.-Fri. 8 a.m.-6 p.m.

Protemps
130 Bush St. (4th Fl.),
Financial District
• 788-3623

Along with your garden-variety temporary secretary, Protemps provides qualified word processors, data processors and even computer programmers. A word processor goes for about $20 an hour.
Open Mon.-Fri. 8 a.m.-6 p.m.

A TAILOR

Walter Fong
459 Geary St.,
Union Square
• 397-7777

This longtime San Francisco tailor does good work for a reasonable price. The service and attitude are accommodating.
Open Mon.-Sat. 9:30 a.m.-6 p.m.

The Tailored Man
324 Stockton St.,
Union Square
• 397-6906

Given The Tailored Man's location facing onto Union Square, it's not surprising that its prices are high (just having a pair of pants taken in costs $15). But the quality of the tailoring, including the custom-made suits, is equally high. There's a large selection of ready-to-wear clothing as well.
Open Mon.-Fri. 9:30 a.m.-6 p.m., Sat. 9 a.m.-5:30 p.m., Sun. noon-5 p.m.

A TRANSLATOR

Berlitz Translation Service
660 Market St. (4th Fl.),
Financial District
• 986-6474

Berlitz can provide you with someone to translate almost every language imaginable, from French to Farsi. Oral translation fees are about $50 an hour, with a two-hour minimum; written translators are paid by the word.
Open Mon.-Sat. 8 a.m.-9 p.m.

A TUXEDO

La Rosa Formal Wear
1780 Haight St.,
Haight-Ashbury
• 668-3746

Not only can you rent new designer tuxedoes in this Haight shop, but you can also buy clean, well-preserved vintage tuxes, dinner jackets and formal gowns at reasonable prices.
Open Mon.-Sat. 11 a.m.-7 p.m., Sun. 11 a.m.-6 p.m.

Selix Formal Wear
123 Kearny St.,
Union Square
• 362-1133

A full line of contemporary tuxedoes, tails, morning suits and dinner jackets rent for $50 to $100 a day. Selix can also fit women in some of the models.
Open Mon.-Fri. 9 a.m.-6 p.m., Sat. 8:30 a.m.-5 p.m.

A VETERINARIAN

Pets Unlimited
2343 Fillmore St.,
Upper Fillmore
• 563-6700

A well-established, always-busy veterinary hospital with four skilled, compassionate vets on staff. Unfortunately, Pets Unlimited does not board animals (see Pet Express under "A Pet Hotel").
Open Mon.-Wed. 9 a.m.-7 p.m., Thurs.-Fri. 9 a.m.-6 p.m., Sat. 9 a.m.-5 p.m., Sun. 10 a.m.-4 p.m.

SIGHTS

BEACHES & PARKS

BEACHES

It may be surrounded by water, but San Francisco is not known for its beaches. The fog is always rolling in, the waves are always crashing against rocky cliffs, and the whole scene seems suitable only for sea lions and squawking gulls. But while most surfers and sun worshippers head south to Santa Cruz or north to such Marin beaches as Stinson, San Francisco does have a few choice spots, and the weather is warm and sunny more often than you might suppose.

Baker Beach
Gibson Rd. off Bowley St.,
Presidio
• 556-0560

A part of the Golden Gate National Recreation Area, this mile-long stretch of clean, sandy beach attracts fishermen, family picnickers and nude sunbathers (tolerated north of the "High Tide" sign). Overnight camping is not allowed, but picnic and barbecue facilities, restrooms and drinking water are all provided by the park service. Although Baker is often warmer than other local beaches, its waves are hazardous and swimming is discouraged.

Land's End Beach
Land's End Trail off Merrie
Way, near Geary Blvd. &
Great Hwy.,
Richmond District
• 556-0560

Swimming is not allowed at this small but picturesque beach, but since the 1960s it has been a favorite of the clothing-optional crowd. Getting there, down a steep trail, is difficult, but protected as it is by the high cliffs, Land's End is private and affords a grand view back on the San Francisco harbor. The crowd at the moment is largely gay, although this has shifted like the tides over the years.

Ocean Beach
Great Hwy. south of the
Cliff House,
Richmond District
• 556- 0560

Where Golden Gate Park ends its long stretch toward the sea, San Francisco's most accessible beach begins. When most city dwellers want surf and sand, this is where they come. The long strip of sand is often heavily populated with joggers, Frisbee throwers, sunbathers and beachcombers. But because of the rough tides and dangerous undertow, wading and swimming are frequently unsafe.

Phelan Beach
Seacliff Ave. off El Camino
del Mar, Richmond District
• 558-3706

At last a beach where you can swim! Nestled into a small cove, Phelan, once known as China Beach, is sufficiently protected from the tides and undertows so that swimming is feasible during the warmest periods of the summer months. Lifeguards are on duty from April to October, but you should call ahead to check on the conditions.

274

PARKS

Aquatic Park

Next to Ghirardelli Square
(900 North Point),
Fisherman's Wharf
• 556-0560

When the sun breaks through the ubiquitous "morning and evening low clouds and fog," this small bayside park fills up with picnickers and sunbathers. Its tiered layout affords a splendid view of the Bay, out to Alcatraz and across the Golden Gate Bridge to Sausalito and Angel Island. There is a large lawn and a small beach for wading, and joggers are a regular part of the landscape.

Dolores Park

Dolores & 18th sts.,
Mission District
• 558-3706

Just two blocks away from Mission Dolores, this small oasis of greenery in the densely populated Mission District is a frequent rallying point for political demonstrations and marches. On most days its quiet setting affords a panoramic view of San Francisco, from downtown to the southern waterfront.

Golden Gate Park

Bounded by Fulton & Stanyan
sts., Great Hwy. & Lincoln
Blvd.
• 558-3706

Inspired by Frederick Law Olmsted's pioneering work with Central Park in New York City, Golden Gate Park is a masterwork of creative urban transformation. In the 1860s, when Olmsted visited the city, this 4.5-mile-long, 9-block-wide expanse was simply dry, sandy land brutalized by rough winds from the Pacific Ocean. Olmsted may have been intimidated, but engineer William Hammond Hall, the park's first superintendent, along with John McLaren, the tireless landscape gardener who took over as superintendent in 1876 and served for the next 55 years, designed, planted, nurtured and tended the 1,000 acres until they flourished with lush, green foliage and over one million trees. The narrow Panhandle, the jogger-filled peninsula between Fell and Oak streets on the park's east side, leads into a dazzling maze of wooded drives. The Hall of Flowers, the spectacular Conservatory of Flowers, the Strybing Arboretum, the Rhododendron Dell, the California Academy of Sciences, the De Young Museum, the Children's Playground, the peaceful Japanese Tea Garden, several lakes (including Stow and Spreckels), a buffalo paddock, a nine-hole golf course, tennis courts, baseball diamonds, handball courts and designated roller skating areas are all brilliantly tucked into their own green havens within the park. The entire realm is a supreme example of man tempering a harsh urban landscape with natural wonders. The park headquarters are in McLaren Lodge, the Romanesque house at Fell and Stanyan streets that served as John McLaren's home during his tenure.

Sigmund Stern Memorial Grove
19th Ave. & Sloat Blvd.,
City South
• 398-6551

For the past 51 years, this 63-acre park has hosted a summer festival of afternoon concerts in its natural tree-lined amphitheater. The music programs feature classical, popular and jazz artists performing in the sylvan setting of redwoods and eucalyptus. The Grove is also a gorgeous place for barbecues and picnics.

EXCURSIONS

Alcatraz Island
Pier 41 (Red & White Fleet),
Powell St. at the waterfront,
Fisherman's Wharf
• 546-2805

The Rock, one of the most notorious prisons in America, has been closed as a penitentiary since 1963. Named Isla de los Alcatraces in 1775 for the pelicans roosting there, the island's isolation made it a prime location for detention facilities. Although the fate of the island is a perennial subject for debate, for the moment it is open to tourists. The Red & White Fleet will ferry you there and provide an optional recorded tour; once you're on the island, rangers from the Golden Gate National Recreation Area conduct guided tours, or you can just wander. Bring a jacket, plan on a two-hour trip and buy your ferry tickets at least two days in advance, especially in summer (advance tickets available through Ticketron).
Open daily 8:15 a.m.-4:40 p.m. Ferries depart hourly from 8:15 a.m.-4:15 p.m. (9:45 a.m.-2:45 p.m. during late fall & winter months); last ferry returns 4:40 p.m. Adults $7.50, seniors $7, children 5-11 $4, children under 5 free.

Filbert Steps
Filbert St.,
Telegraph Hill

To walk down the breathtakingly steep east slope of Telegraph Hill, follow Filbert Street until it turns into a neatly landscaped walkway. From the platforms along the path that snakes down the hillside, you can look from side to side at a rich array of eclectic architecture or out across the redeveloped Embarcadero warehouses to the Bay.

Fisherman's Wharf
Jefferson & Hyde sts.,
northern waterfront

Although now overshadowed by the immense shopping complexes of the Cannery and Ghirardelli Square, Fisherman's Wharf is not without its tacky charm. This quaint relic of tourism boasts such crowd-pleasers as the Wax Museum, Ripley's Believe It or Not! Museum and the Enchanted World of San Francisco mini-cable-car ride, all of which we find dismally dull. Once the city's center of commercial fishing, the wharf still harbors fishing vessels, whose crews can be seen around the docks—though they are far outnumbered by tourists wearing loud T-shirts and toting bags of sourdough bread. Skip the mostly dreadful seafood restaurants in the area and opt instead for the street food, especially the wonderfully fresh sourdough bread and the decent "walkaway" cocktails of shrimp or Dungeness crab from the open-air fish markets. Souvenir trinkets abound.

Fort Mason
Marina Blvd. & Buchanan St., northern waterfront
• 441-5706

Under the supervision of the Golden Gate National Recreation Area, the pier-situated buildings of this former nineteenth-century army post have been transformed into a fine array of workshops, galleries, museums, theaters and restaurants—some of which were damaged in the '89 quake, but all of which are now completely restored. Greens, run by the Zen Center, is a nationally acclaimed showcase of delicious, health-oriented nouvelle cuisine. Life on the Water presents progressive theater and adventurous music programs in Building B, and the new, acoustically marvelous Cowell Theater is used for various arts performances. Two warehouse buildings house annual crafts fairs, and the Great Meadow is home to the rousing San Francisco Blues Festival every September. Just to the weSt.,
extending to the yacht harbor, is the Marina Green, a vast bayside lawn typically dotted with kite-fliers, joggers and sunbathers.

Fort Point
Long Ave. off Lincoln Blvd., Presidio
• 556-1693

Tucked under the southern anchorage of the Golden Gate Bridge, the area surrounding this 1853 fort will be familiar to fans of Alfred Hitchcock's *Vertigo*. The point where Jimmy Stewart meets Kim Novak is perfectly located for an awe-inspiring view of the bridge from underneath. The fort itself, built to protect the city from naval attack, houses a museum of Civil War–era military memorabilia.

Ghirardelli Square & The Cannery
North Point & Leavenworth sts., Fisherman's Wharf
• 775-5500

Just west of Fisherman's Wharf, these two renovated factory complexes house scores of shops, galleries and restaurants. Ghirardelli Square, originally a woolen mill in the mid-1800s and later the Ghirardelli chocolate factory, was converted to its present commercial state in the early 1960s. It boasts a lively outdoor scene, including street vendors and sidewalk performers, a lovely central plaza and some fine upscale chain shops. The Cannery, so called because it was the home of Del Monte's peach-canning operation, was remodeled in 1968 and is another early example of San Francisco's clever commercial redevelopment of old buildings. The mix of shops is less interesting than at Ghirardelli, but both centers are usually packed shoulder-to-shoulder with tourists.

Lombard Street
Lombard St. between Hyde & Leavenworth sts., Russian Hill

The residents on the legendary "crookedest street in the world" have grown impatient with rude tourists jamming bumper-to-bumper down the serpentine maze that they call home. Designed in the 1920s to conquer the steep hill with a switchback scheme, the lovely brick-paved and richly landscaped boulevard allows one-way traffic down the hill. But while it is an irresistible magnet for tourists, Lombard Street may eventually be closed to all but residents if the burdensome traffic and minor accidents finally spark action from City Hall.

Marine World Africa USA
Marine World Pkwy. (off I-80 Fwy.), Vallejo
• (707) 644-4000

Part wildlife preserve, part research center and—mostly—part touristy amusement park, Marine World Africa USA is home to a fascinating collection of exotic animals, many of whom perform in daily shows. Scattered around the 165 acres are various theaters where you can watch killer whales, dolphins, sea lions, colorful birds, tigers, elephants and chimps ham it up for treats from the trainers. Also notable is the Wildlife Theater, where you can get acquainted with rare and often endangered African species, and the Showcase Theater, where animals and humans collaborate on magic tricks. Marine World is well worth a visit for animal buffs (except those who object to animals in captivity) and families. The Red & White Fleet will ferry you north from Fisherman's Wharf to a Marine World bus in Vallejo; call 546-2896 for information.
Memorial Day–Labor Day: open daily 9:30 a.m.-6:30 p.m. Labor Day–Memorial Day: open Wed.-Sun. & holidays 9:30 a.m.-5 p.m. Closed Thanksgiving & Christmas Day. Adults $18.95, seniors $14.95, children 4-12 $13.95, children under 4 free.

Mount Davidson
Rex Ave. & Portola Dr., City South

In the city of hills, Mount Davidson soars above the reSt., climbing to all of 938 feet. Once part of Adolph Sutro's magnificent 12,000-acre estate, the mountain was surveyed in 1852 by George Davidson, who called it Blue Mountain, and is now a city park. Since 1923 Easter sunrise services have been held at the base of the 103-foot cross that rises above the summit.

Pier 39

Northern waterfront near
Beach & Powell sts.,
Fisherman's Wharf
• 981-PIER

Almost exclusively a tourist attraction, this two-level shopping area took over an old cargo pier in 1978, replacing the authentic waterfront buildings with a developer's fantasy of a Barbary Coast village. Other than the architecture, little here is turn-of-the-century, what with the hundreds of tourist-oriented specialty shops, fast-food joints and restaurants. There are, however, a few quaint and crafty respites from the schlock and tack. For the kids, a small-scale amusement park has bumper cars and other rides.

San Francisco Zoo

Sloat Blvd. & 45th Ave.,
City South
• 753-7083

Gradually catching up to the new consciousness in the housing and display of wild creatures, this 70-acre animal park has developed such popular features as Monkey Island, Gorilla World, the Seal Pool, Wolf Woods and other environmentally "natural" showcases for its more than 1,000 exotic wards. There's also a popular children's zoo.
Open daily 10 a.m.-5 p.m. Adults $5, seniors $2, children 12-15 $2, children under 12 free when accompanied by an adult. Admission free first Wed. of the month.

Treasure Island

Midway across the Bay Bridge
(I-80 Fwy.)

Although this artificial island in the middle of the earthquake-damaged Bay Bridge, off Yerba Buena Island, is reputed to be slowly sinking into the Bay, it is still home to a large Navy base. Built as a setting for the 1939 Golden Gate International Exposition, most of Treasure Island's 400 acres are off limits to the public, but a quick stop when crossing the Bay Bridge affords beautiful views of the city.

Twin Peaks

Twin Peaks Blvd. south of
Clarendon Ave., between Noe
Valley & the Sunset District

They may not be the highest points in San Francisco, but on clear days and nights these chilly, windswept peaks offer the grandest view of the city. You can look across the panorama that inspired Adolph Sutro to conjure up a rebuilding plan for San Francisco after it had been devastated by the Great Earthquake.

Union Square

Geary, Powell, Post &
Stockton sts.

Crowding the streets surrounding this one-block oasis of downtown greenery are many of San Francisco's most elite shops and hotels. Union Square is always bustling with shoppers, who are drawn to such magnets as Neiman-Marcus, Saks, Nordstrom, Gump's and Macy's—and to countless smaller shops and boutiques, ranging from Crate & Barrel to Louis Vuitton. Scattered throughout the square and the streets are street musicians, street vendors and street people. When you've charged your cards to the limit, recover in the soothing lounge of the classic St. Francis Hotel facing Union Square.

THE GREAT OUTDOORS

San Francisco has so thoroughly spread its civilization over its hills and valleys that its outdoor sports are confined to an occasional oasis of green or blue, often where man has deigned to install a touch of nature amid the dense development. Most of the Bay Area's best outdoor activities are focused on points north, south or east of the city. But if walking the hills, window shopping and bending an elbow in a neighborhood tavern don't provide you with enough exercise, and you don't want to leave the city limits, there are some fine places to skate, bicycle, golf, jog and sail.

BICYCLING

Golden Gate Park
South off Fell St. entrance
• 666-7200

Although downtown's fast and furious bicycle messengers are legendary, we don't recommend imitating their dangerous weaving through autos and pedestrians. Instead, ride the relaxed way along the 7.5-mile bike path from Golden Gate Park to Lake Merced. Start on the Fell Street side of the Panhandle and, after entering the park, follow South Drive to Sunset Boulevard, which leads to Lake Merced and a pleasant five-mile loop. Or take South Drive to Great Highway and ride along the beach for a few miles. Several shops along the Stanyan Street side of the park rent bikes of every kind.

FISHING

Lake Merced
Harding Park, Skyline Blvd.
& Harding Rd., City South
• 753-1101

Along with the many charter fishing boats that depart from Fisherman's Wharf in search of such deep-sea denizens as rock cod, San Francisco actually has its own large freshwater fishing hole where you can row out and cast for trout during fishing season. Lake Merced, a backup reservoir just south of the zoo, has a boathouse that rents boats; there's a bar, restaurant and plenty of picnic areas.
Open daily 6 a.m.-7:30 p.m. Rowboats $6 per hour, $14 per half day, $19 all day.

GOLFING

Gleneagle's Golf Course
McLaren Park, Sunnydale Ave. & Hahn St., City South
• 587-2425

A tough, hilly nine-hole course, Gleneagle's makes up for the frustrations it imparts with the southern Bay view it allows from the clubhouse. Though on McLaren Park property, the course is privately operated.
Open daily 7 a.m.-8 p.m. Admission $7 for 9 holes, $11 for 18 holes weekdays, $8 & $14 weekends & holidays.

Golden Gate Park Golf Course
Golden Gate Park, 47th Ave. between Fulton St. & John F. Kennedy Dr.
• 751-8987

Once you've been tested by the short but tight fairways, tricky turns, ample hills and surrounding trees, not to mention the wisps of fog that blow in from the nearby Pacific, you might be glad this course is only nine holes.
Open daily 7 a.m.-8 p.m. Admission $4 weekdays, $7 weekends.

Harding Park Golf Course
Harding Park, Harding Rd. near Skyline Blvd., City South
• 664-4690

Formerly the site of the Lucky Open on the PGA tour, the eighteen-hole, 6,637-yard course, beautifully set in lush forest surroundings, is a challenge from hole to hole. Harding Park is also home to the nine-hole Fleming Golf Course.
Open daily 6:30 a.m.-dusk. Admission $7 weekdays, $17 weekends.

Lincoln Park Golf Course
Lincoln Park, 34th Ave. & Clement St., Richmond District
• 221-9911

San Francisco's oldest eighteen-hole golf course is 5,081 yards of rough but scenic terrain. Some holes boast views of the Golden Gate Bridge.
Open daily 6 a.m.-8 p.m. Admission $10 weekdays, $14 weekends.

HORSEBACK RIDING

Golden Gate Park Stables
John F. Kennedy Dr. & 34th Ave., Golden Gate Park
• 668-7360

Unfortunately, these stables do not rent out horses for unescorted riding. But you can take riding lessons, either alone or with a group, and enjoy Golden Gate Park on horseback. Reservations are required.
Open Tues.-Fri. 9 a.m.-6 p.m., Sat.-Sun. 9 a.m.-5 p.m. Group lessons $12-$17 an hour per person, private lessons $30 an hour.

ROLLER SKATING

Golden Gate Park
John F. Kennedy Dr. between
Kezar & Transverse drives
• 666-7200

While the hills of central San Francisco would be death-defying folly on any wheels other than those belonging to autos and cable cars, Golden Gate Park has a designated area for skaters on Sundays. A good stretch of John F. Kennedy Drive is closed to cars, allowing plenty of open space for trick skating and casual rolling. Skate rentals are available from several shops around the park.

ROWING & SAILING

**Lake Merced
Boathouse**
Harding Park,
Harding Rd. & Skyline Blvd.,
City South
• 753-1101

You can explore this long, narrow lake in Harding Park via a rowboat, canoe or pedal boat, all of which are rented (for a mere $6 to $7 an hour) at the park's boathouse. *Open daily 6 a.m.-7:30 p.m.*

**Stow Lake
Boathouse**
Golden Gate Park,
Lake Dr. off John F. Kennedy
Dr.
• 752-0347

The largest body of water in Golden Gate Park has a boathouse that rents rowboats, pedal boats and motorboats for $8 to $12.50 per hour. Take your loved one and a picnic basket, then row over to Strawberry Hill island in the middle of the lake for a romantic rendezvous. *Open Tues.-Sun. 9 a.m.-4 p.m.*

RUNNING

Most runners make their own trails, even through the hilly streets of San Francisco. The city is known for its annual Marathon, Bridge Run and world-renowned Bay-to-Breakers footraces. But some routes are better than others. Our favorites are Lake Merced in Harding Park, with five flat miles of asphalt and dirt; the Marina Green, a very popular one-mile stretch of grass with spectacular views of the Golden Gate Bridge, Alcatraz and the Bay; the Polo Field, just off Middle Drive in the center of Golden Gate Park, with its pleasant tracks and trails; and Stow Lake, a short, scenic course around the water with the option of more difficult dirt trails on Strawberry Hill.

TENNIS

San Francisco Recreation & Parks Department
McLaren Lodge,
Fell & Stanyan sts.,
Golden Gate Park
• 666-7200

One call to the Parks Department will give you the location of more than 100 city tennis courts, most of which are free to use. The most popular courts, located on the east end of Golden Gate Park, cost $2 after 5 p.m. and close at dark. They can be reserved on the weekends by calling 478-9500 from Wednesday through Friday.

LANDMARKS

We can't begin to cover the breadth of architectural and historical gems in San Francisco—there are far too many. But we can present you with a somewhat idiosyncratic list of our very favorites.

Bank of America Building
California & Kearny sts.,
Financial District

A 52-story block dwarfing everything but the Trans-America Pyramid, this early '60s giant escapes the monotonous monolithic look through faceted walls and windows, an odd-shaped top and glazing that reflects light differently throughout the day. For the city's best view, ride the elevator up to the penthouse Carnelian Room for a before- or after-dinner drink (remember to dress up a bit).

Bay Bridge
I-80 Fwy. between
San Francisco & Oakland

Actually two bridges—a double suspension bridge on the San Francisco side and a cantilever bridge on the Oakland side—connected by a tunnel through Yerba Buena Island, this 50-year-old two-level span was brilliantly engineered by Charles H. Purcell—and hit hard by the '89 earthquake, which sent a piece of the top level down onto the lower level. (As we write these words, the bridge is still closed for repairs, but it's sure to be back in action by the time you visit.) The entire structure is more than 8 miles long, on-ramps included, and the bridge spans 4.5 miles of water. The longest steel high-level bridge in the world, it requires a 75-cent toll (which may rise again soon) westbound into the city.

Children's Carousel

Children's Playground,
Golden Gate Park,
Kezar & Martin Luther King
drives
• 666-7200

Constructed in New York around 1912, and arriving in San Francisco after the 1939 World's Fair, these 62 animals, two chariots, one tub and one rocker on a turning platform have been lovingly restored and are housed in a turn-of-the-century Greek temple.
June-Sept.: open daily 10 a.m.-5 p.m.; Oct.-May: open Wed.-Sun. 10 a.m.-4 p.m. Adults $1, children 6-12 25 cents, children under 6 free with paying adult.

China Basin Building

Berry St. between 3rd & 4th sts.,
China Basin

With a horizontal measurement of 850 feet, this chunky former warehouse, built in 1922, is longer than any San Francisco skyscraper is high. It was repainted bright blue in streamlined ocean-liner style in 1973, its warehouse-to-office conversion prefiguring the current SOMA rehabilitation mania.

Circle Gallery

140 Maiden Ln.,
Union Square
• 989-2100

This 1949 Frank Lloyd Wright building, with a brick facing and fine archway opening, features an interior spiral ramp that was the prototype for Wright's famous design for the Guggenheim Museum in New York. It currently houses a gallery stocked with questionable art.
Open Mon.-Wed. & Fri.- Sat. 10 a.m.-6 p.m., Thurs. 10 a.m.-7 p.m., Sun. 11 a.m-4 p.m.

Civic Center

Polk St. to Franklin St. &
Grove St. to McAllister St.

A masterful complex of Beaux Arts buildings, the Civic Center was the brainchild of architect Daniel Burnham, the creation of some of the country's finest architects and the pride of Mayor Sunny Jim Rolph. The first building was completed in 1913, with original construction continuing into the 1930s. The center includes the domed and beautifully detailed City Hall; the War Memorial Opera House, which houses a remarkable foyer with a stunning gilt ceiling; the San Francisco Public Library, which boasts exceptional interior murals; and many other beauties, including the Civic Auditorium, the State Office Building and the Federal Office Building. The Civic Center's latest addition (built in 1980) is the Louise M. Davies Symphony Hall, designed by Skidmore, Owings & Merrill to fit with integrity into the Beaux Arts scheme.

Cliff House

109 Point Lobos Ave.,
Richmond District
• 386-3330 (restaurant &
bar)
• 386-1170 (museum)

Perched on the cliffs near Point Lobos, the westernmost tip of San Francisco, this 1909 relic (which followed several previous resorts that burned down on the same spot) houses a popular restaurant and a museum that showcases one of the world's largest collections of coin-operated automatic musical instruments. The building, a typical turn-of-the-century Newport-style beach house, is up-staged by the spectacular setting, especially the view from the bar.

Restaurant: open daily 11 a.m.-10:30 p.m.; bar: open daily 11 a.m.-1:30 a.m. Museum: open daily 10 a.m.-8 p.m. Admission to museum free.

Coit Tower
Telegraph Hill Blvd.,
Telegraph Hill
• 982-2648

Built in 1934 by Lillie Coit, in memory of her late husband and in honor of the city's firefighters, this example of '30s moderne architecture also contains a series of significant and once-controversial WPA murals depicting scenes from the immigrant and working-class side of California history. Elevator rides can be taken to the top of the tower; there's also a gift shop selling the expected tourist trinkets.
Open daily 10 a.m.-5:30 p.m.

Columbus Tower
Columbus Ave.,
Kearny St. & Pacific Ave.,
North Beach

A classic Victorian office building on the edge of North Beach, the Columbus Tower was owned for several years by director Francis Ford Coppola, who had his offices there. The weathered green building has an unusual triangular design and is wonderfully ornate.

Ferry Building
The Embarcadero
& Market St.,
Financial District

This grand clock tower with dramatic arcades and galleries was built in 1896 and modeled after the cathedral tower in Seville, Spain. Once the gateway to San Francisco, the Ferry Building received millions of ferry-boat passengers before the bridges were built.

450 Sutter Building
450 Sutter St.,
Financial District

A quintessential art deco skyscraper designed by Timothy Pflueger. Finished just as the Depression took hold, this was the last skyscraper to be built in San Francisco for twenty years. The deco/streamline moderne detailing is fabulous.

Golden Gate Bridge
101 Fwy. between San
Francisco & Marin County

One of the longest suspension bridges in the world (with a 4,200-foot clear span), this 52-year-old masterpiece by Joseph Strauss is also one of the most beautiful. Its orange paint flashes brilliantly against the blue of the sky and water, and its grand scale is rendered human and graceful through fine moderne styling. A toll is required southbound into the city.

Grace Cathedral
1051 Taylor St.,
Nob Hill
• 776-6611

This poured-in-place Gothic Episcopal cathedral was begun in 1914 but not completed until 1965. It's as grand as most European cathedrals, with twin towers rising some 170 feet high (the North Tower is stocked with 44 working bells). After inspecting the doors cast from a mold of the famous doors on the Baptistry of Florence, walk inside for a look at the impressive marble and stained glass, including the lovely rose window. The cathedral's most recent addition is a mammoth pipe organ.

Haas-Lilienthal House
2007 Franklin St.,
Pacific Heights
• 441-3000

A spectacular Victorian stick-style house from 1886, this creatively gabled and towered Queen Anne building is open to the public, with guided tours every half hour on Wednesday and Sunday afternoons.
Open Wed. noon-4 p.m., Sun. 11 a.m-4:30 p.m. Admission $4.

Hallidie Building
130 Sutter St.,
Financial District

Built by Willis Polk and Company in 1917 for the University of California, and named in honor of Andrew Hallidie, the U.C. regent who invented the cable car, this historic building was reputed to have the first curtain-wall glass facade. This ahead-of-its-time facade is curiously adorned with of-the-era wrought-iron ornamentation and fire escapes.

Hallidie Plaza
Market & Powell sts.,
Union Square

This modern, terraced, amphitheater-style plaza was created in 1973 as part of the Bay Area Rapid Transit/Market Street Renewal Program. At lunchtime it attracts hundreds of brown-bagging downtown workers who enjoy the open-air seating and the frequent music—an occasional organized concert or, more commonly, performances by itinerant musicians.

Hibernia Bank
Jones, McAllister & Market
sts., Civic Center

Constructed in 1892, this Beaux Arts bank was called "the most beautiful building in San Francisco" when it was built. It is notable on the outside for its gilt copper dome; go inside to see the lovely ceilings and the vaulted glass dome.

Hyatt Regency San Francisco
5 Embarcadero Center,
Financial District
• 788-1234

Even if you'd pass on one of the expensive rooms, at least stroll into the stunning atrium lobby, which rushes upward into twenty stories of space filled with plants, trees, birds and overhanging balconies. One of John Portman & Associates' most distinctive hotel designs, the Hyatt also boasts a gimmicky rotating bar on top.

Kahn House
66 Calhoun Terrace,
Telegraph Hill

A bit of contemporary Los Angeles planted on the Telegraph Hill slope, this Richard Neutra work, a private residence, is similar to his famous Lovell House in the Hollywood Hills.

Mansion Hotel
2220 Sacramento St.,
Pacific Heights
• 929-9444

Built in 1887 by Utah Sen. Richard C. Chambers, this magnificent twin-towered Queen Anne mansion has a garden with the world's largest collection of Benjamino Bufano statues.

Mills Building
220 Montgomery St.,
Financial District

A downtown survivor of the Great Earthquake, refurbished in 1907 by Willis Polk, this unusual ten-story Chicago School building features a beautifully detailed Romanesque archway and a dramatic lobby replete with black marble and large friezes of San Francisco.

Mission Dolores
Dolores Ave. near 16th St.,
Mission District
• 621-8203

Having survived four major earthquakes, this simple Mexican church, built by the Indians of sun-dried adobe between 1782 and 1791 as one of the string of Junípero Serra's California missions, is San Francisco's oldest building. Its three original bells are still in place but are rung only during Holy Week.
Open daily 9 a.m.-4:30 p.m.

Octagon House
2645 Gough St.,
Union Square
• 441-7512

Eight-sided houses were once considered lucky. The luck is still holding for this unusual structure, now the home of the National Society of Colonial Dames. It has endured since 1861. Call for information about tours.

Old Chinese Telephone Exchange
743 Washington St.,
Chinatown

This colorful three-tiered pagoda building, now the Bank of Canton, once housed the operators for the Chinatown phone system, and stands on the site of the long-gone *California Star*, San Francisco's first newspaper, which announced the discovery of gold in 1849.

Old Metropolitan Life Building
Pine & Stockton sts.,
Union Square

This white, terra-cotta-tiled Roman Revival building, consonant with the grand hotels on Nob Hill, was built in 1909 and remodeled in 1930 by Timothy Pflueger.

Old Mint Building
5th & Mission sts.,
South of Market
• 744-6830

A Classical Revival building built in the post–Civil War years (1869–1874), the Old Mint is the oldest stone building in San Francisco and was for many years the country's largest mint. Its solid stone construction saved the Mint when all its neighbors burned in the great fire after the 1906 earthquake. The on-site museum offers free tours on the hour and shows a movie about the building called *The Granite Lady*.

Museum open Mon.-Fri. 10 a.m.-4 p.m. Admission free.

130 Bush Street Building
130 Bush St.,
Financial District

Only twenty feet wide but ten stories high, this George Applegarth Gothic creation is remarkably (and gracefully) slim.

Pacific Telephone Building
130 New Montgomery St.,
South of Market

If all of San Francisco's skyscrapers had been built with the grace and proportion of this 1925 giant by Miller & Pflueger and A.A. Cantin Architects, the skyline might today be a thing of beauty instead of a postmodern mess. The moderne lobby has striking Chinese ceiling.

Pacific Union Club
1000 California St.,
Nob Hill

Built for railroad baron James C. Flood in 1886, this baroque Italianate brownstone (remodeled by Willis Polk in 1910) now houses a private club for modern-day business barons. The imposing 42-room mansion was the only Nob Hill home left standing after the Great Earthquake.

Palace of Fine Arts
Baker St. between
Bay St. & Marina Blvd.,
Marina District
• 563-7337

Constructed in 1915 for the Panama-Pacific Exposition, the Palace stands next to a beautiful lagoon and represents a pinnacle of architect Bernard Maybeck's career. One of the most popular buildings in the city, with its magnificently curving colonnades and classical Roman rotunda, it was completely restored in 1962 and now houses a theater and the Exploratorium, a wonderful hands-on science and technology museum.

Palace of the Légion of Honor
Lincoln Park,
Clement St. & 34th Ave.,
Richmond District
• 221-4811

Designed by George Applegarth after the Palace of the Légion d'Honneur in Paris, this majestic gray-stone museum was a gift from the Spreckels family in 1924. It sits atop a hill and overlooks a breathtaking vista of the city. Although it suffered damage in the '89 quake (notably the pillars), all is now restored and back to normal.

Open Wed.-Sun. 10 a.m.-5 p.m.

Roos House
3500 Jackson St.,
Presidio Heights

Bernard Maybeck's detailing, especially the windows and eaves, highlights the handsome English Tudor styling of this 1909 house, now a private residence.

Russ Building
235 Montgomery St.,
Financial District

Until the "Manhattanization" building boom of the early 1960s, this Gothic Depression-era high-rise, modeled after the Chicago Tribune Tower, was San Francisco's tallest building, rising to a dazzling 31 stories.

San Francisco Gas Light Co. Building
3600 Buchanan St.,
Fisherman's Wharf

Completed in 1893, this small Queen Anne–style brick building is a simply detailed jewel. Recently remodeled, it is now an office building.

Spreckels Mansion
Buena Vista Park,
737 Buena Vista St.,
Haight-Ashbury
• 861-3008

This grand, square Victorian built in 1887 was known to have numbered Ambrose Bierce and Jack London among its guests. Today the Spreckels Mansion is a quiet, discreet bed-and-breakfast inn.

Steiner Street Houses
700 block of Steiner St.,
Western Addition

One of the most photographed blocks in the city, this row features six identical houses—each a Victorian gem—that were built by Matthew Kavanaugh in 1894 and 1895. They have been handsomely restored.

St. Mary's Cathedral
Geary Blvd. & Gough St.,
Van Ness

An ultra-modern cathedral built in 1971, this simply flamboyant church is distinguished by its 190-foot roof formed by four deeply sloping concave sides that meet in a cross at the top. Inside is a breathtaking altar canopy made of fourteen tiers of brilliant aluminum rods.

Stock Exchange
301 Pine St.,
Financial District

The pulse of the Financial District beats in this offbeat blending of art deco and classical styles. Its main facade is adorned with a row of grand pillars, which are flanked by a pair of 21-foot-high moderne statues that are worth a look.

St. Paul's Lutheran Church

Inspired by the frontal design of the Gothic cathedral at Chartres, A.J. Kraft's 1894 church is one of the city's grandest.

Sutro Baths
Sutro Heights Park,
Point Lobos Ave.,
Richmond District

Here lie the ruins (mostly just the old foundation) of Adolph Sutro's ambitious re-creation of Roman-style baths. A three-acre spa with six saltwater pools of varying temperatures sat under a roof of colored glass. The building burned in 1966.

TransAmerica Pyramid
Montgomery St. &
Columbus Ave.,
Financial District

Designed by the Los Angeles firm of William Pereira & Associates, this narrow white pyramid drew much criticism when it was completed in 1972; its many detractors considered it ugly and weird, and denounced it for overly dominating the skyline. Today, however, it has been adopted, with either a certain fondness or simple resignation, as a novel landmark in a city of incredibly diverse architecture. It's the city's tallest structure, towering 853 feet over the Financial District.

MUSEUMS

ART MUSEUMS

Ansel Adams Center
250 4th St.,
Yerba Buena
(South of Market)
• 495-7000

Operated by the Friends of Photography and dedicated to one of its founding members, the great California photographer Ansel Adams, this new 14,000-square-foot museum is at the vanguard of revitalizing the Yerba Buena district around the Moscone Center. (The Museum of Modern Art is scheduled to move nearby in 1993.) Its five galleries reflect the full range and diversity of historical and modern photography. The building also houses a bookstore and library.
Open Tues.-Sun. 11 a.m.-6 p.m. Adults $3, seniors & students $3, children under 12 free.

Asian Art Museum
M.H. De Young Memorial
Museum,
8th Ave. & Kennedy Dr.,
Golden Gate Park
• 668-8921

When Avery Brundage donated his incomparable collection of Asian art to San Francisco in 1966, the city cleared out the West Wing of the De Young Museum to make room for the almost 10,000 pieces. Only a portion of the paintings, ceramics, sculptures, jades, bronzes and textiles can be exhibited at one time; sadly, some of the collection was destroyed in the 1989 quake, but there's still plenty to see. Don't miss the breathtaking blue-and-white porcelains or the Jade Room, where some objects date back more than 3,000 years.
Open Wed.-Sun. 10 a.m.-5 p.m. (first Wed. of the month 10 a.m.-8:45 p.m.). Adults $4, seniors $2, children under 18 free. Admission free first Wed. of the month.

California Historical Society Library
Pacific & Laguna sts.,
Pacific Heights
• 567-1848

A library in the grand old style of large chairs, broad tables, deathly stillness and meticulous librarians who know the collection inside out, the CHS is a primary holder of books, documents, photographs and periodicals on Western history. Its 25,000 volumes and sizable art collection are a vast resource for California historians, and the sandstone mansion, built for paint magnate William Whittier in the 1890s, is an appropriate period setting.
Open Wed.-Sat. 1 p.m.-5 p.m. Admission free.

Chinese Historical Society of America
650 Commercial St.,
Chinatown
• 391-1188

The history of the Chinese in the Americas is woefully under-written, but this small, recently relocated museum houses changing displays of photographs, documents, artifacts and memorabilia that shed light on the heritage of a major segment of the city's population.
Open Wed.-Sun. noon-4 p.m. Admission free.

M.H. De Young Memorial Museum
8th Ave. & Kennedy Dr.,
Golden Gate Park
• 750-3600

Reflecting its age and the character of its benefactors, the De Young Museum houses the most eclectic permanent collection in San Francisco. Although its genesis was the 1894 California Midwinter International Exposition, the building expanded dramatically after 1917, when newspaper baron Michael De Young sparked new construction. The permanent collection includes works from ancient Egypt, Greece and Rome through the Renaissance to the present: specifically Rubens, seventeenth- and eighteenth-century Italian paintings and an extensive American collection bolstered by paintings donated by John D. Rockefeller III. Another gallery contains traditional arts of Africa, Oceania and the Americas.
Open Wed.-Sun. 10 a.m.-5 p.m. (first Wed. of the month 10 a.m.-8:45 p.m.). Adults $4, seniors $2, youths 12-17 $2, children under 12 free. Admission free Sat. morning & first Wed. of the month.

The Mexican Museum
Fort Mason Center, Bldg. D,
Marina Blvd. & Laguna St.,
Fort Mason
• 441-0404

So many immigrant cultures have been laid over one another in California's history that the state's Mexican heritage is often associated only with the Spanish missionary era and the wars for territory. This museum, the first of its kind outside Mexico, pays tribute to the considerable Mexican contribution to California's past. The collection of Mexican and Mexican-American art is displayed in five thematic settings—Hispanic, Colonial, folk, Mexican fine arts and Mexican-American fine arts.
Open Wed.-Sun. noon-5 p.m. (first Wed. of the month noon-8 p.m.). Adults $2, seniors & students $1, members & children under 10 free. Admission free first Wed. of the month.

Museo Italo Americano
Fort Mason Center, Bldg. C,
Marina Blvd. & Laguna St.,
Fort Mason
• 673-2200

Although the Italian influence in San Francisco is still felt in present-day North Beach, its impact has greatly diminished over the years. Thankfully, this museum, the first in the U.S. to collect the work of contemporary Italian-American artists, preserves an authentic touch of Italy in the Bay Area.
Open Wed.-Sun. noon-5 p.m. Admission free.

Museum of Modern Mythology
• 546-0202

You may think our consumer culture is producing artifacts faster than any curator could keep up with. You may think we are living in a disposable world. But in this marvelous—but, at this writing, homeless—museum, Mr. Peanut and the Poppin' Fresh Doughboy are the heroes, and they are surrounded by thousands of advertising signs and symbols. This is the raw material of the late Andy Warhol's vision. The museum's home was destroyed in the '89 earthquake; as 1990 began, it was seeking a new home, which it hopes to have by the time you read this.
Open Wed.-Sat. noon-5 p.m. Adults $2, students & seniors $1.50, children 6-12 $1.

Palace of the Legion of Honor
Lincoln Park,
Clement St. & 34th Ave.,
Richmond District
• 750-3600.

People visit this spectacularly located museum almost as much for the view as for the art. Beautifully situated atop a hill in Lincoln Park, it commands a sweeping view eastward across the city and the Bay. Built in 1924, the palace was a gift of the Spreckels family and was designed by George Applegarth after the Palace of the Légion d'Honneur in Paris. Its permanent collection includes Rodin sculptures, eighteenth- and nineteenth-century French paintings (including Impressionist works by Monet, Renoir and Degas), decorative arts and tapestries. Downstairs, the Achenbach Foundation for Graphic Arts houses more than 100,000 works of art on paper, the largest collection of its kind in the West. Recent jazz and blues series in the gorgeous, intimate and acoustically splendid Florence Gould Theater have added new dimensions to the building's appeal. Pipe organ concerts are presented every Saturday and Sunday at 4 p.m.
Open Wed.-Sun. 10 a.m.-5 p.m. Adults $4, seniors $2, children 12-17 $2, children under 12 free. Admission free first Wed. of the month.

San Francisco Art Institute
800 Chestnut St.,
Russian Hill
• 771-7020

An important focus of the contemporary art scene in the Bay Area and Northern California, the Art Institute, founded in 1871, is the oldest art school in the western U.S. Its four galleries—the Diego Rivera, the Emmanuel Walter,

the Atholl McBean and the Still Lights—show the work of both students and professionals.
Open Tues.-Sat. 10 a.m.-5 p.m. Admission free.

San Francisco Museum of Modern Art

Veterans' Memorial Bldg.,
Van Ness Ave. &
McAllister St.,
Civic Center
• 863-8800

Located in the Veterans' Building, one of Brown and Landsburgh's 1932 architectural contributions to the grand Beaux Arts Civic Center complex, the SFMMA was the first modern art museum in California. It is especially strong in Abstract Impressionism (with a large Clyfford Still collection), photography and works by twentieth-century California artists. Works by Picasso, Matisse and Kandinsky are included in the ever-expanding permanent collection. Lectures, films, poetry readings and the occasional "Jazz in the Galleries" evenings add to the vitality the museum brings to the Civic Center, which is also home to the Opera House, Symphony Hall and City Hall. A fine museum bookshop and an interesting café are accessible without admission to the galleries.
Open Tues.-Wed. & Fri. 10 a.m.-5 p.m., Thurs. 10 a.m.-9 p.m., Sat.-Sun. 11 a.m.-5 p.m. Adults $3.50, seniors & children under 15 $1.75. Admission free Tues. & reduced Thurs. night.

OTHER MUSEUMS

Cable Car Museum

Washington & Mason sts.,
Nob Hill
• 474-1887

After two years of inaction and $60 million in repairs and renovations, the city's famous cable-car system reopened in 1984 with new cables, tracks, brakes, seats and shiny coats of paint. In this refurbished cable-car barn, built in 1887 and rebuilt after the 1906 earthquake, you can not only peruse historical photographs and memorabilia, but from an underground viewing room you can watch the giant gears, pulleys and spinning cables that operate the novel urban transit system.
April-Oct.: open daily 10 a.m.-6 p.m.; Nov.-March: open daily 10 a.m.-5 p.m. Admission free.

California Academy of Sciences

Music Concourse,
Golden Gate Park
• 750-7145

Gorgeously situated near the middle of Golden Gate Park is this endlessly fascinating complex of museums. Across the neatly tree-dotted Music Concourse from the De Young Museum, and bordered by the splendid Rhododendron Dell and the lovely Shakespeare Garden, the Academy of Sciences houses a museum of natural history, a planetarium and an aquarium.
Morrison Planetarium. In addition to the enthralling and spectacular star shows that one comes to expect of a major

planetarium with a 65-foot dome, the Morrison hosts dazzling laser light shows with contemporary high-tech and rock soundtracks. Adults $2.50, seniors and youths $1.25. There's a separate admission charge for the specially scheduled "Laserium" shows. Call 387-6300 for times and prices.

The Museum of Natural History. From Cowell Hall, where an enormous geophysical globe and a 27-foot-long allosaurus skeleton stand, proceed through the Wattis Hall of Man and see life-size models of humans throughout the ages. If you can get past the absorbing, perpetual rhythm of the huge Foucault Pendulum, marking the Earth's rotation by knocking down one peg at a time on a circle, there are more visual treasures to behold. The Simson African Hall and the North American Hall include lifelike dioramas of animal and plant life from the two continents. Children can get closer to nature in the Discovery Room.

Steinhart Aquarium. If something seems fishy here, it must be the nearly 15,000 species of aquatic plants and animals housed in glass-front tanks and nature-imitating environments. In the Roundabout, you proceed up a spiral ramp, surrounded by an enormous ring-shape tank where sharks, tuna, yellowtail, rays and other large ocean fish swim around you in an endless current. The immersion effect is astounding. The Swamp houses lazy-looking alligators and crocodiles that seem to know more than they let on. A simulated tide pool allows you to reach in (with guidance from the monitors) and handle certain rock-dwelling creatures. Dolphins, seals and penguins put on amusing shows every two hours at feeding time. And there are nearly 190 other tanks containing all manner of large and small fish. *Open daily 10 a.m.-5 p.m. Adults $4, seniors & children 12-17 $2, children 6-11 $1, children under 6 free. Admission free first Wed. of the month.*

Cartoon Art Museum
665 3rd St. (5th Fl.), South of Market
• 546-9481

Attuned to the pen-and-ink world of the superheroes and daily-life characters of the comic strips, as well as the commentary and satire of the editorial pages, this specialized gallery offers exhibits that are often timely and always fascinating, such as the 1989 "Batman: The Art of the Dark Knight" show. *Open Wed.-Fri. 11 a.m.-5 p.m., Sat. 10 a.m.-5 p.m. Adults $2.50, children under 12 $1.*

Exploratorium

Palace of Fine Arts,
Baker St. between Bay St. &
Marina Blvd.,
Marina District
• 561-0360

The masterpiece hands-on learning center designed by scientist/educator Frank Oppenheimer, the Exploratorium opened in 1969 and has delighted, fascinated and astounded visitors ever since. Over 500 exhibits allow the child in everyone to explore the principles of physics, chemistry, geometry, math, botany, biology, geology, astronomy and more. Lasers, sound rooms, mirrors, video screens, magnets and fantastically rigged contraptions challenge you to figure out how the world works by getting physically involved. The Tactile Gallery is so popular that it requires reservations and separate admission.
Open Wed. 10 a.m.-9:30 p.m., Thurs.-Sun. 10 a.m.-5 p.m.; open for group tours with advance reservations. Adults $5, seniors $2.50, children 6-17 $1.50, children under 6 free. Admisssion free first Wed. of the month & every Wed. after 6 p.m.

National Maritime Museum and Historical Park

Hyde St. Pier,
Hyde St. at the waterfront,
Fisherman's Wharf
• 556-6435

When commuting across the Bay to San Francisco was a more romantic venture, the Hyde Street Pier was the docking point for the Golden Gate ferries. Docked here today are five antique ships (three of which you can board), including the *Eureka*, the last of the side-wheel ferries to run in the U.S. The most recent addition to the collection is the *Balclutha*, a century-old sailing ship with three masts reaching skyward and classic square rigging. Built in Scotland in 1883, the *Balclutha* has been a cargo ship, a lumber ship, a salmon cannery in Alaska, a carnival ship and a Hollywood prop. Guided tours are held twice daily.
May-Oct.: open daily 10 a.m.-6 p.m.; Nov.-April: open daily 10 a.m.-5 p.m. Admission to museum free; admission to ships $2 for adults, free for children & seniors.

Presidio Army Museum

Lincoln Blvd. &
Funston Ave.,
Presidio
• 561-4115

Originally the northernmost military post of the Spanish when they ruled Mexico, the 1,400-acre Presidio has a fascinating history, much of which is documented in this museum. The museum is the oldest building in the Presidio; it began life in 1857 as the Old Station Hospital.
Open Tues.-Sun. 10 a.m.-4 p.m. Admission free.

Tattoo Art Museum

30 7th St.,
South of Market
• 864-9798

Lyle Tuttle's body is legendary. Covered virtually head to toe with tattoos, his decorated torso and limbs are a walking museum of this needle-meets-flesh art. But since Lyle can't live his life on display, he has assembled the world's largest collection of tools, photos and arcana from his trade. There is a tattoo studio on the premises.
Open daily noon-midnight. Admission free.

NEIGHBORHOODS

Want to discover the *real* San Francisco, not the tourist-shop approximations? Then wander through the picturesque neighborhoods that are often as colorful as their names. Reflecting the ethnic, cultural and economic diversity of the city, many of these neighborhoods are self-sustaining communities with their own unique sights, sounds, smells, architecture and lifestyles.

THE CASTRO DISTRICT - Spilling out from Castro and Market streets, this is the gay capital of the world: proud, close-knit and bustling with foot traffic and a lively outdoor café scene. The charming Victorian architecture and the rather insular small-town completeness give it the air of an independent city.

CHINATOWN - A maze of streets and alleys between North Beach and the Financial District, Chinatown is home to the largest Chinese community outside the old country and is also in some ways a city unto itself. Bordered roughly by Broadway, Bush, Stockton and Kearny streets, Chinatown has been burgeoning since the 1850s and now houses more than 80,000 residents, including many new residents from Southeast Asia. It bustles with the daily activities of any overcrowded urban neighborhood. Throw in thousands of tourists, browsers, shoppers and diners, and you have a magnificent (if sometimes stifling) swarm of humanity. In addition to countless restaurants (of every quality and price range), tea shops (where dim sum prevails), jade stores, curio shops and souvenir bazaars, Chinatown highlights include old-world architecture, a Chinese wax museum and exotic food and herb shops.

HAIGHT-ASHBURY - Just south of the Golden Gate Park Panhandle, the area still contains a few remnants of the Summer of Love, when tour buses used to bring gawking Midwesterners to stare at authentic hippies. But the gentrification of the Haight has resulted in trendier stores, restaurants and bars, and a population that is overwhelmingly affluent and baby-boomer, both gay and straight. A few hippie holdouts (and burnouts) still roam Haight Street, and a few counterculture shops hang in there.

JAPANTOWN (NIHONMACHI) - This concentrated community of businesses is clustered around Geary and Fillmore streets in the Western Addition. The focus is Japan Center, a five-acre mercantile complex featuring gift, jewelry and electronics shops; restaurants, tea houses and sushi bars; the Japanese Consulate; the Miyako Hotel; and the Japanese Trade Center. A new movie theater multiplex is now bringing in even more people from around the city.

THE MISSION DISTRICT - South of Market Street and east of the Castro, the Mission is practically a separate city. Largely Latin, its fascinating mix includes Mexican, Central and South American, Filipino and Southeast Asian populations, along with low-income artists and musicians of every ethnic heritage. Several walls boast elaborate murals depicting the area's culture and history, and the choice of good ethnic restaurants is staggering.

NOE VALLEY - West of the Mission and protected from the foggy breezes by Twin Peaks, Noe Valley is a longstanding enclave of beautifully refurbished row houses. The population is a mix of oldtime families, upwardly mobile professionals and somewhat bohemian artists. The shops, restaurants, coffeehouses and bookstores along 24th Street preserve the small-town atmosphere that has prevailed since this was farming territory.

NORTH BEACH, bounded by Broadway, Columbus and the Embarcadero, is at once the city's most beloved and most rapidly disappearing ethnic neighborhood. The old Italian merchants and family restaurants are gradually yielding to franchise businesses and fast-food outlets. But amid the rampant development, many charms endure: cafés and bookstores from the Beat era; picturesquely peopled Washington Square and the Church of St. Peter and St. Paul (prominently featured in *Dirty Harry*); dozens of fine restaurants; the old shops, saloons and Italian cafés along Grant Avenue; and foot traffic as varied and intriguing as anywhere in the city.

POLK GULCH, along Polk Street near California Street just west of Nob Hill, is a vibrantly gentrified but somewhat less expensive shopping area than Union Street. It is also known for its variety of good restaurants and its gay bar scene.

SOUTH OF MARKET (SOMA) - This neighborhood is a developer's dream come true. In the last several years, the industrial area between Market Street and China Basin has been undergoing a phenomenal renaissance. Warehouses have become Galllerias and Showplace Squares, hosting trade shows and consumer exhibitions. A motel has been turned into a restaurant and rock club. A sleek jazz club rises up next to a Bay Bridge off-ramp. Hipper-than-hip nightspots crop up at an alarming rate. Galleries and artists' studios multiply faster than you can say "art in the age of mechanical reproduction." Fashion and style are the bywords, and they change with the blink of an aloof and distanced eye. Once the province of biker and leather bars, SOMA (a relatively new and commercially contrived title) is now an entrepreneurial heaven—the place to be and an amusing place to watch.

THE TENDERLOIN - Squeezed in between the Civic Center (Van Ness Avenue and Grove Street), Union Square (Powell Street), Market Street and Geary, this is the neighborhood least likely to be a source of civic pride. Dotted with transient hotels, overpopulated with Asian refugees and the destitute and homeless, the Tenderloin butts up against both the theater district and the ballet/symphony/opera center, reminding the better-off citizenry of the oft-forgotten underside of San Francisco society. But the residents have guts and pride, which are captured in a fine neighborhood newspaper, the *Tenderloin Times*. The area also boasts an amazingly high number of interesting eateries—from the classic Original Joe's through diverse Greek, Burmese, Indonesian, Italian, Middle Eastern, Vietnamese, Thai, Indian, French, German and, of course, American restaurants.

UNION STREET (COW HOLLOW) - In the upper Marina, Union Street features scores of upscale boutiques for shopping, galleries and bookstores for browsing, and restaurants and cafés for trendy dining and drinking. It got the name "Cow Hollow" in the last century, when this now-yuppie area was home to the city's dairy farms. The area also boasts some lovely Victorian architecture.

TOURS

Blue & Gold Fleet
Pier 39,
Fisherman's Wharf
• 781-7877

The Blue & Gold's basic tour, which lasts a little over an hour, takes you along the waterfront, under both the Golden Gate and Bay bridges and around Alcatraz. It's as touristy as can be, but, weather permitting, you will be rewarded with some lovely views. Special dinner cruises are offered on Friday and Saturday evenings.
Spring & summer: open daily 10 a.m.-7 p.m. Fall & winter: hours vary. Adults $12, seniors & children 5-18 $6, children under 5 free.

Gray Line Tours
350 8th St.,
South of Market
• 558-9400

Gray Line's package bus tours hit all the expected attractions. The 3.5-hour city tour includes the Mission District, Golden Gate Park, the Cliff House, Fisherman's Wharf and a drive across the Golden Gate Bridge, with stops along the way. It can be supplemented with a Bay cruise package or an Alcatraz walking tour. Tours to Muir Woods, Sausalito and the wine country are also available. Not for the independent or the adventurous.
City tours depart daily 9 a.m., 10 a.m., 11 a.m. & 1:30 p.m. Adults $21.50, children 5-11 $10.75. Times & prices of other tours vary.

Dashiell Hammett Tours
Meets at San Francisco
Public Library,
200 Larkin St.,
Civic Center
• 564-7021

This four-hour, three-mile walking tour takes you through the San Francisco of writer Dashiell Hammett, creator of the legendary Sam Spade. A Pinkerton detective and ad copywriter before his star rose in the murder-mystery firmament, Hammett set most of his pulp magazine stories and his classic hard-boiled detective novels (most notably *The Maltese Falcon*) in these streets.
May-Aug. tours depart Sat. noon. Admission $5.

Heritage Walking Tours
Haas-Lilienthal House,
2007 Franklin St.,
Pacific Heights
• 441-3000

These docent-led tours help preserve San Francisco's history and give residents and tourists alike a look at some of the city's finest architecture. There are several tours, including one of the spectacular Victorian-era Haas-Lilienthal House; one through Pacific Heights, a neighborhood rich with Victorian and Edwardian mansions; and one through the old north waterfront. Call for details, directions to starting points and information on special and custom

tours. Admission fees benefit the nonprofit conservatory group.
Tour times & locations vary. Admission $3.

Hornblower Dining Yachts
Pier 33,
Fisherman's Wharf
• 394-8900

The sumptuous way to cruise the Bay is aboard the spacious and graciously appointed *City of San Francisco*, the flagship of the Hornblower yacht fleet. It accommodates 400 comfortably for dinner-dance cruises every evening, lunch cruises and champagne brunch cruises every weekend. Special events are scheduled almost every time of year, including full-moon cruises, holiday galas, "Big Game" (Cal-Stanford football) cruises and the New Year's Eve dinner-dance. Reservations are essential.
Admission $24-$59. Holiday cruises & special events up to $150 per person.

Levi Strauss & Co.
250 Valencia St.,
Mission District
• 565-9153

A 45-minute guided tour takes you through the cutting and sewing operations of the factory where the world's most famous pants, Levi's blue jeans, are made. Reservations are requested at least a week in advance.
Tours Wed. 10:30 a.m. Admission free.

Red & White Fleet
Pier 41 & Pier 43 1/2,
Fisherman's Wharf
• 546-2805

The Red & White handles commuter and ferry service to Angel Island, Sausalito, Tiburon, Marine World, Vallejo and Stockton and offers group rates and special charters. Its tours include the round-trip ferry ride and tour of Alcatraz Island (see "Excursions" in this chapter), weekend jaunts to Angel Island, and the 45-minute Golden Gate Bay Cruise, which sails under the Golden Gate Bridge and around Alcatraz.
Golden Gate Bay Cruise departs Pier 43 1/2 at 10:45 a.m., noon, 1:15 p.m, 2:30 p.m. & 3:45 p.m. Adults $12, seniors, military & children 12-18 $8, children 5-11 $5, children under 5 free. Hours & prices of other trips vary depending on the destination & the season.

OUT OF
SAN FRANCISCO

RESTAURANTS

The Covey
Quail Lodge,
8205 Valley Greens Dr.,
Carmel Valley
• (408) 624-1581
FRENCH/CONTINENTAL

Let's face it, the main restaurant at the exclusive, golf-oriented, solidly Republican Quail Lodge in Carmel Valley is stuffy and boring. But we like it anyway: the French food—a mélange of standard Continental, nouvelle and minceur cuisines—is very good, and the service is as well executed as the food. We're still using the tableside-prepared Caesar salad we had here a year or so ago as the yardstick by which all others are measured. And if you're offered fresh salmon, by all means order it; the chef has a deft touch with fish in general and salmon in particular. The meandering dining room is artfully designed to give each table its own space at windowside, so that everyone overlooks a pond with a bridge and luxuriant surrounding foliage, all dramatically lit (even the ducks). Lighting in the dining room is on the dim side, a plus for discreet romantics. Dinner for two, with wine, will run about $120.
Open Sun.-Thurs. 6:30 p.m.-9:30 p.m., Fri.-Sat. 6 p.m.-9:30 p.m. All major cards.

Fresh Cream
100F Heritage Harbor,
Monterey
• (408) 375-9798
FRENCH

Nestled close by Monterey's Fisherman's Wharf, within earshot of barking sea lions, Fresh Cream would be a romantic special-occasion place even if the food wasn't terrific. But terrific it is, starring French classics interpreted with frequent "California-eclectic" touches. A tender filet of venison, for example, is first marinated in an East-West blend of honey, ginger, garlic, soy sauce and jalapeño peppers before grilling. And a thick filet of swordfish, moist and meaty, is stuffed with a mélange of sun-dried tomatoes, garlic and oyster mushrooms and served with red-bell-pepper butter and salsa. Roast duckling, succulent and remarkably unfatty, comes with an addictive, not-too-sweet black-currant sauce. But the pièce de résistance is the lamb, an entire eight-chop rack of it, roasted to order with a delicate mustard–bread crumb crust. Definitely last-meal-on-Earth material! So are several of the appetizers, notably the lobster ravioli and fried soft-shell crab in a not-too-potent garlic butter. The dessert menu boasts several selections of like caliber, including several excellent classic tarts and a whimsical sac au chocolat: a chocolate "paper bag" brimming with house-made coffee ice cream. Also, try to find a way to try the ambrosial soufflé Grand Marnier. You can always walk it off after dinner along the picturesque waterfront. Dinner for two, with wine, will run about $125. *Open Tues.-Sun. 6 p.m.-10 p.m. Cards: AE, MC, V.*

Giuliano's
Mission & 5th sts., Carmel
• (408) 625-5231
ITALIAN

11/20

We had high hopes for this charming little jewel box of a restaurant; a tiny hideaway in the midst of Carmel's rabbit warren of shops and galleries. Aside from some very fine appetizers, however, we weren't impressed enough with the food to award Giuliano's a toque. A pasta del mare was billed as containing scallops and sun-dried tomatoes, but when our order came up, we were told that the sun-dried tomatoes had run out. This would have been fine, had the resulting dish not suffered from not-quite-fresh-enough scallops, cooked far beyond tenderness. A rollatino of spinach, eggplant and prosciutto, rolled in a thin pasta and served with tomato sauce, was both lackluster in flavor and overbaked. On the plus side, the house turns out some really choice primi piatti—starters that a grazer could happily combine into a full meal. A gorgeous presentation of carpaccio brought tissue-thin raw beef, showered with good Parmesan and drizzled not with the usual olive oil, but with squiggles of a tangy mustard sauce. An insalata specialità consisted of perfect little mixed lettuce leaves, crisp nuggets of sautéed pancetta and a well-made balsamic vinaigrette. Soups, such as a fine-flavored tomato-basil cream, are freshly made each day. The kitchen also turns out standard veal dishes (piccata, scaloppine alla Marsala, valdostana with prosciutto and fontina), rich sweetbreads with lemon, garlic and olive oil, and a fresh catch of the day. All in all, there's fine potential here; it just hasn't been realized to its fullest as yet. Dinner for two, with wine, should run about $85.
Open Tues.-Sat. 11:30 a.m.-2:30 p.m. & 6 p.m.-10 p.m. Cards: AE, MC, V.

Hog's Breath Inn
San Carlos & 5th sts., Carmel
• (408) 625-1044
AMERICAN

10/20

Everyone's on the prowl at Clint Eastwood's phenomenally successful restaurant/bar in Carmel village. It's casual (in Carmel, that means golf shirt, blazer and hiking boots for men, bimbowear for women), loud and fun. The bartenders pour well and generously. The goofy but great-looking patio is warmed by fireplaces; inside is a charming pub and a relatively quiet separate dining room. The food is honest and good, if not thrilling: burgers, sandwiches, salads, grilled meat. The Dirty Harry burger is unpretentious and therefore excellent, and the grilled steaks and chicken are satisfying and nicely presented by snappy young servers. With a bottle from the good California wine list, dinner will set two back anywhere from $60 to $80; considerably less for a burger-and-beer lunch.

Open daily 11:30 a.m.-3 p.m. & 5 p.m.-10 p.m. All major cards.

Jimmy's American Place
26344 Carmel Rancho Ln., Carmel Valley
• (408) 625-6666
CALIFORNIAN

Jimmy's is a fun addition to the little corner of Carmel Valley that is rapidly becoming Carmel's nightlife center. Owner Kenny Fukumoto owns several popular restaurants, of which Jimmy's may be the best. The sexy decor captures a gray, sea-like feeling using gray and black marble and industrial-chic rubber tile, with hot neon accents refracted in lots of chrome-glass brick (which separates the bar from the dining room). There's usually cool jazz on the excellent sound system. There are usually a half dozen fresh West Coast oysters available at the bar, along with fresh crab and shrimp. The kitchen puts out creditable regional Californian cuisine, which in this region means freshly caught fish from Monterey Bay and the Pacific, and beef from Harris Ranch not far inland. The meats are grilled over oak, as are some of the fish. Pastas are very good, especially the seafood pasta and the herb linguine. Our favorite dish is the baby back ribs from Harris Ranch, which are smoked and then finished on the grill over oak. About $65 for two, with wine. *Open Mon.-Fri. 5 p.m.-10 p.m., Sun. 4:30 p.m.-10 p.m. All major cards.*

Mission Ranch
26270 Dolores, Carmel
• (408) 624-3824
AMERICAN

11/20

Locals love to gossip about trysts of the rich and infamous in the guest cottages on this oldtime cattle ranch restored as a rustic roadhouse/restaurant/motel complex and live-music venue. Actor Clint Eastwood (there's that magic name again) and his partners have preserved the historical feel of the oak-shaded property and its view of the wetlands at the mouth of the Carmel River. It really is like eating in a ranch house—a very full ranch house, usually. The steaks are tender and cooked accurately to order, accompanied by béarnaise and a twice-baked (stuffed) potato. The fresh catch of the day is usually a good bet. Local wines dominate the list, and a corny cocktail pianist dominates the dining room/bar. Later in the evening the bolder elements in the crowd sing along with such hits as "Somewhere Over the Rainbow," which can be fun or hellish, depending on your attitude. Meanwhile, the adjacent barn–cum–music hall features everything from big-band music to rock (with a cover charge), a different flavor each night. Mission Ranch is part of an evening circuit that also includes the Hog's Breath Inn and Rio Grill, but the demographic profile is broader here. You'll fit in best if you dress for success. Dinner for two will run about $55, with a simple wine. *Open Mon.-Fri. 11:30 a.m.-3 p.m. & 5 p.m.-10 p.m., Sat.-Sun. 11:30 a.m.-3 p.m. & 5 p.m.-11 p.m. All major cards.*

HOTELS

Carmel Valley Ranch Resort
1 Old Ranch Rd., Carmel
• (408) 625-9500, Fax (408) 624-2858

Arranged amid 1,700 acres in the balmy Carmel Valley, this is a full-service resort complete with tennis courts, swimming pools, a 50-seat restaurant and an eighteen-hole golf course designed by Pete Dye. One hundred suites, four to a villa, cling to the oak-studded hillside. Each has its own deck—ideal for room-service breakfasts with only deer and birds for company—lavish baths, fully stocked wet bars, fireplaces, Amish bed quilts, original watercolors and soaring cathedral ceilings. Color schemes are muted: moss green, oak gray, dusty rose. The accommodations are extraordinarily large and attractive; an extensive room-service menu is available on very short notice. There is a second pool near the tennis courts and a large clubhouse near the golf course, where guests may prefer to take casual meals. The main lodge restaurant, with its floor-to-ceiling windows overlooking the woods, offers a rustic backdrop for elegant fare, mostly local produce, game and seafood from nearby Monterey Bay.
Singles & doubles: $185-$275; suites: $375-$575.

The Cobblestone Inn
Junipero St. between 7th & 8th sts., Carmel
• (408) 625-5222, No fax

If you like Petite Auberge in San Francisco, you'll probably eat up The Cobblestone Inn, another jewel run by the same family. Fluffy quilts, elegant wallpaper and hand-picked antiques echo the European countryside. But unlike so many small-town inns, the Cobblestone offers private baths for all 24 rooms and a cobblestone fireplace, a television and a refrigerator in most. A courtyard of more cobblestones separates the guest rooms from the main lounge (and yet another stone fireplace), where guests are served tea, wine and hors d'oeuvres. An extensive breakfast buffet includes cereals and baked eggs.
Singles & doubles: $95-$170; suites: $155.

Gosby House Inn

643 Lighthouse Ave.,
Pacific Grove
• (408) 375-1287,
No fax

Cute as a bug, inside and out, the Gosby House nonetheless inspires feelings of claustrophobia. Some of the rooms are small, made even more precious by the hanging of beribboned straw hats on the walls. Perhaps it's worth the cramping to have private baths and fireplaces in most rooms, but travelers who like to spread out will quibble with the tradeoff. The owners, experienced innkeepers, have created 22 accommodations in this 1887 Queen Anne house (which is on the National Historic Register) and an outbuilding (two of the latter units have kitchens). Hot tea, chocolate and cider—provided by an omnipresent innkeeper—and full breakfasts are included in the rates.
Singles & doubles: $85-$125.

Highlands Inn

Hwy. 1, Carmel
• (408) 624-3801,
(408) 626-1574

Perched above the froth of the Pacific since 1916, the Highlands Inn has long commanded a larger-than-life view of the dramatic coastline four miles south of Carmel. For years, the place was doomed by a gloomy Scottish decor, but it's absolutely amazing what a $41-million face-lift can do. Today, shingled clusters of rooms, suites and town houses stagger up the eleven-acre hillside retreat. Most of them—especially the town houses—afford stunning ocean views beyond the central swimming pool. Throughout the property, the color scheme reflects the rose, emerald, aqua and amethyst tones of a Pacific sunset. Nowhere is this shown to better effect than in Pacific's Edge, a spacious oceanfront restaurant. The menu relies heavily on local seafood and produce from the nearby Central Valley; the style is elegant Californian cuisine. An all-day deli, concierge services, several outdoor spas and such amenities as golf umbrellas make this one of the most appealing hideaways on the central coast.
Singles & doubles: $205-$310.

Hotel Pacific

300 Pacific St.,
Monterey
• (408) 373-5700,
No fax

The prettiest hotel in downtown Monterey, the Hotel Pacific provides a series of pleasant discoveries, from the inviting lobby to the luxurious landscaped gardens to the deluxe rooms—suites, actually. More than 100 accommodations (on two to four levels) are connected by bougainvillea-draped walkways, lending the hotel the air of a private Spanish compound. Hardwood floors, custom rugs, fireplaces, four-poster or high-post beds, refrigerators, wet bars and private patios or balconies distinguish each room. Close to historic sites, the Hotel Pacific is the kind of place we'd love to come home to after a hard day of touring the state's oldest city.
Singles & doubles: $129-$199.

Inn at Spanish Bay

1700 17 Mile Dr.,
Pebble Beach
• (408) 647-7500,
Fax <408) 647-7443

The newest addition to Pebble Beach, the Inn at Spanish Bay offers 270 rooms in a three- and four-story buildings that hug the oceanfront golf course. Behind the inn is a grove of Monterey pines. Tiled roofs and wood-framed balconies suggest Old Monterey and its Spanish heritage. Rooms and suites are spacious, with a fireplace, a deck or patio, separate dressing area and room enough for the custom-made furniture groupings. Every restaurant, lounge and guest room is situated to capitalize on views of either the water or the forest, sometimes both. On site are plentiful shopping, a full-service tennis club, a health club with heated swimming pool, and an eighteen-hole championship golf course that meanders through dunes in true Scottish fashion.

Singles & doubles: $250-$385; suites: $700-$875 (plus $15 gratuity per night).

Lodge at Pebble Beach

17 Mile Dr.,
Pebble Beach
• (408) 624-3811,
Fax <408) 624-6357

This is where the Old Money comes, and has come since 1919, when the place was opened as the Del Monte Lodge. This imposing oceanfront lodge, with oversize furniture and fireplaces, serves as a gathering place for golfers and well-to-do families interested in sports and socializing in a pampered, secluded setting. Service is first-rate, as it has to be to please these patrons, who can afford to stay any place they like. Most of the 161 extra-large accommodations lie in twelve separate low-rise buildings; only eleven are in the lodge itself. Most have fireplaces and all have wet bars, well-stocked refrigerators and either a patio or a balcony within earshot of the ocean. Four restaurants include the Cypress Room, which serves a sort of haute regional cuisine, and Club XIX, a lower-level restaurant and bar facing the eighteenth green and Carmel Bay. More than a dozen boutiques, 34 miles of bridle paths through Del Monte Forest, a swimming pool, a beach-and-tennis club and, of course, championship golf courses are among the amenities.

Singles & doubles: $250-$350; suites $775.

Old Monterey Inn

500 Martin St.,
Monterey
• (408) 375-8284,
No fax

Built as a home for a former mayor of Monterey, this fetching Tudor-style mansion enjoys a parklike setting, with dozens of tall trees, a rose garden, fuchsias, hydrangeas and a forest of ferns growing beside a creek bed. Each of ten accommodations is drastically different, from the book-lined Library to the shuttered two-room Garden Cottage with a windowseat overlooking the gardens. Full breakfast is served indoors or out on the patio; wine, coffee and hors d'oeuvres are provided in the parlor in the afternoons. A favorite amenity in this perfect bed-and-breakfast inn is the book of guest-written reviews of local restaurants. *Singles & doubles: $140-$195.*

Quail Lodge
8205 Valley Greens Dr.,
Carmel Valley
• (408) 624-1581

A former dairy farm, the 600-acre Quail Lodge still has that bucolic feel, with several lakes and hills on all sides disguising its present incarnation as a golf resort that's extremely popular with a conservative middle-aged and older crowd. A fairly recent remodeling of most of the hotel's 100 rooms and suites has lightened and modernized the interiors, most of which have views of the golf course. Top-of-the-line are the two-bedroom executive villas, each with its own hot tub, stereo system and cassette deck. The hotel organizes excellent hiking trips into the unspoiled, wildlife-filled hills up above the golf course. Don't miss dinner at The Covey, where updated Continental cuisine is livened up with home-grown herbs.
Singles & doubles: $155-$195; suites: $210-$310. Golf packages available.

Stonepine Estate Resort
150 E. Carmel Valley Rd.,
Carmel
• (408) 659-2245

Once the estate of Henry Potter Russell, this twelve-suite property is now an excellent spot for a very private getaway. The setting in the Carmel Valley is absolutely knockout, which may account for the pilgrimages made by more than a few of Hollywood's best and brightest. The equestrian center will keep those of you who want to be in the saddle happy. There's even an opportunity to learn the fine art of carriage driving. For something special, ask for one of the suites with a wood-burning fireplace. Dinners cost $45 per person.
Suites: $160-$550.

EAST BAY

RESTAURANTS

Augusta's
2955 Telegraph Ave.,
Berkeley
• 548-3140
AMERICAN

12/20

Showing up here with a reservation on a weeknight is almost like going to a friend's house for a dinner party. The sunny, comfortable neighborhood restaurant gets its homey feel partly from being in a shambling old house and partly from the familial aura projected by the staff. Ah, home . . . except Augusta's food is better than anything Mom ever made (sorry, Mom, it's no disgrace). One reason for its success is that the fish, a special focus here, is impeccably fresh and well chosen. We're praying that this will continue to be true, since Augusta's new owners no longer buy from the Monterey Fish Market. However, the menu will be as seafood-oriented as ever: Augusta's pescatorial productions are always good; they do great things with shark and swordfish. Soups and pastas are alsoexcellent, and we have had good luck with nonseafood specials. Garlic-lovers will quickly become addicted to the roast garlic potatoes, and dessert-lovers should reserve something from the daily sweets selection when ordering entrées. Two can eat and drink well for $55.

Open Tues.-Fri. 11:30 a.m.-2:30 p.m. & 5:30 p.m.-9:30 p.m., Sat. 5:30 p.m.-10:30 p.m., Sun. 10:30 a.m.-2 p.m. & 5:30 p.m.-9 p.m. Cards: AE, MC, V.

Bay Wolf Café
3853 Piedmont Ave., Oakland
• 655-6004
CALIFORNIAN

The name has always appealed to us, with its echoes of *Beowulf* and the famous *Sea Wolf* of Oakland writer Jack London. The food has echoes, too—of Chez Panisse, James Beard and Provence—though it is also unique. There's a consistency, call it a kitchen flavor, to the inventive and well-produced cuisine that has created a legion of Bay Wolf devotees; as a result the competition for tables, especially on weekends, makes reservations essential. The dining rooms occupy an expanded Victorian house in the Oakland hills, a comfortable place with an appealing touch of hail-fellow-well-met tavern cheer. We've thoroughly enjoyed everything we've tried here: bluefin tuna sautéed with red and gold tomatoes and lacy, airy onion rings; grilled shrimp on a bed of grilled eggplant; toothsome fettuccine with two kinds of sausage, one spicy and one mild; a very good mixed grill. Perhaps the best thing about the Bay Wolf is the list of drinkable, as opposed to merely trendy, wines. Call the restaurant to receive copies of upcoming menus, which may determine the night you wish to visit. About $50 for dinner for two, with wine.

Open Mon.-Fri. 11:30 a.m.-2 p.m. & 6 p.m.-9:30 p.m., Sat. 11 a.m.-3 p.m. & 5:30 p.m.-9:30 p.m., Sun. 10 a.m.-3 p.m. & 5:30 p.m.-9:30 p.m. Cards: MC, V.

Bucci's
6121 Hollis St., Emeryville
• 547-4725
ITALIAN

10/20

Bucci's is visually one of the most stimulating restaurants in the East Bay. It's particularly appealing at lunch, when sunlight streams in at all angles from big windows placed at ceiling and street level. There's plenty of faux marble and wood trim around, and the people-watching is excellent. With this kind of atmosphere, we wish the food were as exciting as the clientele. Bucci's has become known for

crisp-crusted pizzas and calzones with such upscale toppings as chorizo, red chard, goat cheese, mushrooms and mozzarella. The crustiness is sensational at first but gets soggy quickly. The toppings are intensely cheesy, too much so, and yet they still lack character. What's great about Bucci's is that you can snack or dine from lunch right on through dinner. There's always a wide selection of appetizers at dinner, and two or three of them make for a satisfying meal. A small, unusually reasonable wine list offers a fair number of ready-to-drink California and French table wines for $13 to $15 a bottle. Count on $50 for a dinner for two, with wine.
Open Mon.-Fri. 11:30 a.m.-2:30 p.m. & 5:30 p.m.-9:30 p.m., Sat. 5:30 p.m.-9:30 p.m. No cards.

Café at Chez Panisse
1517 Shattuck Ave., Berkeley
• 548-5525
CALIFORNIAN

Any complaints about this now-venerable Berkeley institution? Well, it's as hard as ever to get in, it hasn't gotten any cheaper, they still run out of the really good stuff (like Hog Island oysters) fairly early in the evening, and the waiters persist in acting as if they were doing you a personal favor by deigning to take your order. So is it still worth coming here? You bet. You could practically shut your eyes and point at the menu and get a fabulous array of fine-tuned flavors. Virtually every wine on the list is not only excellent with the food, but drinkable right now. The ambience has actually improved, both from yuppie attrition and the gradual influx of people who want to have a good time eating instead of worshipping the kitchen. Goat-cheese calzone and roasted-garlic pizza reign supreme, as always, and the salads of tender greens are better than ever, thanks to the organic-produce revolution that this restaurant helped spawn. And there's no substitute for a dish like grilled radicchio with savory beans and aïoli when that's what you really want. Even the basics—like grilled chicken with warm potato salad—are handled better here than they would be anywhere else. But yo! Alice! Talk to your people about attitude, please. About $40 to $50 for two, with wine by the glass.
Open Mon.-Sat. 11:30 a.m.-11:30 p.m. All major cards.

Cambodiana
156 University Ave., Berkeley
• 843-4630
CAMBODIAN

12/20

Cambodiana bills itself as "exotic and nouvelle Cambodian cuisine," which describes its fare admirably. In a town glutted with Southeast Asian eateries, this unpretentious little place, a mere block from the U.C. Berkeley campus, fills a niche all its own. Where else, after all, can you find the likes of rabbit, quail and escargots, in complex and fascinating preparations, without paying French-restaurant prices? Cambodiana organizes its main dishes according to sauces, and the kandal red curry sauce (made with lemon grass, galanga, shrimp paste, garlic, shallots, coconut milk and chili, and spiced to order) boasts the chef's proud signature. His sweet-sour Mekong houseboat sauce, with shallots, garlic, lime juice and chili, works especially well on boneless quail royale, stuffed with a blend of ground pork, shrimp and lemon grass. We especially loved the naga princess sauce—thick, creamy and singing with toasty garlic, coconut milk, tangy tamarind and spices—on simply poached prawns. Among the chef's specialties, the smoky eggplant country style, sautéed to tenderness with ground pork and shrimp, was another clear winner. Minor disappointments included a too-thin spicy coconut soup and a cool prawn salad with green papaya, shredded pork, chopped peanuts and mint, which, until we livened it up with hot sauce, seemed too bland. Cambodiana's wine list, though small, is well chosen and very reasonably priced, with every selection also available by the glass. Dinner for two should come to about $60.

Open Mon.-Thurs. 11:30 a.m.-3 p.m. & 5 p.m.-10 p.m., Fri.-Sat. 11:30 a.m.-3 p.m. & 5 p.m.-10:30 p.m. Cards: AE, MC, V.

Carrara's Café
1290 Powell St.,
Emeryville
• 547-6763
ITALIAN/CALIFORNIAN

Emeryville, a small, mostly industrial town at the east end of the Bay Bridge, has enjoyed a recent surge of surprisingly fine eateries in its sprawling warehouse district. Among the best of these is Carrara's Café, a homey little haven whose name alludes to the marble works that share the building. It's open all day, six days a week, serving up imaginative yet unpretentious bistro fare at the bar or at the tiny knot of no-frills tables. The considerate hosts even provide a rack of books, magazines and games for their patrons' amusement. Carrara's grilled sandwiches, on thickly sliced French bread, make a hearty meal at any time of day. Try the bresaola (air-cured beef) and Havarti, the pepper ham and Brie or the whole-milk mozzarella with watercress and sun-dried tomatoes (complete with a dollop of great pesto). The pesto returns as a savory flourish on a bowl of that ultimate Italian comfort food, polenta. With a swirl of melting Gorgonzola, a slab of toasted French bread and some sliced fresh tomatoes, this dish is hard to beat for soothing away the cares of the world. For incorrigible lily-gilders, the polenta even comes with steamed clams and garlicky aïoli. Desserts are simple but choice: Linzertorte, chocolate truffle torte, apricot-brandy pound cake and assorted gelati with toppings that include the delectable

, fruit wines from Bonny Doon. A carefully assembled wine and beer list rounds out the menu. A snack (sandwich and beer) will run about $10; a full meal for two, $50 or so. *Open Mon.-Thurs. & Sat. 7 a.m.-midnight, Fri. 7 a.m.-1 a.m. Cards: MC, V.*

Chef Paul
4179 Piedmont Ave.,
Oakland
• 547-2175
FRENCH

When Chef Paul took over the former Premier Cru Café early in 1989, he reaped the benefit of its built-in client base from the wine bar downstairs. This has continued to serve Chef Paul's well via special tasting menus, booked through Premier Cru's mailing list, which pair a group of eight wines (such as the 1970 Bordeaux and the 1974 California Cabernets) with a multicourse dinner. As his international background would suggest, Chef Paul pulls out all the stops for these feasts, laying on seven lavish courses composed of everything from sweetbreads with morels and lobster to wild-duck breast with pink peppercorns to a warm Kahlúa soufflé drenched in mocha sauce. His everyday "menu gastronomique" is one of the fanciest in the East Bay, featuring full-scale treatments of lobster with whisky and cream, mesquite-broiled peppered beef filet with Roquefort, and veal filet Strasbourg with foie gras. Pure decadence, and hard on the arteries, but delectable stuff indeed. For two, with wine, dinner will be between $75 and $105. *Open Tues.-Sat. 6 p.m.-11 p.m., Sun. 4 p.m.-11 p.m. Cards: AE, MC, V.*

Chez Panisse
1517 Shattuck Ave.,
Berkeley
• 548-5525
CALIFORNIAN

With each passing year organic baby lettuces become more run-of-the-mill, but these modest, homey tables remain the hottest ticket in the Bay Area, attracting scores of pilgrims eager to pay homage (and plenty of cash) at this shrine of Californian cuisine. Though increased competition in the Bay Area's restaurant scene has knocked Chez Panisse down a point from our earlier rating, what is most worth noting— and the truest measure of Alice Waters's stature as a cultural revolutionary—is that the restaurant is still as good as it ever was. Sure, the staff can be haughty, but let's face it, the clique mentality in restaurants wasn't invented in Berkeley. Californian cuisine was, however—not the ingredients and the general style, perhaps, but certainly its focused, refined form as practiced at Chez Panisse. *Purity* is the watchword here—while the kitchen seems less inventive than it once was, the purity of the ingredients and flavors remains flawless. These last few years, Waters has left the cooking to Paul Bertolli, who has injected an Italian note into many of the fixed-price dinners (which offer no choice whatsoever). But American food is still the focus—the simpler the better.

Our last meal was simple to the point of seeming ordinariness: a modest grilled-duck salad with green beans, a bowl of white-corn soup, a plate of unadorned thin-sliced roast beef, a simple green salad and a homey strawberry semifreddo. No complicated, involved recipes, no costly truffles or foie gras, not even dramatic plate presentations. So what's the big deal? The big deal is found in the first bite of each dish: pure flavors the likes of which even the most dedicated foodie rarely encounters. The corn soup, for instance, was bursting with rich corn flavor; the beef (from the Nieman-Schell ranch), simply coated in rock salt and baked, had more flavor than a dozen tournedos Rossini. Like his boss, Bertolli has a gift for achieving maximum flavor with minimum fuss and folderol.

We still maintain that everyone should dine here at least once. After all these years, Chez Panisse remains the wellspring of Californian cuisine and a guiding light for American contemporary cooking, whether it be rooted in New England or New Mexico. Both Chez Panisse and its lively, more informal upstairs café (see Cafe at Chez Panisse) occupy a big old house in an old Berkeley neighborhood. The main dining room on the first floor has dark-wood paneling, classic furniture and soft lighting, a surprisingly modest American setting for the quintessential new American cuisine. The prix-fixe menu, which changes every few days, is $55 per person, without wine. Remember that a fifteen percent service charge is included in your bill. Don't unknowingly tip twice. Make reservations three weeks to a month in advance.
Seatings Tues.-Sat. 6 p.m., 6:30 p.m., 8:30 p.m. & 9:15 p.m. All major cards.

Christopher's Café
1843 Solano Ave.,
Berkeley
• 526-9444
CALIFORNIAN

Californian cuisine, unlike the classic cuisines of, say, France, Italy and China, means something entirely different depending on who's wielding the whisk or wok. It's a freewheeling style of cooking whose only constants are impeccably fresh ingredients and an offbeat flair for combining them. Born in Berkeley, Californian cuisine has stretched to accommodate the influx of flavors and techniques that the '70s and '80s have brought. At Christopher's Café, at the top of Solano Avenue's "Restaurant Row," those influences begin with the usual Mediterranean in such contemporary classics as Greek spinach salad with Kalamata olives, feta, mint and lemon dressing; egg tagliarini with grilled chicken, prosciutto, eggplant, tomatoes, herbs and Parmesan; and grilled salmon trout with pesto. Then the menu takes a few radical turns: to Scandinavia for a butter-smooth, house-cured gravlax with honey-dill dressing, and to North Africa for Moroccan lamb brochette with papaya-pineapple chutney. There's a Thai peanut sauce on the grilled marinated chicken breast, and Thai chilies in the wonderful sautéed marinated Chinese lamb, spiced also with ginger, jalapeño and cilantro. As if this weren't enough diversity, the kitchen travels to the Southwest and then south of the border with blackened center-cut pork chops with blue-corn blini and fruit salsa; crab chimichanga with ancho-chile sauce and guacamole; and grilled house-made Yucatán sausages made with chicken, pork, cumin, allspice, jalapeño, cilantro and sweet cream. How's that for a world tour! An equally eclectic, reasonably priced wine list, with many selections available by the glass, expands the options even further. Dinner for two, with wine, should run about $75.

Open Mon.-Thurs. 11:30 a.m.-2:15 p.m. & 5:30 p.m.-9 p.m., Fri. 11:30 a.m.-2:15 p.m. & 5:30 p.m.-10 p.m., Sat. 5:30 p.m.-10 p.m., Sun. 5:30 p.m.-9 p.m. Cards: AE, MC, V.

La Crème de la Crème

5362 College Ave., Oakland
• 420-8822
FRENCH/ITALIAN/ CALIFORNIAN

Owner/chef David Nugent grew up on produce from the family farm, anticipating the Californian cuisine trend toward fresh-from-the-garden fruits and veggies. When he opened La Crème de la Crème in 1983, he brought these memories, plus his skills in French cooking techniques, to his new place. You'll find many French-country dishes coming from Nugent's kitchen, such as navarin à la printanière (braised lamb with fresh vegetables), rockfish Provençale (baked with tomatoes, onions, garlic, herbs and olive oil) and grilled lamb tenderloin with aïoli and green beans. He even does a soul-satisfyingly hearty cassoulet with chunks of pork, duck and sausage studding the creamy white beans. But beyond these classics, Nugent has added some highly original, even quirky dishes—pizzas and pastas that bring in some decidedly non-Gallic ingredients. The Creole sausage pasta, for example, contains Louisiana-style chaurice sausages along with niçoise olives, tomatoes, olive oil, garlic and Parmesan. And several pizzas include fresh fruit in their toppings, such as the mango and goat cheese with blackberry sauce and the apple, duck sausage, white Cheddar and nutmeg. If you're skeptical, stick to the margherita, with fresh tomatoes, garlic, mozzarella and a chiffonade of fresh basil. The pizza crusts are chewy and crisp, and flavored with an elusive hint of honey and thyme. It's hard to resist the great house-made French bread and focaccia, served with both butter and olive oil. And for dessert, the flourless chocolate gâteau La Crème de la Crème tempts irresistibly from its puddle of raspberry sauce. Go for it. Also, don't miss the rich and copious caramel sauce on vanilla-bean ice cream, all homemade. Dinner for two, with a decent California wine, should cost about $70.

Open Mon.-Fri. 11:30 a.m.-2 p.m. & 6 p.m.-9:30 p.m., Sat.-Sun. 8 a.m.-2 p.m. & 6 p.m.-9:30 p.m. All major cards.

Fourth Street Grill

1820 4th St.,
Berkeley
• 849-0526
CALIFORNIAN

In 1989, the Fourth Street Grill, along with a slew of other Bay Area restaurants (Augusta's, Hayes Street Grill), celebrated its tenth birthday, which says something about the passing of Californian cuisine from yuppie trend to well-rooted establishment. The good news is that the food at Fourth Street is still looking—and tasting—very good. The restaurant's best-known chef, Mark Miller, has moved on to the Southwest, and successor Amy Shaw, famous for her arsenal of chile peppers, has decamped to the Maltese Grill in San Francisco. But the current chef, Kurt Koessel, worked with both of them, and the kitchen still displays a marked affection for dishes of Southwestern and Mexican inspiration. This is the restaurant where half of the foodies in the Bay Area got their first taste of mesquite-grilled fish, hand-chopped salsas and searing hot chiles, all of which are as ordinary as cheeseburgers today. With its varnished wood tables and bright Southwest-patterned cushions, Fourth Street has a comfortable, lived-in feel. Wood-framed windows look onto 4th Street, and French doors now enclose the former patio, which also features a skylight that slides open on summer nights.

At lunch, you can still order one of the world's best BLTs, made with Acme seed bread, a stack of lean, flavorful bacon, a *real* tomato, romaine lettuce and handmade mayo. The burgers—with cheese and chili if you like—are great, too. And the skinny shoestring potatoes are still the best in town. A favorite, too, at both lunch and dinner is Fourth Street's signature Yucatán sausage, a chunky mix of pork and chicken laced with fresh cilantro and fiery green chiles. The green salad is always a mix of baby lettuces picked that day from Kona Kai Farm's urban garden across the street; the Caesar salad is true to the original; and the guacamole is thick and chunky. Fish is treated with respect: calamari deep-fried in a hot pepper–spiked batter, salmon dipped in cornmeal and topped with enoki mushrooms and ribbons of leek and fresh ginger. The kitchen does its homework when it comes to searching out first-rate suppliers—fish comes from Berkeley's Paul Johnson, beef from the Nieman-Schell Ranch, and so on. To keep her regulars interested, owner Suzy Nelson changes the theme of the specials every few weeks. An emphasis on northern Italian cooking might be followed by Southwestern or regional Mexican menus. About half the dishes are regular items; the rest are such changing specials as poussin in a blood-orange and chile sauce.

So where are the faults? Some of the pasta dishes are ill-conceived, and the short dessert list could be improved. But all in all, the Fourth Street Grill has entered its second decade with skill and creativity. Two will spend about $65 for dinner with wine.

Open Tues.-Thurs. 11:30 a.m.-2:30 p.m. & 5:30 p.m.-10 p.m., Fri.-Sat. 11:30 a.m.-2:30 p.m. & 5:30 p.m.-10 p.m., Sun. 5 p.m.-9:30 p.m. Cards: MC, V.

Gertie's Chesapeake Bay Café

1919 Addison St.,
Berkeley
• 841-2722
AMERICAN/SEAFOOD

12/20

Gertie's is an upscale, down-home, noisy Berkeley institution specializing in crabcakes made from Maryland blue crabs. It's also an oyster bar, and the culinary laboratory for chef Eric Haines, who is particularly adept at cooking seafood. Creative, reasonably priced food comes out of the kitchen, and the staff serves it with great cheer and liveliness. On Monday night the chicken dinners are a steal: for $11 you get an enormous pan-fried free-range half chicken with a choice of eight different trimmings that vary each week. We love the crabcakes, held together with a minimal amount of binding so the sweet, lightly spiced seafood taste shines through. They're served with excellent coleslaw and french fries. Gumbo is kaleidoscopic—light brown in color with delayed-reaction spice and plenty of fresh seafood and sausage to balance out the rice. Daily specials are the most inventive items on the menu—like one unusual brochette of grilled scallops with fresh figs, red and green peppers, jalapeño pepper and a strawberry, served on pecan rice with lemon sauce. If you're into dessert, you'll like Haines's offerings. They're extremely rich, sometimes cloyingly so, but several of the items are wonderful. We relish the chocolate-mousse cake with fresh raspberries, and the flavorful fresh-fruit tarts. Dinner for two, with wine, runs about $70.

Open Mon.-Thurs. 11:30 a.m.-2 p.m. & 5:30 p.m.-9:30 p.m., Fri.-Sat. 5:30 p.m.-10 p.m., Sun. 10:30 a.m.-2 p.m. Cards: AE, MC, V.

Gulf Coast Restaurant & Oyster Bar

736 Washington St.,
Oakland
• 839-6950
SEAFOOD/CAJUN/CREOLE/
OYSTER BAR

Fads come and go, no more so than in the restaurant world. But if you thought the Cajun/Creole phenomenon would fizzle, just check out the full house at Gulf Coast, the East Bay mecca for N'awlins-style gumbo, jambalaya and blackened fish. What sets this place apart is its fresh, updated approach, its personal touches and its immaculately fresh ingredients. The blackened fish (local Pacific snapper, not the overfished Louisiana redfish) comes with oyster crème fraîche and a refreshing cucumber salad; the jambalaya is made with wild rice. Seafood stews contain anything from briny little Olympia oysters to meaty jumbo prawns to perfectly cooked (a rarity!) calamari. Chefs Dan Wormhoudt and Michele Le Prohn fly in much of their seafood from Louisiana and use organic California produce for peak flavor. Desserts, as befits the Southern theme, are good and gooey—if you see a nut tart when you walk in, make sure they save you a slice. Dinner for two, with wine, runs about $75.
Open Mon.-Fri. 11:30 a.m.-2:30 p.m. & 5:30 p.m.-10 p.m., Sat. 5:30 p.m.-10 p.m. Cards: AE, MC, V.

Lalime's

1329 Gilman St.,
Berkeley
• 527-9838
MEDITERRANEAN

From its modest start as a tiny café some five years ago, Lalime's has turned into one of the most popular restaurants in Berkeley, as much appreciated for its easy, low-key ambience as for its delicious food. Haig Krikorian, who owns the place with his wife, Cynthia, and her sister and brother-in-law, explains that while his cooking background is French, his eating habits are definitely Armenian. The food is gutsy, Mediterranean fare, with dishes from France, Italy, Spain and even the Middle East getting equal play on the menu. The partners decorated their newer two-level space (the original Solano Street location is now their café and take-out place, Thyme-Wise) on a shoestring, but with plenty of wit and style. Banquettes along the walls are covered with pastel cotton rag rugs; the ceiling has been sponge-painted in peach. And the windowboxes outside are overflowing with flowers.

Krikorian likes earthy, sharply defined flavors, and his most enthusiastic clients are clearly people who love to eat, including lots of chefs and cooks who come here on their night off. First courses are often a sampling of tastes: perhaps toast topped with shrimp, accompanied with salmon rillettes, homemade pickles and silky Moroccan-style preserved lemons, or Siracusan baked onions served with a head of baked garlic, tapenade and an array of olives. Other good bets include the tasty deep-fried crabcakes served with a tangle of garden greens and aïoli, or the stellar calamari, seared on an iron griddle and served warm, drenched in a lemony vinaigrette. The strong suit here is definitely seafood: sliced, rare ahi tuna and fat roasted prawns with a chile-seared tomatillo salsa and a peppery arugula pesto; warm scallops in a fiery vinaigrette; a sumptuous coulibiac of salmon, a tender pastry crust tucked around a filling of salmon, rice and Swiss chard. But the carnivore is not neglected, as witnessed by the veal chop with creamy polenta, the thick loin lamb chops marinated in Middle Eastern spices, and the New York strip steak served with two subtly different mustard sauces. Desserts are the least interesting part of the menu, but since the entrée portions are hefty, you probably won't have room anyway. Monday nights are reserved for special prix-fixe menus, which are generally about $25. One month, for example, might feature regional French or Italian menus, the next pay tribute to favorite American restaurants, followed by a month of menus by four French women chefs. An à la carte dinner for two, with wine, will range from $65 to $80.

Open Mon.-Thurs. 5:30 p.m.-9:30 p.m., Fri.-Sat. 5:30 p.m.-10:30 p.m. Cards: MC, V.

Nakapan
1971 Martin Luther King Blvd.,
Berkeley
• 548-3050
THAI

11/20

The delicate renditions of Thai favorites here are in direct contrast to the brazen, fire-born dishes served at Siam Cuisine. What is proper Thai, you might ask? We've visited that dreamy country several times and still can't say with certainty whether a given Stateside Thai restaurant is true to form. We think it has to do with the philosophy of individual kitchens. Nakapan's philosophy seems to be that flavors should be arranged like blossoms to make a bouquet on the palate. The ingredients assert themselves individually, and they also coalesce. But enough beating around the bush—to be specific, Nakapan's tom ka gai and som tum are delicious in a delicate way. That doesn't mean they can't blaze, if you so ordain. The decor is handsome, with plenty of wood and indirect lighting, and it's even possible to find a parking space in this transitional neighborhood. Two will spend $45 for dinner with beer.

Open Mon.-Fri. 11 a.m.-3 p.m. & 5 p.m.-10 p.m., Sat. 5 p.m.-10 p.m., Sun. noon-4 p.m. Cards: AE, MC, V.

Oliveto
5655 College Ave.,
Oakland
• 547-5356
ITALIAN/FRENCH

The cuisine of Southern Europe has a near-universal appeal. Who can resist the homey, sun-drenched cooking—its pastas, risotti and polentas; its tomatoes, garlic, peppers, olives, artichokes and citrus fruits; its aïoli, basil and sage; and its biscotti, flan and zabaglione? We certainly can't, which is why we're so fond of Oliveto, a handsome, rough-plastered country restaurant in the middle of Oakland's gentrification district. "Rustic cooking of Italy, France and Spain" is how the management describes the offerings on the daily-changing menu, which will tempt you to order more than you should. Pastas and risotti—with Tuscan sausage and arugula, with red and gold beets and pancetta—are especially successful, as are the various calamari preparations and most of the seafood entrées. The wine list is modest and service is just fine. There's an inexpensive café and tapas bar downstairs. Dinner for two, with wine, will run about $85. *Open Mon.-Sat. 11:30 a.m.-2 p.m. & 6 p.m.-10 p.m. Cards: MC, V.*

Santa Fe Bar & Grill
1310 University Ave.,
Berkeley
• 841-4740
CALIFORNIAN/
SOUTHWESTERN

Jeremiah Tower needs no introduction, but his former showcase needs to be reintroduced in the wake of Tower's departure. The question on everyone's mind, of course, was whether the restaurant would decline in his absence. In our opinion, it hasn't. A few years after his departure, and ostensibly still under Tower's tutelage, Santa Fe's kitchen staff continues to turn out its hybrid Southwestern/French/Californian grill cuisine with flair, and service is as good as it ever was. The rambling white adobe building looks like an old train station on the outside and feels like a hacienda inside. The menu is a primer on the imaginative and deft uses of chiles. About $60 for two, with wine. *Open Mon.-Thurs. 11:30 a.m.-3 p.m. & 5 p.m.-10 p.m., Fri. 11:30 a.m.-3 p.m. & 5 p.m.-11 p.m., Sat. 5 p.m.-11 p.m. All major cards.*

Sedona Grill & Bar
2086 Allston Way,
Berkeley
• 841-3848
SOUTHWESTERN

This is a gorgeous restaurant. Sedona (formerly the Dakota Grill and Bar), just off the lobby of the Shattuck Hotel, has a character and definitive personality that makes it one of the most exciting restaurants in the Bay Area—especially since Southwestern cuisine is still in its infancy here. Sedona has carved out a niche for itself with an inventive menu that changes every couple of weeks. Chiles are a leitmotif, as are corn, onions, and the witty reinvention of Mexican classics. Chimichangas, for example, turn up presented as beautifully as anything in a Japanese kaiseki dinner, stuffed with scallops and black beans in a sweet-and-sour sauce. Tortillas are puréed into a plush, smoky soup holding nuggets of

crisp fried squid. If we have any complaint with Sedona, it's that the chef, Maureen Long, gets so excited about seasonings and sauces that her food can sometimes taste unbalanced. Grilled rabbit with mole sauce barely survived the rich sweetness of its too-generous coating, although the combo of meat and sauce worked well with sweet parsnip fritters and astringent collard greens. Tenderloin of beef was fork-tender, medium rare as ordered, but floundering in an overkill of tomatillo salsa and goat cheese. Despite these imbalances, however, her food tastes marvelous. It's easy to forgive the excess. Desserts at Sedona can be extraordinary: a Bosc pear poached in red wine, stuffed with sweet cream cheese, raisins and candied walnuts, and topped with red-wine ice cream. Dinner for two, with wine, is about $80.
Open Mon. 11:30 a.m.-2:30 p.m., Tues.-Fri. 11:30 a.m.-2:30 p.m. & 5:30 p.m.-9:30 p.m., Sat. 5:30 p.m.-9:30 p.m., Sun. 10 a.m.-2 p.m. & 5:30 p.m.-9:30 p.m. Cards: MC, V.

Siam Cuisine
181 University Ave.,
Berkeley
• 548-3278
THAI

12/20

There's nothing fey or ethereal about this cuisine. The flavors are right there in every bite, and quite welcome at that. If this food were a wine, we'd say it was forward and aggressive. Not that Siam goes for the throat, unless you order the food hot—as we always do. The decor evokes an upscale burger joint more than the Far East, but there's an undeniable wacky charm in eating superb Thai food in a high-backed red vinyl banquette. Perhaps it's for the best that they don't serve martinis. Our very favorite mee krob of all time is served here, and it makes a good foil for such Siam specialties as calamari salad and chicken with sweet basil. Deep-fried tofu with peanut sauce makes an exquisite accompaniment to a spicy seafood dish, such as fresh red snapper in curry sauce. Dinner for two, with beer, will be about $35.
Open Sun.-Thurs. 5 p.m.-11 p.m., Fri.-Sat. 5 p.m.-midnight. Cards: MC, V.

Union Hotel
401 1st St.,
Benicia
• (707) 746-0368
CALIFORNIAN

Here's an intimate little hotel in the sleepy little town of Benicia, 45 minutes from San Francisco. The dining room, under the direction of Israeli filmmaker-turned-chef Lev Dagan, offers some of the most honest, imaginative cuisine in the greater Bay Area. The menu varies twice a day and changes completely every few weeks. We love the fact that much of the produce, the dairy products and even some of the meat comes from local farmers. Pizzettas and pastas have strong, clear flavors. Dagan's not afraid to have fun with garlic and fresh herbs. The mixed organic-greens salad with edible blossoms couldn't be a more effective palate cleanser. Main dishes are equally straightforward and alive with flavor. A New York steak with Jack Daniels sauce, green peppers and roasted red potatoes was a lovely piece of meat, medium rare as requested, its sauce provocative. Pan-fried halibut with fresh mango chutney was nutty, juicy and delicious. Portions are generous, and all the steamed vegetables have clear, clean tastes. The reasonably priced wine list also changes frequently, featuring predominantly Californian wines. Desserts are too sweet for our taste, heavily weighted toward chocolate, although pleasant enough for a bite or two. Dinner for two, with wine, is about $75. *Open Tues.-Sat. 11:30 a.m.-2:30 p.m. & 6 p.m.-10 p.m., Sun. 11:30 a.m.-2:30 p.m. & 5:30 p.m.-9:30 p.m. All major cards.*

Yoshi's Restaurant & Nightspot
6030 Claremont Ave., Oakland
• 652-9200
JAPANESE /SUSHI

10/20

With the huge video screens playing music, constant crowds, two bustling dining rooms and an always-busy sushi bar, Yoshi's is sort of a "Jazzanese" Disneyland. Over the years it has developed a reputation as having some of the best Japanese food in the East Bay. Well, yes and no. The sushi is generally excellent, but on several recent visits we've been disappointed with the cooked offerings, which, though always beautifully presented, have been uneven in quality. An extensive platter that feeds two or three is layed out as exquisitely as a scientific diorama of the Earth, with a medley of tempura, yakitori, teriyaki chicken, grilled beef, raw vegetables and fruit, and a choice of lobster or sashimi. Unfortunately, the teriyaki can be achingly salty, the tempura shrimp and vegetables are suffocated by a too-dense, oily batter, and calamari suffer the same fate. The grilling techniques are solid; it's the sauces that have let us down. Dinner for two, with saké or beer, averages $50. *Open Mon.-Thurs. 11 a.m.-2:30 p.m. & 5:30 p.m.-9:30 p.m., Fri. 11 a.m.-2:30 p.m. & 5:30 p.m.-10 p.m., Sat. 5:30 p.m.-10 p.m. (sushi bar open until midnight). Cards: MC, V.*

Yujean's Modern Cuisine of China
843 San Pablo Ave., Albany
• 525-8557
CHINESE

The only question is whether it's worth finding your way to the darkest depths of the East Bay, to Albany, for a fine contemporary Chinese meal. Wine-lovers will definitely say yes—owner/chef Yujean Kang is a connoisseur with a penchant for Burgundies, red and white, and the richer California wines. He prices them to sell, too, which is good because that style of wine is just right with the focused, well-defined flavors of Yujean's cuisine. Sautéed (actually, dry-fried) French beans have a ginger-garlic zing. Things heat up with Szechuan spicy lamb, which derives a broad range of flavors from frying with several different types of peppers. The best thing we've had is tea-smoked duck, similar to Celadon's version of the classic but with extra dimensions of flavor from smoking over jasmine tea. Chicken with pungent garlic is unexpectedly fiery—just the thing with a luscious, slightly older Chardonnay. If you order 24 hours in advance, the kitchen will prepare such dishes as wild boar with glazed hazelnuts, shiitakes and sesame seeds; venison with green beans and plum-oyster sauce; and sturgeon with kumquats and passion fruit. Despite the sophistication of the wine and food, this is not a fancy place. The room is almost nondescript, with uninspired lighting and a few simple Chinese scroll paintings against cream-colored walls. Customers are often dressed in jeans and athletic shoes. All the drama, all the glamour, is in the food and drink. About $60 for two, with wine. *Open Tues.-Sun. 11 a.m.-2:30 p.m. & 4 p.m.-10 p.m. Cards: AE, MC, V.*

QUICK BITES

The East Bay is heaven for café-hoppers and low-budget gourmands. From Oakland's barbecue houses to Berkeley's diners, you can find every kind of quick meal for very little money. We can't possibly cover the myriad cafés, coffeehouses and joints in the U.C. Berkeley area, but we can tell you to wander Telegraph Avenue and College Avenue near the campus, where you'll be tempted by espresso bars, pizza-by-the-slice joints, ethnic restaurants and lively pubs, all of which offer low prices and great people-watching. And we can tell you about our very favorite East Bay quick bites.

Bette's Ocean View Diner
1807A 4th St.,
Berkeley
• 644-3230

Using the best ingredients—farm-fresh eggs, smoky black beans, fresh salsa and homemade muffins, scones and tortillas—Bette's takes breakfast classics to new heights. The pancake here is actually a huge but delicate soufflé encasing either apple and brandy or banana and rum. On weekends, eggs, linguiça (Portuguese pork sausage), bell peppers, onions and home fries combine into a bountiful, wondrous dish called the Farmer's Scramble. Bette's huevos rancheros comprise two sunny-side-up eggs topped with melted cheese and salsa and served with black beans and tortillas. Because of these creations, patrons are willing to wait interminable lengths of time to get into this bright, new-wavish diner; the owners have tried to accommodate those who won't wait by opening a take-out shop next door stocked with Bette's excellent baked goods, coffee and espresso. The lunches aren't quite as inspired as the morning meal, but they're still well above average. Pizza fans should head for Bette's Bakeshop, 1926 Shattuck. About

$20 for a breakfast feast for two.
Open Mon. 6:30 a.m.-2:30 p.m., Tues.-Sat. 6:30 a.m.-4 p.m., Sun. 6:30 a.m.-4 p.m. No cards.

Café Fanny
1603 San Pablo Ave.,
Berkeley
• 524-5447, 524-5451

Devotees of Californian cuisine make regular pilgrimages to Chez Panisse, the restaurant that started it all. If you're such a devotee, but have neither big money to spend nor patience to wait three weeks for a reservation, then hie yourself to Café Fanny, Alice Waters's gem of a café named for her daughter. The tiny food bar has no tables, just one bench inside and a couple of benches outside. But never mind the setting—we'd eat one of Café Fanny's sandwiches on a refuse heap if it came to that. Waters's love of just-picked garden products shows in these sandwiches, which pair meats and cheeses with watercress, radishes, red peppers and the like. Try the baked ham and watercress on foccacia, a thick, savory, pastry-like bread baked with herbs and olive oil. Or come for breakfast and lose yourself in a bowl of steaming cappuccino and outstanding buckwheat crêpes, prosciutto toast or marvelous eggs from free-ranging hens. About $16 for breakfast or lunch for two, with an espresso or a glass of wine.
Open Mon.-Fri. 7 a.m.-3 p.m., Sat. 8 a.m.-4 p.m., Sun. 9 a.m.-3 p.m. No cards (checks accepted).

Café Oliveto
5655 College Ave.,
Oakland
• 547-5356

That the Rockridge section of Oakland is undergoing rapid gentrification is evidenced by the opening of places like Café Oliveto, a chic tapas bar with a very handsome Mediterranean decor. While patrons at the upstairs restaurant sample large plates of rustic Italian/Spanish food, those at the downstairs café nibble on small savory dishes from the menu of innovative tapas (essentially glorified appetizers). Everything we've tried has been good: calamari in a tomato-caper sauce; chicken and linguiça (pork sausage), an inspired tart of roasted garlic, mozzarella and basil; delectable little pizzas; and more. A few tapas (priced at $2.75 to $3.50 each) and a glass of Chardonnay from the small but select list make for a very pleasant lunch or supper. (The upstairs restaurant also serves tapas on Mondays.) About $30 for two, with wine.
Open for tapas Mon.-Thurs. 11:30 a.m.-11 p.m., Fri. 11:30 a.m.-midnight, Sat. noon-midnight, Sun. noon-10 p.m. Cards: MC, V.

Flint's

3814 San Pablo Ave.,
Oakland
• 658-9912
6609 Shattuck Ave.,
Oakland
• 653-0593
6672 E. 14th St.,
Oakland
• 569-1312

Although upstarts are ever crowding on the horizon, no one has yet managed to usurp Flint's position as the Bay Area's barbecue leader. The sound of surly women hacking away at smoked meats is music to the ears of the fanatic customers who come into the shabby, smoky Flint's outlets to pick up ribs, chicken, links or barbecued-beef sandwiches. Flint's barbecue is a match made in heaven: perfectly smoked meat married to an almost mystical hot sauce. And, of course, it wouldn't be authentic barbecue without the slices of Wonder bread and the scoops of overly sweet potato salad. Flint's only failure is with dessert: the sweet potato pie is depressingly gelatinous and smacks of long hours sitting on a shelf. Nonetheless, the barbecue buck stops here. A whole slab of ribs is about $14, a chicken $8. *Open daily 11 a.m.-2 a.m.*
Open Sun.-Thurs. 11 a.m.-2 a.m., Fri.-Sat. 11 a.m.-4 a.m.
Open Sun.-Thurs. 11 a.m.-midnight, Fri.-Sat. 11 a.m.-3 a.m. No cards.

Kirala

2100 Ward St.,
Berkeley
• 549-3486

Like tapas, its Spanish equivalent, Japanese robata has been slow to catch on in the Bay Area. But if the crowds at Kirala are any indication, that may be changing. The appetizer-like dishes offer a new understanding of Japanese cuisine—a refreshing alternative to the usual teriyaki and tempura. Since Kirala's take on the latter dishes is strictly routine, make a meal of the wonderfully grilled robata items like aspara beef, rivets of perfectly cooked asparagus stuffed between tender slices of beef; tsukune, delightfully spiced chicken meatballs; kaki, oysters cooked in soy and sake. The chef also does impressive things with chicken gizzards, eel and baby corn. Prices hover around $2, so you can sample quite a smorgasbord. About $30 for two, with saké or beer. *Open Tues.-Sat. 5:30 p.m.-9:30 p.m., Sun. 5 p.m.-8:30 p.m. All major cards.*

Picante

1328 6th St.,
Berkeley
• 525-3121, 526-9779

The kind of Mexican food found at the best Mission District taquerias has finally made it to Berkeley. Like all taquerias, Picante has no decor to speak of, looking rather like a college dorm cafeteria, but its tacos, burritos, tostadas and nachos are unimpeachable. The soft-shell taco crammed with exceptionally juicy chorizo is almost a meal in itself, and the nachos—drenched in fine melted jack cheese and crowned with luscious fresh hot salsa—certainly make a meal. The pork, beef and chicken chunks, well grilled and tender, are in no danger of being overwhelmed by runny sauce and tepid refried beans. And the carnitas, tortas and

quesadillas are all superb. About $12 for two, with beer.
*Open Mon.-Thurs. 11 a.m.-10 p.m., Fri. 11 a.m.-midnight,
Sat. noon-midnight. No cards.*

Saul's Restaurant & Delicatessen
1475 Shattuck Ave.,
Berkeley
• 848-3354

While not the Carnegie, Saul's has been doing an adequate
job in filling that most conspicuous of Bay Area cuisine
gaps: the kosher-style deli. Saul's flies pastrami in from New
York and serves melt-in-your-mouth lox, real kippered
salmon, concentrated chicken soup with airy matzo balls,
sandwiches piled high (though not as high as the Empire
State Building), tangy coleslaw and a fabulous cheesecake.
In those deli classics, Saul's shines, though there are a few
disappointments, especially the excessively doughy blintzes.
Moderately dilled pickles and tomatoes are brought to your
table gratis, and dinnertime sees such standards as roast
chicken and Hungarian beef goulash. About $28 for two,
with beer, wine, or Doctor Brown's soda.
*Open Mon.-Fri. 10:30 a.m.-9 p.m., Sat.-Sun. 9 a.m.-9 p.m.
No cards.*

The Swallow
University Art Museum,
2625 Durant Ave.,
Berkeley
• 841-2409

University cafeterias are usually home to the most shocking
food—from mystery "Mexican" casseroles to strange Jell-O
salads. But leave it to Berkeley to surprise us with this
cafeteria on the lower level of the campus art museum. The
chefs here do wondrous things with eggs and cheese,
whipping up inspired quiches and frittatas. We took a lean
"Roast Beast" sandwich (served on excellent homemade
French bread), a buttery shortcake and an espresso outside
to the sculpture garden and ate in the glorious sunshine.
We couldn't have asked for a more satisfying simple lunch.
Between the museum, The Swallow and the wonderful
Pacific Film Archive, one could do much worse than spend
an entire day in this building. About $15 for lunch for two,
with a glass of wine.
*Open Wed.-Sat. 11 a.m.-8 p.m., Tues. & Sun. 11 a.m.-5 p.m.
No cards.*

Taquería Morelia
4481-91 E. 14th St.,
Oakland
• 261-6360

This is not a neck of the woods you're likely to find yourself
in, unless it's to visit Taquería Morelia, which raises the
creation of burritos, tacos and tortas (Mexican sandwiches)
to a high art. There's no pretense to ambience here, just a
loving devotion to good food. As is always the case with a
superior taquería, freshness makes the difference: the meats,
beans and salsas really stand out, instead of congealing into
a blob. Unlike most taquerias, Morelia offers a full menu of
tortas, made with ham, chicken, carnitas and chorizo. If

Morelia is crowded, take your food to the adjoining bar, Talk of the Town, which is under the same ownership. About $16 for two, with beer.
Open Mon.-Thurs. 10 a.m.-11 p.m., Fri. 10 a.m.-1 a.m., Sat. 10 a.m.-11 p.m., Sun. 10 a.m.-10 p.m. No cards.

Top Dog
2534 Durant Ave.,
Berkeley
• 339-0304

The occasional craving for a hot dog should not be denied, but, unfortunately, the Bay Area has few good hot dog stands. Berkeley's phone-booth–size Top Dog stands, however, have been holding the top-dog spot for many years now, offering all kinds of dogs, including a kosher New York–style frank (which holds its own against *any* N.Y. deli dog), kielbasa, smoked Bratwurst, Italian calabrese and Top Dog's own all-American frank. We found ourselves unable to resist trying six varieties, each flawless on a seeded French bun. Our stomachs paid the price, but it was worth it. A couple of dogs and a soda apiece will cost two $8.
Open Sun.-Thurs. 10 a.m.-2 a.m., Fri.-Sat. 10 a.m.-3 a.m. No cards.

Zachary's Pizza
5801 College Ave.,
Oakland
• 655-6385
1853 Solano Ave.,
Berkeley
• 525-5950

Zachary's offers both normal and deep-dish pizza, the latter being the Bay Area's closest approximation of the Chicago-style pizza. Crusts are thick and crisp, and the sauce, cheese and toppings are well layered; the end product is more like an Italian bread casserole than a pizza. But even though a lot of care goes into these pizzas, the fresh-tasting tomato sauce lacks zest. Still and all, Zachary's pizzas are among the very best around. Lines form early, and since the pizzas take longer than usual to cook, it's a good idea to order ahead. About $17 for a pizza for two, with beer.
Open Sun.-Thurs. 11 a.m.-10 p.m., Fri.-Sat. 11 a.m.-10:30 p.m. No cards.

HOTELS

Claremont Resort Hotel
41 Tunnel Rd., Oakland
• 843-3000,
Fax 848-6208

Many millions of dollars in restoration have given new life to this grand old lady of the East Bay, and now the great white Claremont—with its tower, cupolas, 22 acres of grounds and 1915 resort-hotel architecture—is almost as attractive on the inside as it is on the outside. The latest addition is a full-service spa where guests (and nonguests) may get facials, massages and other treatments. Though large, the Claremont is quiet and makes a perfect romantic hideaway, especially if you request a room with a view of

San Francisco. Amenities include an Olympic-size pool, ten tennis courts, a nearby golf course, a bar with a great city view and an equally view-struck stylish restaurant that is a favorite of the Sunday-brunch set. Such details as high ceilings and moldings add period charm to the spacious rooms, which have all been comfortably furnished.
Singles: $145-$210; doubles: $165-$240; suites: $275-$700. Weekend & other discount packages available.

Gramma's Bed and Breakfast Inn
2740 Telegraph Ave., Berkeley
• 549-2145,
No fax

For anyone who never had a grandmother to visit, this house will make up for all the lost years. Never mind that there's no real McCoy on the premises. The closest thing is the portrait of Elizabeth Taber that hangs in the stairwell of the original house. (An Irish immigrant who ran a Boston boardinghouse, Taber was the grandmother of a former innkeeper and probably inspired such practices as keeping full jars of cookies stashed around the house.) Floral wallpaper and handmade quilts still characterize the original accommodations in this Belle Epoque Tudor-style mansion and in the nearby Fay House. Over the years, Gramma's house has evolved into Gramma's compound with the opening of two new buildings, bringing the total room count to 30. The Carriage House is a welcome choice for guests who prefer larger quarters; fireplaces and wicker furniture distinguish the eight rooms in the Garden House. Come dawn, every guest may feel he or she really is at Gramma's bountiful table. Located just a short walk from the U.C. Berkeley campus, this inn is a cozy alternative to the large hotels and tiny motels more typical of the East Bay.
Singles & doubles: $85-$175.

Hotel Durant
2600 Durant Ave., Berkeley
• 845-8981,
Fax 486-8336

This modest old hotel is popular with professors, lecturers and parents visiting their U.C. Berkeley students and children in school just a block away. Though the 140 rooms are plain and rather shabby, the location is perfect for enjoying both the campus and the many restaurants and shops of central Berkeley. The hotel houses a restaurant and a bar. Added bonus: guests can buy passes to use U.C. Berkeley's pool, gym and tennis courts.
Singles: $80; doubles: $90; suites: $99-$180.

MARIN COUNTY

RESTAURANTS

Avenue Grill
44 E. Blithedale Ave.,
Mill Valley
• 388-6003
AMERICAN/
INTERNATIONAL

11/20

The Avenue Grill is one of a new breed of restaurants that try to put the fun back into fundamental American food, but it doesn't always succeed. American heartland standards like meatloaf, mashed potatoes, hamburgers and grilled spit-roasted chicken are dressed up with garlic, unusual sauces or offbeat garnishes. Sometimes this approach works—we love the garlic mashed potatoes with rich brown gravy, even if they're overpriced. And we like the fact that you can order anything from Cajun cooking to sashimi. But sometimes the food comes across as simply gimmicky. The chef is nothing if not inventive. A wacky illustrated calendar, published monthly, advertises nightly specials like Oinker Heaven, paella, turkey dinners with all the trimmings or Caribbean food. There's always an unusual fish and pasta of the day. The regular menu is heavy with good, though pricey, appetizers, like deep-fried coconut shrimp with mango-papaya chutney; delicious whole-kernel corn cakes with black beans, tomato salsa and sour cream; and garlicky chicken wings. One of the Avenue Grill's problems is that it has become so popular, you'll probably have at least an hour's wait. There's a somewhat odd selection of beers, a nice range of California wines by the glass and a decent wine list. Dinner for two comes in at about $60, including wine. *Open Mon.-Thurs. & Sun. 5:30 p.m.-10 p.m., Fri.-Sat. 5:30 p.m.-11 p.m. Cards: MC, V.*

Butler's
625 Redwood Hwy.,
Mill Valley
• 383-1900
AMERICAN/
INTERNATIONAL

Mill Valley is the laid-back, white-on-white heart of California yuppieland. Appropriately, Butler's is practically all white, with a pale hardwood floor. Before sunset, all the wood and the wide wraparound windows, with their views of water and woods, give the place the feeling of a cabin on an anchored yacht. By night, both the art on the walls and the open kitchen gain more visual importance. But day or night, the real show is the soap opera–caliber clientele. Butler's is upstairs from Perry's, the Marin saloon operated by Perry Butler and based on his incredibly successful saloon on Union Street in San Francisco. Butler's is the most serious restaurant of the three. The food is consistently excellent, thanks to chef Heidi Krahling. The menu changes periodically according to her whims and interests, which means there is always considerable enthusiasm behind whatever's coming out of the kitchen. One thing that doesn't change is Krahling's predilection for locally grown organic produce and meats. A splendid sunset supper one evening consisted of a fine Caesar salad of organic romaine from Bolinas, with a bold garlicky dressing and plenty of Parmesan, along with fresh-baked Italian country bread and a glass of Sauvignon Blanc. Another evening a grilled, marinated half chicken was succulent, as were the corn pancakes that accompanied it. And Krahling appreciates Mexican cooking; her carne asada, served with salsa, avocado and black beans, is consistently excellent. Butler's does very well by Mill Valley, and vice versa. About $70 for two, with wine.

Open Mon.-Sat. 5:30 p.m.-10 p.m., Sun. 5:30 p.m.-9 p.m. All major cards.

Cactus Cafe
393 Miller Ave.,
Mill Valley
• 388-8226
MEXICAN

This little laid-back, blue-eyed Mexican place is loads of fun. There's nothing pretentious about the food, but it does have a certain flair and it's uniformly delicious. An added bonus is the location near the Marin Theatre Company and the 2 AM Club. Our favorite dish is the Mexican eggplant—corn tortillas topped with grilled eggplant and attractively served with spicy green and red sauces. Chef Mike Hann also puts together nicely balanced, tasty enchiladas, burritos and rich seafood gumbo, using a lot of grilled meats and vegetables. A very good beer selection matches the food beautifully. About $40 for two, with beer.

Open daily 11:30 a.m.-9:30 p.m. Cards: AE, MC, V.

Caprice
2000 Paradise Dr.,
Tiburon
• 435-3400
FRENCH

11/20

This is one of the most romantic restaurants in the Bay Area. The contrast between a spectacular view of San Francisco and the Bay, and the dreamy, intimate dining room creates a creamy sensuality that is ably abetted by deft service. We're not exaggerating. The food is in the sumptuous vein and is well done, but of an older order, not the kind of thing foodies get excited about these days. But who cares? Foodies have no hearts anyway, and hearts are what Caprice is all about. The wine list has some extraordinary French selections at pretty reasonable prices. Two can spend $100 for dinner with wine without trying too hard.

Open Mon.-Thurs. 6 p.m.-9:30 p.m., Fri.-Sat. 6 p.m.-10 p.m. All major cards.

Casa Madrona
801 Bridgeway,
Sausalito
• 331-5888
CALIFORNIAN

12/20

We love this place, especially during crab and salmon seasons. The view of Sausalito's postcard-perfect harbor is just what we want to see while we munch a little fresh salmon with herb sauce, suck down a few crisp oysters on the half shell, or address a delectable Dungeness or soft-shelled crustacean. A spot of Chardonnay doesn't hurt, either. The food is heartwarming, though not fantastically delicate, and the Californian/French menu has an interesting touch of sunny Italy to it, as telegraphed by the liberal use of pancetta and flavorful vine-ripened tomatoes. Service is friendly, but there's often a wait, even with reservations. We finished dinner around midnight on our last visit, and wished we'd booked a room for the night. Next time. About $80 for a romantic dinner for two, with wine.
Open Mon.-Thurs. 11:30 a.m.-2:30 p.m. & 6 p.m.-10 p.m., Fri. 11:30 a.m.-2:30 p.m. & 6 p.m.-11 p.m., Sat. 6 p.m.-10 p.m., Sun. 10 a.m.-2:30 p.m. Cards: AE, MC, V.

Guaymas
5 Main St.,
Tiburon
• 435-6300
MEXICAN

12/20

Guaymas is yet another of Spectrum Foods' trendy, chic restaurants, and true to the formula that begat Tutto Bene, Prego and Ciao (among others), it is great looking, attracts quite a crowd and serves respectably decent food. Guaymas deserves kudos for attempting to bring regional Mexican cuisine to the masses—it's sort of a go-go version of L.A.'s Border Grill. The restaurant itself is spectacular, with a drop-dead location—right on the ferry pier, with a great waterside view—and a sun-washed, adobe-moderne decor. This is no intimate cantina—the rooms are quite large, and the fact that your waitperson punches your order into one of those infernal little hand-held computerized doohickeys adds to the corporate feel. The dishes range from very good to merely okay; consistently excellent, however, are the salsas (tomatillo, spicy tomato and sweet-hot chile) served with the fat, hot homemade corn tortillas. The guacamole is chunky and freshly prepared, though a bit lackluster—we found ourselves spooning gobs of salsa into it to goose it a little. We enjoyed the green-corn tamales, absolutely fresh and sweet, and the gorditas were quite tasty as well. The carnachas, little tarts filled with a mixture of black beans, tomatoes and cheese, were a bit on the chewy side, though the deep-fried quesadilla oozing with chiles and cheeses was terrific. It's best to stick to the appetizers; the main dishes, especially the seafood ones, are a bit disappointing. As for the desserts, we had a love-hate relationship with the avocado pie (which tasted more like lemon cream); after the first couple of bites, it was cloying. But the frozen-fruit ices are most refreshing. The whole of Guaymas adds up to more than the sum of its parts, though—its liveliness, loveliness and great location truly add a lot to the experience of dining here. Dinner for two, with beer, should run about $60.

Open Mon.-Thurs. 11:30 a.m.-10 p.m., Fri.-Sat. 11:30 a.m.-11 p.m., Sun. 10:30 a.m.-10 p.m. Cards: AE, MC, V.

La Lanterna
799 College Ave.,
Kentfield
• 258-0144
ITALIAN

"Everyone should try being Italian at least once a week." That's the motto of La Lanterna's "adopted Italian" chef/owner, Jim Brown. Having decided long ago that his Italian friends were having more fun—and eating better—than he was, he began to surround himself with things Italian, right down to the temperamental Italian Rototiller he bought to tend the restaurant's Mediterranean garden. The menu at La Lanterna reflects his passion. Both ambitious and authentic, it leapfrogs all over Italy's boot with carefully researched and executed recipes. Brown's specials—which recently have included tagliolini neri con cozze, black squid-ink pasta with New Zealand mussels in a dense cream sauce; risotto con funghi, with a bushel of assorted wild mushrooms; and spiedino di tonno, grilled skewered tuna with polenta and vegetables—make use of the market's daily bounty. Pastas are house-made, including the ingenious two-toned pappardelle topped rustically with sausage, red and yellow bell peppers and tomato sauce. On a separate, heart-healthy menu, "Il Cuore Sano," chef Brown eschews the fat (as well as the salt, sugar and dairy products). Such dishes as linguine di pescatore, swimming with clams, mussels, calamari and prawns, are so good—and so generous—that you'd scarcely know this was diet food. What's more, chef Brown hosts frequent winemaker dinners, whose prix-fixe of $35 includes wine with each course. Despite its unlikely location, in an out-of-the-way shopping center in a small Marin college town, La Lanterna is more than worth the drive, for the taped Neapolitan love songs, the new Pat Kuleto–inspired interior (peach textured walls, faux-marble columns, muted glass sconces) and the lovingly prepared food. Chances are you'll want to be Italian, too, at least once a week. Dinner for two, with wine, runs about $70.

Open Tues.-Sat. 5:30 p.m.-10 p.m., Sun. 5 p.m.-9 p.m. Cards: AE, MC, V.

Lark Creek Inn
234 Magnolia Ave.,
Larkspur
• 924-7766
AMERICAN

The service is as bad as the food is fabulous at this latest avatar of American food messiah Bradley Ogden. But waves of attitude from a smarmy staff can't totally spoil the experience. The eats are worth some annoyance—this is the kind of cooking Mom (the Mom of fable and myth) would have done if she'd been turned on the way Ogden is—he calls his cuisine "American regional cooking with gusto." To begin with, there's a timeless American feeling about the venerable inn and the redwood trees around it. The dramatically remodeled interior focuses on an oakwood-fired grilling/baking station at center stage, which is the source of much that makes this cuisine distinctive. The menu changes nightly, but it always has something to do with the grill, as in an oak-roasted pork loin chop at dinner or an herbed flatbread at lunch. There are usually fresh local oysters available, and two or three fresh fish, along with such newly palatable American standards as liver and braised oxtail. We loved a saffron risotto with crisp duck confit one evening, and have been pleased by several variations on the classic corn fritter, notably the one with shrimp and scallions. Breakfast features such wonders as salmon hash with poached egg, and warm bread-and-butter custard. The wine list is marvelous, although most of the selections are too young. Getting reservations is as difficult as getting tickets to a Broadway hit, but the full menu is available in the bar to walk-ins. About $100 for two, with wine.
Open Mon.-Thurs. 11:30 a.m.-2:30 p.m. & 5:30 p.m.-10 p.m., Fri. 11:30 a.m.-2:30 p.m. & 5:30 p.m.-11 p.m., Sat. 5:30 p.m.-11 p.m., Sun. 10 a.m.-2:30 p.m. & 5:30 p.m.-10 p.m. All major cards.

Marin Joe's
1585 Casa Buena Dr.,
Corte Madera
• 924-2081
ITALIAN/AMERICAN

9/20

It doesn't try to be what it's not, which is a terrific restaurant. It doesn't have to try to be what it is, which is a comfortable, passable restaurant in a perfectly convenient location off Highway 101. We've frequently gone hungry during a road trip just because the choice of roadside restaurants was too awful to face. Marin Joe's easily solves that problem in this neck of the freeway. Its quasi-Italian setting ("ambience" is too strong a word) fits the hearty, Italian-American workingperson's menu. We've had good mushroom omelets and steaks here (the filet mignon is great), but more often than not we go for the no-nonsense spaghetti with meat sauce and garlic bread, or the osso buco and a nice, crisp salad. The wine list is terrible, but there's a decent choice of beers. About $40 for two, with beer.
Open Mon.-Fri. 11 a.m.-12:45 a.m., Sat. 5 p.m.-12:45 a.m., Sun. 4 p.m.-11:45 p.m. All major cards.

North Sea Harbor Village

300 Turney St.,
Sausalito
• 331-3300
CHINESE

11/20

Making reservations at this place can be problematic, but even arriving without reservations, we've generally been seated within ten to twenty minutes. But even if you have to wait awhile, the dim sum is worth it—especially during the day, when you can enjoy a cheerful view of San Francisco Bay and the adjacent docks full of sailboats. There's not enough space between the tables here to accommodate rolling carts, so waiters—many of whom don't speak English—carry trays full of dainty offerings around the two levels of dining rooms. If you want to know what's inside the mysterious, temptingly translucent noodle wrappers, you'll be out of luck. Take your chances, though, because we've had some of the lightest, most delicate dim sum in the Bay Area at this restaurant. The steamed dumplings stuffed with pork, shrimp or mixed vegetables are our favorites. We also loved steamed lotus leaf, wrapped around a mixture of sticky rice and stuffed with pork and egg. What we don't love is the wine list. The prices are so disproportionate to the food prices that it's somehow insulting. Also, on a recent visit, we discovered that of eight interesting-sounding desserts listed on the menu, not one was available. A dim sum lunch for two costs about $20; dinner (less satisfying than dim sum) for two, with wine, is about $50. *Open Mon.-Fri. 11 a.m.-3 p.m. & 5 p.m.-10 p.m., Sat.-Sun. 10 a.m.-3 p.m. & 5 p.m.-10 p.m. Cards: AE, V.*

Ristorante Giramonte

655 Redwood Hwy.,
Mill Valley
• 383-3000
ITALIAN

11/20

Founded and run by the Giramonte family with cooking by chef Adriana Giramonte, this is one of Marin's most popular Italian restaurants. It's situated right on Richardson Bay, so there's a lovely view of the water in the early evening. We recommend skipping the appetizers. Except for an unripe tomato, basil and mozzarella salad and a mixed antipasto plate, the starters tend to be variations on the theme of lettuce. Instead, head straight for the main courses. If you're lucky enough to be served by the waiter who virtually sings the daily specials, you'll enjoy a melodic recitative of such dishes as linguine tutto mare, gnocchi with tomato sauce and cheese, and rabbit in wine sauce with polenta. Eggplant Parmigiana is densely satisfyingd: thick slices of the lightly fried vegetable in a sparkling tomato sauce with tender, melted cheese. Veal scaloppine with steamed vegetables and a wild-mushroom sauce is also a good choice. Save room for the excellent cold zabaglione served over seasonal berries. The wine list is unexciting but competent, with a few California and Italian choices by the glass. Dinner for two, with wine, runs $60. *Open Tues.-Sun. 5 p.m.-10 p.m. Cards: AE, MC, V.*

Royal Thai
610 3rd St.,
San Rafael
• 485-1074
THAI

A few years ago, fans of Khan Toke Thai House in San Francisco were horrified to learn that certain members of the kitchen crew had defected to Marin. The kitchen closed ranks and everything was fine, and the upshot is that now there's an outstanding Thai restaurant in San Rafael. Royal Thai is small, occupying one wing of a large old house that's been converted into a mini shopping mall. The Thai crêpe is the best we've tried, and the pad Thai has a deep, rich flavor with real tang. Don't be afraid of hot dishes—the flavors in everything we've tried have been well balanced. The wine list is unusually fine. Two will spend about $40, including wine.
Open Mon.-Thurs. 11 a.m.-2:30 p.m. & 5 p.m.-9:30 p.m., Fri. 11 a.m.-2:30 p.m. & 5 p.m.-10 p.m., Sat. 5 p.m.-10 p.m., Sun. 5 p.m.-9:30 p.m. All major cards.

Savannah Grill
55 Tamal Vista Blvd.,
Corte Madera
• 924-6774
AMERICAN

10/20

It's hard to say what Savannah has to do with this place. If we're talking Africa, perhaps it's the grilled and house-smoked meats (just like the lions eat); if it's the Belle of Georgia, then we're in nebulous territory. There's little Southern food, but there is a nod to Southwestern, especially in the spicy sauces on some fish dishes. The rest is basic grill 'n' graze, with a well-chosen list of wines by the glass. The location in a shopping mall bodes poorly, but the wood, brass and frosted-glass interior, with comfortable booths, is pleasant. About $60 for two, with wine.
Open Mon.-Thurs. 11:30 a.m.-4:30 p.m. & 5:30 p.m.-10 p.m., Fri.-Sat. 11:30 a.m.-4:30 p.m. & 5:30 p.m.-10:30 p.m., Sun. 11:30 a.m.-9:30 p.m. Cards: AE, MC, V.

HOTELS

Casa Madrona
805 Bridgeway,
Sausalito
• 332-0502,
Fax 332-2537

Some rooms are small, some could have a bit more style, but most have wonderful views of the idyllic Sausalito harbor. It has the size (39 rooms) and amenities of a small hotel but the warmth and ambience of a bed-and-breakfast, including a communal breakfast and evening gatherings for wine and cheese. Depending on the location, accommodations vary greatly in decor: romantic Victorian in the main house, country in the cottages and a mix of contemporary styles in the newer rooms that cascade down the hill toward the waterfront. Moreover, Casa Madrona can also accommodate you in a nearby houseboat. At the hotel itself, amenities include a hot tub and a lovely restaurant that serves some mean seafood.
Singles & doubles: $90-$200.

Mountain Home Inn
810 Panoramic Hwy.,
Mill Valley
• 381-9000,
No fax

With this location—cantilevered off a scenic hillside more than halfway up Mount Tamalpais—just about any inn would suffice. But this inn would be beautiful anywhere. Slim redwood trunks rise through the lobby, stretching to the sky above. The lobby shares the entry level with a small bar and a dining deck with a commanding view to the east and south. A more formal restaurant is located downstairs. Ten large rooms are carved out of the hillside, all decorated with such soothing colors as beige and apricot, and all sporting views. Some have Jacuzzis, private decks and/or fireplaces. This is an exceptionally romantic hideaway located within yards of some of the mountain's best trails. *Singles & doubles: $112-$178.*

Pelican Inn
Hwy. 1, Muir Beach
• 383-6000,
No fax

Marin County is blessed with more public open space than some small states, and, fortunately, with a number of country-style inns close to the action. The Pelican Inn has a strong Tudor personality that may not suit everyone but certainly suits the site, close to both Muir Beach and Muir Woods. Within this old farmhouse are six cozy guest rooms, all with private baths and each decorated with English antiques, canopied beds and Oriental rugs laid on hardwood floors. With its expansive lawn, flowering vines and ground-floor pub—complete with roaring fireplace—the Pelican Inn evokes an English countryside cottage. *Singles & doubles: $115-$145.*

WINE COUNTRY

RESTAURANTS

John Ash & Co.
4330 Barnes Rd.
(River Rd. exit off Hwy. 101),
Santa Rosa
• (707) 527-7687
CALIFORNIAN/FRENCH

Vineyards just outside the large windows set the tone for a quintessential wine-country dining experience. The spacious restaurant gains a design-magazine California-ness from earthenware tile floors and pastel stucco walls, lit to emphasize the wide-window views of producing vineyards. Ash's cuisine can seem eccentric or inspired, depending on how well it works. Sometimes it seems exploratory in nature, as in taking a particular spice (cumin, for example) too far. But the menus are always interesting. And the food merits an additional point above our last rating. We've enjoyed artichoke ravioli with smoked salmon, lamb loin in a hot-sweet mustard sauce, pork with local raspberries, and veal sweetbreads with Zinfandel and fig sauce. And we've always enjoyed the experience. You'll need to make reservations up to three weeks in advance. A five-course prix-fixe meal is offered nightly for $42.50; otherwise, expect to spend $100 for dinner for two, with wine.

Open Tues.-Thurs. 11:30 a.m.-1:45 p.m. & 6 p.m.-9:30 p.m., Fri. 11:30 a.m.-1:45 p.m. & 6 p.m.-10 p.m., Sat. 6 p.m.-10 p.m., Sun. 10:30 a.m.-2 p.m. All major cards.

Auberge du Soleil
180 Rutherford Hill Rd., Rutherford
• (707) 963-1211
FRENCH

From the first impression of rosy adobe, tile, wicker and foliage, this could be the governor's dining room at a French colonial outpost on some subtropical island. It's not, though—it's just an expensive, very good, if slightly reactionary, restaurant with a wine list to dream about and the best restaurant view in the Napa Valley. To look out over the fabled vineyards at sunset, while sipping a properly aged wine from those very vines, is a heady experience. The menu supports the experience adequately, occasionally with brilliance, though if one were to be rigorously objective, it's clear that in any other location this kitchen would really have to compete. But why get hypothetical? An evening here can easily be the high point of a Napa Valley weekend. The chef has replaced our beloved grilled farm rabbit with a pungent mustard sauce and the house-made seafood sausage with a guinea fowl in black currant sauce. There is also steamed live Maine lobster with prawns and an oyster on the half shell. Desserts are perfectly decadent, especially when peaches are in season (chocolate, of course, is always in season), and there are always three sorbets made in the kitchen. Service harkens back to the old surf'n' turf milieu, but it's sincere. The prix-fixe dinner is $52 a head, and the sky's the limit on the wines.

Open daily 11:30 a.m.-2 p.m.; seatings nightly 6 p.m. & 9 p.m. Cards: AE, MC, V.

La Boucane
1778 2nd St.,
Napa
• (707) 253-1177
FRENCH

Perhaps because it is located in the *city* of Napa (which is to the wine country what Bakersfield is to California), La Boucane has eluded the attention of the culinary press. That's unfortunate, because this place is a joy. It serves classic French fare, intricately prepared with an occasional ethnic twist, in a sensuous remodeled Victorian house at extremely reasonable prices. The garrulous Algerian chef and owner, Jacques Mokrani, defines Boucane as a kind of smoky, bawdy, seafaring ambience, and the food follows suit. If the appetizer of prawns is offered, choose it—the shrimp are lightly floured, sautéed, deglazed in Cognac and finished with garlic, tomatoes, butter and lemon juice. Standout entrées include the monkfish Bretonne, the lobster-like fish sautéed in clarified butter, well sauced and served with rice timbales and perfectly finished vegetables; and the medallions of lamb, as tender as can be and well matched with crispy diced potatoes that are both roasted and sautéed. Subtle essences are distinctively combined into the creamed vegetable soups, and a salad snappily dressed in a walnut-Roquefort vinaigrette shows that the chef can be as au courant as anyone. La Boucane breaks with French tradition by not offering pastries for dessert—a shame, though the chocolate and hazelnut mousses will more than suffice. Dinner for two, with wine, will run about $100. *Open Mon.-Sat. 5:30 p.m.-10:30 p.m. Cards: MC, V.*

Cafe Beaujolais
961 Ukiah St.,
Mendocino
• (707) 937-5614
AMERICAN

The redoubtable Margaret Fox and her husband, Chris Kump, are gradually turning their big lot in the heart of Mendocino into a kind of restaurant village. The main restaurant continues to serve simple but very good dinners, featuring ultra-fresh fish and organic beef from the Nieman-Schell ranch in Bolinas. A new pizza hut in the ever-expanding garden turns out California-style pizzas—topped with such goodies as roasted garlic, local chèvre and fresh vegies—from a wood-fired oven. Meanwhile, locals and week-enders alike continue to pack the deck and garden for some of the world's tastiest breakfasts and lunches, not to mention divine cappuccino. Critics say the Pacific air makes the food taste better than it really is. Perhaps that's true, but who cares?—every chef should have such exquisite seasoning. The four-course fixed-price dinner is $39.50 per person, without wine; otherwise, count on about $100 for dinner for two, with wine.
Open Sun.-Wed. 8 a.m.-2:30 p.m., Thurs.-Sat. 8 a.m.-2:30 p.m. & 6:15 p.m.-9:30 p.m. No cards.

Château Souverain
400 Souverain Rd.,
Geyserville
• (707) 433-8281
CALIFORNIAN

During the past several years, the California wine industry has nurtured the natural symbiosis between wine and food. Even the smaller wineries now have chefs on staff, or sponsor recipe contests, or provide handouts pairing foods with compatible wines. The obvious next step is an on-site restaurant. Château Souverain, still the only winery restaurant in Sonoma County, combines the best features of a fine country dining place with the obvious charms of a winery setting. Its dining room, elegant yet cheerily bright, overlooks a picturesque cascade of vineyards. Executive chef Gary Danko takes fullest advantage of "the bounty of the county," Sonoma's endless cornucopia of fresh, top-quality ingredients. From the warm Sonoma goat-cheese salad with walnuts and roasted peppers to the grilled Sonoma lamb tenderloin with wild-mushroom risotto and rosemary lamb essence, the local produce, seafood and meats star in inspired, vibrantly flavored combinations. The menu revolves mostly around fittingly Mediterranean creations such as fettuccine with garlic cream and fresh herbs. Naturally, the wine list is pure Sonoma, showcasing many of the region's small, boutique producers as well as Château Souverain's own. With a modest bottle (the Nalle Zinfandel, one of the best in the state, is a steal at $16), you can expect to spend $100 on dinner for two.

Open Tues.-Wed. 11:30 a.m.-3 p.m., Thurs.-Sat. 11:30 a.m.-3 p.m. & 5:30 p.m.-9 p.m., Sun. 10:30 a.m.-2:30 p.m. Cards: AE, MC, V.

Domaine Chandon
California Dr. at Hwy. 29, Yountville
• (707) 944-2892
CALIFORNIAN/FRENCH

When Moët & Chandon first opened Domaine Chandon in the Napa Valley more than a decade ago, oenophiles and foodies alike ventured to it with the sort of reverence usually reserved more for a healing visit to Lourdes than a cheerful meal in a vineyard. It was then, and continues to be, the only winery in Napa to run a first-class restaurant on its premises, turning the proper blending of wine and food into a task of the highest importance, aided by a magnificent setting overlooking the slowly growing vines. Interestingly, at first, the restaurant was known best for serving a generous lunchtime buffet, a groaning board of pâtés and cheeses that was a perfect accompaniment to the fine champagnes emerging from the winery. But over the years, the food has grown a good deal more serious. The buffet is gone, replaced with loads of wine-country elegance, which means you'll see plenty of rustic vintners here. In a way, Domaine Chandon has turned into the sort of French restaurant we're always looking for in the French countryside but never quite finding. Chef Philippe Jeanty has been cooking here for well over a decade, and his cuisine has evolved into a textbook rendition of the sort of Californian/French cuisine that Jeremiah Tower, Alice Waters and Michael McCarty would all be proud of. Though he says he tries to create food that's compatible with champagne, his food works fine with anything. As the sun has set over the Napa Valley, we've dined on lovely versions of plump prawns, grilled to a turn and served on a musky bed of shiitake mushrooms; a creamy, dreamy tomato soup served in a puff pastry; ravioli filled with potatoes and Gruyère, served over wild mushrooms; and a ludicrously decadent lobster-and-prawn lasagne. For dessert, by all means order the straw-berry milkshake in a chocolate bag, which is unlike anything you ever had at the old soda shop. Dinner for two, with champagne, costs more than $100.

Open Wed.-Sun. 11:30 a.m.-2 p.m. & 6 p.m.-10 p.m. All major cards.

French Laundry
6640 Washington St.,
Yountville
• (707) 944-2380
CALIFORNIAN

Tucked away in a nest of bushes on a quaint corner, the French Laundry offers a dining experience that epitomizes the wine country. Ambience is the main attraction, and it is nigh impossible to resist the charms of this old two-story brick French country chalet. Patrons have their table for the entire evening, and avuncular host Don Schmitt invites everyone to roam the premises over the course of the meal. Pick up your glass of Chardonnay and take him up on the offer: wander into a modest yet bountiful vegetable and herb garden before studying the prix-fixe menu, which perpetuates the French country mood. For the most part, the food delivers, taking you far away from Californian cuisine's trendy excesses and plopping you in the middle of a French village. The basil egg (simply a coddled egg served on a bed of basil mayonnaise with three kinds of basil leaves), the buttery duck liver pâté with shiitake mush-rooms, the creamy sorrel soup studded with bacon . . . each of these starters transported us. Despite occasional disap-pointments, we still think it's a must for romantics—it's hard to imagine a more pleasant evening. About $130 for two, with wine.

Seatings Wed.-Sun. 7 p.m.-8:30 p.m. No cards (checks ac-cepted).

The Grille
Sonoma Mission Inn,
18140 Hwy. 12,
Boyes Hot Springs
• (707) 938-9000
CALIFORNIAN/SPA

If Charles Saunders were cooking in San Francisco, he'd be on everyone's uncontested list of top chefs. As it is, his skill and inspiration have placed this Sonoma outpost on the must-see list, for his fine cuisine as much as for the Euro-pean-style spa amenities the Sonoma Mission Inn is famous for. Since he took over the kitchen in 1988, Saunders has focused and fine-tuned The Grille menu around the bounty of the county, namely, the wealth of local edibles that abound in Sonoma. Hog Island oysters, goat cheese from Laura Chenel, Reichardt duck and Bodega Bay salmon star in creative yet careful combinations of flavors and textures. For those serious about a weight-loss regimen, the menu features a number of spa cuisine dishes, marked with an asterisk, which have far more flavor than calories. (Except for the smaller portion size, you'd never know that the Pacific albacore tuna, served with thin string beans, "bliss"

potatoes, Kalamata olives and capers, could be a guilt-free indulgence.) For both regular and spa dishes, Saunders borrows freely from the cuisines of the world. The Petaluma chicken tostada with Sonoma Cheddar, guacamole and chile salsa has a definite south-of-the-border cast; the chilled mesquite-grilled seafood salad, tossed with sesame linguine, Japanese vegetables, light soy sauce and rice-wine vinegar, happily melds East and West. As if keeping up with Inn guests and pilgrims to the restaurant weren't enough, Saunders handles chef duties for the Sonoma County Auction's gala dinners each summer. Dinner for two will cost about $100, with wine.

Open Mon.-Sat. 11:30 a.m.-2:30 p.m. & 6:30 p.m.-11 p.m., Sun. 10 a.m.-2 p.m. & 6:30 p.m.-11 p.m. All major cards.

Lisa Hemenway's
**Village Court Mall,
Farmer's Ln. (Sonoma Ave.),
Santa Rosa
• (707) 526-5111**
CALIFORNIAN

Is there life beyond the Flamingo Motel? Indeed there is, just down Farmer's Lane. Don't be put off by this restaurant's location in a shopping center on the fringe of Santa Rosa—we love the place for its friendliness and truly fine eats. Large windows make the dining room airy and light, and the contemporary-country decor is attractive. So is the eclectic menu, which chef-owner Hemenway (who also runs a successful catering business) bases on fresh Sonoma County products. The daily specials reflect the results of her foraging. One night fresh red snapper was dredged in blue cornmeal and served with a tangy, chunky salsa fresca that had the unmistakable sweetness of vine-ripened tomatoes. A sautéed breast of free-range chicken was graced with a luscious sauce of sun-dried cherries. Okay, we'll confess—we go to Hemenway's mostly for her Hungarian nut torte, a fantasy in walnuts and caramel. The wine list shows careful attention not just to quality, but also to affinities with Hemenway's cuisine. Dinner for two, with wine, is a very fair $60 to $70.

Open Tues.-Sat. 11:30 a.m.-9:30 p.m. Cards: DC, MC, V.

Kenwood
**9900 Hwy. 12 (Sonoma Hwy.), Kenwood
• (707) 833-6326**
FRENCH/CALIFORNIAN

This wooden building among the oaks in upper Sonoma Valley once housed a popular restaurant called the Capri. In its new life as the Kenwood, it's even more popular. The feeling is decidedly rustic, but the ol' ranch house was never like this. From the parking lot on a warm evening, the softly lit restaurant with its gentle table sounds and laughter is reminiscent of outdoor nightspots painted by Picasso and Renoir. You come to this romantic little country dining room to feast on such goodies as grape leaves stuffed with wild rice and ground lamb, or fried polenta, mixing and matching with pastas—we loved the fettuccine with

salmon, mahi mahi and mussels in tomato-basil sauce—and such fresh fish as poached salmon with a lemon-cream and caper sauce. The emphasis is on fresh Sonoma County produce, and the wine list is suitably chauvinistic, too. The prices are as agreeable as the setting: about $60 for two, with wine.
Open Sun.-Thurs. 11:30 a.m.-9 p.m., Fri.-Sat. 11:30 a.m.-10 p.m. Cards: MC, V.

Madrona Manor
1001 W. Side Rd.,
Healdsburg
• (707) 433-4231
CALIFORNIAN

As long as you're having dinner in the lovely old house on the Dry Creek Benchland, why not stay overnight? The grounds are lovely, an oasis in the dry madrona-chaparral country hereabouts. Chef Todd Muir, a Chez Panisse graduate, prepares a straightforward regional cuisine, the region being northern coastal California as illuminated by the cuisines of Europe and Asia—that is, Californian cuisine. The three elegant, Victorian dining rooms in the 1881 mansion overlook lawns and gardens, the source of many of the vegetables, herbs and edible flowers that appear on the table. Muir learned the art of making pizza from Alice Waters, so naturally Madrona Manor has a wood-fired oven for pizza and breads. Goat cheese is glorified in a tangy herbed soufflé, and there are always meats and fish from the mesquite grill. Dessert embraces such heady delights as prune-Armagnac ice cream. After a romantic meal in these storied rooms, the canopied bed upstairs seems truly inviting, all the more so because breakfast comes with the price of the room. And breakfast on the Madrona Manor veranda is very fine indeed. Dinner, either à la carte or prix-fixe, will run about $100 for two, with wine.
Open Mon.-Sat. 6 p.m.-9 p.m., Sun. 11 a.m.-2 p.m. & 6 p.m.-9 p.m. All major cards.

Matisse
620 5th St.,
Santa Rosa
• (707) 527-9797
CALIFORNIAN/FRENCH

All the best wine-country restaurants seem to be artisan ventures, and Matisse is one of the best. The artisan is chef/owner Michael Hirschberg, who has evolved from neophyte to accomplished practitioner over about fifteen years in the same premises (he sold it ten years ago before traveling to Europe, but bought it back on his return). Matisse is a comfy California bistro occupying its own little building in charming downtown Santa Rosa. Much of the market-driven menu changes daily, and the repertoire changes seasonally. We've enjoyed Hawaiian spearfish sautéed with brown butter and pistachios, grilled swordfish with a Kalamata-olive tapenade, and a grilled duck breast with a tangy cherry sauce. The all–Sonoma County wine list fits the cuisine quite well. For example, an appetizer of

chilled asparagus with chèvre dressing was wonderful with a local Gewürztraminer. On several occasions the servers have been pretty full of themselves, but that tends to happen in successful restaurants off the beaten track. Let them know you're deeply honored to be allowed to eat there, and they'll knock themselves out to please you. Two will spend about $75 for dinner with wine.
Open Mon.-Fri. 11:30 a.m.-2:30 p.m. & 6 p.m.-9:30 p.m., Sat. 6 p.m.-9:30 p.m. All major cards.

Mustards
7399 St. Helena Hwy.,
Yountville
• (707) 944-2424
CALIFORNIAN

This was the prototype for such new temples of hedonism (though not necessarily gastronomy) as the Fog City Diner in San Francisco and the Rio Grill in Carmel. Chef Cindy Pawlcyn took her cue from the delights of noshing—she observed that the appetizers were often the best part of a menu and began tampering with such nibble items as tapas, canapés and zakuski. The result has been dubbed, for lack of a better description, grazing cuisine. And there's no question that the grazing cuisine here is a cud above the imitators. The Napa Valley was a perfect birthplace for the concept, what with two-thirds of the clientele ordering food pretty much as an excuse to taste various wines, a pastime that calls for wild flavors in discreet packages: pan-fried green tomatoes with salsa, Sonoma goat cheese with an herb vinaigrette, cold strawberry-nectarine soup, crisp onion rings, rabbit with mustard seeds, strawberry-rhubarb pie. Two will spend about $60, with wine.
Open daily 11:30 a.m.-10 p.m. (Nov. 1-May 1: open Sun.-Thurs. 11:30 a.m.-9 p.m.). Cards: MC, V.

Piatti Ristorante
6480 Washington St.,
Yountville
• (707) 944-2070
ITALIAN

From day one in 1987, both the cognoscenti and the just plain folk of Napa Valley began flocking to this little wine-country hideaway to check out its pizzas, pastas and grilled specialties. Could Claude Rouas, maestro of the tony, up-valley Auberge du Soleil, really make it with a place so, well, homey? There's no question: he could, and he has. Piatti is serious competition for the "best Italian in Napa Valley" honors, with many stalwart *paesani* standing squarely in its camp. The ambience is deliberately unprepossessing; simple wooden furniture and casual service underscore the informal, trattoria mood. In the de rigueur open kitchen, young chefs scurry about as the fragrances of garlic, good olive oil and grilling permeate the room. The pizza chef covers her mop of red hair with a Campagnolo bicycling cap. Blink, and you could be in Tuscany. From the unusual antipasti (grilled fennel root with fontina cheese, pancetta, basil and caramelized onion vinaigrette; sautéed

sweetbreads with wild mushrooms; sliced baby eggplant rolled with goat cheese, arugula and sun-dried tomatoes) to the killer desserts (rich hazelnut ice cream, tiramisu), the food carries out, for the most part, the expectation of fine Italian country fare. Pizza crusts are perfectly chewy and crisp. House-made pastas come with such varied goodies as smoked salmon and cream, duck ragoût and a simple tomato-basil-garlic combination. The orecchiette Piatti, "little ears" pasta with cabbage, pancetta, fontina, garlic and butter, is flavorful and hearty. From the grill, everything, from assorted vegetables and polenta to porterhouse steak, is cooked to order. A recent mixed grill of seafood—thinly sliced salmon, halibut and ahi tuna on wilted greens—was perfectly cooked, tender and moist. The wine list combines Napa Valley favorites with a choice selection from the old country. Dinner for two, with wine, runs $75.
Open Mon.-Fri. 11:30 a.m.-2:30 p.m. & 5:30 p.m.-10 p.m., Sat. noon-10 p.m., Sun. 11:30 a.m.-10 p.m. Cards: MC, V.

Plaza Grill
109A Plaza St., Healdsburg
• (707) 431-8305
AMERICAN

This is probably the best restaurant in Healdsburg. The owners have made the most of a deep storefront that evokes a railroad car; howver, the high gray walls, mod furniture and cool lighting make it pleasant. Located on the town's charming old square, it's convenient to wine touring in Alexander Valley, Dry Creek Valley, Russian River Valley and the immediate Healdsburg vicinity. The menu is decidedly California wine country—standout dishes include pork tenderloin with Pinot Noir sauce, rib chop with Merlot butter, fresh salad creations and a tasty appetizer of lightly breaded artichoke hearts fried in garlic butter. Two will spend about $90 on dinner with wine.
Open Sun. & Tues.-Thurs. 11:30 a.m.-2:30 p.m. & 5:30 p.m.-9 p.m., Fri.-Sat. 11:30 a.m.-2:30 p.m. & 5:30 p.m.-9:30 p.m. Cards: AE, MC, V.

Starmont
Meadowood Resort, 900 Meadowood Ln., St. Helena
• (707) 963-3646
FRENCH/CALIFORNIAN

Napa Valley society has tended to rhapsodize over the lost glories of former chefs Hale Lake, who is said to have invented lamb chops, and Cyndi Pawlcyn, who ordained quail and went to Mustards, Fog City and Rio Grill fame. The current chef, Hervé Glin, has brought the dreamers back to a splendid present with such Franco-Californian delights as halibut with a two-basil sauce (green and opal), Hog Island oysters from the Marin coast served with a sun-dried-tomato mignonette, an intense but ethereal garlic custard and a succulent roast duck in ginger-Cabernet sauce. *Magnifique* and then some. Naturally, the wine list is mostly Napa Valley and has good vintage depth. Entered past a huge, dramatically lit boulder, the dressy, lodge-like dining room feels like a getaway for the rich and famous, which is exactly what it is. The corporate golf-croquet set is ubiquitous, along with pillars of the local wine community—a well-balanced crowd, all in all. This is no place for the frugal: dinner for two, with wine, will set you back $120. *Open Mon.-Sat. 5:30 p.m.-9:30 p.m., Sun. 11 a.m.-2 p.m. & 5:30 p.m.-9:30 p.m. All major cards.*

Sun Dial Grill
13500 S. Hwy. 101,
Hopland
• (707) 744-1328
CALIFORNIAN

The enthusiastic Fetzer Vineyards family has been trying to civilize the town of Hopland in Mendocino County for two decades. This unpretentious, well-run wine bar and grill is a giant leap forward. The booths and tables in the natural-wood and glass dining room are inviting. The menu is based on fresh, seasonal ingredients, and it provides a showcase for produce from the Fetzers' ambitious organic garden project on their nearby Valley Oaks estate. This isn't Chez Panisse; the kitchen tends to fail when it flies too high. But it's easily the best eatery in the Ukiah Valley. The straightforward items are best: fresh grilled salmon, a salad of sweet vine-ripened tomatoes and baby lettuces with a tangy vinaigrette. Breads and desserts are exceptional. Many Mendocino County wines are available by the glass, so the comfortable bar area effectively doubles as a county-wide tasting room. Dinner for two, with wine, is about $80. *Open Mon. & Wed.-Sat. 11:30 a.m.-2 p.m. & 5:30 p.m.-9 p.m., Sun. 10 a.m.-2 p.m. & 5:30 p.m.-9 p.m. All major cards.*

Terra
1345 Railroad Ave.,
St. Helena
• (707) 963-8931
ITALIAN/INTERNATIONAL

11/20

One of the newest additions to the St. Helena restaurant scene is Terra, just down the road apiece from the sublime Miramonte. Just a year old, Terra was opened by Hiro Sone, a former head chef under Wolfgang Puck at Spago, and his pastry-chef wife, Lissa Doumani, also late of Spago. This solid, simple stone structure is cozy and comfortable (wonderfully restored, it was originally the Hatchery, erected in 1884); unfortunately, the structure is more of a wow than the food served in it. The menu suffers not only from being a bit too compact, but from not delivering what it promises; it's too erratic. For example, the baked mussels in a fragrant garlic butter were voluptuous and delicious, but the panzanella, that most simple of Italian peasant dishes, suffered from overly soggy chunks of bread paired with tasteless, cottony tomatoes—yet they were bathed in a delicious, drinkable olive oil. The success of the main courses also wavers. The seared pepper salmon with a tomato-ginger vinaigrette was perfectly cooked and piquant, and the osso

buco with a creamy risotto milanese was rich and meltingly good. But the pastas were lackluster, as was the grilled rack of lamb with an eggplant-potato gratin. Doumani, however, should take a bow for her sinful desserts: the tiramisu is light and dreamy, with an earthy dusting of cocoa; the shortcake with an assortment of fresh local berries and a mountain of snowy whipped cream is a comfort-food lover's fantasy. This newcomer does have a lot of promise; hopefully, the food will soon match its perfect surroundings. Dinner for two, with wine, will run about $90.
Open Mon. & Wed.-Sun. 6 p.m.-10 p.m. Cards: MC, V.

Tra Vigne
1050 Charter Oak Ave.,
St. Helena
• (707) 963-4444
ITALIAN

Dreams of a recent vacation to Tuscany might resemble the interior of Tra Vigne ("among vines"), currently the Napa Valley's hottest restaurant. All the fantastic elements are present within the old stone building, a former wine cellar: a stately carved-wood bar, stone lions, a pastoral fresco, acres of all-important marble, terra-cotta and pastel earth tones everywhere, Italian art deco posters, a fountain gurgling in the courtyard. Fortunately, the food more than lives up to the invocation. Breads (baked on the premises) are superb, particularly the rosemary/raisin and the fennel, and each table has a little tub of olive oil for dipping. The trick is to order a bunch of dishes and pass them around. Our favorite appetizer is mozzarella alla griglia, small leaf-packets of tangy, creamy cheese and prosciutto grilled until the cheese is smoky and soft. The small pizza (from the wood-burning oven) topped with roasted garlic and rosemary is also quite wonderful. Pastas are dreamy, featuring sauces of fresh seasonal vegetables and herbs, and quail figures prominently in various preparations, notably wrapped in prosciutto and grilled. Service has been shaky in the past but seems to be improving. Ditto the wine and bar selections; insiders know that the bar's pride is a formidable selection of rare grappas. From $60 to $75 for two, with wine.
Open daily noon-10:30 p.m. Cards: MC, V.

Tre Scalini
241 Healdsburg Ave.,
Healdsburg
• (707) 433-1772
ITALIAN

Tre Scalini means "three steps"—and that's how far it is to the piazza in the heart of Healdsburg. From the vineyards surrounding the town to the pastoral mural on the wall to the breadsticks on the tables, the small-town atmosphere here recalls a feeling of rural Italy. The menu, too, would be right at home at a family trattoria in the old country. Raw ingredients come from local farms and market gardens. Flavors are full and assertive in both traditional dishes and the occasional fanciful ones. It would be easy to make a meal of first courses: melanzane e peperoni alla griglia to open,

perhaps, with marinated black olives and Roma tomatoes joining the grilled eggplant and three colors of sweet peppers; then the ocean-fresh antipasto alla buranella, with calamari, mussels and scallops marinated in olive oil and lime; then perhaps a carpaccio alla fiorentina, the raw beef laced with extra-virgin olive oil, or the pesce spada alla Tre Scalini, swordfish stuffed with mango, mandarin orange and water chestnuts and grilled with lemon-lime butter. A hearty bowl of zuppa di ceci, a thick, old-fashioned soup of chickpeas, fresh vegetables and garlic sausage, would round things out nicely. You'll find no vampires at Tre Scalini—the garlic level is uncommonly generous in such potent concoctions as steamed mussels in cream sauce (you'll need some extra bread to sop it all up) and tagliarini alle vongole, fresh basil-garlic pasta sauced with fresh Manila clams, Roma tomatoes, white wine and plenty of excellent olive oil. If you should ever get to the main dishes, try the definitely upstream braised salmon Alexander, finished with local Sonoma Cabernet and sweet butter, or the stone-grilled lamb chops with garlic, rosemary and red wine. According to the menu, "Time allowing, all special requests are welcome." So if you don't see exactly what you want on the menu, just ask. A full dinner for two, including a bottle of Sonoma or Italian wine, should cost about $80.
Open Mon. 6 p.m.-10 p.m., Tues.-Fri. 11:30 a.m.-2:30 p.m. & 6 p.m.-10 p.m., Sat. 6 p.m.-10 p.m. Cards: MC, V.

Trilogy
1234 Main St.,
St. Helena
• (707) 963-5507
FRENCH

Driving through St. Helena later in the evening, you can often see couples with their heads together inside Trilogy, looking dreamy and content. It's that kind of place. Chef-owner Diane Parisseau and her partners serve French cuisine inspired by the local abundance of fine ingredients. Entering the small, brightly appointed dining room through an iron gate off Hunt Street, one is welcomed twice—first by the host, then by delectable aromas presaging the wonders to come. And the food is wonderful, indeed. Not terribly inventive, but beautifully deft, as in a toothsome sautéed chicken breast with Dijon mustard sauce, or the steamed halibut with saffron threads, chives and shallots. The gallantine of rabbit with cranberry compote, an appetizer, is superb. So is the fettuccine with a mushroom-garlic cream sauce. As might be expected, the wine list is one of the area's best, with extraordinary vertical depth. Trilogy is definitely worth an overnight stay in St. Helena. About $85 for dinner for two, with wine.
Open Tues.-Sat. noon-2 p.m. & 6 p.m.-10 p.m. Cards: MC, V.

Truffles

234 S. Main St.,
Sebastopol
• (707) 823-8448
CALIFORNIAN/
INTERNATIONAL

Sonoma County, renowned for its fine wine and pastoral landscape, has also emerged as a mecca of gastronomy. Many of its choicest restaurant finds, such as Truffles, are situated in remote corners of the county but are more than worth the hunt. The menu at Truffles is a kaleidoscopic crazy quilt of reinterpreted Californian/French classics and Asian-themed inventions of the talented chef-owner, Mark Malicki. Sautéed sweetbreads, for example, are served with a bittersweet sauce of melon and saffron. Steamed mussels come with a cilantro-mint Southeast Asian pesto sauce. The East-West touch is also evident in the Thai-inspired barbe- cued prawns with green-onion pancakes and spicy peanut sauce. Akin to a make-it-yourself tortilla, this dish is a perfect balance of the smoky, meaty prawns, warm, chewy rounds of flatbread and a complex sauce containing over a dozen ingredients (including tamarind, galanga, Kaffir lime leaves, coconut and Thai chilis). The stuff is addictive— once when it disappeared from the menu, irate regulars clamored to have it reinstated. Truffles' multiethnic hodge- podge also includes Hawaiian-style poki sashimi (cubes of raw fish marinated with spices, rice vinegar and sesame oil), Korean barbecued pork tenderloin with spicy fried cabbage, and curried roast free-range chicken and prawns. The wine list centers on the best local offerings—we loved a Gewürztraminer with the rillettes of pork with Asian pears, and a berry-like Merlot alongside the roast venison with raspberries and huckleberries. A complete dinner for two, with wine, will run about $100.

Open Tues.-Thurs. & Sun. 6 p.m.-9 p.m., Fri.-Sat. 6 p.m.-10 p.m. Cards: MC, V.

QUICK BITES

Big Three Fountain

Sonoma Mission Inn,
18140 Hwy. 12,
Boyes Hot Springs
• (707) 938-9000

The farthest outpost of the Sonoma Mission Inn, the Big Three goes back to well before the time when the inn was a favored training camp for pro football teams. The soda- fountain ambience is casual, but the food is serious. Carne asada presents one of the finest marinated, grilled skirt steaks around, and the cheeseburger is archetypal. But the jewel in the crown is SMI executive chef Charles Saunders's chocolate malt, made with a chocolate sauce made from scratch. About $20 for lunch for two.

Open daily 7 a.m.-3 p.m. & 5:30 p.m.-9:30 p.m. All major cards.

The Diner
6476 Washington St.,
Yountville
• (707) 944-2626

Before beginning a rigorous day of wine tasting, stop into The Diner for a marvelously fortifying breakfast. Your day will start right with a cup of Graffeo's coffee, continuing with such joys as cornmeal waffles with bits of bacon in the batter, ultra-fresh eggs, homemade spicy sausage and great home fries. The plain white interior won't assault your senses before you've had a chance to wake up, though it is given interest with an old-fashioned soda fountain. The best breakfast in the wine country will cost two about $20. *Open Tues.-Sun. 8 a.m.-3 p.m. & 5:30 p.m.-9 p.m. No cards.*

Forty Karats
109 Plaza,
Healdsburg
• (707) 431-8181

Every town needs a diner, and this is Healdsburg's. The '50s motif passes through a '60s filter and stops just short of psychedelia. It's all yellow (or gold) and chrome, with the businesslike linoleum counter that is the center of every diner's self-contained universe. The fare is basic and well done—a very good patty melt indeed, and an excellent chocolate malt to go with it. An added bonus is the espresso machine, which makes Forty Karats one of the only places in the Russian River area for a serious caffeine pit stop before that long drive back to the city after a grueling day of wine tasting. About $15 for a sandwich meal for two. *Open Sun.-Thurs. 7 a.m.-4 p.m., Fri.-Sat. 7 a.m.-9 p.m. Cards: MC, V.*

HOTELS

With its sprawling vineyards, charming towns, lush countryside, brilliant weather, romantic restaurants and excellent wine-tasting opportunities, it's no wonder the wine country is thick with hotels and inns. But don't count on breezing into a room. During the season (April through October), getting a reservation can be difficult, especially on short notice. Two organizations would like to help: Wine Country Reservations (707-257-7757) and Napa Valley Reservations Unlimited (707-252-1985).

In the winter months—when rain falls—it's a different story. Hotels practically beg for you to be their guests, some offering discounted rates and special packages. We find this to be the best time of year to visit the wine country—it's peaceful, and there are no lines at the wineries.

Auberge du Soleil
180 Rutherford Hill Rd.,
Rutherford
• (707) 963-1211,
Fax (707) 963-8764

Auberge du Soleil is considered by many to be the crème de la crème of wine-country inns, and the staff knows it. Problem is, they can be a little rude in letting *you* know it. Make no mistake, this place caters to the upper crust, and in the busy summer months anyone less than a movie star, multimillionaire or member of the Royal Family can get short shrift. (We know a few people who were shunted from room to room more than once, presumably to make way for more eminent guests.) And this gets the "highest nose in the air" award: Auberge du Soleil is so pretentious that, here in the heart of America's wine country, each of the twelve adobe-style buildings (containing four rooms each) is named after a *French* wine region. Oh, please.

All that said, we must add that in luxury and setting, Auberge du Soleil is unparalleled in these parts. Each building is gently terraced up the hills of an olive grove high above a valley of vineyards. No room is without a view and a deck from which to appreciate it, and the interiors include fireplaces, stocked wet bars, tiled floors, tasteful furnishings and baskets of fruit and other goodies. Amenities include tennis courts, a large pool and the inn's namesake restaurant, which is not as wonderful as when Masa Kobayashi was the chef, but which still boasts a lovely outdoor patio with the best view of any restaurant in Napa.

One-bedroom suites: $220-$385; two-bedroom suites: $510.

The El Dorado Hotel
405 1st St. West,
Sonoma
• (707) 996-3030,
Fax (707) 996-3148

The El Dorado Hotel reopened just as we went to press, making it impossible for a personal inspection. Accomplished hotelier/restaurateur Claude Rouas (who owns Napa's Auberge du Soleil) remodeled the 27-room hotel, making the rooms somewhat smaller than in the original. Each room has a four-poster bed and a private balcony, though as the prices would indicate, the El Dorado is more modest than Rouas's other ventures. The cuisine at Piatti is the same northern Italian cooking that has made Rouas's Napa Valley Piatti a great success. There is extra seating in the courtyard, which also has a swimming pool. Rates include complimentary Continental breakfast in the lobby.

Singles & doubles: $100-$125.

Inn at the Tides
800 Coast Hwy.,
Bodega Bay
• (707) 875-2751,
Fax (707) 875-3023

Staggered up and down the rugged Sonoma Coast hills, the Inn at the Tides is a modern hotel (actually, a collection of freestanding two-story structures) that conforms well to its salty, foggy environs. Warmth is provided by fireplaces (in most rooms) and an indoor-outdoor heated pool, which has adjoining sauna and massage facilities. The rooms are crisp, immaculate and stocked with fresh flowers, and refrigerators are filled with snacks; there are comfortable sofa beds and terrycloth robes. Guests are greeted in the morning with a complimentary breakfast and daily newspaper. The Bay View dining room takes full advantage of the inn's proximity to the ocean and serves a range of fresh seafood; the wine list draws extensively from the wine-country communities to the east.

Singles & doubles: $110-$160; deluxe: $185.

Madrona Manor
1001 Westside Rd.,
Healdsburg
• (707) 433-4231,
Fax (707) 433-0703

Perhaps the best example of the efficacy of converting an old private mansion (in this case a Victorian circa 1881) into a guest house, the Madrona Manor combines antique opulence with modern luxury. Much of the original furniture remains—ancient dressers with marble tops, beds with carved headboards—in the nine mansion rooms. As for the eight more rooms in the carriage house behind the mansion, they are outfitted with furniture purchased in Nepal. All rooms have private baths, some have balconies, and none have phones or television. Accommodations in two recently developed outbuildings are adequate but far inferior to the size and style of those in the main house. The magnificent eight-acre grounds, replete with fruit trees, an herb garden and soaring palms and redwoods, complement the picture, as does the superb mesquite-grill-anchored restaurant run by Todd Muir. Muir learned his Californian cuisine craft from Alice Waters and is a whiz with baked goods and victuals smoked on the premises. Breakfast, included with the accommodations, is quite substantial. With a swimming pool to boot, Madrona Manor is a wine-country best bet.
Singles & doubles: $90-$122.

Meadowood Resort Hotel
900 Meadowood Ln.,
St. Helena
• (707) 963-3646,
Fax (707) 963-3532

Meadowood is our slice of heaven: total luxury, with just enough rusticity to permit a sense of proportion. Ten lodges are insouciantly scattered around the forested acreage as if they were backwoods cabins. And though each lodge (containing four suites and a studio) looks stolidly modest from the outside, inside are stunning, spacious nests of opulent seclusion. The architecture is New England in style: exposed beams, peaked roofs in soft whites and grays. Details are carefully thought out: brass door and drawer handles, warmed floor tiles in the bathrooms, Krups coffee makers, well-stocked wet bars, fireplaces made of Silverado stone, terrycloth robes. Newer lodge rooms—some near the tennis courts and swimming pool, others closer to the nine-hole fairway and the croquet courts—bring the total number of accommodations to 58. Hervé Glin, a French-trained chef, is now in charge of the Starmont Restaurant, located in the gray, white-railed main lodge.
Singles & doubles: $155-$185 (Sun.-Thurs.), $195-$255 (Fri.-Sat.); suites: $195-$265 (Sun.-Thurs.), $255-$365 (Fri.-Sat.).

Mount View Hotel

1457 Lincoln Ave.,
Calistoga
• (707) 942-6877,
Fax (707) 942-6904

Get enough of a concentration of hotels and you're sure to find one that uses a gimmick to attract customers; this one employs art deco. The entire 34-unit building is done up in the style of the '30s, with rooms named after Tom Mix and other Hollywood stars of the period. This might seem like the kind of urban pretension that people would come to Napa Valley to escape, but there's no doubting that the Mount View offers charm, comfortable quarters and full hotel amenities—at a very good price. The atmosphere is lively, and guests come here for fun: to listen to the live swing jazz in the Deco Lounge, to dance in Fender's Lounge, to sip bubbly drinks poolside and to prowl the delightful town of Calistoga and the surrounding wine country. Unfortunately, as of this writing, the once-superb dining room is between chefs, so there is no dining other than the complimentary Continental breakfast.
Singles & doubles: $60-$85; suites: $110.

Napa Valley Railway Inn

6503 Washington St.,
Yountville
• (707) 944-2000,
No fax

The idea of converting turn-of-the-century railroad cars into guest rooms is a cute one, but if these are the conditions rail travelers had to face back then, we're glad to be living in the space age. With a New Orleans bordello theme, the rooms are as spacious as you'd expect from a large box, but the ventilation is poor, the noise level high and the bathrooms less than pristine. And, where are the telephones? One benefit: location. It's just a short walk to Vintage 1890, a complex of shops, and to The Diner, the best breakfast place in the wine country.
Singles & doubles: $95 (Sun.-Thurs.), $104 (Sat.-Sun.).

Rancho Caymus Inn

170 Rutherford Dr.,
Rutherford
• (707) 963-1777,
No fax

In the shadow of Auberge du Soleil sits the relatively new Rancho Caymus Inn, another theme house. The inn evokes California's Spanish history, with suites named after such figures as Black Bart and such places as Bella Oaks Mine. Much is made of the artistry behind the construction—furniture hewn of California oak, black walnut and fir, Ecuadoran wrought-iron lamps and the like—but the all-suite Caymus is nonetheless très Best Western. There's a pleasant floral courtyard where you can munch your complimentary breakfast; fancier rooms have fireplaces and Jacuzzis.
Doubles: $95-$150; suites: $225-$295.

Silverado Country Club & Resort

1600 Atlas Peak Rd.,
Napa
• (707) 257-0200,
Fax 257-2867

Its size alone makes Silverado a wine-country anomaly. With 350 condominiums, 280 of which are available for guest lodging, the 1,200-acre spread is reminiscent of a Florida retirement community, with the adjacent city of Napa filling the Miami shoes. Some of the condos are rather attractive, but many are ordinary and furnished unexceptionally, though they are large and comfortable enough. As for the resort, it offers everything one could want except rusticity and seclusion. Golfers love Silverado for its two eighteen-hole golf courses, tennis players have twenty courts at their disposal, and swimmers can choose from nine pools. Rounding out the sports facilities are jogging trails and rental bikes. As for the food, you won't find any of that froufrou nouvelle, spa or Californian cuisine here, just good old steak and seafood at the Royal Oak Grill and a mundane Continental menu at the Vintner's Court. *Rooms & studio condos: $130-$165; one-bedroom condos: $195; two-bedroom condos: $330; three-bedroom condos: $465.*

Sonoma Hotel

110 W. Spain St.,
Sonoma
• (707) 996-2996,
No fax

Located on the northwest corner of the historic Sonoma Plaza, the three-story Sonoma Hotel is as close as you can get to the nineteenth century in the wine country. The lower two floors were built of adobe well over a century ago; the high-gabled third floor was added in the 1880s. Once a combination dry goods store and meeting hall, the building is now a lovely seventeen-room hotel decked out mostly in French and English antiques, including bookshelves and marble-topped tables in the hallways (where guests find glass jars of lemon drops to sweeten their passage). The Vallejo Room is special, furnished with a hand-carved walnut bed and dressers that once belonged to Gen. Mariano Vallejo's sister. Continental breakfast is served in an antiques-filled lobby reached through a beveled-glass door. You'll get a lot of charm for not very many bucks. *Singles & doubles: $58-$98.*

Sonoma Mission Inn & Spa

18149 Sonoma Hwy. 12,
Boyes Hot Springs
• (800) 862-4945

The Sonoma Mission Inn is geared toward the sybarite who wants to get in shape—which is, of course, almost oxymoronic. We certainly don't come to the wine country for abstinence, preferring instead to sample its rich wines and creative food. Yet the Sonoma Mission Inn is a tremendously popular spa that attempts to combine luxury with a low-calorie intake and a high-calorie expenditure. Celebrities swear by the five-day spa package ($1,200 to $1,800), an intense, personal-trainer-led regimen of aerobics, weights, swimming and so on, accompanied by spa-cuisine meals. But Tammy Faye Bakker would feel comfortable here, too, getting beauty treatments and consuming more plentiful and traditional fare. For a luxury hotel, the ambience is quite casual; the breezy concierge dresses informally and immediately tries to put stressed-out executives and matrons at ease. No one could object to the accommodations, which are modestly elegant. There are two parts to the inn: the smallish, older rooms in the main building, in brown and white earth tones, with minibars and canvas canopies; and the larger, somewhat sterile new rooms, done in pink pastel, equipped with capacious baths and ample closets. A few have fireplaces or small patios; of course, all rooms are near the spa facilities. The Grille, a wellspring of spa cuisine, is now being run by chef Charles Saunders, who presents stunning plates, whether you're ordering from the seductive standard listings that show off local produce and game, or from the spa side of the menu, which won't leave you feeling one bit deprived.

Singles & doubles: $195-$290 (less mid-week & off-season); suites: $475-$525.

Whale Watch Inn
35100 Hwy. 1, Gualala
(Mendocino Coast)
• (707) 884-3667,
No fax

Never mind the name, the word "quaint" thankfully doesn't apply to the Whale Watch Inn. There's not a single turret or lace curtain to be found at this oceanfront enclave where, during the winter, it is possible to sight migrating whales without leaving your room. Five very different buildings, scattered as casually as wildflowers beside the cliff's edge, offer sweeping views—usually through the branches of pine and cypress trees—of the Pacific and the coastline to the south. Best of all are the sleekly contemporary accommodations on the upper level of Pacific Edge, the main lodge; their wildly unconventional configurations will make you wonder why so many hotel rooms have only four walls. Some rooms have skylights; most, sliding doors that let in the aroma of pine and the sound of ceaseless surf. Service, geared to comfort rather than rigid rules, comes with a smile, whether you want a late-night snack or a glass of wine. After an in-room breakfast worthy of a four-star hotel, guests may climb down— we're talking *way down*—a staircase leading to a virtually private beach.

Singles & doubles: $135-$210.

CITYLORE

NATIVE SAN FRANCISCANS

One of the proudest claims a San Franciscan can make is that of being a "native." But the real natives of the Bay Area didn't fare well enough to boast. By the time explorer Sir Francis Drake "discovered" the Northern California shores in 1579 and dubbed the region Nova Albion, the area had been inhabited by the Ohlone and other Native American tribes for several thousand years. It wasn't until the fall of 1775 that Captain Juan Bautista de Anza set out with 250 soldiers and colonists from Sonora, Mexico, to establish Spanish settlements on the Bay of San Francisco. The following year, Father Junípero Serra's vision of a chain of missions throughout California gained its sixth link when Father Francisco Palou established a temporary church next to the Laguna de los Dolores (the Lagoon of Sorrows). The mission was originally named for the founder of the Franciscan order, Saint Francis of Assisi, but is known today as Mission Dolores. According to many accounts, however, most of the sorrows were heaped upon the indigenous population, the targets of true missionary zeal. One visitor reported in 1821 that the 1,000 Native Americans being "civilized" at the mission were dying off at rate of 300 per year.

LET'S MAKE A DEAL

The original civilian settlement on San Francisco Bay was founded by such enterprising merchants as William A. Richardson and Jacob Leese. It was called Yerba Buena and remained a small, relatively unremarkable frontier village until Richard Henry Dana commented on its charms in his 1840 book, *Two Years Before the Mast*. Describing the climate "as near being perfect as any in the world," Dana predicted, "If California ever becomes a prosperous country this bay will be the center of its prosperity." President Andrew Jackson may have sensed such a promising future in 1835 when he proposed to buy the bay from Mexico for $500,000. Today that sum probably wouldn't buy a condo in Pacific Heights.

MORMONS DETOURED

The population of fledgling Yerba Buena doubled on July 31, 1846, when the chartered ship *Brooklyn* arrived carrying 238 Mormons who planned to meet up with Brigham Young. It must have been a typical summer day on San Francisco Bay—"a gray fog distilled the dampness and shrouded the landscape in gloom," one diarist wrote. The Mormons' gloom deepened when they discovered that Young's overland trek had ended at the Great Salt Lake. But the party's leader, Sam Brannan, a Maine native trained as a printer in Ohio, turned the woeful circumstances to his own advantage. A swaggering peacock of a man, Brannan established California's first flour mill and founded the California Star, the city's first newspaper. When charged with using Mormon funds for personal gain—an allegation that put him on trial before California's first jury—Brannan mustered up his best rugged individualist spirit and said, "Go tell Brigham Young that I'll give up the money when he sends me a receipt signed by the Lord."

GOLD!

James Marshall was going about his routine business on January 24, 1848, constructing a mill for John Sutter at Coloma, when he found a sizable nugget of gold in the millrace. It was the enterprising Mormon named Sam Brannan who shouted out the news on the streets of San Francisco, 115 miles to the southeast, and set into motion the great Gold Rush of 1849. (Brannan also just happened to have opened a prospector's outfitting store at Sutter's Fort.) In the first three years of the boom, over 200,000 fortune seekers came to California by land and sea. Fifty thousand '49ers landed in San Francisco, gateway to the gold country, alone. Enterprising journalist Mark Twain, sniffing out the story, called the burgeoning city "a wild, free, disorderly, grotesque society!" Another observer wrote that "a perpetual carnival reigns"—not unlike many outsiders' comments today. And prices started a spiral that would make any current inhabitant feel most at home. "Women of easy virtue," it was said, could be had for $200 to $400 a night, and a low-ceilinged, earthen-walled cellar room, only twelve-foot square, rented for $250 per week.

EMPEROR NORTON

San Francisco has never wanted for colorful characters, but few have dominated their era or endured so belovedly in the civic memory as Joshua Abraham Norton. He arrived in the city from South Africa in 1849, another speculator on the trail of easy money. Almost immediately he turned a quarter-million-dollar profit in the commodities market. But his failed attempt to corner rice left him penniless and he vanished from sight. He reappeared a few months later and delivered a proclamation to the newspapers declaring himself "Emperor of the United States and Protector of Mexico." That was just the first of his flamboyant pronouncements. "Emperor" Norton paraded through town in outlandish uniforms and printed up beautiful 50-cent promissory notes, on which "The Imperial Government of Norton I" pledged to pay the holder, in the year 1880, "with interest at 7 percent per annum from date." His antics were so kindly regarded—he was a newspaperman's dream come true—that Norton was able to live off the generosity and free lunches of his fellow San Franciscans for 25 years, until his death in 1880 (ironically, the year his promissory notes became due). Over 10,000 people reportedly attended his funeral. Not all of the Emperor's proclamations were pure fantasy: one called for building bridges from Oakland Point to Yerba Buena (San Francisco), "from thence to the mountain range of Sausalito, and from thence to the Farallones." His imperial majesty will have to settle for two out of three.

LOTTA'S FOUNTAIN

Conspicuously situated on a downtown corner of Market Street (at Kearney) is a cast-iron column that one historian calls "charmingly ugly." Although it has no logical purpose, it has its origin in San Francisco's thriving theater life of the antebellum and post–Civil War eras. The city's uniquely cosmopolitan-frontier population of working folk, speculators, social climbers and millionaires was notably fond of theatrical entertainments, and especially smitten by such female celebrities as the scandalous Lola Montez and her mesmerizing "spider dance." Montez, who entertained herself with a pet bear, made a protégé out of a British-born, dimpled and ringlet-haired little girl from the Mother Lode mining town of Grass Valley. In turn, Lotta Crabtree, the Shirley Temple of her day, became the rage of music halls around the country, parlaying her girlish charms into a $4 million fortune. She was easily America's highest-paid actress by the time she retired in 1891. Upon her death in 1924, Crabtree's will made generous bequests to favorite charities. But back in 1875, she had already presented her novel cast-iron tribute to the city that loved her best, and it has been known ever since as Lotta's Fountain.

HANG 'EM HIGH

The population explosion that accompanied the Gold Rush brought more than a few disreputable characters to San Francisco. By the end of 1849, enough gangs were roaming the streets to make present-day urban warfare seem mild by comparison. Among the most notorious hoodlum outfits were the Sydney Ducks, a band of English criminals who had escaped their banishment to Australia, and the equally violent Hounds. They ran protection rackets and enforced their rule with fire. After two years of business blazes, enough citizens were sufficiently outraged to take justice into their own hands. A Committee of Vigilance was organized in 1851, and one of its signal acts was the capture and subsequent hanging in Portsmouth Square of a Sydney Duck named John Jenkins. For more than three months, the vigilantes returned the gangs' terror blow for blow. Among their leaders was none other than the ubiquitous Sam Brannan. A second Vigilance Committee arose in 1856, when a reformer newspaper editor who called himself King of William was shot by a city council member whose shady past he had exposed in print. Defying the authority of Mayor James Van Ness, 5,000 enrolled, and the movement took electoral shape with the founding of the People's Party, which dominated city politics through the Civil War.

INTRO TO SUTRO

Like Brannan, Van Ness and other names of pioneers emblazoned on street signs throughout the city, Adolph Sutro's moniker has been immortalized in San Francisco—in the ruins of his famous Baths (saltwater swimming pools near the Cliff House), in his library and even on a TV transmitting tower and mountaintop named after him. Born in Prussia, Sutro arrived in San Francisco as a tobacco merchant, but he found a way to cash in on the mineral bonanzas. When a great vein of silver (known as the Comstock Lode) was discovered near Virginia City, Nevada, Sutro developed a fantastic ventilation and drainage scheme to overcome some of the geological difficulties encountered in the extraction of the ore. It called for building a great seven-mile tunnel, 2,000 feet underground. In July 1866, Congress awarded Sutro the right of way and significant mining rights, but the enterprising engineer had alienated many of the Silver Kings, as well as Billy Ralston, San Francisco's reigning financial genius (founder of the Bank of California and builder of the Palace Hotel), and construction of the tunnel didn't begin until 1869. The project was finally finished in 1878, after the silver rush had subsided. When former President Ulysses S. Grant led an opening-day parade through the tunnel in October 1879, Sutro was nowhere to be seen. In a move of impeccable timing, he had secretly sold his own stock in the tunnel and retired to his mansion overlooking the Cliff House.

GOLDEN GRAINS

Golden Gate Park, more than 1,000 acres of beautifully landscaped gardens, playing fields, lakes and waterfalls, is one of the country's great urban parks. But it might never have taken root without a humble, accidental planting. The sandy northwestern section of the peninsula was known in the mid-nineteenth century as the Outside Lands. Ambitious developers, sensing the city's expansion, had their eyes on these vast, untamed properties. But certain civic-minded powers, including Billy Ralston, envisioned a city project along the lines of New York City's Central Park, even though the Outside Lands were little more than windblown sand dunes. In 1868, the Board of Supervisors purchased an enormous rectilinear parcel and, on the advice of Central Park architect Frederick Law Olmsted, hired William Hammond Hall to survey the site and supervise its reclamation. Hall camped out on the Outside Lands while mulling over the task of conquering the drifting dunes. When his horse refused a handful of barley, Hall tossed the grains on the ground. A few days later he noticed the barley had sprouted. Now he had an anchor in the shifting soil, on top of which he could plant lupine, then grass, and ultimately the shrubs, cypresses and other botanical wonders so carefully plotted and groomed by Scottish landscaper John McLaren. By the late 1870s, 150,000 trees graced Golden Gate Park, and the land was barren frontier no more.

NOB HILL

Westward expansion under the banner of "Manifest Destiny" reached its continental limits at San Francisco, and for the men in power, it reached its crowning glory at the crest of California Street. Today, Nob Hill is home to Grace Cathedral, the Fairmont and Mark Hopkins hotels, and the Pacific Union Club, a wealthy men's retreat held over from the Gilded Age. The hill owes its glittery character to the wealth created by the railroads that finally spanned the nation in 1869. After engineer Theodore D. Judah conceived the Central Pacific Railroad as the western link in the transcontinental network, four Sacramento merchants financed the construction and built an empire that eventually included the mighty Southern Pacific—the infamous "Octopus." The Big Four—Mark Hopkins, Leland Stanford, Collis Huntington, Charles Crocker—and others, including such famed mining-stock "Bonanza Kings" as James Flood, amassed ludicrous fortunes and in the 1870s set about outdoing one another in building ostentatious residences on California Street Hill. Mine owner and lawyer James Ben Ali Haggin built a mansion with 60 rooms; William Sharon's house boasted the first hydraulic elevator in the West; Crocker's estate set him back $2.3 million, so Hopkins spent $3 million; Flood shelled out $50,000 for a bronze fence. Before long, the hill took on a new name, "Nob," after its lofty population of social "nabobs."

GOOD FENCES MAKE BAD NEIGHBORS

If you've ever experienced strained relations with your next-door neighbor, consider the plight of poor Nicholas Yung, a San Francisco undertaker who had the nerve to stand up to the railroad robber baron Charles Crocker. It seems that Yung had purchased a small slice of land at the top of California Street before it came to be known as Nob Hill. When Crocker and his industrialist cronies starting turning the hill into an enclave for millionaire mansions, Yung refused to sell his paltry parcel to Crocker, who had built his mansion on the enormous contiguous plot. In retaliation, Crocker built a 40-foot-high fence around three sides of Yung's tiny house, essentially imprisoning his neighbor. The "spite fence," as it was popularly known, became the subject of editorial cartoons and countless lampoons. To the working classes it was a symbol of the selfishness and arrogance of the rich.

CHINATOWN

Although San Francisco's Chinatown remains a picturesque and popular destination for thousands of tourists, its real-life history is far less quaint than the curios in souvenir stores. The great wave of immigration started when news of the Gold Rush reached Canton, China, and accelerated when Charles Crocker hired an all-Chinese 50-man crew to work on the Central Pacific in 1865. Soon his railroad employed 10,000 Chinese workers, and immigration swelled to a rate of 16,000 per year. By the 1870s, the Chinese in San Francisco were turning to other occupations. They held half the factory jobs in the city in 1872, and virtually monopolized labor in the cigar-making and garment industries. When economic depression hit in the 1870s, the Chinese became easy scapegoats for unemployed white workers. Prohibited from owning land, applying for citizenship or even testifying in court, "coolie" workers became the target of physical violence as well. On July 23, 1877, rioters burned and pillaged Chinatown, killing 21 Chinese and destroying property. William Tell Coleman, a leader of the 1856 Vigilance Committee, was recruited to lead a Committee of Safety, which helped inhibit the angry mobs. But a failed small businessman–turned–sandlot orator, Dennis Kearney, continued to agitate against the Chinese and was active in the formation of the Workingmen's Party of California. Kearney and others tainted the grass-roots labor politics of the party with their virulent racism, injecting the slogan "The Chinese Must Go!" into the working-folk unrest generated by the growing social and economic chasm between the classes. The Chinese didn't go, and despite the negative images of opium dens, sweatshops and nefarious "tongs," Chinatown has remained a vital, inextricable and politically and culturally important segment of San Francisco society.

MICKEY FINN

Fictional detectives Sam Spade and Philip Marlowe could hardly get through a Roaring Twenties caper without being "slipped a Mickey" in some seedy bar. Today, the Mickey Finn is the stuff of jokes and legends, but for the unlucky sailor or innocent waif in a Barbary Coast bar such as the Thunderbolt or Dew-Drop Inn, the surreptitious poison was the gateway to hell. From the 1860s through the turn of the century, the rough-and-tumble waterfront near Pacific Street (now Pacific Avenue) harbored tawdry bars, bordellos, dance halls and gambling dens. The area was named after the pirate-populated section of coast in northern Africa. According to one story, a Scottish chemist and fugitive from justice named Michael Finn became a Barbary Coast bartender and invented a clear, odorless liquid that he could slip into the drinks of unwary sailors and civilians. Over the years the formula derived from several sources—a powerful horse laxative, chloral hydrate or tartar emetic—but it invariably put the victims out of their senses, made them rubbery and subject to easy exploitation. The men were "shanghaied" (another term that allegedly originated in San Francisco) and forced into labor aboard merchant ships, and the women were sold into white slavery. Likely hundreds died by poisoning from too heavy a dose. Despite felony penalties, use of the Mickey Finn continued into the mid-twentieth century, to control unruly drunks or retaliate against political enemies.

A REAL FREE LUNCH

Any drinking establishment worthy of being called a genuine "San Francisco bar" provides some sort of comestibles to accompany the libations. The tradition goes back to the free lunch of the nineteenth century. The rivalry for drinkers and diners was heavy in a city that featured cuisine from every corner of the world and lubricated its population with alcohol by the gallon. The City Directory of 1875–1876 commented, "Nowhere on Earth is the temptation to drink as strong as here. Business is brisk, competition sharp and the climate the most constantly stimulating anywhere to be found." Rudyard Kipling observed during his visit to the city that in San Francisco, "Drinking is more than an institution, it is a religion." And a tankard of ale or shot of liquor typically entitled the customer to a full spread of food—the legendary free lunch. Even in the midst of hard times during the 1870s depression, Kipling noted, "You paid for a drink and you got as much as you wanted to eat . . . for something under a rupee a day a man can feed himself sumptuously even though he be bankrupt."

CABLE CARS

A ride up one of San Francisco's steep hills on a cable car may be a quaint attraction for tourists, but it was born of that age-old combination of necessity and ingenuity. By the mid-1870s, city public transportation was dominated by a half dozen companies operating horse-drawn streetcars. In addition to passengers, the cars hauled produce, lumber, masonry and animals up the imposing inclines of Nob, Russian and Telegraph hills. But in 1869, a horrible accident occurred when a team of horses with a heavy load broke down trying to negotiate a slippery slope. One of the witnesses was an immigrant from London named Andrew Hallidie who had been manufacturing wire rope for the quartz mines of the Mother Lode. Hallidie dreamed and schemed for three years and came up with a wild plan for an endless underground steel cable to which the streetcars would latch themselves through a slot and thus be towed up the hills. The cable was to be kept in motion by giant flywheels driven by steam engines and enclosed in large barns. The first cable car went into operation in 1873. It was a high-tech invention back then and remains a marvel today. In 1964, the cable car was designated the only mobile historical landmark in the United States.

SHAKE & BAKE

The prediction that all of California will someday slip off its geological shelf and sink into the sea may be most strongly supported by the Great Earthquake and Fire of 1906. San Francisco residents had long been familiar with tremors and temblors, but nothing prepared them for the rocking and rolling that hit at 5:13 a.m. on April 18, 1906. The San Andreas fault gave way with a two-minute shift that has been estimated as measuring 8.3 on the Richter scale (devised later). Some 120 aftershocks continued to wrack the already rattled citizens. Memorable images endure, such as that of Italian tenor Enrico Caruso, who had just sung the role of Don José in *Carmen* the night before, pacing the lobby of the St. Francis Hotel, puffing a cigar and vowing never to return to San Francisco. But there is little to make light of in the physical damage, 80 percent of which was caused by the ensuing fires. In three days, nearly a third of the city's buildings were destroyed. Losses were valued at $400 million, in addition to the 250,000 people left homeless (out of a population of

400,000) and the more than 500 deaths. One of the early fatalities was fire chief Dennis T. Sullivan, who had anticipated just such an inferno should a massive quake ever hit. He was killed when a firehouse caved in on him.

SUNNY DAYS ARE HERE AGAIN

The Great Earthquake and Fire had laid waste to city planner Daniel H. Burnham's grand scheme, revealed in 1905, for a "City Beautiful." "Make No Little Plans" was his motto, but the possibility for massive development went up in smoke in 1906. The city did rise from the ashes, and one of the political beneficiaries was James Rolph, who handled public relief efforts after the catastrophe. Mayor John Schmitz and Boss Abe Ruef were caught up in the wave of graft trials that swept City Hall with some 3,000 indictments in 1907. The dapper and genial Mr. Rolph was nicknamed "Sunny Jim" for his cheery, gladhanding personality and won the mayoral election of 1911. He served five terms to 1930, and his administration saw the construction of the bold new Civic Center, many parks and schools, a municipal streetcar system and public water and power programs. Rolph's limited imagination, his inability to cope with the onset of the great Depression and his many ill-considered political judgments later in life left him in disrepute when his final term expired. But he was remembered fondly by bootleggers and others for his ability to address certain scofflaws with a wink and a nod. San Francisco's famous madame Sally Stanford wrote of Summy Jim, "First and foremost he was for Live and Let Live, Let Sleeping Dogs Lie, and Don't Stir Up Muddy Waters. Also, If You Haven't Tried It Don't Knock It."

THE GREAT RAT HUNT

Edgar Allan Poe could have had a field day in the aftermath of the 1906 apocalypse. As if the horror of earthquake and fire were not enough, the threat of bubonic plague returned to terrify the public. A 1900 outbreak of the dread disease had been centered in Chinatown, but when doctors reported 55 cases of the plague in 1907, Mayor Edward Taylor petitioned President Theodore Roosevelt for federal assistance. The government responded with sixteen government public health officers who set up headquarters on Fillmore Street. Their main targets were the rodents suspected of carrying and spreading the disease. More than 400 paid workers and several times more volunteers were enlisted for the roundup. Information about the plague and its carriers was disseminated on 700,000 printed flyers. Some 14,608 traps were set and a half million buildings examined. More than 150,000 rats were captured and examined and, as the diseased rats were destroyed, the number of new plague cases rapidly declined. In what was perhaps a synchronous event, the rodent population was cleaned up about the same time that the city government was rid of certain political rats—Mayor "Handsome Gene" Schmitz and Boss Abe Ruef.

PAPER PALACES

Well before the Great Earthquake struck in 1906, San Francisco was in the running as the site for the World's Fair that would commemorate the opening of the Panama Canal. The seismic cataclysm only postponed the plans. Early in 1907, civic leaders regained momentum for the city's bid by organizing the Pacific Ocean Exposition Company, which later became the Panama Pacific International Exposition Company. San Franciscans subscribed to $4 million in bonds for the venture, and the city voted another $5 million with a state-legislature pledge for matching funds. The 1915 Panama-Pacific International Exposition became more than a celebration of the Panama Canal's completion. It showed the world that San Francisco had recovered from nature's devastation and was capable of unparalleled architectural glory. A 635-acre landfill was prepared on the tidelands between Fort Mason and the Golden Gate. Ten main exhibit palaces were constructed, in addition to a racetrack, stadium and airfield. More than nineteen million people visited the fair between February 4 and December 4, 1915. The most elaborate construction was the 432-foot Tower of Jewels, glittering with 50,000 pieces of colored glass. The most lasting was the Palace of Fine Arts, with its grand neoclassical rotunda and Corinthian colonnade, designed by architect Bernard Maybeck. With the foresight that housing would someday be scarce in San Francisco, or out of fear of another earthquake, nothing was built to last. All of the glorious buildings except the Palace of Fine Arts were demolished after the exposition closed, and the Marina area was built up with the houses and apartment buildings that surround the Palace today.

COIT TOWER

As you climb Telegraph Hill and admire the tall, fluted column that graces its peak, and peruse the populist WPA mural inside, consider the tower's unusual origin. Lillie Hitchcock Coit had been a Confederate sympathizer during the Civil War, in keeping with her North Carolina heritage, and had been married briefly to mining engineer Howard Coit. She adopted San Francisco as her home and earned a reputation for outlandish behavior by dressing up in male drag to gain access to the city's wilder nightspots. Lillie was also renowned for the great affection she felt for the city's firefighters. The Knickerbocker Number Five Fire Company made her an honorary member, and when she died in 1929, Lillie Coit left $100,000 for the city to build a tower honoring her beloved firemen. The tower was erected in 1933 on the site of Telegraph Hill's signal station. Does it look like a hose to you?

THE CASE OF THE MYSTERIOUS MARTINI

More than one amateur historian has attributed the birth of the elegant cocktail called the martini to San Francisco, but no one is really sure of its exact origin. Columnist Herb Caen, who called the gin-and-vermouth concoction "the straight world's hallucinogenic," invested well over 30 years of first-hand research in the matter and came up with at least one joke—about the "mental" martini: "You pour the gin, I'll think vermouth"—and several birthright stories. The gibson, he relays in *One Man's San Francisco*, was invented by stockbrokers who replaced the martini's olive with an onion in order to kill the odor of the gin. The martini may have been the invention of Jerry Thomas, a bartender at the Occidental Hotel in 1860. The barkeep splashed together a hangover cure that remotely resembles today's dry tiddly and named it for his customer's destination that morning, the small town on the interior of the bay, Martinez.

THE THROES OF LABOR

For much of the twentieth century, San Francisco has been known as a great labor town, where working folk could live a decent and respectable life thanks to the stalwart protection of powerful trade and industrial unions. But the history behind that reputation is one of dogged and sometimes violent struggle. One of the early symbols of the battle between labor and capital was Tom Mooney, a Socialist labor leader who moved to California from the Midwest in 1910. On July 22, 1916, during the Preparedness Day parade held on Market Street as a patriotic display of readiness for World War I, a pipe bomb exploded, killing ten and wounding more than forty. Because the period had been marked by intense union fighting over the "open shop," unionists Tom Mooney and Warren Billings were speedily pegged as the suspects. Their trial, conviction and sentencing were equally speedy. Billings was destined for hanging. Conservatives and liberals took heated sides over the case. But later inquiries found crucial evidence that the pair had been framed. In 1939, Governor Culbert Olson pardoned Mooney and commuted Billings' life sentence. (Billings was pardoned in 1961.) Neither man figured significantly in public life after his release, but the cry to "Free Tom Mooney" had become an indelible part of San Francisco labor history.

Labor history took a particularly brutal turn in 1934. The Great Depression had motivated labor organizers to mobilize for better working conditions and more power in hiring practices on the docks. Under the leadership of Australian-born Harry Bridges, workers regained control over the previously boss-dominated longshore union, and 12,000 members of the resuscitated International Longshoreman's Association went on strike on May 9, 1934. They fought for hours, wages and authority in the hiring halls. The owners' Industrial Association, urged on by such newspapers as the San Francisco *Examiner*, was determined to break the union and escalated the conflict by hiring thugs to ram their trucks through the picket lines at the port. On Thursday, July 5, a full-scale waterfront war broke out. The bloody battle between strikers, hired hoodlums and police left two dead and at least 100 injured. But the strikers held their ground. Bridges rallied the support of other unions and shut down the city (but kept food, water and electricity flowing) with a four-day general strike, the largest in American history. The ILA won most of its demands and solidified San Francisco as a proud union town. The power of trade unions may have slipped in the latter decades of the century, but Bloody Thursday and the general strike have never been forgotten on the docks or in working-class bars around the city.

BEAT ME, DADDY-O

A leisurely walk through North Beach takes you past such legendary hangouts as Caffè Trieste and City Lights Bookstore, which have endured for more than 30 years as symbols of San Francisco's longstanding hospitality to bohemian culture. In the mid-1950s, artists, poets, writers and musicians, disgusted by the materialism and shallow values of the Eisenhower Era's mainstream, suburbanized, commercialized and televised "uncool" culture, migrated to the city and established a refuge in the Italian-dominated neighborhood below Telegraph Hill. Allen Ginsberg read his impassioned epic lament against modern degradation called *Howl*, and his publisher, Lawrence Ferlinghetti, was put on trial for disseminating obscenity. Jack Kerouac immortalized the notion of the Beat pilgrimage in his novel *On the Road*, capturing the experimental, experiential, jazz-accompanied flow of life in his use of language and dubbing his peers the "Beat Generation." Before long the dominant culture beat them at their own game, though, creating such caricatures as Maynard

G. Krebs on the *Dobie Gillis* television series, and inundating North Beach with newshounds and photographers, inspiring a whole new population of fakes and publicity seekers. Novelist Herb Gold wrote about the legacy: "The Beatnik begat the Hippie and the Hippie begat a lifestyle that touches us in ways that extend from fashion and drugs and sexuality to politics and race and a sense of what American might be." Unfortunately, even Gold's choice of words betrays the objectification that attempts to freeze a movement in time, as if to preserve it in amber. Ginsberg, Kerouac, Cassidy, Ferlinghetti and others never called themselves Beatniks—the term was the invention of the city's most cogent daily chronicler of popular culture, Herb Caen.

"ARE YOU NOW OR HAVE YOU EVER BEEN?"

Everybody knows that the Free Speech Movement, which erupted on college campuses in the 1960s, was ignited at U.C. Berkeley in 1964, when the administration ruled that students could not solicit funds on campus for social and political activities. But an important precedent was set on the other side of the Bay in 1960, when the House Committee on Un-American Activities scheduled a series of hearings in San Francisco's City Hall. The McCarthy Era was drawing to an ignoble close, and hundreds of angry students and civil libertarians showed up to protest the presence of the congressional inquisitors. The response of the authorities was little less than a police riot. Officers beat protestors with billy clubs and turned on the firehoses inside the City Hall rotunda. The television image of citizens being violently washed down the slippery marble steps marked a new turn in the civil-rights and free-speech struggles of the '60s. Counterculture hero Abbie Hoffman acutely observed that from the event "a generation had cast its spirit into the crucible of resistance."

LOVE/HAIGHT

"If you're going to San Francisco, be sure to wear some flowers in your hair." So sang Scott MacKenzie in the 1967 Top-10 hit that beckoned young idealists to make their "flower power" pilgrimage to the city during the Summer of Love. Even by then, however, many of the most important events in the rise of hippie culture had passed. The first formal dance/concert organized by the Family Dog commune took place on October 16, 1965, at Longshoreman's Hall on Fisherman's Wharf. The event featured the Jefferson Airplane, the Great Society and the Charlatans. Shows continued with such titles as "A Tribute to Sparkle Plenty" and "A Tribute to Ming the Magnificent." Bill Graham, having previously hosted a fundraising party for the San Francisco Mime Troupe, leased the Fillmore Auditorium on December 10 and triggered a whole new wave of musical/cultural events that he would eventually parlay into a multimillion-dollar entertainment empire. Ken Kesey threw his first San Francisco Acid Test at the Fillmore on January 8, 1966, and two weeks later hosted his three-day "Trips Festival" with the freshly rechristened Grateful Dead as the central act. In between, on January 14, the first Human Be-In was held in Golden Gate Park. The combination of psychedelic music, long hair, Zen, drugs, communal living and "free love" was most intensely focused in the Haight-Ashbury district bordering Golden Gate Park, and ostensibly reached its peak in 1967. But by then Gray Line Tours had already set up a "Hippie Hop" ride along "the street called Love," supplying tourists with a handy dictionary guide to hippie ways and language; the end was in sight.

BASICS

AT YOUR SERVICE

FOREIGN EXCHANGE

When the banks are closed, you can still change money at a few convenient downtown locations. Amparo's Foreign Exchange, 1 Hallidie Plaza (956-5503), is open on weekends from 9 a.m. to 3 p.m.; Bank of America Foreign Currency Services, in the international terminal at San Francisco International Airport (742-8081), changes money daily from 7 a.m. to 11 p.m.; and Foreign Exchange Ltd., 415 Stockton St. (397-4700), stays open Saturday from 9 a.m. to 1 p.m.

LATE NIGHT

BABYSITTER

- Bay Area Baby Sitters Agency, 991-7474. Overnight sitters are provided, though they must be reserved during regular business hours.

CAR REPAIR

- Transportation Guarantee Co., 555 1st St., South of Market, 431-4700. Open 24 hours Monday through Friday, and until 8 p.m. Saturday.

DENTIST

- Dr. Jeffrey I. Stone, 334-2600. His staff is on call 24 hours a day.

DOCTOR

- Dr. Benjamin Fong, 421-6441. Answers calls 24 hours a day for seniors and people with acute illness.
- Dr. Eugene Gaenslen, 752-4028. Makes house calls 24 hours a day.
- Dr. Ernest Levinger, 752-6770. Makes house calls 24 hours a day.

LIMOUSINE

- Luxury Limousine Service, 824-6767. Lincolns and Cadillacs (both stretch and squat) are available 24 hours a day if reserved in advance. Prices range from $40 to $55 an hour with a three-hour minimum.

LOCKSMITH

- Campbell's, 861-5882. A 24-hour emergency locksmith service.
- San Francisco Locksmith & Safe Co., 681-4000. On call 24 hours.

NEWSSTAND

Believe it or not, the city does not have a newsstand that stays open all night. If you must find the latest copy of *Pravda* at 3 a.m., you'll have to venture across the Bay to De Lauer Super Newsstand, at 1310 Broadway in Oakland (451-6157), which is open 24 hours.

PHARMACY

- Walgreen's Drugstore, 3201 Divisadero St., Pacific Heights, 931-6417. Open all night, but doesn't make deliveries (see Pickup & Delivery below).

PHOTOCOPY

- The Copy Factory, 47 Spear St., Financial District, 641-7555. If you're downtown and need to drop off documents to be copied, this place is open 24 hours, Monday through Friday.

PICKUP & DELIVERY

It's not a universally known fact, but most cab drivers will act as errand runners for you. If you need something delivered to you, call a cab, prepay the driver for the cost of the item to be purchased, then, upon delivery, pay what's on the meter plus a negotiated extra fee (usually a couple of dollars).

RESTAURANTS

San Francisco's cosmopolitanism diminishes significantly when you consider how hard it is to get a decent meal after 10 p.m. However, the situation is improving, especially when it comes to Asian and Mexican food.

- Basta Pasta, 1268 Grant Ave., North Beach, 434-2248. The fare is standard North Beach Italian and the clientele is touristy, but at midnight, the pasta and seafood dishes will surely satisfy. Open until 2 a.m.
- Clown Alley, 42 Columbus Ave., North Beach, 421-2540. The best hamburger stand in town, and a welcome sight in the middle of the night. The fries and shakes aren't as good as the burgers. Open until 3 a.m.
- David's Delicatessen, 468 Geary St., Union Square, 771-1600. Like all delis in San Francisco, it's ersatz and overpriced, but in the wee hours you might not notice. Open until 1 a.m.

- Everett & Jones Barbeque, 5130 3rd St., Bayview, 822-7728. Some of the best barbecue in the city. Succulent ribs, chicken and links, all smoked in a brick oven, are served until midnight Sunday through Thursday and until 2 a.m. Friday and Saturday. Not the best neighborhood in the middle of the night, but it's worth the trek.

- Golden Dragon, 833 Washington St., Chinatown, 398-4550. Sheer heaven for carbo-loaders, Golden Dragon serves every variation of Chinese noodle dish. All are topped with savory sauces, meats, fish or vegetables, and all are good. Open every night until 1 a.m.

- The Grubstake, 1525 Pine St., Van Ness, 673-8268. Decorated like a dining car, The Grubstake is, true to its name, grubby. But if you find yourself carousing in the Polk district after hours, you can land a decent burger here. Open 22 hours a day (it closes from 5 a.m. to 7 a.m. for cleanup).

- Hamburger Mary's Organic Grill, 1582 Folsom St., South of Market, 627-5767. This madhouse is packed with a colorful mix of yuppies, housewives and transvestites, who come for the good salads, omelets, steaks, grilled fresh fish and so on. Open until 2 a.m. every night of the week.

- Korea House, 1640 Post St., Japantown, 563-1388. Korea House will take the chill out of any damp midnight with its fiery, delicious fish stews, noodle dishes, steamed fish and do-it-yourself barbecue. It's open every night until 3 a.m.

- Lori's Diner, 2336 Mason St., Union Square, 392-8646. Basic American diner fare in a neo-'50s setting, complete with Elvis posters, vinyl booths and lots of chrome. The burgers are fried, the french fries authentically greasy and the salads appropriately drab. Don't mistake the "fried chicken steak" for chicken-fried steak. Open 24 hours.

- Max's Diner, 311 3rd St., South of Market, 546-6297. The owners of Max's Opera Café have combined elements of the deli, the fern bar and the neo-American diner in this trendy spot. Buffalo chicken wings, meatloaf with mashed potatoes, and Dr. Brown's sodas are served until midnight Sunday through Thursday, and until 1 a.m. Friday and Saturday.

- Max's Opera Café , 601 Van Ness Ave., Civic Center, 771-7300. A slick and stylish deli that is ever-popular in spite of its inedible lox, barely edible sandwiches and massive but disappointing desserts. Try the smoked chicken breast or one of the tasty salads. Open until midnight Tuesday through Thursday and until 1 a.m. Friday and Saturday.

- Los Panchos, 3206 Mission St., Mission District, 285-1033. Salvadoran pupusas (seasoned flour patties stuffed with cheese and grilled) make a heavenly meal on their own or with one of the other treats on the Salvadoran-Mexican menu here. Open daily until 4 a.m.

- La Rondalla, 901 Valencia St., Mission District, 647-7474. Excellent Mexican food is served in a noisy, chaotic setting until 4 a.m. every night except Tuesday. After a Mexican beer and an order of great guacamole, you'll join in the fun and sing along with the mariachis.

- Sparky's Diner, 240 Church St., Castro District, 621-6001. The pizza is atrocious and the burgers mediocre, but Castro District denizens keep this trendy 24-hour neodiner hopping until the sun rises.

- Tommy's Joynt, 1101 Geary St., Van Ness, 775-4216. A collection of more than 90 great beers keeps sports fans piling into this garish pub until the wee hours. Sandwiches are hefty, but dry and tough, and the dishes (Italian or Mexican) aren't much better. Open daily until 2 a.m.

- Yuet Lee, 1300 Stockton St., Chinatown, 982-6020. Excellent Cantonese preparations of Maine lobster, Dungeness crab, fried squid and poached chicken are some of the delicacies served here daily until 3 a.m. Bring your own beer or wine, and be warned: this is not cheap Chinese food.

- El Zocalo, 3230 Mission St., Mission District, 282-2572. Above-average Mission District Mexican food served until 3 a.m. Sunday through Thursday and until 4 a.m. on Friday and Saturday.

TELEPHONE NUMBERS

Ambulance, 911
Amtrak, 982-8512
BART (Bay Area Rapid Transit), 788-BART
BASS (Bay Area Seating Services) Ticketmaster Outlets, 762-BASS
Camping Information, (800) 444-7275
Chamber of Commerce, 392-4511
Children's Emergency Services, 665-0757
Coast Guard, 911
Directory Information, 411
Fire & Rescue, 911
Highway Conditions, 557-3755
Highway Patrol, 911
Library Information, 558-3191
MUNI (San Francisco Municipal Railway), 673-MUNI
Oakland International Airport, 577-4000 (call airlines for flight information
  and booking)
Paramedics, 911
Poison Control, 911
Police, 911

Postal Information, 550-0100

San Francisco International Airport, 761-0800 (call airlines for flight
  information and booking)

San Francisco Ticket Box Office Services (STBS), 433-7827

Taxis, 626-2345 (Yellow), 673-1414 (De Soto), 282-4141 (Luxor),
  552-1300 (Veteran's)

Ticketron, 546-9400

Time, 767-8900

Visitors' Information Bureau, 391-2000

Weather Report, 936-1212

GETTING AROUND

AIRPORT TRANSPORTATION

SAN FRANCISCO INTERNATIONAL AIRPORT

San Francisco International Airport is one of the busiest airports in the world.
If that's not enough, it also sports horrific delays and a bad safety record, and
unfortunately, there isn't much the increasingly beleaguered traveler can do
about it. Luckily, getting to and from the airport is a fairly painless and civil
experience. Located fourteen miles south of the city, off Highway 101, the
airport is served excellently by a number of transportation companies.

Fierce competition among a profusion of van shuttle services means you can
get a quick ride to or from your flight from any part of the city at any time of
day for just $8 or $9. The shuttles prefer 24-hour advance notice, but they will
usually pick up with less warning. At this writing, Bay Area Supershuttle
(558-8500) seems to be the best staffed, followed by Good Neighbors Airport
Shuttle (777-4899) and Yellow Airport Shuttle (282-7433).

Slightly more economical but slightly less convenient are the SFO Airporter
buses (495-8404), which pick up at the major downtown and Fisherman's
Wharf hotels every fifteen or twenty minutes; you can also board at the
downtown terminal, 301 Ellis Street, until 2 a.m. The fare is $5 one way and
$8 round trip.

Taxis, of course, are an easy, if less cost-effective, way to get to the airport; from downtown, expect to pay about $25 plus tip. Cabs can be shared to reduce cost. The city has a plethora of limousine companies that will whisk you to your plane in style; ask your hotel concierge to steer you to a reliable firm.

OAKLAND INTERNATIONAL AIRPORT

A much smaller sister to SFO, the Oakland airport is nevertheless seeing an increase in business, thanks to the public's aversion to the increasingly long waits and the confusing connections at SFO. But unless you either rent a car, leave your own car in the parking lot, or hop a ride with a friend, getting to and from the Oakland airport is more of a chore and an expense than getting to SFO. Located five miles from downtown Oakland on Highway 880, the airport is about a $32 (plus tip and $1 bridge toll) cab ride from downtown San Francisco. Lorrie's Travel & Tours (334-9000) charges $49 plus $1 bridge toll for five to seven passengers and expects 24-hour advance notice.

If flight juggling sends you from one airport to the other, Bay Area Bus runs buses every hour, on the hour, from either airport for a mere $7. Regrettably, the buses stop nowhere in between.

If you're traveling light, consider BART (Bay Area Rapid Transit, 788-BART), which will get you to Oakland from downtown San Francisco in 25 minutes for $1.90. BART trains run every fifteen minutes during the day and every twenty minutes at night; they stop running at midnight. To reach the airport, take a Fremont train to the Coliseum stop, then (for another dollar) take an Air-BART shuttle, which runs every fifteen minutes and takes five minutes to reach the airport. But be prepared to add another half hour to your trip if you take BART after the evening rush hour or on Sunday—Fremont trains don't operate in San Francisco at those times, so you'll have to take a train to Oakland and transfer to the Fremont line.

CARS

With public transportation as good as it is and parking as hopeless as it is, a car is the last thing you'll want in the city. But if you plan to venture afield to Marin, the wine country or perhaps Lake Tahoe, you'll need to rent a car. Hertz (771-2200) and Avis (885-5011) both have offices around the city and plenty of standard-issue cars. Somewhat less expensive than the two giants are Budget (875-6850, 800-772-3773) and Alamo (882-9440), along with a host of agencies along O'Farrell Street near Union Square. If you plan to pick up a car at the airport, Bob Leech's Autorental (583-2727) is highly recommended for its low rates and quality cars, but you'll need to reserve a week in advance. For those seeking something other than a Ford Fiesta, try Rent-a-Wreck (776-8700) for a fun jalopy or Autoexotica (885-6655) for a Rolls or a Lamborghini.

PUBLIC TRANSPORTATION

BART (BAY AREA RAPID TRANSIT)

The underground railway that links San Francisco to the East Bay and Daly City, BART is the best way to travel to Berkeley and Oakland. Trains are remarkably clean and quiet, and fares are reasonable. They vary depending on distance traveled; a round trip to Berkeley will run about $4, and travel anywhere within San Francisco is 80 cents. The high-tech system is entirely automated: machines dispense magnetic-card tickets valued at anywhere from 80 cents to $20, and these tickets are read by computers at the turnstiles when you enter and exit. The computer will calculate your fare and automatically subtract it from your ticket. Die-hard rapid-transit buffs may want to purchase a special $2.60 excursion ticket, which allows you to ride the entire 71-mile system in one trip. BART trains run Monday through Saturday 6 a.m. to midnight, and Sunday 9 a.m. to midnight. Call 788-BART for more information.

CABLE CARS

San Francisco would not be San Francisco without its treasured cable cars. These old-world, open-air trollies—driven by gregarious bell-ringing brakemen and powered by a vast underground cable network—transport thousands of tourists and locals a day, roller-coaster style, up and down the awesome hills of downtown and the waterfront. The fare is $2, or $6 for a ticket that's good for the whole day, including rides on MUNI buses (see MUNI, below). Cable-car transfers are also accepted on MUNI buses and trains. Tickets can be purchased from machines at the terminals (at Powell and Market streets downtown, and Hyde and Beach streets at Fisherman's Wharf) or on the cable cars themselves if you have exact change. Tips on avoiding long lines: Ride early in the day or late at night, or skip the terminal points and board midroute. Cable cars run daily from 6 a.m. to 1 a.m.; call 673-MUNI.

MUNI (SAN FRANCISCO MUNICIPAL RAILWAY)

MUNI is, quite simply, one of the best public transportation systems in the world, and a bargain to boot. There's nary a square foot of the city that isn't within spitting range of either a MUNI diesel bus, electric bus, streetcar or cable car. And MUNI vehicles are modern, efficient and clean, except for the pervasive graffiti.

Fares are 85 cents for all MUNI lines except cable cars, which cost $2, and exact change is always required. Fares include a transfer good for *two* connections on any line, in any direction, within a 90-minute period. All lines run until midnight, after which a more limited—but still ample—number of "night owl" buses take over for the rest of the night.

The official MUNI map, available at hundreds of stores for $1.50, is comprehensive and clear, and it serves well as a general street map of the city. Call 673-MUNI for route information.

OTHER TRANSPORTATION

AC Transit (839-2882) is the East Bay's bus system, with service to San Francisco over the Bay Bridge. Golden Gate Transit (332-6600) transports commuters over the Golden Gate Bridge to Marin and farther north. Samtrans (761-7000) offers local bus service to the San Francisco airport and cities on the peninsula. And Caltrain (557-8661) provides commuter rail service to San Jose, including points along the way.

TAXIS

Although taxis aren't the cheapest way to get around the city, they can be the most fun (if you get a good driver) and the fastest (if you avoid rush hour). We have had great success with San Francisco's cabbies, finding 90 percent of them to be friendly, amusing, informative and honest. Most of the time, cabs are easy to flag down (look for the lighted sign on the car's roof), but empty ones become almost extinct at rush hour, when cab companies' telephone lines seem hopelessly busy. The best bet during rush hour is to wait for a cab outside a good hotel. Gypsy cabs are increasingly common, especially at the airport, but you're safer in a city-licensed cab; they come in all colors, but all sport a city insignia on the front doors.

At this writing, taxi meters start at $1.40 and add 15 cents for every tenth of a mile (or $1.50 a mile). Drivers should be tipped about 15 percent. The major companies are Yellow (626-2345), De Soto (673-1414), Luxor (282-4141) and Veteran's (552-1300).

GOINGS-ON

A combination of rich culture and heavy tourism ensures that there is always some sort of celebration going on in San Francisco. We've put together a calendar of the more prominent and/or interesting events, providing dates and phone numbers when possible. For up-to-date information on all these events, call the San Francisco Visitors' Information Bureau at 391-2000.

JANUARY

▪ ACT (American Conservatory Theatre) performances (through late May), Geary Theater, 415 Geary St., Union Square, 749-2228.

- San Francisco Performances (through mid-May), Herbst Theater, 401 Van Ness Ave., Civic Center, 392-4400.
- San Francisco Symphony (runs year-round), Davies Symphony Hall, Grove St. and Van Ness Ave., Civic Center, 431-5400.
- San Francisco Ballet repertory season (through early May), War Memorial Opera House, 301 Van Ness Ave., Civic Center, 621-3838.

FEBRUARY

- Chinese New Year Celebration and Parade (early Feb.), Chinatown, 982-3000. Colorful, firecracker-punctuated parade through Chinatown's streets.
- Volvo Tennis/San Francisco tennis tournament (early Feb.), San Francisco Civic Auditorium, Civic Center, 239-4800.
- American Ballet Theatre (through March), War Memorial Opera House, 301 Van Ness Ave., Civic Center, 621-3838.

MARCH

- St. Patrick's Day Celebration, downtown, Civic Center, the city's pubs and the United Irish Cultural Center, 2700 45th Ave., Sunset District. Festive parade, ceremonies and parties on the Sunday closest to St. Patrick's Day (March 17).
- San Francisco International Film Festival, AMC Kabuki 8 Cinemas, Japantown and Pacific Film Archives, Berkeley, 221-9055 or 931-9800. Acclaimed film festival that has been running for more than 30 years.
- Mostly Mozart Festival (last weekend of March), Davies Symphony Hall, Grove St. and Van Ness Ave., Civic Center, 431-5400; Herbst Theater, 401 Van Ness Ave., Civic Center, 392-4400.

APRIL

- Cherry Blossom Festival, Japantown, 922-6776. Parades, performances and tea ceremonies throughout Japantown.
- San Francisco Giants season opens, Candlestick Park, 467-8000.
- Oakland Athletics season opens, Oakland Coliseum, 430-8020.
- Macy's Easter Flower Show, Macy's, Stockton and O'Farrell sts., Union Square, 397-3333.
- Easter Sunrise Service (Easter Sunday), Mount Davidson. A San Francisco tradition. Easter services are held at the base of the giant cross atop Mount Davidson; you'll have to hike to the top.
- Yachting season opens, first day of daylight saving time, San Francisco Bay. Floating bands and boats of every kind parade through the water.

MAY

- Black & White Ball, Civic Center, 431-5400. This gala ball, to which the whole city is invited, benefits the San Francisco Symphony. Several thousand don black and white and cough up $200 apiece to take part in the great fun.
- Cinco de Mayo celebration and parade (first weekend in May), Potrero del Sol Park, 25th St. and Potrero Ave., Mission District. Mexican celebration and parade through the streets of the Mission.
- San Francisco Historic Trolley Festival (through October), Market St., Union Square. Vintage trolley cars from around the world run all summer on downtown's train tracks.
- Bay to Breakers Race, San Francisco, 777-7770. Famous 7.5-mile foot race through the city's streets.

JUNE

- Union Street Spring Festival, Union St. from Gough St. to Fillmore St., Cow Hollow, 346-4446. A merchant-sponsored street fair.
- Ethnic Dance Festival, Herbst Theater, 401 Van Ness Ave., Civic Center, 552-3656. Dancers from around the world perform.
- Haight Street Fair, Haight St. between Masonic St. and Stanyan St., Haight-Ashbury, 346-4446. Haight merchants and craftspeople put on this street fair, which attracts a crazy quilt of locals—yuppies, hippies, punks, oldtimers—with some tourists thrown in for good measure.
- Carnaval, Mission and 24th streets, Mission District, 826-1401. Lively festival modeled after Rio's Carnaval, with dancing and parades.
- Stern Grove Midsummer Music Festival (through August), Sigmund Stern Memorial Grove, 19th Ave. and Sloat Blvd., City South, 398-6551. This acclaimed music festival, which showcases classical artists but also features jazz and pop, has been going strong for more than 50 years.
- San Francisco Symphony Beethoven Festival, Davies Symphony Hall, Grove St. and Van Ness Ave., Civic Center, 431-5400, and Herbst Theater, 401 Van Ness Ave., Civic Center, 392-4400.
- Lesbian-Gay Freedom Day Parade, from Market St. to the Civic Center. A vibrant and outlandish celebration of the city's substantial gay population, 864-3733.

JULY

- KQED International Beer Festival, Concourse Exhibition Center, 8th and Brannan sts., South of Market, 553-2200.
- Jazz and All That Art on Fillmore Festival, Western Addition. A celebration of the rich history of this melting-pot neighborhood.
- Fourth of July Celebration and Fireworks (July 4), Crissy Field, Presidio waterfront. Celebration goes on all afternoon; fireworks start at 9 p.m.

- Midsummer Mozart Festival, Davies Symphony Hall, Grove St. and Van Ness Ave., Civic Center, 431-5400, and Herbst Theater, 401 Van Ness Ave., Civic Center, 392-4400.
- San Francisco Marathon, San Francisco, 681-2322. Thousands complete a 26-mile route around the city.
- Comedy Celebration Day, Polo Field, Golden Gate Park, 777-7120.
- San Francisco Symphony Pops season (through Aug.), Civic Auditorium, Civic Center, 552-8000.

AUGUST

- Nihonmachi Street Fair, Japantown, 563-5626. Merchants and food vendors line the streets of Japantown.
- San Francisco Hill Stride, San Francisco, 546-6150. A walker's workout up and down the hilly city streets. The most recent stride drew 5,000.
- Shakespeare in the Park, Liberty Meadows, Golden Gate Park, 221-0642. This reputable company performs one play, through September, for free.
- San Francisco 49ers season opens, Candlestick Park, 468-2249.
- Ringling Brothers and Barnum & Bailey Circus, Cow Palace, City South, 469-6000.

SEPTEMBER

- Renaissance Pleasure Faire (through September), Blackpoint Forest, Novato, 892-0937. Food, crafts, entertainment, clothing and whimsy of the fifteenth and sixteenth centuries.
- Reggae Explosion, Fort Mason, Pier 3, Fisherman's Wharf, 921-8030.
- San Francisco Opera season (through mid-Dec.), War Memorial Opera House, 301 Van Ness Ave., Civic Center, 864-3330.
- Today's Artists Concerts (through April), Masonic Auditorium and Herbst Theater, 401 Van Ness Ave., Civic Center, 392-4400. Chamber orchestras and string quartets are featured in this series of concerts.
- San Francisco à la Carte à la Park, Golden Gate Park, 383-9378. Food festival featuring samples from some of the city's best restaurants.
- San Francisco Blues Festival, Great Meadow, Fort Mason, 826-6837. A weekend festival that showcases the best blues talents in the Bay Area and the country.
- Folsom Street Fair (late Sept.). More than 200,000 people come out to celebrate this fair, which features the weird and wacky.
- San Francisco Fair and Exposition, Civic Center, 557-8758. A wonderful urban version of a county fair, with food and wine tastings and performers of every kind. (The fair is sometimes held in October, so call first.)
- Fiesta Italiana, Pier 45, Fisherman's Wharf. Italian street fair.

OCTOBER

- Columbus Day Celebration and Parade, North Beach and Aquatic Park, 274-0400. The city's Italian heritage is celebrated with a parade up Columbus Avenue, a boccie ball tournament, general festivities and a blessing of the fishing boats in Aquatic Park near Fisherman's Wharf.
- Fleet Week U.S. Navy Celebration, Pier 32, Fisherman's Wharf, 391-8000. The Navy displays its air and sea muscle.
- International Street Performers Festival, Pier 39, Fisherman's Wharf, 981-8030.
- San Francisco Fall Antiques Show (late Oct.-early Nov.), Pier 3, Fort Mason, 921-1411. Antiques dealers display their wares.
- Great Halloween Pumpkin Festival, Clement St. between 3rd and 8th aves., Richmond District, 346-4446.
- Halloween Night (Oct. 31), along Castro and Polk sts. The gay community (and its straight friends) dress up in wild costumes and parade informally.

NOVEMBER

- El Día de los Muertos (Day of the Dead) (Nov. 1), Mission St., Mission District, 826-8009. Parades and ceremonies honoring the dead.
- KQED Wine and Food Festival, Concourse Exhibition Center, Eighth and Brannan sts., South of Market, 553-2230.
- San Francisco International Auto Show (late Nov.-early Dec.), Moscone Center, 3rd and Howard sts., South of Market, 974-4000. Car makers show off their newest models and their prototypes for cars of the future.
- Run to the Far Side Race, Golden Gate Park. Race with cartoonist Gary Larson.

DECEMBER

- Pickle Family Circus, Palace of Fine Arts Theater, Marina District, 826-0747. Like Cirque du Soleil, a circus with panache.
- *The Nutcracker*, San Francisco Ballet, War Memorial Opera House, 301 Van Ness Ave., Civic Center, 621-3838. This Christmas classic is the San Francisco Ballet's money-maker.
- *A Christmas Carol*, ACT (American Conservatory Theatre), Geary Theater, 415 Geary St., Union Square, 673-6440. No Christmas-season excursion to San Francisco would be complete without seeing ACT's fine performances of this beloved Dickens play.
- San Francisco Symphony New Year's Gala (Dec. 31), Davies Symphony Hall, Grove St. and Van Ness Ave., Civic Center, 431-5400. Culture vultures can welcome the new year in with style.
- New Year's Eve Extravaganza, Cow Palace, Geneva Ave. and Santos St., City South, 469-6000. Pop-rock musicians sing in the new year.

MAPS

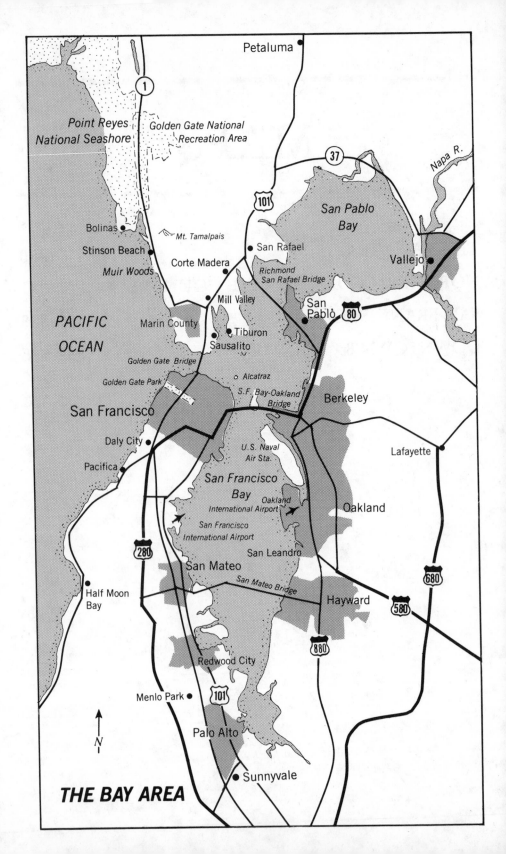

THE BAY AREA

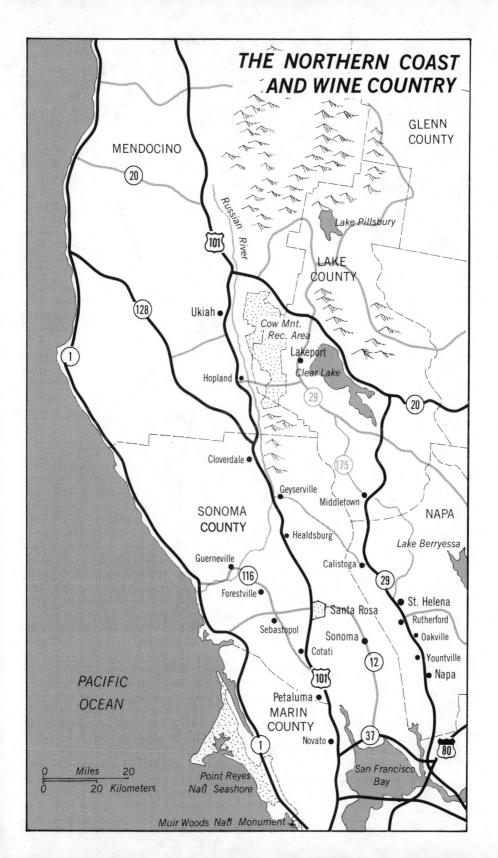

THE NORTHERN COAST AND WINE COUNTRY

GLENN COUNTY

MENDOCINO

20

Russian River

101

Lake Pillsbury

LAKE COUNTY

128

Ukiah

Cow Mnt. Rec. Area

Lakeport

Clear Lake

1

Hopland

29

20

Cloverdale

175

Geyserville

Middletown

NAPA

SONOMA COUNTY

Healdsburg

Lake Berryessa

Guerneville

Calistoga

116

29

Forestville

St. Helena

Rutherford

Santa Rosa

Oakville

Sebastopol

Sonoma

Yountville

Cotati

12

Napa

101

PACIFIC OCEAN

Petaluma

MARIN COUNTY

Novato

37

80

1

San Francisco Bay

0   Miles   20
0   20 Kilometers

Point Reyes Nat'l Seashore

Muir Woods Nat'l Monument

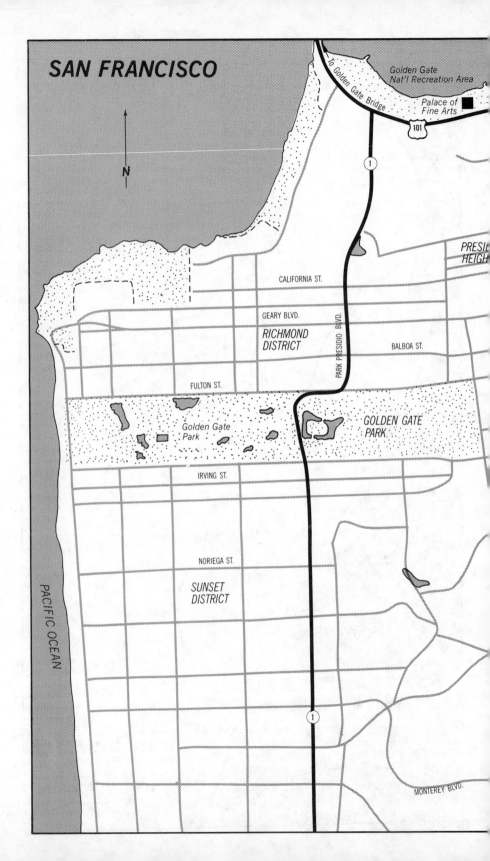

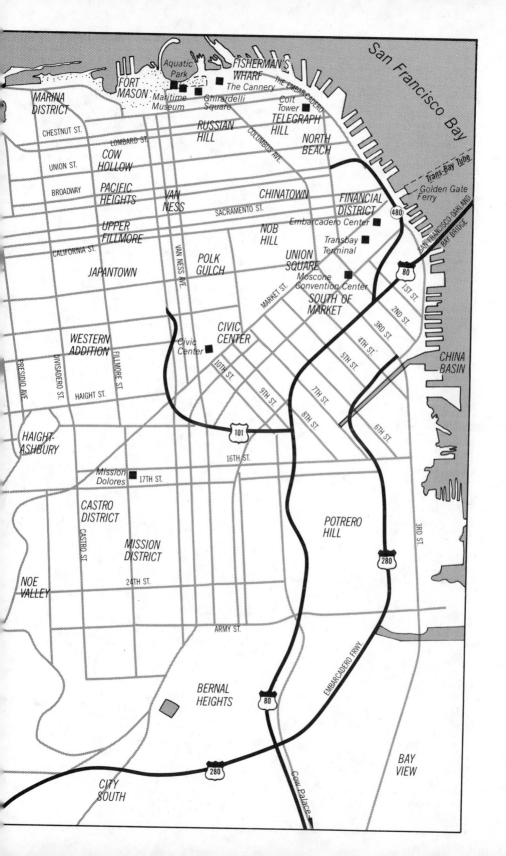

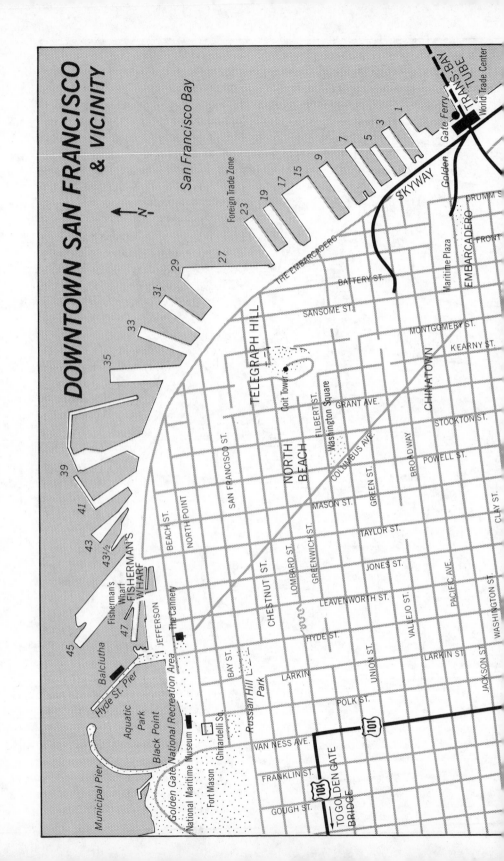

INDEX

MORE GAULT MILLAU "BEST" GUIDES

Now the guidebook series known throughout Europe for its wit and savvy reveals the best of major U.S., European and Asian destinations. Gault Millau books include full details on the best of everything that makes these places special: the restaurants, diversions, nightlife, hotels, shops, arts. The guides also offer practical information on getting around and enjoying each area. Perfect for visitors and residents alike.

Please send me the books checked below:

☐ The Best of Chicago $15.95
☐ The Best of London $16.95
☐ The Best of Los Angeles $16.95
☐ The Best of New England $15.95
☐ The Best of New York $16.95
☐ The Best of Paris $16.95
☐ The Best of San Francisco $16.95
☐ The Best of Washington, D.C. $16.95
☐ The Best of France $16.95
☐ The Best of Italy $16.95
☐ The Best of Hong Kong $16.95

PRENTICE HALL TRADE DIVISION
Order Department—Travel Books
200 Old Tappan Road
Old Tappan, NJ 07675

In the U.S., include $2 (UPS shipping charge) for the first book, and $1 for each additional book. Outside the U.S., $3 and $1 respectively.

Enclosed is my check or money order made out to Prentice Hall Trade Division, for $ _____

NAME_____

ADDRESS_____

CITY _____STATE _____

ZIP_____COUNTRY _____

André Gayot's
TASTES
with the Best of Gault Millau

THE WORLD DINING & TRAVEL CONNECTION

P.O. Box 361144, Los Angeles, CA 90036

- Latest news from an international team of critics
- The best restaurants, hotels, nightlife, shopping and fashion
- What's hot from Hollywood to Hong Kong, via Paris

☐ **YES,** please enter/renew my subscription for 6 bimonthly issues at the rate of $30. (Outside U.S. and Canada, $35.)

Name_____

Address_____

City_____State _____

Zip_____Country _____

☐ **ALSO,** please send a gift subscription to: *

Name_____

Address_____

City_____State _____

Zip_____Country _____

Gift from_____
(We will notify recipient of your gift)

* With the purchase of a gift subscription or a second subscription, you will receive, **FREE,** the **Gault Millau guidebook of your choice**—a $17 value. (See reverse for a complete list of Gault Millau guides.)

☐ CHECK ENCLOSED FOR $ _____.
☐ PLEASE SEND ME, **FREE,** THE GAULT MILLAU GUIDE OF MY CHOICE: _____

302/90